Operation Black Thunder

An Eyewitness Account of Terrorism in Punjab

Sarab Jit Singh

Sage Publications
New Delhi • Thousand Oaks • London

First published in 2002 by

Sage Publications India Pvt Ltd
M 32 Market, Greater Kailash I
New Delhi 110 048

Sage Publications Inc
2455 Teller Road
Thousand Oaks, California 91320

Sage Publications Ltd
6 Bonhill Street
London EC2A 4PU

Published by Tejeshwar Singh for Sage Publications India Pvt Ltd, type-set by Line Arts Phototypesetters, Pondicherry in 10 pt Charter BT and printed at Chaman Enterprises, New Delhi.

Second Printing 2002

Library of Congress Cataloging-in-Publication Data

Singh, Sarab Jit, 1935–
    Operation Black Thunder: an eyewitness account of terrorism in Punjab/ Sarab Jit Singh.
        p. cm.
    Includes index.
        1. Terrorism—India—Punjab. 2. Punjab (India)—Politics and govern-ment. I. Title.
    HV6433.I4 S5535   954'.552052—dc21   2002   2002066788

ISBN: 0–7619–9596–X (US-Pb)   81–7829–158–4 (India-Pb)

Sage Production Team: K.E. Priyamvada, Proteeti Banerjee, Neeru Handa, N.K. Negi and Santosh Rawat

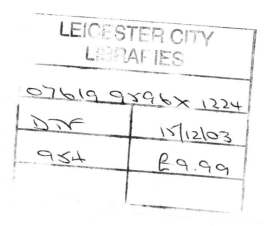
This book is dedicated to the magic of faith that is the
Darbar Sahib

Kujh lok vee shehar de zalam see
Kujh mainu maran da shauq vee see

(In part the townfolk were cruel
And partly I nursed a death wish)

The above couplet is from a Punjabi poem by a Pakistani poet which I happened to see in *Punjabi Dunia*. About 20 years later, in 1990, in the Senate Hall of the Guru Nanak Dev (GND) University I faced an angry and belligerent crowd of students. They were agitated because the police had tried to arrest one of them from the campus a day earlier. This verse suddenly came to my mind and, as I quoted it, their anger began to melt and we parted as friends.

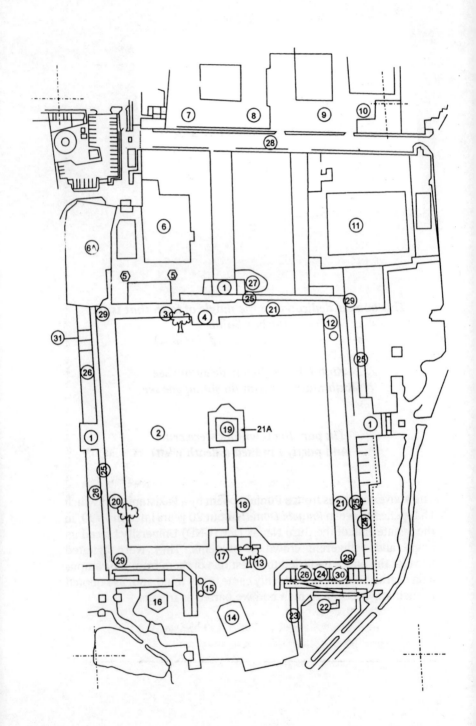

1. Entrances
2. Sarovar (Holy Pool)
3. Dukh Bhanjani Beri
4. Ath Sath Tirath (Shrine of 69 Holy Places)
5. Watch Towers
6. Langar
6A. Braham Buta Akhara
7. Guru Ram Dass Sarai
8. Teja Singh Sumundri Hall
9. Guru Nanak Sarai
10. Guru Hargobind Niwas
11. Manji Sahib Dewan
12. Baba Deep Singh Shrine
13. Lachi Ber (Guru Arjan Dev's Tree)
14. Akal Takht
15. Nishan Sahib
16. Thara Sahib (Shrine of Guru Teg Bahadur)
17. Darshani Deorhi
18. Causeway
19. Harmandar Sahib
20. Ber Baba Budha Ji
21. Parikrama
21A. Inner Parikrama
22. Dilapidated building where DIG S.S. Virk was hit by militants.
23. Roof of Prashad Point from where the terrorist fired at the police party injuring S.S. Virk.
24. Shops opening on the roadside.
25. Varandahs
26. Parikrama Rooms
27. Debris of Akal Takht Building where 46 dead bodies were recovered.
28. Roads.
29. Water Booths.
30. Room Nos. 13 and 14. (Office of Khalistan)
31. Room Nos. 45 and 46. (Torture Rooms)

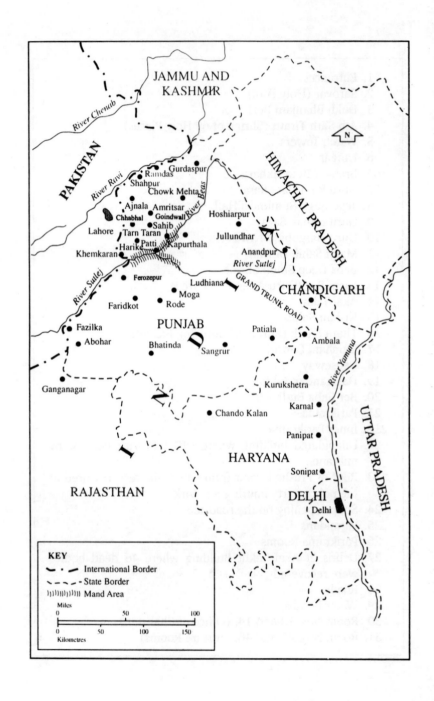

Contents

Foreword   11

Preface   16

1. The Golden Temple: In the Eye of the Storm   23

2. The Sikh Heritage and the Punjab Problem   35

3. The Rajiv–Longowal Accord: The 'Secret' Healing Touch   57

4. S.S. Barnala's Government: The Healing Touch Impaired   71

5. Governor Ray's Tenure   86

6. The Politics of the Clergy   96

7. January–March 1988: The Killings Increase   103

8. April–May 1988: Measures to End the Killing   115

9. Operation Black Thunder   122

10. The Militants Surrender   133

11. Trial at Midnight   149

12. Restoring the *Maryada*   158

13. Demoralisation versus a Gun Battle   163

14. The SGPC's Dilemma   168

15. Jasbir Singh Rode's Dismissal   175

16. The Corridor Plan   181

17. Jasbir Singh Rode Resurrected   187

18. *Panchayat* Elections Postponed: Missed Opportunities   197

19. The Militants and the Police: Between the Two Terrors   207

20. The 'National Games'   214

21. A New Government at the Centre   222

22. The 'Civil Face' of Governor Mukerji's Administration   230

23. Governor Varma's Tenure   241

24. 1990: The Killings Continue   249

25. Governor Malhotra Takes Charge   263

26. Attempts to Restore Democracy   273

27. Delhi's Inconsistent Punjab Policy   292

28. Elections by February 1992   300

29. From President's Rule to an Elected Government: The Return of Democracy   314

30. In Retrospect   323

Glossary   340

Index   345

About the Author   359

Foreword

It was pure coincidence when, some years ago, an old colleague and friend talked to me about the exceptional qualities of head and heart of Sarab Jit Singh, the author of this volume. He spoke of him in words of high praise. I too had heard that during his tenure as Deputy Commissioner of Amritsar during the troubled days of militancy, he had performed outstandingly. Having handled that extremely difficult job for a full five years, he had acquired a wealth of first-hand experience. It seemed to me that his experience deserved to be put down in black and white. My friend H.S. Gurm, told me that he was already doing it. This prompted me to get in touch with him.

The outcome is here in the reader's hands. It took the author virtually four years to write this book. Even though he had some material at his disposal, he made the effort to collect further material and write several drafts. I had the privilege to look at each one of them, and make certain suggestions which, for the most part, were found acceptable by the author. It goes without saying that both the factual details and views expressed are entirely his own.

I cannot say that I agree with everything that is said here, even though I have lived with this book, to the extent any outsider can. In certain matters particularly, in regard to what happened in the closing stages of the 'lost decade' I do not agree with the author beyond a point.

Sarab Jit Singh's contention that these things happened after he had left is factually correct. But the fact of the matter is that both the militants and the police carried out a large number of indefensible actions. Towards the end, when the militants were on the run, the police took advantage of the situation. Some of the subsequent developments have shown that for every wound that was inflicted by either side, there was always a residue of pain and suffering. The police too suffered in certain respects, though it is another matter that a substantial number of them got away with what they did.

At one stage, I had publicly suggested that an enquiry should be held into the details of the assets and the property acquired by a large number of policemen during the preceding 10–15 years. Had this suggestion been acted upon, this would have shown that, in addition to other motives, pure and simple greed was a powerful motive. But nobody took that suggestion seriously and the issue has receded to the background. More to the point, however, is the picture of Punjab during those eventful days that emerges from a reading of this book.

In my judgement four things stand out. One is Sarab Jit Singh's basic thesis that Indira Gandhi had evolved a strategy of political survival for herself, in the early 1980s and an important part of it was to demonstrate that she could take a tough line in Punjab, if required. In this particular case, she deliberately allowed the situation to deteriorate to such an extent that sending the army into the Golden Temple became more or less unavoidable in the eyes of a substantial number of people. This was done but with ghastly, and entirely avoidable, consequences. At the time this strategy was planned, little did she realise that by playing the communal card she was giving birth to a monster of which she herself, and her party, would become the victims. Since the author has written at great length about this, it is not necessary to dilate upon this issue.

The second point that emerges from this narration is that in certain key areas, the Centre and the Punjab Administration were working at cross purposes. The latter followed one approach, whereas the approach adopted by both the Ministry of Home Affairs as well as the Central Intelligence agencies was more or less in contradiction to it. In V.R. Narayanan's book on this subject, there are many references to this state of unconcealed confrontation between the two. That this basic inconsistency between the two crucial agencies of the government was bound to lead to certain tragic consequences could have been anticipated. But this dimension of the problem was overlooked.

Since the author of this book had inside knowledge of almost everything that was happening, it would be instructive for political analysts to track down these details further. Should any of the actors in the drama enacted behind the scenes choose to unveil some of the murky goings-on, it would be a significant contribution to contemporary history. I find some of these details (to the extent I know them) damaging both to Indira Gandhi and her son's Home Minister, who, between them, inflicted incalculable suffering upon the people of Punjab.

The third issue which the author takes up is of the nature of terrorism that gripped Punjab for a number of years. Was it fundamentalist in its ideology and character? With his first-hand knowledge of what was happening, the author answers in the negative. According to him terrorism did not develop spontaneously. It was the outcome of state inaction and even its deliberate sustenance in certain cases. The role of the Intelligence agencies at the Centre was short-sighted and even disruptive at times. If terrorism was eliminated towards the end, this came to pass largely because the police forces had been considerably strengthened and an elected government had come to power.

In regard to the character of fundamentalism, the author tells an interesting story in the last chapter of his book, where he refers to his presence as the chief guest at his alma mater at Amritsar. While he was being welcomed, the students demanded that the student poet who was delivering the welcome address should also recite his poem about the elimination of a terrorist by the police in a fake encounter. Much to the embarrassment of the Principal, the author saw nothing wrong with the student doing so.

At the end of the function, this very poet joined in the singing of the national anthem and as the author comments, 'This was the correct picture of the younger lot'. If we were to take note only of the criticism of the 'fake encounter' and ignore the act of joining in the national anthem, it would be a half truth. This was the reality of Punjab which was ignored, even deliberately distorted, by the Centre for a whole decade.

Fourth, he discusses the question: to what extent was the Beant Singh government justified in claiming credit for wiping out terrorism. As the author has demonstrated with the help of facts and figures, by the time the state went to the polls in 1991–92, terrorism had run its course and almost exhausted its deadly grip. The Akalis through an act of sheer miscalculation and downright political cowardice, boycotted the polls. This gave a walkover to the Congress party. Beant Singh's main contribution was to give a free hand to the police. Most of the excesses committed by the police were committed in this period while in the proceeding couple of years the boot had been on the other foot. Most of the details are public knowledge already. What this book does is to put things in their proper perspective.

It is not the purpose of a Foreword to dilate only upon the merits of the book. In this case I have been so personally involved with the author that I could not but draw attention to some of the more important points which emerge from a close reading of the book. Interestingly enough, this book and a collection of articles by Satya Pal Dang, a Communist leader based in Amritsar, entitled 'Terrorism In Punjab' published recently, suggests an uncanny convergence of views between the two.

That a known critic of the government and the Akalis and one of its principal officers, should in retrospect, think more or less alike, points to only one fact: both of them were objective in their approach and have had time for reflection. If in the ultimate analysis, there is not much serious divergence of views between the analysis of those days presented by these two persons, it only goes to show that we are nearing the true reading of the situation. If one may put it this way, what happened in Punjab was partly the infusion of a virus from across the border, partly the desire to grab power, and largely an outcome of what had been planned in Delhi. That certain sections of politicians then in power colluded with this kind of approach makes it tragic beyond words.

One thing more may also be added here. While this book is an authoritative analysis of what happened during those fateful years, no one who was involved in policy making in Delhi has written a similar book. Were such a book to be written, only then will we have a full picture of how things were mishandled in Punjab as has happened time and again in Jammu and Kashmir for decades together. The factors at work in both cases were the same: a limited political vision, the selfish interest of certain individuals who at that point of time were in charge of decision making and, no less important than anything else, an insane desire to continue to wield power even at the cost of hurting the long range interests of the country. More than anyone else, it is the Congress party which is responsible for what happened in these two states. And in both cases, the stability of the country was seriously compromised.

I commend this book to the attention of prospective readers as a significant and insightful contribution towards understanding what happened in the state of Punjab at a crucial period during the last decades of the twentieth century.

23.10.2000   **Amrik Singh**

Preface

Soon after I took over as Deputy Commissioner of Amritsar in July 1987, I had a hunch that, in addition to leading the fight against terrorism, I might have to write about it. I knew for certain that in this kind of battle of arms although guns made the news, ultimately if peace has to prevail, organising the people was the more important part of my job. It was pure coincidence that had placed me in a post which enabled me to witness all the facets (some of them even repulsive) of militancy, for five long years.

Within a year of my posting, I got the opportunity to initiate and sustain action against the militants lodged inside the Golden Temple in an operation named 'Black Thunder'. Considering the anti-terrorist measures taken till then, it was indeed an epoch-making event. But the approach of the Central Government to it appeared to be neither straightforward nor open. Sometimes the reaction of the Centre was so illogical that at times I just failed to understand their objectives. It was shocking indeed. But for Governor Siddharth Shankar Ray's confidence in me, and his direct access to the Prime Minister, the action would have been abandoned halfway through and the most merciful punishment for me would have been transfer from Amritsar, on the basis of some pretext or the other. It was then that I began keeping notes and preserving newspaper clippings. Whenever I had free time I would often reflect on the important events relating to the Operation, and later, plan further moves on the basis of every-day happenings. Such 'rehearsals' have been etched on my mind and are still fresh enough to bother me at times.

When it came to writing this book, I felt that it had to be a full account of the militant movements in the Punjab and not merely the memoirs of a posting in the district of Amritsar. I had dealt with militancy in one way or the other in my capacity as Additional Deputy Commissioner (Development) Patiala (April 1984 to April 1986), and thereafter as Secretary, Punjab State Agricultural Marketing Board till July 1987. During this period, the significant events that occurred included Operation Blue Star, the assassination of Mrs. Gandhi, the anti-Sikh riots in Delhi, the September 1985 Assembly elections, the release of militants from jail by the Surjit Singh Barnala government, the resurgence of militancy and the dismissal of the S.S. Barnala government.

I had had the opportunity of interacting with and rehabilitating the migrant victims of the Delhi riots and the alleged militants released by the S.S. Barnala government. While at the Marketing Board, I had the opportunity to meet politicians of all kinds and at all levels who were members of the Board, or of the 132 Market Committees spread over the state. All of them were affected by the growing militancy. Many of them had participated in various peaceful agitations for a Punjabi suba since 1955. A helpless angry lot, they were keen observers and would often point an accusing finger at the Central Government for the trouble in Punjab. One of them reminded me of a British Governor of Punjab, W.M. Hailey. That able administrator had persuaded the then Government of India to compromise with the Akali agitators the moment it was felt that the militants were likely to take over the agitation. The agreement of 1924–25 was supposed to be the result of that policy. He added ruefully, 'Look at our own government, it is encouraging militants to foil our agitation just to corner some votes.'

As Deputy Commissioner (DC) Amritsar, militancy was my direct concern. It had grown using the Golden Temple as its sanctuary. This district was also the arena of the entire range of militancy-related controversies of the political parties; the Shiromani Gurudwara Prabandhak Committee (SGPC) the clergy, the Damdami Taksal, the Sikh Students Federation, and the Panthic Committees. A major portion of border crossings, smuggling of weapons, and nearly 70 per cent of the state's killings took place in this district till the end of 1990.

I held that office for five years (from July 1987 to May 1992) which in itself is a record till date. This is the longest stay in Amritsar by any District Magistrate in the last 140 years. Within limitations, therefore, I have attempted to cover the complete story of militancy in Punjab.

But, there were many missing links in the notes that I had kept. I therefore, spent months at the State Archives at Patiala, located in the famous 'Baraan Dari Gardens', before I could write the book. This magnificent mansion—one of the royal residences during the princely days—and its beautiful environs were a good recompense for the dusty smell of its record rooms. During these months, I could fill the gaps and complete my notes. But, perhaps, it was the weird vibes of intrigues lurking from the princely days, under the roof of the mansion, that enabled me to delve deep and understand the various machinations that politicians and their governments had employed to camouflage their respective roles in the rise and growth of militancy. As a result, besides recounting the chronicle, I could analyse it as well.

It was the peculiarity of those dark times, that those who were 'heroes' for some, were 'villains' for others and vice versa. In such a situation, recording the events as I have endeavoured, was a sure invitation for trouble. Sahir Ludhianvi, the Urdu poet, has put it beautifully in two couplets of a ghazal:

> *Aayeene se bigad kar beth gayae*
> *jin kee surat jinhen dikhai gayee.*
> *Dushmanon hi se beyr nibh jaaey*
> *doston se to aashnai gayee.*

These can be literally translated into English as

> 'With the mirror they got cross
> Whose real faces it portrayed
> Let hostility with enemies last
> For, the love of friends stands betrayed'

Sahir was right. The truth often melts friendships like snows in March, but enmities last. I would like to believe that the truth has emerged from my narration. For example, the truth is that militancy in Punjab was never a people's movement. It had been planted with a purpose—divide and rule. The truth is that some people in the ruling Congress party tried to undermine Operation Black Thunder and sabotage the other peace efforts of Governor S.S. Ray. The truth is that Governor's N.K. Mukerji and V. Varma did a great deal to raise the people's morale and had laid firm foundations for the decline of militancy. This fact was not only downplayed, but both Governors were eased out before long. Their actions could not be condoned because of the mindsets of those who controlled things in Delhi.

Governor O.P. Malhotra sustained the campaign of his predecessors so effectively that the end of militancy could be seen around the corner. But he had to resign because the newly elected Congress government at the Centre cancelled the June 1991 elections without taking him into confidence, indeed this decision was taken behind his back. Not only that, the government also withdrew the army which was deployed in the state at the time. Crime in such a situation could not but flourish and it did. Soon after when the army was re-deployed, crime began decreasing. The hiatus cost many more civilian lives. But it enabled the Beant Singh government to claim the entire credit for wiping out militancy. This way, the government felt, a grateful people would forget who had manipulated the rise of militancy.

Many other similar twists have been unveiled here. The book may therefore be unpalatable to several of my friends. But this cannot be helped. I have not tried to hide facts, nor have I tailored them in order to support any of my inferences. My intention is not to denigrate or eulogise any leader or official. I do not possess the proclivities of either an iconoclast or a sycophant. Those who do not come out well in this account may have excelled in other situations, before the rise of militancy or after it, or even in other fields. The picture that I have painted is that of Punjab militancy and their roles in it.

Whenever significant decisions were taken at my suggestion made in a meeting I have mentioned the names of the participants. For computing statistics of killings I have depended on my personal information and the figures released to the press by police spokespersons. These generally tally with statistics appearing in *Tryst with Terror* (Ajanta Publishers, 1996), written by V. N. Narayanan, then Chief Editor of *The Tribune*.

This book got really going when I got a computer which my nephew Gurmeet (Happy) lent me. I gave it back to him after my son bought one. I am grateful to both of them. For encouragement to write the book, I am indebted to my wife, Sukh, who often walked into my study and indeed, stood behind me as I was typing the last lines. My son, Amitoj, prompted and nagged me whenever I felt lazy. My daughters Tanvir and Kamal, wished me success and prayed for it. Bhai Sahib Kirpal Singh ji, founder President of the World Spiritual Foundation, based at Sydney and Kuala Lumpur happened to be with us at Patiala. He must have guessed my hesitation in writing my first book, for he asked me if I really intended to write the book. 'Tell me. I feel like praying to God today that it should be a meaning-ful and excellent one.' With these words the wise sage closed my options.

God evidently heard Bhai Sahib's prayers. The moment I felt that I could show the draft of my book to some knowledgeable person, there came a telephone call from Dr. Amrik Singh, a former Vice Chancellor of Punjab University, Patiala. I had not met him before, but I knew about him. He had come to know about my book from a common friend, Dr. H.S. Gurm, currently Vice Chancellor of the Tech-nical University, Jalandhar. His personal interest in the book and valuable guidance took care of the 'excellence' part of Bhai Sahib's prayer. I remain indebted to him both for encouragement, guidance and more than that for the pains he took to go through the book more than once. My thanks are due to Dr. Harbir Singh of GNDU Amritsar, who also helped me throughout with characteristic diligence.

I cannot forget the valuable advice Khushwant Singh gave me. One fine morning I forced myself on him. In the 15 minutes he had promised me, I got a feeling that the art of writing was no more alien to me than to several others. I am also indebted to Dr. H.K. Puri for his very fine advice on various sensitive issues.

I cannot get over the strange remorseful feeling of having written about the travails of my own people which I could not assuage as much as I wanted to, particularly during the peak days of terrorism. Yet I have audaciously agreed with the general assessment that my tenure was very successful. I crave their indulgence, and hope the large hearted people of Amritsar and all Punjabis will understand. I have no words to record my sorrow at the senseless killings. The only justification I occasionally give to myself is that I had done my best, and all signs of militancy had almost ended in Amritsar by the time I left it. The flickering revival of killings were the desperate gasps of dying militancy. In fact it was decreasing in the other dis-tricts as well.

I ought to pay my tribute to the victims of this tragedy. One has to remember the entire families, including the infants that were eliminated. I cannot forget the faces wrinkled with age but shocked into silence by the obliteration of their entire male progeny at the hands of militants. Many will bow their heads with me in memory of the martyrs who held their principles and the quest for peace dearer than their lives. They hailed from all walks of life—education, politics, business, professionals, all the services—specially the police, and above all from the mass of common people.

In all humility, I record my heartfelt sympathies for all those who lost their kith and kin and who suffered prolonged agonies at the hands of the kidnappers. I am also very sorry for the parents whose sons were led astray; and pity the young wards who without understanding and knowing what they were doing, brought ruin all around them and also perished in it themselves.

I am grateful to all the others who stoically bore the hideous trauma and let the business of life go on as usual. I remain indebted to my colleagues, those working at the grass-roots level in the civil and police hierarchy, including those in the semi-governmental and private organisations who never failed me. I also would like to record my gratitude to my seniors for their unsolicited support and appreciation, without which I could not have accomplished half as much as I did.

I am indebted to the army officers who never let me down and were very good friends. Last but not the least I must thank the media persons who, generally speaking showed great kindness throughout my long stay in Amritsar.

In the end I must crave the indulgence of my readers and all those who have been mentioned in the book, for any factual mistakes, errors of judgement and expression which may have crept in despite all the precautions that I took in writing this account.

Amritsar   **Sarab Jit Singh**

1

The Golden Temple: In the Eye of the Storm

The Golden Temple, Amritsar, had not fully emerged from the shadows of Operation Blue Star—the Army operation of June 1984—nor had the Sikhs recovered from the shocks of the first half of the 1980s when the political situation began to deteriorate again. Another storm was looming in Punjab and very sadly, the Golden Temple was again going to be its eye.

In the wake of Mrs. Indira Gandhi's assassination by two of her Sikh security guards on 31 October 1984, hundreds of innocent Sikhs were not only murdered but burnt alive in Delhi. The law of the jungle also prevailed in several cities of the Congress-ruled states as the law and order machinery was rendered inactive. The Sikh community accused of being secessionist stood isolated and ostracised. The feeling that, like Operation Blue Star, the killings in November 1984 had also been contrived, amounted to adding salt to the wounded Sikh psyche. The warmth and the prevailing sympathy of the saner Hindus were not enough to assuage the feelings of persecution of the entire Sikh community for a crime committed by some misguided persons.

To heal the wounds of the Sikhs and to restore peace in Punjab, the newly-elected Prime Minister, Rajiv Gandhi, signed an accord with Sant Harchand Singh Longowal, the President of the Shiromani Akali Dal in July 1985. But it was torpedoed in such a subtle manner that in essence it remained unimplemented. The various Commissions appointed by the Central government, to adjudicate disputes between Haryana and Punjab, either could not come to a conclusion, or their recommendations remained unacceptable to the disputing parties.

On 26 January 1986, the Republic Day of India, a gathering of extremists, styling themselves as *Sarbat Khalsa* (like the meetings of the Sikh *Misls*—confederacies—in the eighteenth century), dismissed all the legal and elected religious organisations of the Sikhs and appointed a Panthic Committee to replace them. On that very day the dismantling of the newly repaired Akal Takht building, which had been mutilated during Operation Blue Star, began. A new Akal Takht had to be erected in place of the existing structure which was tainted by 'unholy hands' and sullied money provided by the Central government for its repair. However, when *kar-sewa* (work by voluntary labour) first to demolish and later to reconstruct the Akal Takht commenced, the extremists used this as a handy cover to flock to the Golden Temple. In April 1986 the Panthic Committee resolved to struggle for the attainment of Khalistan and publicised this fact widely. This was accompanied by an ominous increase in the killing of innocent persons. In brief these were the signs of resurgent terrorism.

The only implemented clause of the much publicised Rajiv–Longowal Accord was also undone on 11 May 1987, when the 19-month-old Akali Government in Punjab headed by Chief Minister Surjit Singh Barnala was dismissed on the grounds of a supposed breakdown of law and order in the state. The succeeding Governor Siddhartha Shankar Ray's administration toiled hard to restore peace. In the first two months, the increased pressure on terrorist affected areas resulted in more and more militants moving into the Temple complex where they had already established their headquarters. The wheel had come full circle and the situation in the Harmandar, though not as alarming as in 1984, was certainly reminiscent of conditions prevailing before the Operation by the Army.

As a result of the large scale transfers of bureaucrats which the newspapers called a 'shake up' ordered by the Governor, I was tipped to head the most sensitive district of Amritsar as its Deputy Commissioner. This office also combined the functions of the District

Magistrate and the Collector. Normally such a posting would be a matter of pride for any officer of the Indian Administrative Service but for me it was much more. I hailed from this district. My moorings are in village Jethuwal, founded and named by my ancestors in the eighteenth century. I was also actively looking after our ancestral land. According to the prevailing practice, officers are generally not posted to their hometowns. At the beginning of my career I had sought a posting here but the government did not agree to make an exception even for the period of my training. The exception had now been made for a challenging job which carried an obvious risk for the lives of my kith and kin as well as my own.

Amritsar is a vast district spread over 5,000 sq km covering five sub-divisions. It has a 265 km long international border with Pakistan, which zigzags along the boundaries of the agricultural fields of several villages of Lahore and Amritsar districts. The artificial line that cyril Radcliffe drew in 1947 to demarcate Pakistan from the existing Punjab, caused the cross-migration of populations on the basis of religion. But it could not break the age-old ties of a common language, shared culture and social customs. After the Partition, normal trade between the two districts was transformed into smuggling with fabulous profits not known earlier. Only the construction of a 'Berlin Wall' could have stopped this illegal trafficking, but we had only *kacha* (rough) tracks on either side of the no-man's-land. Understandably the international border remained quite porous. It had become a matter of serious concern from the early 1980s onwards when lethal weapons, ammunition, RDX and trained terrorists began flowing increasingly from Pakistan into India.

Amritsar has for long been the hub of political activity. Therefore, it is important both for the government and the media. The Golden Temple complex houses the headquarters of the Shiromani Akali Dal, SGPC and the All India Sikh Students Federation (AISSF). It is from the Akal Takht (within this complex) that the Akali Dal launched its *morchas*. The orthodox Damdami Taksal, numerous *deras*—hospices—of *sants* and historical gurudwaras commemorating the martyrs of the eighteenth century Sikh struggle against the Mughals and the Afghans, are spread all over the district. The Jallianwala Bagh, known for the merciless shooting on an unarmed assembly on Baisakhi day, 13 April 1919, ordered by General Dyer, lies almost adjacent to the Golden Temple. The Guru Ka Bagh, where a long drawn agitation by Akalis attracted international attention in the

1920s and forced the British to concede a moral victory to the Akalis, is only 25 kms from the city.

With such a background and the addition of what Governor S.S. Ray called the 'Smugglers, Police and Politicians nexus', the availability of unemployed youth, their training by the Inter Services Intelligence (ISI) of Pakistan and the short-sighted approach by the State and Union Governments, this district became an ideal breeding ground to spawn and nourish the monster of terrorism.

In such a situation, a conscientious administrator has not only to take many a risk and put one's career at stake, but also remain circumspect at all times. As a devout Sikh, I decided to visit the Golden Temple before formally taking over as DC Amritsar. My predecessor intended to lay down his office at 10.00 A.M. on 7 July 1987. Therefore, I planned to be in the Harmandar Sahib at 7.30 A.M. on that day to give myself two hours in the sacred precincts.

A couple of fatal incidents, came to my mind then. In April 1983 the militants in the Golden Temple had shot dead A.S. Atwal, a DIG of Police, who had gone to the Temple incognito. On 7 March 1987, militants had killed a police constable in mufti whom they spotted in the *parikrama* of the holy place. Twenty policemen who went in to rescue their colleague were also fired at, resulting in injuries to some of them while their officers waited helplessly outside. Though the police succeeded in evacuating the injured and the dead, the administration could not do anything against the militants. I was also aware that the morale of the militants was up again because the S.S. Barnala government had been dismissed in May 1987 on the allegation of having failed to control the revival of militancy in the state.

In addition to all this, a terrible incident on the night of 6 July 1987 had shocked the nation and had badly shaken the Punjab and Central Governments. Some terrorists had hijacked a Haryana State Roadways overnight bus on the Chandigarh–Ambala highway, forced it on to a link road and then shot dead 40 of its passengers, mostly Hindus. Thirty occupants of the overloaded bus were also injured. This incident was the most terrible till then. Retaliatory violence against the Sikhs in some of the neighbouring states was feared. Some people apprehended a serious fallout in Punjab as well. To my mind, however, the chances of any disturbance appeared remote.

I had to reconsider my planned visit to the Temple which, even in normal circumstances, was risky. All the odds were against such a move. The ominous incident had greatly increased the likelihood of embarrassing the government in case of any mishap; such as holding me hostage, or even interrogating me in their torture chambers. I even imagined people reading my obituary if things were to take an adverse turn. But the optimist in me prevailed. The call of duty and my faith in God coalesced and provided me with strength. I had to see for myself how the protagonists of bloodshed could be at ease in God's house where every visiting soul is uplifted with the peace and beauty that prevails there.

Any lurking doubts were dispelled by the weather gods as the first monsoon showers greeted me the moment our car moved towards the Harmandar Sahib. The cool rain in sweltering summer gladdens the heart of man, bird and beast, but at that moment, thinking practically I realised that the drizzle could provide me with a valid and safe excuse for tarrying at some places for shelter inside the Temple complex. In fact, I could begin my visit with a stop under the main entrance on the Ghanta Ghar side as the drizzle turned somewhat heavy.

I cherished the sight of the serene and beautiful Harmandar and its immaculate cleanliness in keeping with its mystical and spiritual ambience. The number of devotees was visibly less than usual for this season. The proportion of Hindus was perceptibly lower. This was evidently due to the presence of the militants inside. However, the militants presence did not seem to affect the day's visitors. As soon as they entered the Darbar Sahib the people were transformed into joyous looking pilgrims.

The Golden Temple complex is bigger and much more beautiful than can be visualised from the various accounts and pictures available. I remember how the Chief Constable (Wales, UK) Mr. Dear, who visited the Golden Temple after Operation Black Thunder, could not hold back his surprise. He said, 'Back home as I followed the Operation, I was wondering why you people cannot drive out the militants instantly. Having seen it now I appreciate your problem. I could never imagine that it was so vast.' Sir David Goodall, the then British High Commissioner to India came to visit the Temple in October 1987 when it was under the sway of the militants. He agreed to my suggestion that he view it from the top of Braham Buta Akhara. Spellbound, he watched it for nearly 20 minutes. When he turned around he seemed intoxicated with its incredible beauty and was whispering to himself 'a breathtaking beauty!' After the militants were driven out of the Temple, he visited again in the year 1988, and stayed for hours in the *parikrama*. This time he tried to capture the beauty of the Temple on canvas. The reflection of religious sentiments in the setting has been noted beautifully by Percy Brown. In his book, *Indian Architecture: Islamic Period*, he says:

> As an example of religious emotion materialised in marble glass colours and metal, the Golden Temple at Amritsar is equalled only by Shwe Dagon Pagoda in Rangoon; the former symbolises the faith of the Sikhs and the latter is the highest expression in a very similar range of material of another Indian religion, that of the Buddhists.

Coming back to my visit on 7 July 1987, the scene of splendour and magnificence of the Harmandar that we saw that day was rare. The low, dark grey clouds were in the background and the rain occasionally stopped, letting the sun peep through a break in the clouds. The glitter of the many golden domes, the marble and its reflection in the rippling azure waters around the Harmandar sent me into a state of ecstasy. My wife, who had come to know of my intended visit, and had insisted on accompanying me was equally awed. In acceding to her wish I had thought that it would be a good precaution. As we descended the marble steps from the portico to the *parikrama*, she said, 'Where is the danger you were cautioning me about?' I only reminded her of our agreement that in the *parikrama* we were to keep a reasonable distance between us, so that she could ignore me in case of any contingency. In the *parikrama* we turned to our left and joined a small group of pilgrims. I hastened towards the head of the group.

The *parikrama*, a marble pavement around the 150 sq m holy tank has a width, except at a few portions, of 60 feet. The outer side of the pavement is covered by a *verandah* on three sides behind which there are large rooms. The Braham Buta Akhara, Bunga Ramgharian and the arched entrance from the side of the Guru Ramdas Sarai, form the outer wall of the first half of the eastern side of the *parikrama*. Adjoining the remaining side of the eastern *parikrama* there is an open space for a garden, but at that time the debris of the Akal Takht building which was pulled down in 1986, formed a sizeable mound here. Next to the mound is some open space and the sprawling Manji Sahib Hall. The new *langar* (community kitchen) building is behind Bunga Ramgharian and it faces Manji Sahib Hall. Alongside these is a wide metalled road. The SGPC and the Municipal authorities both lay claim to this road. On the other side of the road are located the Akal Rest House, the Guru Ramdas Sarai, Teja Singh Samundari Hall and Guru Nanak Niwas. This complex houses a bank, the secretariat of the SGPC and the AISSF office. The office of the Shiromani Akali Dal is at the end of the road behind the Manji Sahib Hall.

The sanctum sanctorum, in the middle of the *sarovar* (tank) can be reached only from the western side of the *parikrama* over a 240 ft. long causeway, access to which is through a beautiful arched entrance known as the Darshani Deorhi. On the other end of the causeway is the solid 57 sq m platform supporting the magnificent Harmandar Sahib. It is the place of audience for devotees with their God. The surrounding tank known as Amrit Sarovar (Pool of Nectar) after which the city gets its name—Amritsar—is 17 ft. deep. Facing the Darshani Deorhi stands the Akal Takht, then under reconstruction.

Although my ostensible purpose was to pay obeisance in the Harmandar, for the purpose of my surveillance, three points were specifically important. The first was the two room nos 45 and 46, which were at the corner formed by the end of the northern side of the *parikrama* into which we had descended. The second comprised of room nos 13 and 14 which were located near the corner, diagonally opposite room nos 45 and 46. The third was the area where the Akal Takht building was under construction.

By now, the drizzle was mild. To enable a stop at the first corner, I made use of the *chhabil* located there. Here as well as at the other three corners, water is provided for the thirsty. I picked up a bowl and moved into the *verandah* to be close to the infamous rooms. The rooms were rather quiet. Suddenly a voice shouted, 'How can the Assistant Manager (an official of the SGPC) refuse to provide us with another fan? He is not going to pay from his father's money. Go and tell him to make sure that the fan is installed by the evening, failing which he will personally face the consequences.'

A teenager darted out of the room and, without looking at the group of villagers sitting in the *verandah* or noticing me, ran to fulfil his errand. Through the open door one could see some coloured photographs of teenaged boys on the inner walls of the second room. Obviously these were of the 'boys' who may have been killed in encounters with the police. It appeared as if the group of villagers had also been summoned. I curbed my urge to talk to them or to stay longer near the rooms.

I turned to come out of the *verandah* when I noticed two teenagers standing on the other side of the pillars of the *verandah*. They were obviously watching me. Ignoring them I started surveying the Braham Buta Akhara and the Bunga Ramgharian, which is next to it. I reverentially tarried at the *Dukh Bhanjani Beri*—Reliever of all pain and sorrow—a tree alongside the holy *sarovar*. It is believed that a dip at the site heals many diseases. When I turned to resume my perambulation, both the boys were behind me. I realised I had stayed rather long outside the rooms which were avoided by most people. I thought if I continued ignoring them they would keep on shadowing me and perhaps draw ugly conclusions. I took the initiative. Looking at them I asked, 'Are you Singhs (a title assumed by militants), or employees of the SGPC or, are you associated with some *dera?*' They looked at each other sheepishly, but smiled at me. The elder one of them nodded and said, 'We are Singhs'. The saints and Singhs use the plural pronoun for their individual selves.

'And what do you do here?' I asked. They seemed to be at a loss for words, not knowing what to say.

'What job has been entrusted to you?' I tried to be more specific.

'Whatever our seniors tell us to do,' said the younger one who also appeared to be the sharper of the two.

'Upto which class have you studied in school and what is the name of your village?' I kept them at the answering end.

They were from village Sur Singh. They gave up school after passing the seventh class because their parents placed them with a *dera* which was participating, on a voluntary basis, in the reconstruction of the Akal Takht. Here they got involved with the Singhs. In reply to their only question I informed them that I was a visitor from Udaipur in Rajasthan. They had never heard of the beautiful city. After ascertaining this they turned back towards their rooms.

The drizzle was becoming heavy. I moved into the *verandah* of the southern *parikrama*. Just short of the next corner opposite my last stop, a tall and hefty man surrounded by a small group was proudly narrating a recent incident which took place in one of the rooms in that corner. The story was that he heard the cries of an old man from one of the rooms close to room nos 13 and 14. His enquiries revealed that two young boys, were torturing an old man, to extract more money from him. This Akali leader brought it to the notice of the so-called Lt. General of the organisation. He got very furious and immediately dispatched the two boys and their leader, bag and baggage, from the temple.

Because of the drizzle, no construction activity was going on at the Akal Takht site. Some marble slabs and other material were being stored. Some artisans were supervising the placement. The scene was dominated by the youth in their long *cholas* (loose shirts reaching below the knees). Officially the *kar-sewa* had been entrusted to a panel of five saints. The Damdami Taksal had staked exclusive claim to this holy task which was not acceptable to the SGPC. Nevertheless, they dominated the group. Some baskets and boxes had been placed at various places around the *parikrama* for collecting donations for the task. The baskets were covered with a transparent, waterproof plastic sheet. One could see that many people had offered gold jewellery as their contribution. Contributions worth lakhs of rupees were lying unattended. This was evidence of the faith of both the donors and the organisers. After seeing this I moved towards the Darshani Deorhi.

It did not take me long to reach the Harmandar Sahib where my wife was waiting for me. We sat inside to listen to the *kirtan*. When we moved out, the mild storm began to wane. I was getting late so we hastened towards the main entrance through which we had come. Just near the stairs the two young boys that I had talked to earlier were standing accompanied by two other young men. It appeared as if they were waiting for me. These men were also in long flowing *cholas*. I had not expected this. I felt that the report that the young boys may have given to their seniors perhaps raised their suspicion, so they wanted to cross-check my antecedents. The situation was piquant. They accosted me with their usual greeting *Wahe Guru ji ka Khalsa Wahe Guru ji ki Fateh*, and as I came close they asked, 'You live in Udaipur?' I nodded and replied in the affirmative. They looked at each other. I told my wife to go up the stairs and buy some souvenirs from a particular shop. I was planning to send her so that I could dash out if it was necessary. But she lingered on, to be with me in this moment of apparent crisis.

'If we come to Udaipur can you help us buy marble from a mine nearby?' one of them asked quite politely. We relaxed and my wife started moving up the stairs. 'The mine is at Nathdwara, about an hour's drive from Udaipur,' I informed them. I also advised them to reach the gurudwara and contact the *Granthi* if they wanted to reach me. 'But the quality is quite unfit for this holy place.' I gave my decisive opinion. Instead of giving my name I gave them the name and address of my elder brother who actually lives in Udaipur (Rajasthan).

From the conversation that ensued, I elicited from them their opinion of the rebuilding of the Akal Takht as well as of the Punjab situation. They were convinced that because of the rebuilding of the Akal Takht they were very popular with the people. They pointed to an old peasant couple who, after placing some currency in a basket were also offering a gold ring. They alleged that it was government agents who were responsible for carrying out the killings and extortion demands in order to defame their movement. They refused to identify any such agency while emphatically denying any connection with the killings. One of them maintained that they had respect for the brave militants who were risking their lives and comforts for avenging the honour of the *Panth*.

'We cannot do anything for these martyrs, we therefore hang their photographs on our walls,' he said, 'The Government of India is still behaving like Aurangzeb and is out to destroy our temples and us. What happened during the Blue Star Operation and during the Delhi riots of 1984, the whole world knows. If there are no laws to book the perpetrators of these crimes, the present day Massa Ranghars and Mannus (Mughal administrators) then Sukha Singh and Mehtab Singh and Bota Singh (Singhs of the eighteenth century) have to avenge the wrongs. It is true that Rajiv Gandhi signed an accord, but what is the outcome, where is the accord now? It died with Longowal.' They spoke with passion and conviction, supporting each other. 'The SGPC has many corrupt employees just like the people in the government. They are also committing many irregularities and blaming the "boys".' Their contempt for the SGPC was obvious. 'Unless the government does not support the bad elements how can the weapons come into the Temple when the Central Reserve Police Force (CRPF) is guarding and frisking people at all the entry points to the Darbar Sahib? We are not against the Hindus. The government arranges all such killings in order to malign us as separatists and communal.'

I had elicited their views, by pointing out the dangers to which the Sikhs in the rest of India were exposed as a consequence of their activities, particularly the killing of Hindus. I also referred to the efforts of the Government of India, particularly by Rajiv Gandhi, to assuage the hurt psyche of the Sikhs. At this point I felt that pursuing the topic any further would only irritate them, so I left. Each of them shook my hand with both of theirs, which were as powerful as the jaws of pliers; I was glad that I did not have to test my physical prowess in any effort to escape from their cordon. I was glad that I had not cancelled my visit. I now had some first-hand information about the thinking of the militants inside the Temple and the kind of brainwashing that they had undergone. I considered that some of their arguments could be countered through an information campaign.

I returned to the DC's office. The dull red brick building, an 18 ft. high single storey structure, erected by the British immediately after annexing Amritsar in 1849, looked very sombre. A few old magnificent trees enlivened the atmosphere. The war souvenir, (a Patton Tank, one of the 100 odd abandoned by the retreating Pakistan Army at Aasal Utaar in Amritsar district during the 1965 war) stood at the entrance to the Deputy Commissioner's office enclave. This was a symbol of the unfriendly relations between the two countries, which was also reflected in the prevailing terrorist situation in Punjab. Ramesh Inder Singh (IAS) my predecessor, had completed his tenure of three years and had performed quite creditably. He welcomed me with a big smile. The papers were ready for our signatures. As soon as the formalities of my assuming the post were over, the telephone rang. A press reporter wanted to know the steps taken in view of the previous night's killings. As briefed by Ramesh Inder Singh, I informed him about the increased patrolling etc. 'How is the situation in the city, Sir?' was his next question.

Apart from what I had seen in the temple, I had not noticed any visible uneasiness during my drive through the city to my office. But that would amount to making light of the overall situation. The press and the administration had often used the non-committal phrase 'tense but under control' to evade a precise assessment of any situation. I had earlier ridiculed this phrase saying that the tension was on the part of the administration, and the control that of the militants, who could choose the mode, place and time for provocations. I could not, therefore, use this convenient but trite phrase. Choosing my words with care and wondering how he would react, I said 'I do not think there is going to be any reaction in this district to last night's ghastly killings. As far as terrorist crimes are concerned that cannot be predicted, the initiative unfortunately is the prerogative of the devil.' On hearing my response, he said 'Thank you, and welcome to Amritsar.'

I saw off Ramesh Inder Singh and returned to the huge empty room. I could not help a few moments of reflection before the officers and senior staff members were expected to pour in. I reflected that approximately 100 Deputy Commissioners before me must have spent many anxious moments in this room. I thought of Miles Irving who had sat in the same chair when General Dyer exhausted his ammunition on defenceless people at Jallianwala Bagh on 13 April 1919. I thought of the last British Deputy Commissioner who had to contend with the Hindu-Muslim riots in 1947 and of the first Indian DC, in independent India, who dealt with famished, dispirited and penniless hordes of refugees coming from Pakistan. What was so unique in the design of this roof that it showered tremendous challenges on the incumbents of that chair? Suddenly I thought of the national flag fluttering on top of the building. It was this symbol of state authority which had to be upheld at all costs. Currently it had been challenged by the resurgent Sikh militants who occasionally hoisted their own flag in the Golden Temple. I wondered what impelled these boys to rebel. Their ancestors had been in the forefront of those who had sacrificed their lives in defending the motherland against the invaders from the north and later in the national struggle for freedom. Our heritage remains a powerful—at times dangerous—influence on our thinking and actions. It can take you by surprise and it can also be exploited by others.

Years ago in the Coffee Bar of the Supreme Court of India, a Muslim lawyer was taunting his Hindu colleagues: 'Though we were few and had come from other countries yet we ruled over you for centuries.' Then he turned to me, 'Am I right Sardar ji?' I was the only Sikh present. I shook my head and said, 'It was true so long as we had not appeared on the scene. After that no one could enter India at least through Punjab.' He pondered for a moment, had a long pull on the cigarette he was smoking and then agreed with me. I also became pensive. Such a boast was certainly alien to my ethos but it was my heritage as a Sikh and a Punjabi. Let us look at the fascinating story of the people of Punjab in order to understand its bearing on the turmoil of the 1980s, and also to note how ignorant youths were exploited in the name of their history.

2

The Sikh Heritage and the Punjab Problem

The Sikh heritage is a fascinating saga of 'Sparrows battling hawks' and 'One fighting against a lakh and a quarter'. These prophetic and emotionally charged phrases uttered by Guru Gobind Singh (1666–1708) were vindicated within 10 years of his having created the Khalsa on Baisakhi day in 1699. Banda Singh Bahadur, perhaps the last 'Singh' to have been baptised by the Guru himself at Nanded, was sent by Guru Sahib to Punjab with a *hukamnama* directing his Sikhs to support Banda. Banda led the enthused Sikhs to victory over the Mughals. He himself speared the Mughal Governor of Sirhind on 12 May 1710 in a battle at Chhappar Chiri and established Sikh rule from the Yamuna to the Sutlej.

The rule lasted for only four years, when the Mughals launched a counter campaign to exterminate the Sikhs completely from the empire. Over the next 50 years, three Mughal Governors of Lahore—Abdus Samad Khan, Zakaria Khan and Moin Ul-Malik (Mannu)—in succession, devised and used the most cruel and inhumane methods of torturing the Singhs, including their children, to death. The latter organised themselves into small groups to protect a limited number of villages. Such groups were known as *rakhi*. A group of *rakhis* would combine to form a *misl* to deal with a larger enemy force and the *misls* would combine to form a *Dal Khalsa* to take on the army of the enemy. In resisting the carnage, the Sikhs raised their guerrilla fighting to the level of a people's war and won it. As part of this campaign they also dared repeated raids on Nadir Shah's train on his way home after the loot and massacre of Delhi.

The Guru's words were vindicated again in 1765 when an alliance of the Sikh *misls* captured Lahore and struck a new coin to proclaim their rule. This rule of the *misls* was consolidated by Ranjit Singh, the sardar of the Sukherchakia *misl*, to establish the first Sikh Empire which extended up to Kabul. Thereafter, no conqueror dared attack Punjab from that direction. The history of repeated incursions into India from the North had literally been reversed when the Sikhs invaded the land of Pathans.

Hari Ram Gupta, in his well known book *The Sikh History*, evaluating the achievement of Sikhs during this period states that they '...maintained the struggle between good and evil, between sovereign will of the people and divine rights of kings and the opposition of liberty to despotism;... avenged the insults, the outrages and the slavery of many generations past.' He goes on to say that they are the 'people who won for the Punjab the envied title of the "land of soldiers"; who alone can boast of having erected a "bulwark of defence against foreign aggression", the tide of which had run its prosperous course for the preceding eight hundred years; and to whom all other people of Northern India in general, and of Punjab in particular, owe a deep debt of gratitude.'

The learned historian was commenting on the 'soldier'—*Miri*—aspect of their struggle which the Mughals had forced on the Tenth Guru. Their initial struggle as 'saints'—*Piri*—is in fact much more important and significant. Guru Nanak, (1469–1539) the First Sikh Guru, had introduced a different approach when he preached that there is 'no Hindu, no Musalman', nor any high or low castes. There is only one self-created, eternal God. He alone is the creator of the universe and of all life. Thus, all humans are equal. To make his Sikhs (from *Shish*—disciple) live his teachings, he used to make them congregate and sing the praises of God, and later cook and eat in the *langar* sharing the same roof and floor, irrespective of their caste and social status.

The Fifth Guru, Arjan Dev and the Ninth Guru, Teg Bahadur had willingly accepted martyrdom rather than bow to the threat to accept Islam. This had shaken the people to wake up to their rights.

The Sixth Guru, Har Gobind, after the martyrdom of his father had asked for two swords to wear; one for *piri* and one for *miri*—symbolising that he was not only the spiritual guru but also the temporal head of the Sikhs. Guru Gobind created the *Khalsa* on the *Baisakhi* of 1699 after the martyrdom of his father Guru Teg Bahadur.

Shortly after they became organised, the Sikhs came in conflict with the Mughal rulers who were oppressing the people in many ways; including forcible conversion. Later, they passively resisted the British who supported the unlawful possession of historic gurudwaras by corrupt hereditary priests—*mahants*. The challenge was to the state's interference in their religious affairs and the assertion of their rights to manage their own shrines. Many a time, even after Independence, the Akalis complained of interference in religious affairs. They were not always wrong.

In the Sikh ethos, their faith is sovereign. They had begun referring to the Harmandar as 'Darbar Sahib' during the lifetime of Guru Arjan Dev. The word Sahib means the 'Master'. The implication was that the Court of their Master is the Darbar Sahib and not the Mughal Court. Similarly, the throne they bowed before, was the Akal Takht (throne of the Timeless—immortal God) and not the Mughal throne. Their defiance of the Mughals was staunch and unwavering. Even Maharaja Ranjit Singh, the builder of the powerful Sikh Empire, was summoned to appear at the Akal Takht and awarded religious punishment—*tankhah*—for having consorted with a Muslim woman, which is forbidden by the Sikh moral code. In the present day, the President of India, Giani Zail Singh; and Buta Singh the Home Minister complied with the summons of the Akal Takht. Their explanations were eventually accepted, but S.S. Barnala, the Chief Minister willingly submitted to his sentence. He cleaned shoes and utensils in five gurudwaras besides paying other penalties.

After the annexation of the Punjab, the British ultimately recognised and came round to respect the Sikh identity. They did all that was possible to win them over. They recruited a large number of soldiers of the Sikh army and dispersed them in various British regiments. Sikh symbols were not only respected in the British army, but each Sikh in the army was required to observe them. In 1860 they started digging two canals in the province to add to the prosperity of the Punjabis. Despite their efforts, they could not suppress the Sikh spirit.

In the year 1862, Baba Ram Singh, a former soldier turned a man of God and founded the *Namdhari* order. They organised a mutiny against the British. Unfortunately, information about the D day was leaked out. As a consequence, 60 odd Namdharis, including some in their teens, were tied to the mouth of canons and publicly blown to pieces in Malerkotla. This took place within five years of the uprising of 1857.

But an open conflict between the Sikhs and the British Government appeared inevitable on account of the religious reform movement of the early 1920s. The hereditary priests, (*mahants*) in control of the historical gurudwaras, many of which contained great wealth, had British support. A Gurudwara Reform Movement was launched by the Akalis to evict the corrupt *mahants* but it was entirely peaceful and non-violent. This agitation to liberate Sikh gurudwaras (1920–25) became, in a way, the spearhead of the national freedom movement. Supporting this fact, Mahatma Gandhi congratulated Baba Kharak Singh, the President of the SGPC, who had managed, without any resort to violence, to compel Mr. Dunnet, the then Deputy Commissioner of Amritsar, to release the Sikhs arrested during the agitation for the keys and also to hand over the keys of the *Toshakhana* (treasury) of the Golden Temple. Mahatma Gandhi's telegram to Baba Kharak Singh, on this occasion read: 'First Battle of India's Freedom Won. Congratulations.'

Another political innovation of this movement was that the Sikhs were the first organised group to demonstrate in actual practice that Gandhi's doctrine of non-violent passive resistance could be used on a mass scale in liberating their gurudwaras. *Mahant* Narayan Dass, with the help of hired killers trapped and killed all the 131 unarmed Sikhs who had come to liberate the gurudwara at Nankana Sahib. Not only that, he also dared to cremate the dead bodies to destroy evidence. Mahatma Gandhi, after an in-depth analysis of the incident, lauded the stark courage of those who had laid down their lives without offering any resistance. He also praised the newly formed Akalis, who visited the site of the martyrdom of their colleagues at Nankana Sahib without displaying any anger. They continued their passive resistance at Guru Ka Bagh, Tarn Taran and Jaito in Nabha State for another five years.

Despite great provocation and severe injuries inflicted on them during the police *lathi* charges ordered by an obdurate British administration, the Akali *jathas* had remained remarkably peaceful.

Jawahar Lal Nehru and Pandit Madan Mohan Malviya were deeply moved by their forbearance and patience. The young Nehru had participated in the Jaito agitation. Pandit Malviya publicly advised that each Hindu family should enrol one son of theirs into the Khalsa fraternity. This custom was followed by many even after the Partition of the country in 1947.

Ultimately the British had to relent. The government passed the Shiromani Gurudwara Prabandhak Committee Act of 1925. Consequently the SGPC was given the control and management of the historic gurudwaras located in the Punjab.

In his speeches, the Mahatma cited and lauded their sacrifices as justification of his theory of non-violence and truth. The SGPC and the Akalis who had come into existence to help the former, had incontestably established their credentials as *satyagrahi* nationalists.

The new credo of the Sikh organisation was in direct contrast to the traditional Sikh love of soldiering. At the end of the First World War, the number of Sikhs in the Indian Army was vastly disproportionate to their population in the country. They were also in the forefront of the struggle for freedom. Statistics show that out of every 100 Indians who suffered punishment for joining the freedom struggle, more than 70 were Sikhs. Of, the 2,175 Indians who fell to the bullets of the British, 1,575 were Sikhs. Out of 2,646 sentenced to life imprisonment and sent to *Kala Pani* (Cellular Jail in the Andaman Islands), 2,147 were Sikhs. Of the 127 sent to the gallows, 92 were from amongst the followers of the Gurus. Of the 20,000 strong Indian National Army raised by Subhash Chandra Bose from amongst the prisoners of war, 12,000 were Sikhs.

The Sikhs were justifiably proud of their significant contribution in the struggle for freedom. This had been recognised and, on various occasions, they had received assurances from senior leaders of the Indian National Congress that they, too, would share in the 'glow of freedom'. Soon after independence, however, they began to feel that they had been let down. In the early 1950s they again found themselves agitating for a *Punjabi Suba*—a state with Punjabi as its official language. This was vehemently opposed by the Hindu Maha Sabha, the Arya Samaj, and the Save Hindi organisations.

On the one hand, these organisations had been claiming that Sikhs were a part of the Hindu *parivar*; and on the other, during that period, the Punjabi language for them was like a red rag to the bull. In many an anti-*Punjabi Suba* procession, some of the slogans raised were that Punjabi was a '*langri bhasha*', and a '*gandi bhasha*' (lame and dirty language).

The States Reorganisation Commission was formed in 1953 to examine the issue of reorganising the states on a linguistic basis. One of the directions to the Commission was that the states on the national border should have a larger size, keeping defence considerations in mind. This direction had come from Jawahar Lal Nehru, the then Prime Minister of India. One can surmise that the experience of Pakistan's aggression in 1948 on Jammu and Kashmir, (a part of which is still under the control of that country), was at the back of his mind. But it did pre-empt the formation of a *Punjabi Suba*.

The Akalis, however, were happy with the outcome of the Commission's report as accepted by the government. According to one of the recommendations the union of Punjabi-speaking Sikh princely states, known as PEPSU, was merged with Punjab. The recommended merger of Himachal Pradesh with Punjab was put off for 10 years to appease the angered people of that state. In the Punjab thus made larger, both Punjabi and Hindi were to be the official languages in their respective areas, known as the Punjabi and Hindi regions. Quite surprisingly the predominantly Punjabi speaking districts of Kangra and Shimla were included in the Hindi region and the Akalis did not object to it, perhaps in order to have a Sikh majority in the Regional Committee. A Regional Committee for each region comprising of the legislatures from the region was to legislate on the listed subjects for their respective regions. The Akalis not only accepted this arrangement, but gave up the demand for the *Punjabi Suba*, entered into a truce with the Congress at the legislative level, and also contested the 1957 general elections on the Congress ticket.

But even this generous arrangement was not acceptable to the protagonists of Hindi. This was really unfortunate. The Regional Formula was a brilliant innovation which was in several parts of our multilingual country, particularly the eastern region. The Hindi protagonists were once again out in the streets with the same gusto under the banner of Mahan Punjab Samiti. They rejected the Regional Formula in April 1958. Master Tara Singh began a counter agitation.

As a result the chances of the Regional Formula turning out to be an acceptable arrangement dimmed. The agitation for a *Punjabi Suba* and a counter agitation for Mahan Punjab became increasingly aggressive. Renowned religious personalities from both camps went on fasts unto death, to be broken on one pretext or the other. The Prime Minister of India while replying, to a debate on the issue in the Rajya Sabha on 20 August 1961, said that the division of Punjab on a linguistic basis '... would be no protection to Punjabi. In fact it would harm it by linking (confining) it to a small area. There would be a dangerous division of Punjab on communal lines leading to the growth of fissiparous tendencies and bitterness.' The firm stand by the State and the Central governments resulted in the failure of the Akali agitation. They also fared badly in the 1962 election securing only 19 seats.

The demand for a *Punjabi Suba* was revived in 1965. Sant Fateh Singh had announced that he would go on a fast unto death on 10 September 1965, but he agreed to postpone it in view of Pakistan's aggressive designs. The people of the area displayed overwhelming support to the armed forces during the fighting. While retreating, the Pakistan army had to abandon its pride, a 100 Patton Tanks, near Bhikhiwind. Prime Minister Lal Bahadur Shastri announced the formation of a three member Cabinet Committee under Mrs. Gandhi to consider the demand of the *Punjabi Suba*. Another parliamentary Committee under the Chairmanship of Hukam Singh, the Speaker, was also formed to advise the Cabinet Committee. By that time some interests in the Haryana area and Himachal Pradesh had also decided to have separate states. The *Punjabi Suba* this time was therefore formed quite easily. The three states came into being on 1 November 1966.

However, Chandigarh, the capital of Punjab was made a union territory. The Akalis felt cheated. They launched an agitation to get their capital. Again fasts unto death and threats of self-immolation were announced. Darshan Singh Pheruman, after remaining on hunger strike for 75 days breathed his last. After him Sant Fateh Singh undertook a similar pledge, vowing to immolate himself. Within three days of his fast, Mrs. Gandhi the Prime Minister, announced an award in 1970 which was to be implemented by 1975. Chandigarh was to go to Punjab. Haryana was to get Abohar and Fazilka from Punjab with a furlong wide corridor from Rajasthan along the border. This award was to be implemented after five years. Haryana had to vacate Chandigarh after two years. But it did not do so on the plea that the transfer of Abohar, Fazilka and Chandigarh was a package deal. K.C. Pant, the Minister of State for Home Affairs clarified in Parliament that 'they were not in the nature of a package deal.'

That is where things rest even today. The Akalis once again felt cheated and agitated in Delhi with a charter of their grievances and demands. They had earlier pointed out the irritants that had spilled over as a result of the implementation of the Reorganisation Act of 1966. The Akalis who had boycotted the proceedings of the Shah Commission, were upset over some of the provisions of the Reorganisation Act as well as the demarcation of the *Punjabi Suba*. They had some objections which were part of their charter of demands in the early 1980s. They enumerated the wrongs done to Punjab. In essence these were as follows:-

A. The Census of 1961 was the outcome of the severe linguistic conflict going on at that time. As a result, a substantial number of Punjabi-speaking Hindus wrongly gave Hindi as their mother tongue. The communal conflict and the violent linguistic agitation had thus vitiated the report.

B. The Hindi and Punjabi speaking areas had been correctly demarcated in the Sachar formulae of 1949 which had been followed in the Regional formula that had remained operative for decades and been accepted by all. This should have been the basis of the division rather than the Census Report distorted by narrow, momentary prejudices.

C. Besides the above anomaly, they pointed out that Chandigarh, Ropar and the Morinda Assembly Constituencies of Ambala district formed part of the Punjabi Region. To unsettle this arrangement, instead, the Tehsil was made a unit for consideration by the Commission. As a result Chandigarh came to be made a Union Territory.

D. The river waters and hydel power which, according to the Constitution of India, are State subjects had been taken over by the Central Government under the Reorganisation Act of 1966. The control of the river Yamuna has been given exclusively to Haryana. This, they rightly pointed out, violated the Constitution of India and amounted to despoiling the Punjab of its basic developmental resource. Punjab being a predominantly agricultural state felt hurt.

E. They also pointed out that, similarly, the water which was being given to Rajasthan was not lawful. Rajasthan has no riparian claim to Punjab water even if the princely state of Bikaner had been buying water from the Punjab state during the British regime.

F. The Akalis also pointed out that it was because they insisted that these matters be referred to the Supreme Court for a decision, that Mrs. Gandhi had made the Congress Chief Ministers of these States sign agreements for sharing the water, and thus preempted their approaching the Supreme Court.

G. Another unconstitutional decision of Mrs. Gandhi about which the Akalis felt sore was the executive order restricting the recruitment to the army on the basis of population. As a result, the proportion of Sikhs who had formed 17 per cent of the Defence Forces was reduced to 1.5 per cent.

Undoubtedly Punjab had not been treated equitably. It is difficult to identify the compulsions of Mrs. Gandhi and the rationale behind them. One may detect a hint in the observations of Mohan Lal, a former Finance and Home Minister of Punjab. He was a votary of the larger Punjab. As a close confidante of Pratap Singh Kairon, a sincere Punjabi and an old Congressman, he remained involved with political developments. In his book, *Disintegration of the Punjab* (Sameer Parkashan, 1984, Jalandhar), he records:-

> In this small book, it is not possible to mention all the material particulars relating to the partition of Punjab and the declaration of Chandigarh as a Union Territory. That by itself would need a separate book. I would, therefore, confine myself to the actual position as it emerged as a consequence of the partition.

It very clearly indicates that there is more to the government's stand than is apparent. The hint is that there were some compulsions or some fears and possibly a secret policy framework behind the completely negative attitude of Mrs. Gandhi's government towards the Akali demands. If a vigorous party is kept on a path of agitation for too long, it is likely to lose the goodwill of the people. After nearly 20 years of agitation the Akalis passed the Anandpur Sahib resolution in 1973, which they revised in 1978 when they had formed a coalition government with the Janata party. This resolution was dubbed as separatist because of which they lost much of their positive image. They suffered a further setback with the rise of killer squads of Sant Bhindranwale. It must be remembered that both the Sant and the Akalis were at that time aggressively against the Sant Nirankaris—a formation unacceptable to orthodox Sikhs. We will come across more evidence in support of the suspicion that the Congress had sponsored Punjab terrorism for electoral gains.

Mrs. Gandhi in her book *My Truth* has very candidly said that she made serious efforts to stall the formation of the *Punjabi Suba* but Hukam Singh with the support of the then Prime Minister Lal Bahadur Shastri, outmanoeuvred her. The Akalis alone had sustained an organised agitation against the Emergency imposed by her. Although this single agitation of theirs was entirely for the love of liberty and freedom and not for any political advantage, yet it was bound to annoy her further. If they repeatedly went about pointing out her indefensible and unjust dispensation, she would look for an escape by painting them as fundamentalists.

I am not trying to justify her reaction, but I want to make the point that the Akalis should have thought of the counter moves of Mrs. Gandhi and looked for an escape route. There was not enough justification for their boycotting the Shah Commission. If they claim to have proved before P. C. Sethi, the then Home Minister, that the Census Report of 1961 was incorrect, they could have done so before the Shah Commission as well. Second, they are also guilty of looking for an area where they could have a Sikh majority under the slogan of the interests of the Punjabi language. This was not only an unhealthy approach but also quite an impractical one, because in Punjab, the Sikhs are a strong constituent of almost all political parties. If their number in the BJP is negligible, all Akali governments, with the exception of the S.S. Barnala government in 1985, were formed in coalition with it. In that very government, one third of the Akalis formed a separate party. Surely Punjabi could flourish better in a larger Punjab.

After the formation of the *Punjabi Suba* none of their governments paid the requisite attention to the use of Punjabi in government offices. Even the militants thought of it in early 1991 when they realised that their movement was very much on the wane. They used the cause of promoting the Punjabi language in order to resuscitate themselves. Implementing the use of the Punjabi language was the government's legal obligation. The government could not ignore Punjabi even though it was the militants who appeared to have boosted its implementation.

Let us consider the changes in the political scenario in Punjab and in Delhi after the reorganisation of Punjab. A significant change was the move by the secular Congress, in a stark reversal of its traditional policy, to win over the vast Hindu vote even at the cost of provoking fundamentalist opposition; even terrorism.

In the first four Assembly elections after the reorganisation of Punjab, the Congress could win only the 1972 election, which was held in the wake of the euphoria of liberating East Bengal, as independent Bangladesh, in December 1971. The Akalis, had won the remaining three elections and had formed coalition governments. Although the Congress was responsible for pulling down their first three coalitions, it was the elections in 1977 that unnerved the Congress. That year, in addition to Punjab, non-Congress governments had been formed at the Centre and some other states. The nemesis in a way was complete. The Akalis and the Jan Sangh who were opposed to each other had come together to form governments in Punjab and at the Centre, and the Congress leaders, including Mrs. Gandhi and Zail Singh, having lost very badly were being hounded as criminals. It had become necessary for them to break this alliance even if the secular Congress had to encourage fundamentalism in order to obtain the Hindu vote.

The first steps in this direction were taken in 1978. The Congress, under Zail Singh, revived the *Dal Khalsa* and the All India Sikh Students Federation. Zail Singh, at this stage, was trying to get a foothold in the SGPC. In the 1979 election of members of the SGPC, the Congress sponsored 40 candidates with the support of the *Dal Khalsa*, AISSF and Sant Bhindranwale. But they could win only four seats. The Congress had suffered a similar failure when Giani Kartar Singh had contested the SGPC elections under the name of the Sadh Sangat Board. It was thus obvious to the Congress that some other strategy would be needed to dent this alliance. What they were seeking seemed to be at hand.

The Damdami Taksal under Sant Jarnail Singh Bhindranwale, in Chowk Mehta of Amritsar, had come into conflict with the Sant Nirankaris. Trouble had started brewing some time earlier but had taken a serious turn around 1978. On Baisakhi day in 1978 it burst out in the killing of 11 persons belonging to the Sant Bhindranwale faction and the Akhand Kirtni Jatha of Bibi Amarjit Kaur, whose husband was amongst the victims. Allegedly the followers of the Bibi and the Sant had gone to the Sant Nirankari function merely to request them not to keep the Guru Granth Sahib at a level lower than the seat of their guru. But the Nirankaris fired and killed 11 of the group. Both Bibi and Bhindranwale vowed to avenge these killings. But no one was killed in retaliation, presumably because a criminal case had been registered against the Nirankaris, including Baba Gurbachan Singh. The latter was killed by Ranjit Singh only after the appeal filed against the acquittal order of the Sessions Judge, Karnal, was withdrawn by Jaisukhlal Hathi, the Governor of Punjab, in 1980 at the behest of the Congress Government at the Centre.

The killing of the Baba was an individual's act. The Congress needed the Nirankari votes as well as Bhindranwale's support in the SGPC election in 1979. It somehow managed to retain the support of both. Bhindranwale supported the Congress candidate, Mrs. Bhinder, who won from Gurdaspur in the 1980 parliamentary election. That year the Congress won 12 seats out of the 13 parliamentary seats in Punjab. Therefore, there was no need for the Congress to be obliged to the Sant to the extent that they did. He later extended support to the Congress candidates in the Assembly elections too.

With the return of the Congress to power in 1980, first at the Centre and later in Punjab, new doors of recognition and power began opening for the Sant. Though changes in the Punjab political scene suited the Congress plan they did not augur well for peace in Punjab. The state had come under unfavourable stars. The admirable traits of Punjabis inherited by them through centuries of turbulent history, were being manipulated to plague them.

With this background, I would identify the years 1980 and 1981 as the time when the storm of terrorism began to gather. It could easily have been, nipped in the bud by timely administrative and political measures. But, on the contrary, the hidden agenda of both the Central and the Punjab governments was not concerned with sustaining peace in the Punjab but perpetuating Congress rule in the country. Their possible compulsions at that time may be described as follows:-

(1) The Prime Minister, Mrs. Indira Gandhi, who had been harassed by the Janata Government, was scared of being

eased out of power again. She was determined to win over the Hindus who were more inclined to support the Jana Sangh—later renamed the BJP. She was also in a vengeful mood. Zail Singh, her Home Minister, who had undergone similar harassment, was in a similar frame of mind.

(2) Bhindranwale as a phenomenon rose to power with the government's support. His killer groups and smugglers felt secure and unaccountable when they were under his umbrella. Therefore, his area of influence expanded rapidly. This simple country preacher, with power newly acquired through Congress support, forgot the basic Sikh tenet of not attacking the unarmed enemy. One of his main aides, Harmandar Singh Sandhu, was suspected to be under the influence of the Central Intelligence agencies. The media did the rest. He could not resist this flow of power going to his head. Or, maybe he was led either by his own instincts or by the manipulation of Congress agents around him to defy his benefactors.

(3) The alleged clash of egos of Zail Singh, the Home Minister of India and Darbara Singh, the Chief Minister of Punjab, was a very small factor in the spread of the evil of violence. The latter's ego had been hurt because Zail Singh was junior to him in the party. Darbara Singh on the advice of some police officers equated the terrorist acts with the Naxalite situation in the late 1960s in Punjab, and also believed with them that this movement would also die with the killing of a dozen or so of the militants. This kind of approach in fact was responsible for the further growth of militancy and violence.

(4) The rise of Bhindranwale in that situation, threatened the very existence of the Akalis. They also had to sustain a relentless parallel agitation for their demands. Their agitation was therefore, significantly termed as *Dharam Yudh*—religious war—in order to survive as a political entity.

Let us now have a more detailed look at the above factors.

After the death of her son, Sanjay, in a plane crash in June 1980, Mrs. Gandhi was eager to evolve an electoral strategy which could produce a 'wave' to sweep the forthcoming polls. In the 1980 election, the Congress slogan had been 'vote for a government that works'. The situation, however, changed so rapidly that in 1982 the opposition wrested both Andhra Pradesh and Karnataka, two important south Indian states ruled by the Congress since independence. The urgency to have a slogan to counter this trend had increasingly become a dire compulsion. The Congress that had been boasting of secularism, in desperation tried the plank of 'Hindutva' (not as a cult, but by giving an impression that its leader alone could protect them from the fundamentalists) in the elections to the Delhi Metropolitan Council as well as in Jammu. It worked like magic even in the two BJP bastions. The Congress had found the 'mantra' it had been searching for. In the customary Aryan *havan*, when mantras are chanted, *ahuti*—sacrifice—has to be offered. The Congress chose Punjab to be the sacrifice.

Since October 1981 the Akalis had been negotiating their numerous grievances and demands with the Central Government. These included the transfer of Chandigarh and the sharing of river waters. In her very first meeting, Mrs. Gandhi had told them to reduce their long list of 45 demands to around 15. The Akalis held 26 meetings with the Central Government (of which the Prime Minister herself chaired 4), but not a single demand was conceded.

The fact that in three of her meetings she had included P. V. Narasimha Rao, the Minister for External Affairs, but that the concerned Minister, the Home Minister, was present at only one meeting, is enough to indicate that she was not interested in a solution. At one stage, Swaran Singh, a widely respected politician, who had held several portfolios in the cabinets of Jawahar Lal Nehru and Lal Bahadur Shastri, intervened and arrived at an agreement acceptable to Mrs. Gandhi and the Akalis. But the Prime Minister later amended the draft to a degree not acceptable to the Akalis. She was thus able ultimately to portray the Akalis as separatists and supporters of Bhindranwale.

There are many accounts available detailing the manner in which she rejected each of the Akali demands. I recall only the disposal of the Akali threat to burn photocopies of Article 25 of the Constitution of India if the 'Sikhs' were not excluded from its purview by an amendment of the Constitution. They had only wanted an assurance to the effect that it would be considered. In February 1984, the Akalis were looking for a face-saving excuse to suspend their *Dharam Yudh*. In fact they had precipitated this issue, having been given an informal understanding that such an announcement would be made. However, the announcement was made only in March, after photocopies of the Article had been burned. It is a different matter that all the Sikhs and Akalis have actually benefited financially because of their inclusion in the said Article. Political analysts have pointed out that the systematic isolation of the Akalis in the political field, while dealing with the charter of their demands, was calculated to ensure that by the time the army is sent into the Temple, the public would become unsympathetic to them.

Inder Kumar Gujral, a proud Punjabi and the first from the state to become the Prime Minister of India, said on 24 May 1984 that 'It is ironical but true that on each time the approval was denied in the name of the Prime Minister.' He was commenting on the series of meetings between the Akalis and the Central Government.

Here I recount an incident of one of these meetings narrated to me by G.S. Tohra, an Akali stalwart who remained President of the SGPC for a quarter century. He was under detention in 1990 and was shifted to Amritsar for eye surgery. I had lodged him in a rest house which I had declared a jail.

G.S. Tohra told me that, during one of the meetings with various emissaries of the Prime Minister, he happened to mention his suspicion that the Congress was wooing Hindu voters to Rajiv Gandhi and therefore, they were not willing to accept any Akali demands. According to G.S. Tohra, Rajiv Gandhi spontaneously remarked that, if that had been the objective, the government would have sent the army into the Golden Temple. Rajiv Gandhi was a Joint Secretary of the Congress Party with less than three years experience in Indian politics at that time. When the deputation met PM Indira Gandhi later the same day, G.S. Tohra protested against such an idea to the Prime Minister. He assumed that once such a plan had been formulated, it would surely be put into action at some point. Mrs. Gandhi assured him that, even in the worst of situations, she would not allow the army to be sent into the Golden Temple.

A brief look at the sequence and developments and the trajectory of violence, will reveal how the beginnings of separatism became enmeshed with the agitation.

On 16 June 1980, nearly a decade after Dr. Jagjit Singh Chauhan in the UK issued advertisements announcing the formation of Khalistan, Balbir Singh Sandhu 'Secretary General' of the Council of Khalistan, made a bold announcement regarding the formation of Khalistan. On 20 March 1981, a *kesri* flag of the supposed new republic was hoisted before a huge gathering at the Hola Mohalla festival at Anandpur Sahib, by the AISSF. This organisation had been revived allegedly with the support of the Congress. In March 1981, Chief Khalsa Diwan of Chandigarh organised a Sikh Educational Conference. Ganga Singh Dhillon from the United States attended this conference and postulated the thesis that the Sikhs who are a distinct nation, must have Khalistan. The Chief Khalsa Diwan of Chandigarh, however, disassociated itself from this statement. On Baisakhi, 13 April 1981, Sandhu handed down a blue and golden passport of the Republic of Khalistan to one Gopal Singh Shahid in front of the Akal Takht. Later, a 5 dollar currency note and a postal stamp were also released.

Darbara Singh, the Congress Chief Minister of Punjab, took no notice of such seditious activities. Evidently, he did not require any sanction from the Central Government for ignoring them. The violence in its incipient stages could certainly have been prevented. But even Delhi did not take any serious notice of the developments. In fact on 22 April 1981 the Home Minister, in reply to a question told the Lok Sabha that 'there is no substance in the demand (for Khalistan)... the people who raised the bogey would themselves forget it very soon'. Despite the similarity of their views on the situation at that stage, the State Government cannot be absolved of its continued inaction.

Serious acts of violence began with the arrest of Bhindranwale on 20 September 1981 for the murder of Lala Jagat Narain. On the same day, 3 Sikh youths on motorcycles opened fire in a Jalandhar marketplace killing 3 Hindus, and injuring 12 of them. A similar incident was repeated the following day in Tarn Taran killing 1 and injuring 13. On subsequent days, bomb explosions occurred in a post office at Patiala, at the residence of the Sub Divisional Magistrate at Tarn Taran, Hoshiarpur, Moga and in another office in Bhatinda; railway tracks were damaged in Amritsar, Murthal and Hoshiarpur; an Indian Airlines plane was hijacked to Pakistan. Even after the release of Bhindranwale on 15 October, bomb explosions and the killing of Nirankaris continued.

In 1982, bomb explosions, and the killing of Nirankaris and Hindus increased. In addition, desecration of some Hindu temples also started. There were cases of desecration of gurudwaras too. Hindu–Sikh tension was mounting. On 20 August, the emboldened militants attacked the Chief Minister himself with hand grenades in a public meeting at

Rahon. In 1983 the focus shifted to bank robberies. Petty robberies of shopkeepers were also rampant. On Republic Day, 4 bomb explosions took place in Amritsar and, in April, a DIG of Police was killed outside the portals of the Harmandar. From October onwards, the killings were directed at Hindus.

No effort was made to organise public opinion against the killings or to assert the spirit of communal harmony. A sense of fear and panic was spreading, suppressing the basic instinct which impels a man to defend himself. All that the State government did was to periodically shuffle around police officers, including the Director General. However, no serious effort was made to analyse the crime situation, reorganise the outdated police system or to provide new equipment to it and build its morale by adequate reinforcement. The public continued to distance itself from the police. The only major steps taken by Delhi were to declare the National Council of Khalistan an unlawful organisation on 3 May 1982 and to dismiss the Darbara Singh Government in September 1983.

This meant that, with the imposition of President's rule, the Central Government took over the administration of the state with the Governor at the head of the state administration. But things continued to deteriorate further. Crime kept on increasing. In the first five months of 1984, it almost equalled the figures of the entire previous year. One can legitimately ask: where was the fault of Darbara Singh?

In the beginning of 1984, Hindu temples and some idols were also damaged. In the second week of February, 11 Sikhs were killed in three towns of Haryana—Panipat, Kaithal and Jind—in retaliation for Hindu killings in Punjab. Communal tensions and the sense of horror had begun increasing.

I have given these details only to show how the political situation deteriorated during the early 1980s without the administration ever putting the terrorists on the defensive. Given the acknowledged toughness of the Punjab police, this was quite incredible. They had doubtless been impressed by the political reach and influence of the Sant. Apparently no effort was made to dispel their belief. During my five years stay (1987–92) in Amritsar we had the worst of the situation for the most part. But each time we managed to overcome the hurdles. At our level the fight was never given up and we won on every occasion. But during the period under review, it was quite contrary to the tradition of the Punjab administration which leads to the inescapable conclusion that the government not only sponsored terrorism but by its inaction helped it to grow and flourish.

Despite a continuously worsening situation even after the dismissal of the Darbara Singh government, the army was never inducted to help the civil administration. I have later elucidated, with monthly statistics of crime, the immediate improvement in the law and order situation in Amritsar after the induction of the army in December 1990. But in the 1980s the army was only called to march into the Golden Temple in 1984, which would tend to prove the obvious objective of the whole game.

The rise and fall of Sant Bhindranwale also supports my inference elaborated above. He had a limited but committed following in the Chowk Mehta area, and for that reason he was chosen by Zail Singh to create a foothold in the SGPC. He was used in the parliamentary election in 1980 and became more powerful since the police was apparently unwilling to arrest him; indeed, giving rise to the feeling that they were afraid to do so. The government ultimately agreed to arrest him in the manner desired by the Sant. Having earlier demonstrated a lack of political will, and ample evidence of dereliction of duty, the government exonerated Bhindranwale suggesting that he had no hand in the murder of Jagat Narain. After his release, Bhindranwale went on an illegal jaunt to Bombay and back with a posse of his men, all of whom were armed to the teeth, some with weapons which were prohibited.

To my mind, the police would not risk the arrest of such a prominent person unless conclusive evidence was available. If his men ran amok on his arrest and randomly, killed people, it is safe to presume that they had killed Jagat Narain who had been provided with fairly effective security. The killers had chased the car of the victim and shot at Narain on national highway no. 1. The murky aspect of the whole drama of arrest and release apart, the administration, merely by bowing before the Sant, had made a hero of him.

The impression on the public mind at that time was that the state was not doing anything to check him or his men. In fact, Delhi continued asserting that Bhindranwale was a man of religion. For his followers, the trip to Bombay and of his having dictated the terms of his arrest were enough to see miraculous powers in the Sant who henceforth became a phenomenon for them. Because of such a widespread belief, the number of his followers, which included dreaded criminals and smugglers, increased rapidly.

After the arrest of his principal aide, Amrik Singh, Bhindranwale shifted from Chowk Mehta to Nanak Niwas in the Golden Temple complex on 19 July 1982. The Sant called for a demonstration for the release of Amrik Singh, outside the office of the Deputy Commissioner, Amritsar, which had to be called off as it could not pick up any momentum. This should reveal the Sant's lack of general popularity beyond his direct followers. Earlier, he had won only four seats out of the 40 that he had contested in the SGPC election. On 4 August 1982, both Sant Bhindranwale and Sant Longowal joined hands to activate their failing agitations—nahar roko (to stop digging of the Sutlej–Yamuna link canal) and the release of Amrik Singh. Despite this unholy alliance which gave the requisite boost to the movement, the two Sants were not on speaking terms. The independent agitations of both the leaders were showing signs of failure, most probably because of the taint of violence; due to which people were hesitating to participate. Besides, by the third week of August the paddy harvest becomes the first priority of the farmers who are the backbone of Akali campaigns to court arrest.

After shifting to Amritsar, Bhindranwale also started holding court at the Akal Takht. Pressmen started visiting him. Harmandar Singh Sandhu, his personal secretary, would expound on the Sant's plans and rationalise the interviews he gave. He availed of the opportunity to justify his notion that Sikhs were being treated as 'slaves' in India. He suggested that each village should have a squad of three young motorcyclists with weapons. Killing of Hindus by such squads, according to him, could lead to cross-migration of Hindus and Sikhs as happened during the Partition of India and the result would be the formation of Khalistan. The Sant could easily have been arrested for his subversive activities as he was residing in Nanak Niwas, a rest house adjoining the SGPC offices. In mid-December 1983 he moved into the Akal Takht. G.S. Tohra had reportedly pressurised a reluctant Giani Kirpal Singh, the Jathedar of the Akal Takht, to let the Sant shift in.

The Government of India had never tried to arrest Bhindranwale earlier, but after his moving into the sanctuary of the Akal Takht it asked Sant Longowal to hand him over to the government which, obviously, the latter could not do. It is interesting to speculate that, had the Sant moved into the Temple without his first having been arrested in the murder case and all that followed, could the media at the national and international level have taken any notice of him?

Second, when the Government of India asked Sant Longowal to hand over Bhindranwale, was it serious? The Punjab Government with the best police in the country could arrest Bhindranwale only on his specific conditions which really meant succumbing to him. How could Sant Longowal fulfil the government's wishes? The Government of India was merely attempting to make the people believe that there was a conspiracy between the two Sants and the Golden Temple was being used as a sanctuary. The exercise had been undertaken well in time to let the notion of the alleged conspiracy sink into the minds of the people before Operation Blue Star was to occur.

The fact that many illegal and provocative events were happening or, perhaps being allowed to happen, strengthens the suspicion that the government was planning an operation like Blue Star.

Soon after he moved to the Akal Takht, General Shabeg Singh (retired) joined Bhindranwale there and preparations to face an attack by the army commenced. Bhindranwale also sent messages to some other retired army officers to join Shabeg Singh. But no one accepted. It is puzzling to reflect; how could Bhindranwale anticipate such an attack? It is believed that Harmandar Singh Sandhu was a double agent named 'falcon', and was aware of the governments plans. He was the only man close to Bhindranwale who surrendered before the army authorities after Operation Blue Star was over. The outgoing Congress Government of India also released him from jail in November 1989. This was obviously to create trouble for the incoming V.P. Singh Government, a task he readily undertook with great zeal but his opponents shot him dead in early 1990, cutting short his ambitious and unscrupulous plans.

The conventional Akali politicians were beginning to lose face in their own state, particularly because they had been unable to obtain a single concession from the Central Government. This was also justification for Sant Longowal to continue his parallel agitation. But the most important purpose that it served was to show that the majority of Sikhs backing him were not for Khalistan nor for a solution through violent means. They maintained their religious, political and economic demands, for which they had been agitating, but they were willing to discuss them across the table.

Sant Longowal must have got wind of the impending army action when he announced that he would be raising a cadre of 100,000 *marjiwade*—suicide squads—to face similar government onslaughts on the Sikh agitators. He announced this after 21 Akalis had been killed in police firing on 4 April 1983 in a *rasta roko* (block traffic) agitation. He did not need such a huge cadre for the protection of the participants in his various *roko* calls. Such a large number would be needed only if a human wall around the Golden Temple was planned in order to impede the army. During 1983 the violence was being directed more and more against Hindus. Referring to this trend Sant Longowal had blamed the Darbara Singh Government for fomenting communal trouble in the state (*Spokesman*, May 1983) and in July he suggested that the government wanted to liquidate the Sikhs (*Spokesman*, July 1983). This would support my inference that he had an inkling of the army action, which G.S. Tohra might have shared with him. Nevertheless, Sant Longowal made no attempts to meet Bhindranwale to discuss the implications of such an eventuality.

The agitation that the Akalis under Sant Longowal pursued did not rule out negotiations at any stage, nor did they threaten to join hands with Bhindranwale. After the 24 April agitation, Sant Longowal called for a continuous *nahar roko* agitation from 24 May 1982. Volunteers tried to stop the digging of the Sutlej–Yamuna link canal and the police continually arrested them. By October 1982, the arrests went up to 25,000. In April 1983 a one day *rasta roko* agitation was organised on the main roads. This was followed in August by *rail roko* (block trains) and *kam roko* (stop work) agitations. Sant Longowal had given a call for *anaj roko* for 3 June 1984 to stop the movement of grains out of Punjab, but this could not take place because of Operation Blue Star.

I happened to visit the temple on 30 May 1984 to pay my obeisance. Armed militants on watch were going round the *parikrama*. A group of young boys stood in square formation on the first floor of the rooms and the *verandah* along the *parikrama* as if they were being given instructions. The attendance at that hour (8.30 P.M.) was certainly thinner than usual for that hour, but considering the presence of the militants in the Temple and the tension in the city, the number of people present could be rated as very good. I also happened to notice two newly married Hindu couples seeking blessings. This was quite surprising considering the tension, but it was a very pleasant reminder of the basic fraternal ties between Hindus and Sikhs. When I stood before the Akal Takht, I had a foreboding that I may not see the Takht again in the same shape. Unfortunately my foreboding proved right.

On 2 June 1984, Punjab was formally placed under curfew and handed over to the army. What happened thereafter has been documented by many eyewitnesses. Operation Blue Star started on the night of 5 June and the fight finally ended, barring stray firing from isolated spots, in the small hours of 7 June 1984. The losses suffered, as given out by the army, were four officers killed and 13 wounded; four JCOs killed and 16 wounded and 75 other ranks killed and 219 wounded. On the side of the militants, 492 of them including Bhindranwale were killed and 86 wounded. However, Chand Joshi in his book *Bhindranwale: Myth and reality* (Vikas, 1984, New Delhi), puts the army losses at 700 men and of the civilians at 5,000. In all, 1,592 had been taken into custody including 309 women. Of the 927 weapons recovered, 41 were LMGs, 84 SLRs, 52 Chinese rifles and 399 rifles of .303 bore.

Though the Operation had achieved the desired objective shock and sadness had struck all sane hearts including those of the army and the leaders involved. The savaging of the Temple in the eighteenth and the nineteenth centuries at the hands of foreign invaders was perhaps understandable. But what happened in the twentieth century in independent India surely was not. It is of no consolation to anyone that Bhindranwale did not expect the government to send the army into the Temple or that the government expected the militants to surrender merely at the sight of the army. Many army officers had told their relations and friends that they would be having lunch with them as the operation would be over within a few hours. But it turned out to be a much tougher Battle.

The assassination of Mrs. Gandhi by her Sikh guards, the retaliatory killing of the Sikhs in Delhi and elsewhere, and the well-documented scenes of carnage were entirely contrived acts of violence. One can only feel sad and wish that these unnecessary deaths had never occurred.

3

The Rajiv–Longowal Accord: The 'Secret' Healing Touch

The massacre of Sikhs during November 1984 in Delhi and at some other places in northern India in the wake of the assassination of Mrs. Gandhi, was an unparalleled barbarity on two counts. First, some senior Congress leaders were suspected of organising the violence and second, when violence did break out, the police, did not prevent it for the first three or four days. It was the darkest time for the Sikhs and must also have been quite shameful for the concerned administrations. Fortunately many right-thinking Hindu organisations, mostly Punjabi, and other communities stood up in support of the Sikhs. In course of time they bared the conspiracy through public enquiries, which ultimately opened the way to bring the culprits to book. It is unfortunate that, in spite of the passage of 15 long years, not too many of the culprits have been punished.

For the Congress, however, a strong sympathy wave was rising in its favour. The young Prime Minister Rajiv Gandhi decided to hold the parliamentary election in December 1984. He won with more than a three-fourths majority and formed his new government. He had trained as a commercial pilot and had wanted to remain away from politics. But fate had decreed otherwise. The death in an air crash of his younger brother, Sanjay Gandhi, who was assisting his mother, forced Rajiv Gandhi to take his place and help Mrs. Gandhi as a Joint Secretary in the Congress. In that capacity he had been participating in meetings held with the Akalis over their grievances to find a solution to the long-standing problems of a disturbed Punjab. He, therefore, gave priority to finding a solution to the Punjab problem in his party's election manifesto. After his victory in the election he affirmed to the nation in his first broadcast that, 'The Sikhs are as much a part of India as any other community.'

This was a meaningful declaration as it implied an acknowledgement of the fact that the Sikhs had not been treated fairly. As soon as the Prime Minister took some steps in a positive direction, the militants stepped up their violent acts. It was an indication that terrorism had not ended with the killing of Bhindranwale, Operation Blue Star and the massacre of the Sikhs in November 1984. Therefore, a different approach to the imbroglio was indicated.

The Prime Minister initiated steps towards a new beginning. On 11 March 1985, the government ordered the release of eight senior Akali leaders detained since June 1984. Sant Harchand Singh Longowal, G.S. Tohra, Prakash Singh Badal and Jagdev Singh Talwandi were among them. Arjun Singh, a former Chief Minister of Madhya Pradesh, who was a confidante of the Prime Minister, was appointed Governor of Punjab with an apparent brief of bringing the Akalis to the negotiating table. Orders that had declared the AISSF as an unlawful body were also withdrawn. On 14 March, the PM waived the condition of giving up the Anandpur Sahib Resolution by the Akali Dal before any talks with them. On 23 March, the Prime Minister visited Hussaniwala in Punjab to pay homage to Bhagat Singh, Raj Guru and Sukhdev, the legendary martyrs of the freedom struggle who were cremated there in 1936. At the martyr's memorial, he announced that a judicial enquiry would be held into the Delhi riots. As a Baisakhi gift the formal orders for the enquiry were issued on 11 April 1985.

For the released Akali leaders it was quite a predicament. It was difficult for them to face the people. It was under their leadership that things had come to such a pass. Sensing the initiative taken by the PM for talks, Baba Joginder Singh, the father of Bhindranwale, dissolved both the Akali Dals and announced the formation of the United Akali Dal. The AISSF supported the Baba. The embarrassed leaders, Sant Longowal, G.S. Tohra and P.S. Badal submitted their resignations. In the last week of March, the District *Jathedars* i.e., the Party Presidents of the districts, assembled and unanimously affirmed their faith in these leaders and persuaded them to withdraw their resignations, thus keeping Baba Joginder Singh out. Sant Longowal undertook a tour of Punjab and of the areas which had Sikh populations outside Punjab. His conclusion was that people wanted peace.

The militants had been watching these developments. Peace moves would obviously threaten their identity. In order to sabotage the negotiations between the Centre and the State, they suddenly became quite active. Sporadic violence erupted simultaneously with the announcement of the economic package for Punjab by the Prime Minister. On 24 March 1985, a BJP leader was shot dead in Hoshiarpur which provoked attacks on Sikhs in that district. On 19 April 1985 R.L. Bhatia, a senior leader of the Congress, was wounded in Amritsar. On 10 May 1985 in a series of blasts of bombs concealed in transistors and such other gadgets, randomly planted, 81 people were killed in Delhi, UP and Haryana. On 23 June 1985 the Air India Jumbo jet, 'Kanishka', carrying 329 passengers crashed into the Atlantic Ocean due to a bomb allegedly planted in it by some Sikh militants based abroad.

In view of the volatile times, complete secrecy was essential for the success of the peace talks. Arjun Singh, therefore, kept his moves to prepare the background for talks confidential. The Prime Minister invited Sant Longowal for talks on 23 July 1985. No one could get wind of the developments in Delhi. An agreement was signed on 24 July 1985 and its announcement that day took every one by surprise, including the two Akali stalwarts, P. S. Badal and G. S. Tohra. The Sant had taken into confidence only the next two senior leaders Surjit Singh Barnala and Balwant Singh. This discrimination, as we shall see later, caused fissures amongst the Akalis and became a major hurdle in establishing peace in the state.

The agreement signed between the Prime Minister and the President of the Akali Dal came to be known as the 'Rajiv–Longowal Accord'. It provided that Chandigarh was to be given to Punjab on Republic Day, 1986. By that date a commission was to determine the area that Punjab was to cede to Haryana for the construction of its capital. Another commission was to adjudicate the sharing of river waters between Punjab, Haryana and Rajasthan. A third commission

was to look into the claims of both the states for the inclusion of contiguous areas on the basis of language spoken in the villages. It was
also agreed to consider an formulation of an All India Gurudwara
Bill in consultation with the Akali Dal. The Anandpur Sahib Resolution, hitherto considered 'separatist' and 'controversial' was to be
referred to the Sarkaria Commission, which had been established
to review Centre-State relations. Elections to the Punjab Assembly
were also to be held as early as possible. There were provisions for
the release of the Jodhpur detainees and rehabilitation of soldiers
who had deserted their units on hearing about the attack on the
Golden Temple in June 1984.

Barring the militants, the people heaved a sigh of relief and generally welcomed the Accord as a harbinger of peace to the Punjab. But
there was strong criticism by a section of the Akali Dal and the
Hindutva lobby of the 'avoidable speed and secrecy' of the talks, as
also the contents of the agreement. Almost simultaneously the anti-
Punjab lobby, the protagonists of sustaining the Hindu vote with the
Congress, as also the militants, resolved to sabotage the implementation of the accord by any means.

P. S. Badal and G.S. Tohra, having felt slighted by their exclusion
from the secret negotiations, were very angry. They maintained that
the agreement was a sell out as it only held out promises without
actually giving anything. Sant Longowal managed to get the approval
of the Akali Dal on 26 July 1985. But he could not assuage the heart
burning and the sense of humiliation of the two stalwarts and their
supporters. Rajiv Gandhi may not have gauged the full implications
of ignoring P. S. Badal and G. S. Tohra, but the Sant surely knew
how unacceptable it could be. Ordinarily, he would not have opted
for the signing of the Accord at the cost of destroying the otherwise
fragile unity of the Akali Dal, which, at that moment, was facing a
challenge from the combined forces of Baba Joginder Singh, the
AISSF and the militants. The Sant had never betrayed the slightest
inclination to head the government, but if he so desired, as President of the Akali Dal he could have easily become the Chief Minister.
It is, therefore, not clear why the Sant did not take P. S. Badal and
G.S. Tohra into confidence before signing the Accord.

One explanation current at that time was that Balwant Singh had
apprehensions that if P. S. Badal became the Chief Minister he would
not take him into his cabinet because of the latter's ditching P. S. Badal
during his previous tenure as Chief Minister. He, therefore, conspired

to keep P.S. Badal out of the negotiations either through Arjun Singh or his contacts in the Congress party. My own feeling is that either Arjun Singh suspected that they would take a hard line on some issues, or Rajiv Gandhi who had dealt with the Akalis during the early 1980s, may have found them to be obdurate. Since the PM was keen to settle the Punjab dispute he might have suggested either to Governor Arjun Singh or the Sant to exclude P.S. Badal and G.S. Tohra in the interests of the Accord. The latter alternative appears to be more likely because of what I learnt from G.S. Tohra.

While under detention in 1988, G.S. Tohra happened to be shifted to Amritsar for the treatment of his eyes. Because of the threat to him from the militants in Amritsar Jail, I kept him in a remote Canal Rest House at Khalra which I had declared as a jail. Since this is located right on the Pakistan border, he suspected it to be a conspiracy to eliminate him and refused to eat his food. I met him to explain my reasons for keeping him there and managed to allay his fears. After that, a relaxed G.S. Tohra told me that during one of the meetings in 1983 Rajiv Gandhi had told him that if the Congress were to please the Hindu vote bank they would send the army into the Temple. G.S. Tohra took exception to this observation and expressed his views to Rajiv Gandhi. Later he protested to Mrs. Gandhi that since such an idea had come into their minds they would surely send the army into the Golden Temple one day. Mrs. Gandhi took pains to assure G.S. Tohra that, come what may, no such thing would ever happen.

G.S. Tohra may then have protested vehemently only to embarrass Delhi but, seemingly, he did not take Rajiv's slip seriously when he said so. It was allegedly he alone who pressurised Giani Kirpal Singh, the *Jathedar* of the Akal Takht, to let Bhindranwale move from the Nanak Niwas into the sanctuary of the Akal Takht in December 1983. I did not ask G.S. Tohra whether the other leaders joined him in the protest. But his narration had implied that he alone had protested. The advisors of Rajiv Gandhi may have felt that the signing of the Accord and the give and take in its implementation would be easier with S.S. Barnala rather than with G.S. Tohra and P. S. Badal. If someone was to insist that Chandigarh be transferred to Punjab before the accord was signed, it would have led to a deadlock. In the atmosphere of mutual suspicion that prevailed at the time, it was difficult to identify the reason for 'secrecy' or the 'hurry' in which the Accord was concluded.

After the Accord was signed, the terrorists' killings, though few, were nevertheless stepped up. A sub-inspector of police was killed in Amritsar, about the same time that Lalit Maken, an MP, his wife and an associate, were shot dead in Delhi. On 20 August 1985, the birthday of the Indian Prime Minister, Sant Longowal was killed in Sherpur in District Sangrur, where he was addressing a large gathering of his followers. That day he was supposed to have persuaded P. S. Badal and G.S. Tohra to let Surjit Singh Barnala lead the party. The government, however, ignoring the threats, rightly pressed for an early election in the Punjab. The polls were held on 25 September 1985 under heavy security. More than 65 per cent of the voters came to the polls ignoring the call of Baba Joginder Singh to boycott the same and elected 73 Akali MLAs to the Punjab Assembly.

Bimal Khalsa, widow of Beant Singh, an assassin of Indira Gandhi, lost both the Assembly and the Parliamentary constituencies that she had contested simultaneously. Tarlok Singh, father of Satwant Singh, the other assassin of the late Prime Minister, also lost the Assembly election. The victory of the Akalis was a loud and clear verdict of the Sikh masses that they were in favour of the accord, secular democracy, nationalism and the territorial integrity of India. This, apparently, was not realised in Delhi amidst the noise of violence by a handful of militants. On the basis of incorrect premises it continued to assume, while framing its policies on Punjab, that the Sikhs were separatists. Such a stance assisted terrorism to grow faster under the newly elected Akali Government.

Surjit Singh Barnala was unanimously elected leader of the Akalis and took the oath as Chief Minister of Punjab on 29 September 1985. The sagacious and experienced lawyer from Barnala had had successful stints as Education Minister in Punjab and a Cabinet Minister of Agriculture in the Morarji Desai Government at the Centre. At this time, he had the support of 73 MLAs in a house of 117, the promises of the Accord in his pocket and the backing of the entire nation along with a pat on his back by the Rajiv Government. All these factors should normally have gone into making S.S. Barnala a powerful Chief Minister and enabled him to inaugurate a new chapter of peace in the Punjab. Unfortunately, it was not to be. Within weeks of his taking the oath of office, S.S. Barnala found himself in the vortex of pressures and counter pressures of betrayals, opposition from supporters, rivals and the high expectations of a hurt people who had been affected by the misdeeds of the militants and the government.

It is important to take note of the achievements claimed and propagated by Sant Longowal after signing the accord, and later orchestrated by his followers in the election campaign. The accord was projected as a victory and an acknowledgement of the Akali demands as being genuine. These demands, it may be recalled, had led to the *Dharam Yudh* in 1982. After the signing of the accord they gave up the religious war since all their demands had been conceded. Consequently, it was claimed that the accord was also a condemnation of Operation Blue Star. The people of Punjab hoped to get back their capital after nearly two decades. The accord thus formed the bedrock on which the peace of Punjab could be founded. It was for this reason that the newly constituted Punjab Legislative Assembly, in its very first session resolved unanimously that the accord should be implemented faithfully by the Central Government.

The faith of the people in the accord and their expectations from it, reiterated by the State Legislature, was a mass effort to shake off the trauma of the past few years. The accord was to rid them not only of violence and bloodshed but also from the tensions of nearly two decades of agitation to get back their capital as well as their rightful share in the river waters. It also had the potential to act as a balm to heal many a psychic wound. But the accord and the aspirations of the entire populace were sacrificed at the altar of the political interests of the Congress. The installation of an Akali Government in Punjab was by no means a panacea. It was only a means to an end. The volte-face by the Government of India turned the accord into a Trojan Horse out of which poured forth all the old issues, still burning and alive. This could only promote terrorism, not peace. And it did.

S.S. Barnala, however, chose his priorities correctly. It was not the Sikh psyche alone that had been hurt because of the armed action by the state; the Hindus and Nirankaris had also been traumatised by the militants. Because of the failure of the accord, this issue became hypersensitive and very difficult to resolve. For the Hindus, Operation Blue Star was an euphoric success as it rid them of the fear of their lives. A jubilant Hindu friend of mine after a visit to Delhi in the third week of June 1984, had told me that the thinking in Delhi was that the three border districts, Gurdaspur, Amritsar and Ferozepur, could be converted into a union territory (border belt).

The remaining districts could be tagged onto Haryana. I said, 'Dear, this is a brilliant solution. The trouble is in Punjab; just change the name of Punjab and the trouble would disappear *ipso facto*.'

As if by coincidence, on the same day I happened to meet an old acquaintance, a retired chief engineer, who was in his late 1970s, 'Sardar Sahib, when did you return from America?' I asked casually. His face became red and his lips began to tremble. In a fit of rage he was speechless. I was wondering what was my insolence, when with a great effort he started murmuring, 'I landed on seven ... sev ... seventh of June, the day that woman had sent the army to the Harmandar Sahib.' These were the two extremes of people's opinions; these were the psychological barriers that S.S. Barnala had to break.

These extremes were not diluted when the anti-Sikh riots took place after the assassination of Mrs. Gandhi in October. These sponsored riots had inflicted too great a shock on the Sikhs and their psyche. How could things have become normal in 10 months? Before the signing of the accord, only the thoughtful Hindu organisations, mostly Punjabi, led by men of real eminence—Justice S.M. Sikri for example—had taken the initiative for a return to amity between the two communities. The revival of communal harmony was the first priority of the Barnala government.

The pressure on the Chief Minister for the release of the jailed youth was also instant. They had been in jail for quite some time. In the psychological tension among the communities, it was a very sensitive issue. But it was a desirable exercise; there were many boys who were innocent. However, the logic the AISSF had used in its clamour for their release was quite provocative. They argued that S.S. Barnala was in the Chief Minister's chair because of the policies of Bhindranwale and not because of Sant Longowal. Therefore, he was obliged to release all those who had been arrested since 1983. Chief Minister S.S. Barnala appointed a four member panel headed by Ajit Singh Bains, a former judge of the Punjab and Haryana High Court who is presently involved with the Punjab Human Rights Organisation, to look into the cases registered after 1 August 1981, in connection with the political agitation.

The new government released 224 persons detained under the National Security Act on 30 September. Bibi Amarjit Kaur of the Akhand Kirtni Jatha was also freed with this group. She had lost her husband in the Nirankari shootout on 13 April 1978 and was reportedly associated with the Babbars. In three weeks the Bains Committee recommended the release of 309 persons, a recommendation that the government accepted. The Committee listed 776 cases and recommended to the government to withdraw them in three instalments. The number of militants involved was around 1,761. After this exercise, about 1,100 remained in Punjab jails.

The measures taken to rehabilitate those released from jail were inadequate. The government had some constraints but due importance was not given to this fact. As Additional Deputy Commissioner, Patiala, I interviewed the boys released from Patiala and Nabha jails and recommended their cases for absorption in various government departments and other statutory organisations of the government. In April 1986, I was posted as Secretary of the State Agricultural Marketing Board, Chandigarh. I happened to interview and absorb a 100 odd released boys in that organisation. None of them strayed back into militancy. All of them got married within months of their getting a salaried job.

The government provided soft loans for self-employment but very few of the rural youth could make any headway in such ventures. As Deputy Commissioner of Amritsar, I was able to grant permits to ply mini-buses on rural roads to some of the so-called Jodhpur detainees after their release in 1988 and 1989. This was a vocation they could easily manage. Not a single one strayed back into militancy. There was a lot of scope for opening this avenue to the unemployed youth but the powerful lobby of the transporters put hurdles in the way of further expansion in this sector. As Governor S.S. Ray toured Amritsar during 1989, I would point out bus after bus overloaded with passengers, with dozens of people sitting on the roof, to him. He decentralised some powers and authorised the DCs to grant such permits for mini-buses. Unemployment has certainly been the fuel that has kept the flame of militancy burning. In fact, the number of unadjusted youth was many times higher than their lucky colleagues who got some kind of employment. They were, therefore, frustrated and angry with the 'system'.

There were a large number of victims of Delhi riots who had migrated to Punjab. Their experience was reminiscent of the migration during the Partition of India in 1947 though comparatively on a much lesser scale. Many families bemoaned that they had been ruined and rendered homeless in communal violence for the second time in their lives. They were not satisfied with the relief given to them during the first 10 months of their refuge in Punjab. The installation of the S.S. Barnala government had raised their hopes so much that they became aggressive due to their sense of frustration at not getting adequate relief.

For S.S. Barnala even this had become quite a sensitive task. His government came up with schemes of soft loans but these did not satisfy them. They wanted much more from the Akali government. S.S. Barnala's problems were thus increasing by the day as was the threat to his life. To add to his miseries the anti-Punjab lobby, under the cover of the difficult forthcoming elections in some of the states, was using all sorts of means to scuttle the accord in totality. Bhajan Lal was secretly spearheading that lobby and he had the reputation of never failing in such conspiracies. No wonder the Punjab accord was kept on the back burner.

Two clauses of the accord, elections in Punjab and referring the Anandpur Sahib Resolution to the Sarkaria Commission, had been implemented. But none of the others. Mark Tully in his book from *Raj to Rajiv Gandhi* notes the reasons behind the failure of the accord. He writes, 'He (Rajiv Gandhi) backed down on the sensible accord he had signed to end the confrontation with the Sikh religious party in Punjab when his party told him it was damaging his electoral prospects in the crucial Hindi speaking states of north India.' In fact this lobby was even unhappy over the young Prime Ministers referring the Anandpur Sahib Resolution, till then dubbed as a 'separatist document', to the Sarkaria Commission.

Doubts about the implementation of the agreement had arisen almost simultaneously with its publication. The first difference arose over an admitted typographical error. Recommendation for territorial readjustment of areas surrounding Chandigarh, Abohar and Fazilka were to be made by different Commissions on the basis of the language spoken and contiguity alone. A village was to be treated as a unit. But in the draft an apparently mischievous phrase 'other factors', had been added. The implication of this addition could enable the transfer of large areas of Abohar and Fazilka to Haryana. When this was pointed out to the Centre, the Prime Minister clarified that it was a clerical error and ordered its rectification.

In terms of the accord, three independent Commissions were to adjudicate the three main issues: (*i*) Chandigarh was to be transferred to Punjab on 26 January 1986. A Commission was to determine the Hindi speaking areas to be transferred from Punjab to

Haryana in lieu of Chandigarh. (*ii*) Another Commission was to adjudicate on the claims of both States for the transfer of villages on the basis of affinity of language and contiguity of territory. This was also to be the guiding principle for transfer of areas in lieu of Chandigarh. (*iii*) A third Commission was to adjudicate on the distribution of river waters between Punjab, Haryana and Rajasthan ensuring the continuation of the present supply.

Here, I feel it relevant to recall the observations made by Pranab Mukerji at Chandigarh on 17 January 1987. He was addressing a round table conference organised by ex-servicemen and the Punjab Nagrik Manch. Pranab Mukerji, as a Minister in the Government of India, had attended most of the 26 meetings which were held with the Akalis by the Central Government. He had left the Congress only recently. He said that the 'Accord did not link the transfer of Chandigarh to Punjab with the transfer of certain Hindi speaking areas of Punjab to Haryana. This was done at a later stage for political considerations.' (*The Tribune*, 18 January 1987) This would appear to be correct because in terms of the issue to be decided concerning point (*ii*) above, all Hindi speaking areas falling in Punjab and contiguous with Haryana could be claimed by and transferred to Haryana. After doing this, no other area would be left that could be transferred to Haryana within the parameter, of linguistic and territorial contiguity. If we also recall the remarks of Mark Tully about the Prime Minister's backing away from the accord, we can appreciate the ultimate reports of the Commissions.

Justice K.K. Mathew, retired judge of the Supreme Court of India, was to submit his report by 31 December 1985 to enable the transfer of Chandigarh on Republic Day of 1986. But on 26 January 1986, the Commission reported its inability to determine the Hindi speaking areas to be transferred to Haryana in lieu of Chandigarh. Justice Venkataramiah who succeeded Mathew, came to a 'firm finding' that 70,000 acres of Punjab territory should be transferred to Haryana in lieu of Chandigarh. Haryana had maintained before the Commission that the reference was itself unworkable and stillborn but on 29 May 1986 it claimed 483 villages and 30 towns. In its report submitted to the Government of India on 12 June 1986, the Commission regretted that it could determine only 45,000 acres. The Commission requested that someone else should be entrusted with the work of determining the reminder.

The city of Chandigarh is built over 114 sq km. In suggesting 70,000 acres for Haryana the Commission was recommending an area comprising 282 sq km, which was twice the area of the City Beautiful. The government had fixed 21 June 1986, for the transfer of the city. On 20 June, Justice D.A. Desai was asked to fulfil the task in 12 hours but later the date of transfer was changed to 15 July 1986. By then, apparently, S.S. Barnala saw through the game. He stuck to the transfer of 45,000 acres determined by Venkataramiah and conceded that the rest could be determined by the Government of India after transferring Chandigarh, of course, within the parameters of linguistic and territorial affinity. It was clear that only those Punjabi and Hindi speaking areas were to be reallocated that were contiguous. One may ask, where was the need to first quantify the area in lieu of Chandigarh and then to regret that the balance was not available?

Actually one Punjab village, Kandu Khera, on the border of Punjab and Haryana, broke the contiguity of many villages of Abohar and Fazilka, claimed by Haryana from Punjab. The Haryana administration was sure that it would manage to prove that the said village was Hindi speaking. But the vigil of the Punjab Government and the day and night presence of Punjab Ministers, including Amarinder Singh, in the contested village foiled Haryana's manipulations of enticing the people of the village to give Hindi as their mother tongue. But for Kandu Khera, Haryana would have got Abohar and Fazilka.

I do not wish to impute motives to the various Commissions but I must highlight certain puzzling facts. When the first Commission regrets its inability to determine the area to be transferred, by the date designated for the transfer of the capital, the successor Commission only quantifies the area which was not included in the terms of reference. Haryana keeps on contesting the legality of the reference to the second Commission but on the last day of the Commission's tenure puts in a claim on hundreds of villages. A third Commission is expected to do the needful in only 12 hours. To me as an Indian, the violation of the sanctity of the institution of Commissions is more painful than the denial of Chandigarh to Punjab.

If the functioning of various Commissions was intriguing to say the least, the manner in which Prime Minister Indira Gandhi had settled the river water dispute between Haryana and the Punjab was quite amazing. To begin with, the provisions for the division of water in the Punjab Reorganisation Act, 1966 are *ultra vires* of the Constitution of India. According to our Constitution the Central government, or the Tribunal appointed by it, can settle disputes between states for sharing the waters of inter-state rivers i.e., the rivers that flow through the claimant states. Since the rivers Sutlej and Beas flow through neither Haryana nor Rajasthan, the claims of these non-riparian states are not justiciable. The Punjab Reorganisation Act, nevertheless, provided that should Punjab and Haryana fail to come to an agreement to share the river water within two years, the Central Government would decide the issue. Mrs. Gandhi had consequently given her award. When Punjab placed this illegal decision for review before Prime Minister Morarji Desai in 1978, he asked the claimants to show him on a map where the river Sutlej (the Beas merges with the Sutlej at Harike in Amritsar district) flows through their states. Since it did not, the Prime Minister upheld Punjab's contention. However, he did not rescind the decision of Mrs. Gandhi. At the same time he had no objection to the Akalis filing a writ in the Supreme Court, seeking the relevant provisions of the Reorganisation Act to be struck down, which they did.

Mrs. Gandhi became Prime Minister again in 1980. She summoned the Congress Chief Ministers of the three states on 31 December 1981, and made them sign an agreement to share the river waters. Punjab was compelled to withdraw its writ pending before the Supreme Court. According to the agreement of December 1981, the allocation of water in million acre feet (maf) for various states was: Punjab 4.22 maf, Haryana 3.50 maf, Rajasthan 8.60 maf, Delhi 0.20 maf and Jammu and Kashmir 0.65 maf. But according to the terms of the Rajiv–Longowal Accord, the farmers of Punjab, Haryana and Rajasthan were to continue to get water that would not be less than what they were getting from the Ravi–Beas system as on 1 July 1985. The actual usage of water by each of the states, according to the records of the Bhakra Beas Management Board on the given date was: Punjab 9.655 maf, Haryana 1.334 maf, Rajasthan 4.500 maf.

The Eradi Tribunal was to submit its report in January 1987, but this date was postponed to June, just weeks before the election in Haryana. It is evident that the report was welcomed by the Haryana farmers. Haryana's share had been raised to 3.83 maf, that of Rajasthan to 8.6 maf, but Punjab was given only 5 maf water against its actual consumption of 9.655 maf. Even this magic did not help the Congress win the Haryana election. But, it surely gave a boost to militancy in the Punjab which was manifest in the unprecedented spurt in killings in July 1987.

I feel that it is pertinent to recall the figures of initial allocation of river waters in independent India in January 1955: Punjab (it then included Haryana) 7.20 maf; Rajasthan 8 maf; Jammu and Kashmir 0.65. It would seem that subsequent re-allocation from time to time approximated this distribution. But there was some urgency at that time. The World Bank was overseeing the allocation of river waters to India and Pakistan. It had made it clear that the allocation would depend on the relative utilisation potential for these waters. For this purpose both the countries had to establish their capacity to absorb the river water to feed their respective canal irrigation systems. It was, therefore, necessary for India to develop schemes and means to show the utilisation of the Ravi and the Beas waters. The approval given to the projections of each state in the January 1955 meeting was guided by national interests in the context of the World Bank's directions.

Even otherwise, if we go by the agricultural needs of Punjab and Haryana the requisite quantities would be different. For, in addition to its present allocation of 3.83 maf, Haryana has the exclusive use of the Yamuna waters i.e., another 5 maf. But in Punjab, not only is there a shortage of overground water, but the ever falling level of underground water is also a matter of concern. Punjab has been permitted to use water allocated to Rajasthan till that state develops the means to use its allocation. This concession itself poses the question: what will Punjab do after Rajasthan begins using its full share? Punjab has been using 9.655 maf of water, how will it survive when it is left with only its allocation of 5 maf.

In addition to such manoeuvering, the Rajiv–Longowal Accord was also being undermined by other means.

4

S.S. Barnala's Government: The Healing Touch Impaired

The non-transfer of Chandigarh was a great shock to all Punjabis. As a protest, the militants provided them with another shock on Republic Day 1986. After about 150 years, the defunct institution of *Sarbat Khalsa* was resurrected and organised at the Akal Takht on 26 January 1986 by the AISSF activists and militant organisations. During the eighteenth century, when *Sarbat Khalsa* was convened, all the *misls* were represented and the consensus, arrived at after free discussion, had the sanctity of a *Gurmata* (a decision taken in the presence of the Granth Sahib) and was binding on the *Khalsa*. Most people could not realise the dangerous potential of the present manipulated meet at that time. Many felt that it was a tactic to divert public attention from the government's failure to transfer Chandigarh to Punjab. Others dismissed it as a gathering of megalomaniac fundamentalists. Another view was that it was intended only to ensure that the SGPC entrusted the reconstruction of the Akal Takht to the Damdami Taksal. The *Sarbat Khalsa* was organised for these reasons as well as for something much more dangerous. This can be seen from the decisions announced at the gathering on that day.

The SGPC was dismissed. A Panthic Committee, comprising of five members, was formed to look after the religious affairs of the Sikhs. The existing Akal Takht structure, repaired under the aegis of the Central Government was to be demolished and rebuilt. Jasbir Singh Rode, a nephew of Bhindranwale, was named the *Jathedar* of the Akal Takht. Since he was in jail, Gurdev Singh Kaonke was named the acting *Jathedar.* He was eager to assume office and reportedly visited the Golden Temple on the same day. This was a virtual militant coup to oust the SGPC and put the nucleus of a militant movement in its place.

It may be recalled that Baba Santa Singh, the Chief of the Budha Dal of Nihangs had been specially selected by Buta Singh to repair the damaged Akal Takht. The fabulous sum of four crore rupees was placed at his disposal for the purpose in 1984. By November 1986, Buta Singh favoured its demolition and construction of a new Akal Takht, by supporting G.S. Tohra who had made such an announcement immediately after his release in March 1985. We see, here, an 'unholy' alliance of G.S. Tohra, Buta Singh and the Panthic Committee of (Gurbachan Singh Manochahal), working against S.S. Barnala's Akali government that had come into existence consequent to the Accord. At the same time, Buta Singh was seeking readmission to the Sikh *panth,* so that, according to some, he could become a leader of the Sikhs like Giani Zail Singh. To most Akali leaders, their ego was more important than peace in the state. In this context, terrorism was bound to flourish in the Punjab at the cost of many lives and the honour of many a proud son and daughter of the soil. With this background, let us proceed to examine further developments.

The *Sarbat Khalsa,* in the context of the unimplemented accord, became a singular landmark in the story of terrorist violence in the post-Blue Star period. This was a subtle move on the part of the intelligence agencies who appeared to be behind the manipulation. To install a relation of Bhindranwale, as *Jathedar* of the Akal Takht, was like reincarnating the Bhindranwale syndrome. J.S. Rode who was in jail at that time had instantly been made functional by the proxy of Gurdev Singh Kaonke who was meant to act as *Jathedar* until J.S. Rode was released. The takeover of the Temple was manifest in the demolition of the restored Akal Takht taken up on the same day. The demolition was accomplished by 14 February 1986. Henceforth the militants could remain in the Temple for the purpose of the reconstruction of the Takht. The pre-Blue Star scene had been recreated. In addition, a resolution to establish Khalistan, passed by a committee formed by a spurious procedure, was introduced on 29 April 1986. The result was that the figure of some 60 odd killings during 1985 increased to 520 the following year.

In spite of all that had happened to them, including the contrived Delhi riots, the Sikhs had not even once thought of rebellion. They accepted the Accord readily. The dictates of the political interests of the Congress—the forthcoming elections in various states beginning with Haryana in June 1987—persuaded them to continue to woo the Hindu vote, albeit by pandering to sectarian instincts. In the process it completely disregarded the anger, indignation and disappointment of the Sikhs, which the Rajiv–Longowal Accord had assuaged to a large extent, which now returned with an added feeling of having been fooled and cheated. The outrage was now more widespread. It had become simple to get the *Sarbat Khalsa* launched and much easier for the terrorists to swell their ranks. Ironically, and it came as a consolation to the Sikhs, in spite of the Congress regime having bled Punjab for another seven years, it could not fool the people of Haryana who voted Devi Lal to power. Subsequently, in most of the other seven states that went to the polls, the Congress suffered defeats. It also lost the parliamentary elections of 1989.

My inference that the *Sarbat Khalsa* was connived at by government agencies finds support from the simple fact that in March 1988, J.S. Rode was released by the Government of India at a point of time when the SGPC had no option but to appoint him as *Jathedar* of the Akal Takht. This was in fulfilment of the 26 January 1986 *Sarbat Khalsa*. After the militants had been driven out of the temple by Operation Black Thunder, the Central agencies again attempted in October 1988 to facilitate their re-entry. If J.S. Rode became the beneficiary of the *Sarbat Khalsa*, it cannot be dismissed as just a coincidence. His position suited the suspected objectives of the Government of India and coincided with the purpose of the militants. It is sad that all these moves had been contrived.

The Central Government's interests and those of the militants appeared to be common in some other crucial respects as well. The S.S. Barnala faction complained to the Prime Minister that Home Minister Buta Singh had helped G.S. Tohra to win the SGPC election in November 1986. The allegation was that the Home Minister manipulated the release of Harcharan Singh from jail on the eve of the SGPC President's election and he was instrumental in winning over some members to G.S. Tohra's side although he appeared to canvas openly for Kabul Singh, the S.S. Barnala candidate.

According to a report in *The Tribune*, on 2 December 1986, the PM was unhappy with the action of Buta Singh. G.S. Tohra managed the dismissal of the 'task force', within minutes of his election as President of the SGPC on 30 November 1986. This task force had been created by Kabul Singh, the previous President of the SGPC who was from the S.S. Barnala group. By 24 December 1986, the SGPC under G.S. Tohra had sacked the Head *Granthi* of the Darbar Sahib and secured and accepted the resignation of Kirpal Singh, *Jathedar* of the Akal Takht. Both of them had been supporting the 'task force' in keeping the Temple free from the militants. Darshan Singh Ragi who had been appointed by the new SGPC as the *Jathedar* of the Akal Takht, joined his post on 31 December 1986. On 23 January 1987 the new SGPC also dismissed the three head priests. In their place, it appointed Giani Puran Singh, Giani Savinder Singh, Giani Jaswant Singh and Giani Kashmir Singh as head priests. The *Sarbat Khalsa* held on 26 January 1987 endorsed the resolution of 29 April 1986 for Khalistan and also the appointments of the head priests. A recorded message of G.S. Manochahal (who had been appointed by the *Sarbat Khalsa* in 1986), was played to the gathering in which he announced his resignation as *Jathedar* of the Akal Takht to accommodate Darshan Singh (the appointee of the new SGPC) in the larger interests of the *panth*. The five head priests decided to dissolve all the Akali Dal factions to form a single united party and sought the resignations of the office bearers of all the factions.

The pro-militant faction of the SGPC had pulled off a coup in the religious hierarchy. But S.S. Barnala refused to comply with this order on the ground that the party Constitution did not provide for the dissolution of the party. As a result, he was dismissed even from the primary membership of the Akali Party. In place of the dissolved parties the priests declared the formation of a Unified Shiromani Akali Dal on 5 February 1987. Simran Jit Singh Mann was declared its President. Till his release from jail, a presidium of five members and an 11 member council was to look after the affairs of the party. Darshan Singh did not meet the delegation sent by S.S. Barnala to explain the party's position. S.S. Barnala who was still the Chief Minister of the State organised a mammoth conference on 20 February

1987 at Longowal to demonstrate that the people still supported him. The gathering rejected the edict of the priests against S.S. Barnala.

I consider that the chain of events recounted above, tend to support the conclusion that they were part of a single plan and there was one mind (perhaps an Intelligence Agency) behind the chain of events. The Home Minister of India was accused of helping one faction which, immediately after coming into power, dismissed the priests who were against the militants and appointed new pro-terrorist priests.

We shall soon see the role that Darshan Singh played to negotiate peace, first through the People's Accord of Chandra Shekhar's Janata Dal and, later, after the dismissal of the S.S. Barnala Government, through the World Sikh Conference. Darshan Singh was a renowned *kirtania* (singer of verses from the holy Granth) because of which he was very popular among the masses. Perhaps, he did not realise that by allowing himself to be used by the secret agencies and the militants, he had harmed himself more than he had damaged S.S. Barnala's stature. He claimed to have received hundreds of letters from Sikhs abroad in support of the proposed 'Sikh World Conference'. I happened to meet him in his strongly guarded abode on the first floor of Santokhsar Hall. He could show me only one such letter; and even that was from someone in India.

The proceedings of the *Sarbat Khalsa* and the impetus that it gave to militancy, have been cited as the causes of the Accords failure. Within a month of the declaration at Amritsar, there was a significant change in the pattern and character of violence. The militants were no longer indulging only in stray revenge killings. They began arming themselves in a big way by snatching weapons and robbing armouries. For the first time after Blue Star, they looted 16 rifles and 440 rounds from an armoury in Tarn Taran on 24 February. Three weeks later they looted 28 rifles from an arms dealer of Batala in Gurdaspur District. On 20 February the AISSF men besieged this town with the help of farmers, holding back supplies of milk, fresh vegetables and fruit. On 21 March the UAD (Baba Joginder Singh) men blocked the Punjab Legislative Assembly and in the resultant firing by the police, five people were killed and 37 injured. On 27 March at the Holla Mohalla festival Anandpur Sahib, which lasts for three or four days and where all major political parties hold their conferences, the Federation's men forcibly occupied the stage that was actually meant for the members of S.S. Barnala's Akali Dal.

The Chief Minister and his colleagues had to be whisked away under heavy police cover. The police was compelled to open fire in which 12 people were killed and 24 injured. On 28 March 1986, the day J.F. Ribeiro took charge as DG of Punjab Police, 13 people were killed and 17 injured in a terrorist shootout in Ludhiana. The following day 12 persons were killed in Jalandhar district. On 5 April, in the District Courts of Jalandhar, militants freed five of their men from police custody after killing six policemen. One of the militants freed was the dreaded Sukha Sipahi. Violence had returned with vengeance.

At a *Shaheedi Samagam* (congregation to commemorate martyrs) held in the first week of June in memory of those who had died during Operation Blue Star, the militant organisations resolved to take direct action. The Dashmesh Regiment, which had set on fire 37 railway stations on the night of 14 April 1984, was revived. Three other regiments—Khalistan Armed Force, Khalistan Liberation Army and Liberation Front of Khalistan—were formed to operate in four districts; Ferozepur, Gurdaspur, Kapurthala and Amritsar. On 7 June they killed 10 persons in Amritsar district followed by four on the 8th and another four the following day. Shiv Sena workers reacted to the killing. In Jandiala there was a clash between the two groups. The administration imposed curfew. When the curfew was lifted, the Sena gave a call for a *hartal* in the town which shut down. There was a demand by the BJP for deployment of the army. The all-party committee (*samiti*) formed to check the migration of the Hindu population had not yet commenced working. The administration had to arrest 9 persons under the National Security Act. Some migration from the town had also started. The pattern of future violence, reactions to it and its handling by the administration, had become established.

Another pattern of killing, and the resultant reactions, emerged in the killing of 15 Hindu bus passengers after hijacking the bus to a link road in Muktsar. To quell the consequential communal riots the next day in Delhi (in which four persons had been killed and 45 injured), the army had to be called with orders to 'shoot at sight'. Curfew was imposed in Moga. In Amritsar, in addition to the curfew, the army had to carry out for a flag march.

It became clear that militancy was back in Punjab. Alarm bells should have rung in the Akali camps. It was time to forget their differences and unite in the interest of peace. But their feuds only intensified.

It would appear that the ISI of Pakistan found this moment to be opportune to more actively assist the movement. Many militants including G.S. Manochahal had been in touch with intelligence agencies across the border. A large number of Sikh youth had crossed over to Pakistan fearing arrest under the Terrorist and Disruptive Activities Act (TADA) during what came to be known as 'Operation Wood Rose' in June and July 1984. Included among these were a number of boys who were sent by Bhindranwale himself just before Operation Blue Star when curfew was relaxed by the army. Many of them, on return from Pakistan, told the BSF guards at the border that they had been sentenced to 18 months imprisonment in Pakistan. In jail they were kept in isolation and given training in insurgency. Their sentences were coming to an end and they were being sent back to India in batches. Some were killed while trying to sneak back, some surrendered to the BSF but many must have been successful. For the smugglers operating on this border these militants were a convenient source of manpower.

The failure of the Accord strengthened S.S. Barnala's opponents in the Akali party. P.S. Badal had dubbed the Accord as a sell-out. Compared to the award of Mrs. Gandhi in 1970, in terms of which the transfer of Chandigarh to Punjab was linked with the transfer of Abohar and Fazilka to Haryana, the present accord was more liberal. However, with the failure of the accord, it seemed P.S. Badal's assessment had been correct.

The other opponents, Baba Joginder Singh, Bimal Khalsa and the AISSF had tried to increase their presence in the Temple within a month of S.S. Barnala taking the oath as Chief Minister. They had pulled down a part of the Akal Takht on 31 October 1985 to pre-empt the demolition to be undertaken by the SGPC. Giani Sahib Singh, the head priest of the Darbar Sahib, was shot at and injured by them on 27 November 1985.

The Akali Dal and SGPC had to take the cover of another spurious *Sarbat Khalsa* on 16 February 1986 in order to get support for a resolution designed to help in clearing out the rowdy militants and improving the worsening atmosphere in the Temple. A Task Force of ex-servicemen was raised by the SGPC to keep the Temple free from such elements. This proved quite effective. In June a member of this Force was killed while forcing out the 'boys' who were converging here for the 4 June *Shaheedi Samagam*. But G.S. Tohra managed to have the Task Force disbanded. When I met G.S. Tohra in 1988,

I questioned him about his reasons for wanting to abolish the Task Force. He replied that he had actually ordered its screening but not its dissolution. But facts indicated otherwise.

The militants had, however, been moving fast. The five member Panthic Committee had called a press conference at its headquarters in the Golden Temple and declared the formation of Khalistan. It was quite an intriguing affair. The press reporters were given sealed envelopes with directions to open them only after an hour or so, seemingly to give themselves some time to slip away. The next day, on 30 April 1986, the police was sent into the Temple in search of the elusive Committee. I learnt from some of the political members of the Marketing Board that Arun Nehru, the Minister of State for Home had rushed to Amritsar and insisted on sending the force inside even though the administration was sure that there was no militant in the Temple any more. Captain Amarinder Singh, who was a senior member in the S.S. Barnala cabinet, resigned in protest, as the Chief Minister had not taken him into confidence before sending the police inside the Temple.

A show cause notice was issued to S.S. Barnala, threatening excommunication from the Sikh *panth* for this sacrilege of the temple. Ultimately the *Jathedar* of the Akal Takht pronounced the *tankha* (punishment) to clean shoes and utensils in five gurudwaras. S.S. Barnala's compliance of the sentence was picked up by the Doordarshan TV teams. This humility may have cleansed S.S. Barnala's sins of ego, if any, besides generating some amount of sympathy for the Chief Minister. But the militants must have assumed that their use of the Golden Temple for irreligious activities was no violation of the *maryada* of the Temple.

On 5 July 1986, the P.S. Badal group formally split from the ruling party and declared itself to be the real Akali Dal later named as UAD. P.S. Badal dismissed S.S. Barnala and his supporters from his party and started functioning as an opposition group, accusing the government of eliminating some of the militants through extrajudicial means. They frequently squatted in the well of the House by way of protest. S.S. Barnala was left with the only option of naming his party the Akali Dal (Longowal). The split in the Akali Dal, when the need was for unity, was a boon for the militants. As violence spurted, the migrations of Hindus increased. This added to the communal tension.

Neither S.S. Barnala, personally, nor his administration can be accused of being soft on the militants or having any narrow communal outlook. There were allegations against one or two ministers for being pro-militant but that was mostly for political reasons. In the three months, April to June 1986, when the killings started increasing, all out efforts were made to bring the situation under control. His administration claimed to have accounted for 23 of the 40 hardcore militants, 471 suspected militants had been taken into custody in connection with various acts of violence committed by them. Of the 164 civilians killed, 55 were Sikhs, one Muslim, two Christians and 104 Hindus. The forces had lost 18 of their personnel. In all, 941 families had migrated mostly from Amritsar and Gurdaspur districts, of which 156 had shifted within the state. S.S. Barnala himself tried to persuade the migrants to return from Delhi.

Heavy security was stationed in the Temple complex in view of the *Shaheedi Samagam* to be held on 4 June 1986. The administration made 1,700 preventive arrests. As tension increased inside the Temple, police in plain clothes went in to control the situation. S.S. Barnala had been paying personal attention to the promotion of communal amity. He set up an all-party state level Communal Harmony and Integration Council where all issues were discussed by the state level leaders of the principal parties. His Ministers and local leaders would visit the affected villages to hold *Qaumi Ekta* conferences. They would also visit the victims of violence and the migrants. The principal minority community was encouraged to gear up for self-defence. Arms licenses were issued to them quite freely.

The DGP, J.F. Ribeiro, reorganised the functioning of the police. For more effective control, he proposed reducing the areas of unwieldy police stations, and the creation of new revenue subdivisions and a separate police district, Tarn Taran. Focal villages were identified for stationing the force. For a cluster of 10 villages, an adequate number of platoons was made responsible. On 19 July 1986, a massive raid was organised in the Mand area which was known as the 'Capital of Khalistan'. It is a huge marshy tract falling between the confluence of two rivers, Sutlej and Beas. It touches four districts making it easy for professional criminals—like illicit distillers permanently settled there—to escape to any of the districts whenever the police came chasing them.

About 2,000 personnel, bulldozers, tractors and motorboats were employed in the operation. Although only 50 persons were arrested in the combing of the area yet, psychologically, it was quite a setback to the militants. By the first week of August, J.F. Ribeiro had inducted 60 more companies of the Central Reserve Police Force (CRPF) and Border Security Force (BSF). Manbir Singh Cheharu and Tarsem Singh Kohar, two powerful senior leaders of the movement, were also arrested. By the end of August, the police claimed discernible improvement in the law and order situation. The press also agreed with this version. Migrations, which had risen from 69 families in May to 489 and 325 respectively in June and July, decreased to 46 in August 1986.

When the militants came under real pressure, they attacked the force. In the last week of August, there were four attacks on the BSF and CRPF posts. But this did not help them at all. And Surjit Singh Barnala, on the completion of one year in office could claim that the greatest achievement of his government had been the return of normalcy. On 27 September, he told pressmen that 200 migrant families had returned to Punjab. On 12 September he had pleaded with the National Integration Council for political inputs to sustain normalcy. As per the reports in *The Tribune*, 13 September, he had observed that political complacency was far more dangerous than administrative complacency. 'Political issues have become terrorism in Punjab,' S.S. Barnala was quoted to have said. He certainly seemed to be right, and he had done well despite the betrayals of his own colleagues and the Government of India.

The lack of confidence in the S.S. Barnala Government primarily because of communal tension was dangerous and posed a threat to peace. If violence and similar tensions are manipulated, they can only lead to greater tragedies. So it was in Punjab. We have earlier noted the implications of the *Sarbat Khalsa* of 26 January 1986, the SGPC elections of November 1986, the consequent dissolution of the Task Force and the *Sarbat Khalsa* of January 1987. We have also noted the way the Rajiv–Longowal Accord was scuttled. But for these developments, terrorism could not have assumed such dangerous proportions, nor could Pakistan have aggravated it at will. In this climate of distrust it was easy for the terrorists to rise again.

Communal tensions during this period were intense and out of proportion to the incidents of violence, including loss of human lives. It would seem that a whispering campaign fanned them, augmented perhaps by memories of the pre-Blue Star period. Similarly, the contrived communal anti-Sikh riots of November 1984, may have taught the ruffians that they could kill and loot and thereafter escape retribution. In the case of all major killings there was a greater reaction in Delhi than counter violence in Punjab. What was more surprising was that many political parties did not seem to have faith in the impartiality of the S.S. Barnala Government. There was a persistent demand by these parties, particularly the BJP, to deploy the army. It is likely that such a stance was felt to be necessary in order to counter the Congress effort to earn Hindu votes.

The opposition parties also demanded that the Central Government should use the powers vested in it under Article 249 of the Constitution of India and takeover the maintenance of law and order in the border districts. On 13 August 1986, the Parliament had actually passed the requisite resolution empowering the government to do so, even though it was more important to protect the minority community in Punjab rather than to prevent reactive communal violence outside Punjab. This was imperative because the aim of the militants was to spread communal riots on the same scale as had preceded the Partition of the country.

It is true that in Punjab some Sikhs did not come to the aid of their Hindu brothers when attacked by terrorists. Nevertheless, they sympathised with them and never wanted them to migrate. During the whole decade of violence, there was not a single instance of the looting of a Hindu family or a Hindu house lying locked because of migration. Whereas, outside Punjab, in many situations, looting of the Sikhs, seemed to be the primary motive or perhaps a bait to perpetrate the violence. The S.S. Barnala administration always took serious note of communal tensions, but somehow could not nurture the existing, centuries old relationship between the two communities in Punjab. The bonds of common ancestors, culture and the shared ideals of *Punjabiat* could have been invoked to build a strong movement to counter the divisive aims of the militants and of other vested and political interests. This, I firmly believe, was possible despite the occasional vitiation of the atmosphere.

In 1986, for every 22 Hindus, 19 Sikhs were killed. They could surely have combined to defend themselves. But the communalists on both sides continued to exploit the situation and to project themselves as the saviours. The militants began to forcibly snatch weapons from the Sikhs. The police made them deposit their weapons in the police stations instead of organising both the communities to unite and resist the attacks.

After a month's lull, the militants, on 25 October, shot seven and injured 10 people belonging to the minority community near Malout, then in Ferozepur district. The town had to be put under curfew. Curfew was an instant remedy to prevent anticipated communal clashes. Such a remedy was used, at times for weeks in places like Batala, Fatehgarh Churian, Jandiala, Amritsar, Hoshiarpur and Jalandhar. Its long-term effects were, however, quite dampening. Both the curfews and violence were back. In the month of November about 40 people were killed, but in the first week of December alone, 45 persons fell to the bullets of the militants. When terrorist violence spreads, incidents of kidnapping, robbery, and loot also increase, ostensibly to finance the movement. In fact, crimes of this type had continued all along, but because of the killings, their damage and nuisance paled in comparison.

Violence had taken root in Punjab and had reached intolerable levels. In 1985, 63 civilians and eight policemen were killed in Punjab. In 1986, the killings of civilians rose to 420 of which 193 were Sikh, 224 Hindu and three others in addition to 78 policemen. That year 42 militants also lost their lives. The same pattern of killing and communal tension continued into the following year as well. The SGPC, the clergy and the P.S. Badal factions continued to oppose the S.S. Barnala Government.

Prime Minister Rajiv Gandhi had not achieved much from the Punjab muddle. The political situation in the country was also becoming complicated. The State Assembly elections in Haryana were due in June 1987. It would be an important test for the popularity of the Congress. Bhajan Lal had evidently sensed the changing winds against the Congress a year earlier. He had resigned from the post of Chief Minister in June 1986. His resignation may also have scuttled the transfer of Chandigarh to Punjab, scheduled for 21 June (Bhajan Lal was later elected as Member of the Rajya Sabha and included in Rajiv Gandhi's Cabinet). Devi Lal, the *Jat* leader of Haryana—who at the national level had formed an alliance with N.T. Rama Rao, a former Chief Minister of Andhra Pradesh, and V.P. Singh who had parted company with Rajiv Gandhi—was threatening Bansi Lal, the Chief Minister of Haryana. These three leaders were stirring up a countrywide movement against the 'misrule' of the Congress. Therefore, for the Congress to defeat Devi Lal was literally a question of life or death. This was the main reason behind Prime Minister Rajiv's cooling off on the Punjab Accord.

It was realised by the Government of India that, though S.S. Barnala was a nationalist Sikh, as long as he remained Chief Minister, the Punjab Accord remained alive. Therefore, he had to go. Nor did the Central government want to risk any strong reaction by the Sikhs to his dismissal. Therefore, Professor Darshan Singh, the *Jathedar* of the Akal Takht and other priests were offered another memorandum of settlement. Through this it was ensured that the clergy would tolerate the dismissal of the S.S. Barnala government. This could also be construed as the demise of the earlier accord.

The new formula dubbed as the People's Accord was finalised in January 1987, at a meeting held at Chandigarh, by the Janata Dal government led by Chandra Shekhar. The six-page document summarised the pending problems of Punjab in 14 points and suggested their solutions. On 2 May 1987, Acharya Sushil Muni, an activist of the Janata Dal met the *Jathedar* of the Akal Takht with the draft of the document which was approved by the *Jathedar* and the four head priests. The Muni also claimed that a copy of the new accord had been sent to the SGPC four months earlier and that he had come with the approval of the Prime Minister. Buta Singh, the Home Minister of India, denied the Government's involvement in the move while answering a question in Parliament on 8 May. S.S. Barnala ordered the registration of a case against the *Jathedar* for a speech given by him on 27 February 1987 in Khalsa College Amritsar. According to the *Jathedar*, Acharya Sushil Muni was very perturbed because the registration of the case meant the torpedoing of the talks between the *Jathedar* and the Muni.

By April 1987 violence had greatly increased. Killings by the militants became a daily affair. In addition, the militants had greatly intensified their social reform movement. To popularise themselves among the masses they had embarked on a campaign against the sale of liquor, tobacco and meat. Fifty liquor vends in country areas were not allowed to operate. In villages, many of these vends functioned from wooden structures known as *khokha*. It was easy for the militants to burn them. They would also loot the cash before setting it on fire. The government's inability to establish these vends was an embarrassment. They also required the people to restrict the number of persons in a *barat* to 11. Instead of sumptuous meals, only vegetarian food, restricted to three dishes, was permitted to be served. For any violation, they would spill the entire food and force back the marriage party if it exceeded 11. A larger *barat* in the winter months was made to wade through the cold and dirty water of the village pond before being sent back. These reforms were welcomed only by the economically weaker sections who had to incur debts to comply with costly social customs. But the government could not do much to counter the militants actions.

On 4 May 1987 the Government of India notified elections to the Haryana State Assembly to be held on 17 June. In the prevailing communal tension, the dismissal of the Akali Government in Punjab would have been widely welcomed in Haryana. The S.S. Barnala Government was thus dismissed on 11 May 1987. This decision was based on the report of Governor Siddharth Shankar Ray. The S.S. Barnala Government was accused of not having done all that was possible for stemming militancy. The state was now under President's rule. The *Jathedar* welcomed the dismissal as the end 'of an unworthy' government according to *The Tribune* dated 12 May 1987. Both the Muni and the *Jathedar* maintained that other steps would follow. *Jathedar* Darshan Singh must have hoped to play a greater role in the Punjab administration. Nothing came from the Government of India, but Acharya Sushil Muni did go to the USA—which was perhaps his reward—and the *Jathedar* called a Sikh World Conference to solve the Punjab problem.

The dismissal of a government which still had a majority in the house came under severe criticism. The Home Minister had praised the performance of J.F. Ribeiro, who, as pointed out by S.S. Barnala, was a part of his government. Where had S.S. Barnala then erred? Interference in the police functioning was only a convenient explanation by the police as a cause of increased violence. S.S. Barnala's dismissal was welcome to the militants. They had much to celebrate.

There was only one gain in the dismissal which was neither felt nor mentioned. A sizeable faction of the Akalis, from the P.S. Badal group, sympathised with the militants and criticised alleged police excesses. With the continuous increase in killings, communal tensions also began to increase in Punjab. Fear and intimidation were in the air. A senior Sikh leader, Kirpal Singh, told me in Amritsar that they were unable to readily go for condolence visits, even when lifelong Hindu friends had been killed. S.S. Barnala had tried to mobilise all the political parties to meet the people and try to lessen communal tension, but the parties successively deserted him. Communal amity was necessary to curb militancy. Governor S.S. Ray's presence as the head of the state allayed the apprehensions of the minority community and they keenly hoped for the return of peace to Punjab.

5

Governor Ray's Tenure

Article 356 of our Constitution ignores the repeated assertion of British Prime Minister Cambell-Bannerman (1905), supported by many a liberal political thinker, that a good government could never be a substitute for government by the people themselves. The provision in this Article has frequently been used to dismiss elected governments in Punjab. Even illiterate villagers are aware of the *dhara* 356 of the Constitution. It thus became one of the consistent demands of the Akali Dal, supported by almost all the regional and leftist political parties, that the said Article be abrogated. When Governor S.S. Ray, had recommended the imposition of President's rule, he well knew that his office would virtually turn into a war office. With the issue of the presidential notification on 11 May 1987, the burdens of S.S. Barnala were shifted on to S.S. Ray's shoulders.

A lawyer by profession, a former Law Minister in Mrs. Gandhi's Cabinet and an erstwhile Chief Minister of West Bengal, Siddharth Shankar Ray had direct access to Rajiv Gandhi. This was an asset for the job he had chosen to accept. He did not, therefore, need to go through the Home Ministry to obtain the Prime Minister's consent to his proposals. S.S. Ray could not be unaware that this situation would not always be palatable to the Home Minister, Buta Singh, who is a Punjabi and had detailed knowledge of Sikh religious organisations and their clergy in Delhi and Punjab. S.S. Ray's principal handicap was that he did not know Hindi or Punjabi. But he ensured that this did not hamper his interaction with the masses. S.S. Ray remained concerned and was confident about soon finding a solution to the problems of Punjab. He seemed to have become enamoured of Punjab and revered the Harmandar. After it was cleared of militants, the Rays visited the Temple many times and invariably sat in the sanctum sanctorum without publicising their visits.

Immediately on assuming direct charge of the state, the Governor announced that his first priority would be to restore a semblance of law and order in half the districts of the state in which so-called social reformers had disrupted normal life and intimidated the people. He resolved to deal with the situation with 'compassion and firmness.' He expressed the hope that President's rule would be 'short enough to be sweet and long enough to be effective'. Quite ironically, it turned out to be the longest stretch of President's rule in the history of independent India during which four more Governors, besides S.S. Ray, wrestled with the problems of bringing peace to Punjab.

The redoubtable Governor arranged for 26 more companies of the CRPF and had them sent to the disturbed areas within 48 hours. To curb the highly menacing and demoralising nuisance of the social reform movement, 412 activists of the AISSF and Damdami Taksal were taken into custody within three days; their number doubled in another three days. By way of compassion he announced that those promising good behaviour could be released on the recommendations of the DGP. This concession, however, was withdrawn after a few weeks. To my mind the reason behind this was dictated by caution, lest the release of the boys impair the improving situation.

DGP J.F. Ribeiro, after four weeks of President's rule, claimed that the situation had improved and that the police now had the upper hand. The crime figures supported his claim. The average of killings in the first four months of 1987 during S.S. Barnala's regime was 10 militants and 70 civilians including policemen. In the first month of President's rule, 23 militants and 61 civilians were killed. The killing of civilians had fallen by about 12 per cent and that of the militants had increased by more than a 100 per cent. There was also some decrease in the activities of the so-called social reformers. Agreeing with the super cop, the Governor also told the press that there was appreciable success against the militants' reform movement. The government succeeded in opening many liquor vends which were earlier auctioned by the S.S. Barnala government. The performance of the Governors administration after four weeks was surely promising but it was only the beginning, and we had 'miles to go'.

J.F. Ribeiro also told the press that he had stopped the system of grading the militants. This was a good decision. The confusing classification into A, B, C and D, was of no help to the administration, either to keep surveillance on the militants or to analyse the prevailing situation. Seemingly, the police system of categorising the bad characters in the area of each police station had been applied to the militants also but with disastrous results.

Bad characters did not appear overnight; therefore, the classification in their cases was valid. In the prevailing ambience of killing and dying for nothing, the availability of a few weapons would give birth to a new 'Regiment'. If the courier of a smuggler decided to keep one AK 47 from the weapons he was carrying for others, and if he procured two country made .12 bore pistols, and two .12 bore guns with half the barrel length sawed off, he could easily form a killer group of eight to 12 members. He could announce his affiliation to any of the existing terrorist outfits or assume a new name, give it to a reporter on the phone (one group in Amritsar called itself Cobra Regiment) and then begin the process of causing havoc in the area familiar to him. This capability of amoebic growth completely defied the existing arithmetic of classifying the bad characters by the police. Interestingly, J.F. Ribeiro in his 12 June 1987 press conference claiming the 'upper hand' had said that all B, C and D category terrorists had been killed.

Though the terrorists were spread over half the districts of Punjab, their nerve centre was the Golden Temple in the shape of their respective headquarters and the Panthic Committee. They were able, therefore, to hit back immediately after a press conference in which J.F. Ribeiro claimed success against any of them. Between 11 and 19 June, 35 civilians and 3 policemen were killed. On 6 July 1987 they hijacked an overloaded late night bus on the Chandigarh–Ambala highway to a link road near the Punjab–Haryana border and massacred 40 of its passengers injuring 30 others. On the night of 7 July 1987, in the same manner they killed 30 passengers on another bus. The two incidents compelled the Governor and his DGP to admit that this was a great setback to their campaign.

These killings all but drove the northern states of Delhi, UP, Haryana and even the placid Himachal Pradesh into mob violence against Sikhs. The governments and the administrations of these states had been chastened by the mass killings of Sikhs in Delhi and other towns in the wake of Mrs. Gandhi's assassination. In spite of that, six Sikhs were killed. In many places they had to temporarily seek refuge in the local gurudwaras to save their lives. Hissar, from where one of the ill-fated buses had left, was naturally more disturbed. The army had to be called. By the 10th, the position became normal and people began returning to their homes from the gurudwaras. In their absence some houses had been looted. The administration claimed to have arranged the return of goods to the owners. But the army had to stay till 12 July 1987.

There was strong criticism of Delhi by various parties and organisations. Lal Krishna Advani of the BJP asked the Prime Minister to step down. Delhi itself was deeply concerned as the crime revealed that the militants had developed a strong support structure in other states as well. Consequently, a meeting of all the northern states was held to evolve a system to jointly combat terrorism and check its spillover from Punjab to other states.

The terrorists kept up their killing spree. The killings in July mounted to 173; the highest in any month till then. The intrepid Punjabis seemingly took it in their stride. But the gruesome killing of 12 Hindus in village Jagdev Kalan on the night of 7 August, shattered public confidence. That night, the militants, pulled out the male members from five Hindu homes, made them stand in a line in the village centre and shot them dead. The migration of these families to safer places, with a cascading effect in other places, was an imminent prospect.

Izhar Alam, the SSP Amritsar, and I did everything we could do to prevent the migration. The Governor and his wife Maya Ray visited each of the five households consoling the bereaved in sombre silence; eloquent tears made up for the language barrier. We provided a permanent CRPF post in the village. Our repeated visits, government grants, promises of security combined with pleadings of the entire Sikh population of the village, grieving with them and with shame in their hearts, could not persuade the surviving women to stick to their village. 'For whom should we stay back?' a weeping widow asked me. I pointed to the two-year old boy she was holding. 'For him and his rights to the place of his ancestors.' She looked up,

'Yes I am leaving for him.' I felt like snatching the boy from her, and taking him to the Sikh village elders, standing just a few paces away and asking them if they could be his guardians and protectors. Prannoy Roy, with a Delhi Doordarshan team, was filming the shocking occasion and I consider that, but for the presence of the cameras, I may have acted upon my impulse. With the CRPF post the village was far more secure than many others, yet I had to yield. It was a moral defeat for me as well as for Izhar Alam.

We may not have succeeded here but another village nearby, Mehal Kalan, responded positively to our assurances. They took up weapons and made arrangements to guard the village day and night by themselves. Half the village was Hindu, but it was also related to the Sikh half because of the Khatri caste they shared. Only one elder came to me in my office. He revealed that after the Jagdev Kalan incident his village also feared an attack by the militants any night. He asked that their village be protected for four days, by which time they would procure weapons for themselves. I arranged for their protection. The following day at the village meeting, the SSP and I freely issued them with gun licenses. Izhar Alam even gave them some weapons. No terrorist dared to visit that village. By an arrangement, the CRPF night-patrol approached the village after exchanging code signals. It was quite a morale booster for us. We could quote their example to others so that they would emulate these villagers. But most of the villages did not have the ethnic homogeneity, nor property interests that existed in Mehal Kalan.

Hindus from many other villages were migrating to Amritsar. The government sanctioned monthly grants for their sustenance. Though desirable as a humanitarian gesture, it could prove counter-productive. Hindu migration from the Punjab and promotion of Hindu-Sikh tensions was the primary aim of the militants and their mentors in Pakistan. The only viable solution would be to organise each village to defend itself. Izhar Alam and I took every opportunity to encourage threatened villages to defend their territory like Mehal Kalan. There were no takers. We, however, got a breakthrough in the tragedy of village Chananke.

Chananke is a Congress dominated village near Chowk Mehta. The terrorist killings in this village on the evening of 30 September 1987 were distinguishable from other such incidents in two respects. First, they had struck at 6.30 P.M. without waiting for nightfall; second, even after the shooting they remained there for more than 45 minutes. They killed three young sons of three Hindu shopkeepers and three sons of another clean-shaven Sikh. They were searching for another Sikh youth who had succeeded in dodging them. In the village meeting, a day later, we advanced the idea that if people had their weapons and stood on guard duty by turn, such a tragedy could have been avoided. Only the village *Sarpanch* was holding on to his weapons while the others had deposited theirs, in the police station at Chowk Mehta at the behest of the police in 1986. We offered to give them more weapons and returned those they had surrendered. There were some ex-army men whom we asked to this challenge. The villagers agreed to defend themselves but they reneged on their promise even before we left. Their concern was the safety of the weapons during the daytime when they went out to their fields.

We had to leave the meeting abruptly, as Izhar Alam got a message that a top terrorist, Jhamke, had been spotted while entering the Chowk Mehta gurudwara. I accompanied the SSP in his bullet-proof car. On the way I said to him:

'I am thoroughly convinced, that it would be futile to persuade villagers to take weapons or even give them weapons without providing them with a couple of trained armed men who should form the nucleus of the fighting unit. To begin with, can you spare some?'

We had to experiment before asking for the government's approval. Izhar Alam, always seemed to be exhausted because of the stress of sustained interrogations and the excessive touring that he had to undertake. His reaction was positive. He was confident that he could spare some constables, borrow some home guards and recruit some SPOs (Special Police Officers) in order to provide the nucleus of a fighting unit. Izhar Alam made a small beginning immediately. In a couple of threatened villages where suitable vacant premises were available, we stationed two policemen, two home guards and two young boys (appointed as SPOs on daily wages), and gave them some .303 rifles after some training. This was designated as an SPO post. The policemen were provided with a walkie-talkie set. In most cases the villagers willingly agreed to co-operate with the new experiment. It worked well and appeared to be promising. We put our proposal at the next state level review meeting convened by the Governor in Chandigarh a few weeks later. The proposal was approved.

We did not then realise that the SPO posts would become the widest network to fight militancy, but I had been certain all along that it would be accepted by the people in the countryside. Under the police rules, in case of an emergency, the District Magistrate was empowered to appoint any person(s) as SPO(s) for a specific time and occasion. The SPOs could be paid on a contingent basis. We, therefore, did not require any special sanction. The SPOs not only risked their lives for a miserly daily wage of Rs. 30 but some of them were even killed.

It was not difficult to find accommodation for these posts in villages. The requisite training was given to the SPOs in the use of weapons, walkie-talkie sets and the basics of defence. If they were not as efficient as the regular units, they were certainly more useful at little additional cost. The presence of SPOs and Home Guards in these units added to their acceptability by the villages. Unlike the police, they were not meant to keep an eye on them but only to protect and help them. Barring some exceptions, they got full cooperation from the people. Most of them were eager to get 'promoted' into the police and many of them did succeed by their sheer devotion to duty. If they faulted, it was easy to get rid of them. Last but not the least, by roping them as SPOs, we undermined the source of recruitment by militants. In spite of some lapses, this innovation played an important role in combating terrorism.

The migration of Hindus from many villages did not stop altogether but instead of shifting to the city they sought refuge, in other villages; preferably those with a regular CRPF, police or SPO post. From here the men folk could commute with ease to tend to their shops in their own villages. This saved us a lot of demoralising embarrassment and also huge expense which we would have to bear if the families were to migrate to Amritsar.

Governor S.S. Ray gave great importance to involving the people in fighting terrorism. In July, the bloodiest month till then, he constituted The Punjab State Communal Harmony cum National Integration Council, which met regularly in Raj Bhawan, Chandigarh. Two representatives from each of the State's recognised political parties were its members and represented the people. The Administrative Secretaries, the senior police officers, Divisional Commissioners, the Deputy Inspectors General of Police, Deputy Commissioners and Senior Superintendents of Police from all the districts were represented in the Council.

In its first meeting the Governor made an impassioned appeal to all political parties to organise rallies and educate people against terrorism and divisive forces in the state. Most parties (the major Akali factions did not join) made out a case that ultimately only a political solution would solve the problem. They, nevertheless, agreed to join the mass-contact programme. The Deputy Commissioners were required to organise conferences in sensitive villages, which were addressed by the representatives of political parties. In addition, the DCs were required to organise separate meetings for a group of villages, to redress public grievances and involve people in the developmental schemes of the area as well as for the maintenance of peace. Along with the SSP, I addressed two such meetings every week. The state level Council monitored the progress regularly. The Governor made it a point to attend these meetings by turns in the disturbed districts.

Both types of district level meetings proved effective. As speaker after speaker condemned terrorism and violence and talked of Indian and Punjabi/culture, the teaching of the Sikh Gurus, the common bonds of struggle through the centuries, fear-ridden stolid faces would suddenly begin to react. Describing the barbarity of a killer group active in the area, I narrated the previous night's killing in which they had not shown any mercy to a two-month old girl. The crowd of about 500 men and women grunted 'Hai Hai!'. After a few days the gang again killed another family in a nearby village sparing only a set of twins whom they left with the neighbours of the deceased. In addition to the success of these meetings, at times, they became forums for letting off steam and acted as a sort of catharsis.

The Akalis did not attend the state level meeting but they could not afford to be absent from the meetings held in the country side, particularly in their respective areas. At the end of one such a meeting, Shishupal Singh, a senior and popular local leader and a Cabinet Minister in the dismissed S.S. Barnala Ministry, told me to keep the campaign going. 'The People listen to you and it does make a difference in keeping their morale up.' Even the supporters of militants came to these meetings and complained about the missing 'boys'. I used to condemn terrorism in no uncertain terms. Twice someone posing as the Deputy Chief of the Khalistan Commando Force (KCF) wrote to me that the killings were not done by them but by the police to malign their movement.

These meetings were also development oriented. We approved some of the development proposals on the spot. Grievances and complaints were attended to and resolved as far as possible at the meeting itself. To begin with, people were afraid to complain against harassment by the police. In the course of time we were able to gain their confidence and encouraged them to bring police excesses to our notice. However, rarely would people from the village condemn terrorism from the stage.

The district heads of the departments concerned with rural development, as also their respective field officers, were required to attend these meetings. Such meetings thus also became a means to discourage absenteeism of officials in rural areas in the terrorist ambience. Public administration was thus literally being taken to the doorstep of the people during the darkest days seen by the state. The then Chief Secretary of Punjab, P.H. Vaishanav, presided over some of these meetings held in the worst terrorist affected areas.

The usefulness of these mass meetings was praised by the press. The response of the people boosted the morale of the administration. As a mass contact movement, it was successful and the state Council acknowledged the fact. J.F. Ribeiro also attended many of these meetings. On many occasions he asked for special meetings to be arranged for him. The tall, cheerful DGP spoke broken Hindi in his Goan accent. His bearing impressed the robust Punjabis, and his speech amused and at the same time charmed them. Through this forum, he was successful in washing off some of the criticism and blame of extra-judicial elimination that was laid on his force. In the *Lok Shakti Samagam*—the name given to these meetings—held at Jaitu on 20 November, J.F. Ribeiro attributed much of the credit for the success in curbing militancy to these meetings. He also paid tribute to the people for their warmth, co-operation, fortitude and, above all, their resilience.

Although these meetings, held under full security, were designed to counter militancy, the militants neither tried to disturb them in any manner nor threatened people to keep away from them. I think people welcomed them because of the definite public utility of these development-oriented *samagams*. Therefore, the boys did not attempt to deter them in any manner. Indeed, the damage came from representatives of the political parties, who began to blame each other for the rise of terrorism in the state.

Most fingers were pointed at the Congress party. There were also ego problems; everyone wanted to sit in the front row of the improvised small stage. The Congress was the first to walk out of this arrangement. They embarked on their own mass contact campaign which *The Tribune* (8 September 1987) labelled as 'lacklustre'. The Communists were the next to bow out. But it must be said to their credit that because of their fearlessness and their policy to stand against the militants, many Communists lost not only their lives but in some cases their entire families. The loss suffered by the members of other political parties was comparatively less. They had not picked up the gauntlet of the militants in the way the 'Comrades' had.

In this connection, I must acknowledge that the health department under a programme launched by the World Health Organization were able to organise some of the biggest gatherings in Amritsar district. The Secretary Health to Government of Punjab, S.S. Boparai who presided over these massive meetings did not object to my condemning terrorism in that forum as well. However, at the end of one of these meetings he asked me if I had adequate security.

In the last quarter of the year there were increasing signs of the waning of militancy. The village *Sarpanches* and local political leaders who joined us in the *samagams*, voiced the need for political inputs to give the final push to militancy. Governor S.S. Ray and other well meaning leaders were repeatedly saying the same. But the Central Government stuck to its hardened stand that militancy should first be eliminated in the state.

These *samagams*, in a way, were of great help in narrowing the divide between the people and the bureaucracy. The role played by these meetings proved a useful tool in the hands of Governor S.S. Ray to keep away an Advisory Council dominated by members from the political party ruling at the Centre. Communal tension disappeared completely because we now had a platform to remove many misgivings which got aired in these interactive sessions with the people. Succeeding Governors and the regime at the Centre did not dispense with this forum. I will dwell upon some changes made subsequently in the character of these *samagams* but let us first take a look at the role the Sikh clergy played during this period and how they were handled by Governor S.S. Ray's administration.

6

The Politics of the Clergy

With the month of July turning gloomier every day, Governor S.S. Ray agreed to a convention being arranged by Darshan Singh, *Jathedar* of the Akal Takht on 4 August 1987. The *Jathedar* had invited representatives of all militant organisations, Sikh intellectuals, all factions of the Akali party—barring the S.S. Barnala group—all the Sikh Students Federations and the Taksal. This was the Sikh World Conference the *Jathedar* had announced, when he had failed to solve the Punjab problem through the People's Accord brought to him by the Janata Dal Activist Acharya Sushil Muni.

He succeeded in allowing only the invitees to enter the hall. Though the deliberations were short for a world conference—and they also seemed to have ended rather abruptly—the newspapers reported the next day that the convention had resolved that, in place of Khalistan, an area in north India may be given to them, where the Sikhs could experience the 'glow of freedom'. We had kept a watch on this closed door conference with the 'out laws' from the Akhara Braham Buta, within hearing distance of the venue. We noticed the militants' group leave the venue abruptly while the conference was still going on. We had also heard snatches of slogans of 'Khalistan Zindabad!' (long-live Khalistan!) from the youth standing outside the hall, as they had not been invited. Later we were told by our local intelligence that their withdrawal was not a walkout, but a move by the *kharkoos* (militants) to evade any plan of the administration to arrest them at the end of the conference. Our intelligence report was that the youth had insisted on demanding Khalistan.

The triumph of *Jathedar* Darshan Singh lasted only 24 hours. The very next day, the Panthic Committee, through a two-page note delivered to pressmen, rejected the recommendations of the convention, and dismissed the *Jathedar;* ruling that these issues could be considered only in a *Sarbat Khalsa* which would be held on Diwali day in October. The *Jathedar* fled from Amritsar on 8 August 1987, after announcing that he was 'leaving the field to the youth.' The general secretary of the SGPC, Mal Singh Ghuman, also resigned. The militants had manhandled him on 7 August at Ludhiana. Jathedar Sekhwan, the President of the United Akali Dal (UAD) withdrew his party from the Sikh scene. The militants seemed to be bulldozing all other institutions. But the SGPC and other UAD leaders intervened and persuaded the acting president of the UAD as well as the general secretary of the SGPC to continue. Darshan Singh did not respond to their request to come back.

The militants had set their eyes on the *Sarbat Khalsa* they were planning to hold on the forthcoming Diwali. They threatened the high priests to side with them so that the militants could legitimise themselves. They pressurised the four high priests to appeal to the people to support the Panthic Committee. The priests were in a fix. According to press reports, they agreed to abide by the result of a toss before the Guru Granth Sahib. The slips of paper indicating 'Yes' and 'No' were jumbled up. One slip was picked up. To the dismay of the militants it indicated 'No'. But the militants went back on their word and coerced the priests to issue the dictated statement. The obliging priests did not use the word Khalistan, but did agree to convey to the Sikh masses that the 16 militant organisations had amalgamated in order to provide leadership to the *Qaum* and gain *azadi* for the Sikhs. Therefore, they deserved support. Later, one of the priests disassociated himself from the joint statement.

Those priests who sided with the militants, enjoyed the de facto power that they shared. They began dictating terms to the SGPC and compelled them to decide appointments in their favour. The SGPC transferred Kashmir Singh from Amritsar to Tarn Taran. He refused to join at Tarn Taran, and challenged the right of the SGPC to shift him because the *Sarbat Khalsa* of January 1986 had appointed him. In terms of the principles followed in the Civil Service

Rules, the high priest was definitely talking sense, although it is a different matter that the *Sarbat Khalsa* also had no authority to hire or fire any one.

At this juncture a very intriguing proposal came from the leaders of the Federation. They asked the militants and the UAD to secure the release of Jasbir Singh Rode who was in jail and who had earlier been appointed *Jathedar* of the Akal Takht in January 1986. The Khalsa Liberation Force also requested the high priests to hold parleys with Darshan Singh. Noticing these moves, the Panthic Committee warned its organisations that the Central Government might surreptitiously install its agents through the SGPC. They were obviously hinting at J.S. Rode. The UAD joined hands with the SGPC and appealed to the militants to accept the supremacy of the Akal Takht; in other words, to accept *Jathedar* Darshan Singh. They also requested the latter to return to Amritsar. The *Jathedar* agreed only to resile, maintaining that the Central Government wanted a confrontation between the Akal Takht and the youth, but he wanted to avoid it. The militants desperately wanted their own nominee as *Jathedar* of the Akal Takht on the forthcoming Diwali.

The SGPC had already split into two groups since their 1986 election. Unmindful of the tussle going on in Amritsar, both the Tohra and Longowal factions, held their separate election meetings and elected G.S. Tohra and Harcharan Singh Hudiara as their respective Presidents. The crises through which they were passing, evidently did not induce any introspection or fresh thinking since they could not overcome their egos.

The government had decided to foil the proposed *Sarbat Khalsa*. Both factions of the SGPC decided to keep away because the Panthic Committee had summoned it. Chandra Shekhar, of the Janata Dal, rushed to Amritsar but failed to persuade the priests to defuse the situation. The priests, on the contrary, reportedly suggested that he have a dialogue with the youth, just as Baba Amte of the Knit India Movement had when he made similar efforts only six weeks earlier. Baba Amte, in a meeting he had with the SSP and me told us that after talking to the boys he was convinced that the solution of this national problem lay at the national level, where the causes behind the situation could be removed. Fighting terrorists with guns could only eradicate some terrorists but would add to the larger problem. Sunil Dutt, a matinee idol turned politician, also met the 'boys' in the Temple in April 1987 and came to a similar conclusion. It was, therefore, difficult for Chandra Shekhar, who could give the boys only some words of wisdom, to dissuade them from holding the *Sarbat Khalsa*. Interestingly, during S.S. Barnala's rule two *Sarbat Khalsas* had been held in January 1986 and 1987 without any obstruction by the State or the Central government. But presently, the Central government was anxious that it should not be held, in order that J.S. Rode's installation should give an impression of unanimous choice by all militant organisations.

Thousands of devotees come to have a dip in the holy *sarovar* on the auspicious day of Diwali. If the government had no reason to obstruct this tradition, preventing the *Sarbat Khalsa* was merely a law and order problem and not very difficult to handle. We searched the Temple complex a couple of days earlier. On Diwali day we searched some buildings in the Temple complex again, keeping a sufficient area around the temple under curfew for eight hours on the 21st and from 2.30 A.M. to 4.30 P.M. on Diwali, preventing even the pilgrims from going to the temple. When the curfew was lifted, virtually within seconds, people were in the holy *sarovar* as if they had been fish out of water. I told the Doordarshan team that no *Sarbat Khalsa* was held in the Golden Temple. I had been watching the Temple the whole day along with the SSP and K.P.S. Gill, the then ADGP of the CRPF. We did not see a soul except for the priests at the hour of the change of shifts. Through the media, I also thanked the people for magnanimously bearing with us and with our predicament. I acknowledged my gratitude to them, since I had not received a single complaint. This was a clear indication that people did not approve of the terrorists nor of their stay in the Temple.

The militants, with their usual obstinacy, maintained that the *Sarbat Khalsa* had been held and 12 resolutions had been passed. These were detailed and a two-page hand-written press note was delivered to the newsmen. The all-important resolution, according to the note, was that Baba Gurbachan Singh Manochahal had been appointed as acting *Jathedar* of the Akal Takht. The note bore five signatures. At the *Sarbat Khalsa* of January 1987, the same G.S. Manochahal had made room for Darshan Singh in this post. Obviously, there was politics behind the systemised series of *Sarbat Khalsa* meets. For future manipulations, the support of the defunct eighteenth century institution was no longer required. So, it was being given up.

I could understand why the militants and their mentors within India, Pakistan and other countries needed to revive the institution of the *Sarbat Khalsa*. I knew that the militants wanted to have control of the Temple and the SGPC but I wondered if it was necessary to flout the existing institutions with the support of resolutions adopted at the so-called *Sarbat Khalsa*? They could achieve such control directly with the might of their arms, but in this way they were able to acquire only a fraction of authority and that too only over the SGPC officials. Their mentors suggested that they organise a *Sarbat Khalsa* which they did on 26 January 1986, to defy the established religious hierarchy. They thought that the magic of the words 'Sarbat Khalsa' would be enough to convince the Sikh masses about their legitimacy. But it did not work.

The ideologues did not realise that the struggle to gain control of the historic gurudwaras had been going on in this district for five long years. People from almost every village of Amritsar must have participated in the fight in some manner. Memories of the Guru Ka Bagh agitation during British rule are still alive in the minds of lakhs of people through family stories narrated orally from generation to generation. For the Sikhs, therefore, there could never be a more memorable *Sarbat Khalsa* than the one which resolved to launch the agitation that forced the British administration to pass the Shiromani Gurudwara Parbandhak Committee Act of 1925. It was a pity that the SGPC itself got scared and resorted to holding a counter *Sarbat Khalsa* on 16 February 1986.

I think that such a decision was made because they continued to be divided into two SGPCs despite such a crisis. The January 1986 *Sarbat Khalsa* was not recognised by the SGPC or by any eminent Sikh. Only the militants hailed it. By banning such meetings, we were perhaps the only ones who were giving it some recognition. Even if the two-page note was the result of the deliberations of the militants, taking advantage of the normal gathering before the Akal Takht, the only sanction behind it could have been the might of their guns. Their note did not and could not have the support of the Sikh masses who had given an overwhelming verdict in favour of Indian nationalism during the elections of September 1985.

Nonetheless, our having prevented the holding of *Sarbat Khalsa* was hailed as a success. The press also reminded the public that in the case of the January 1986 *Sarbat Khalsa*, the government had acquiesced to its being held. The sensitive consideration before us, in October 1987, was the avoidable hindrance that we put in the way of religious worship on Diwali day which, besides the sacred sentiment, is also a right, guaranteed by the Constitution. But this time the decision had already come from Delhi to prevent the holding of the *Sarbat Khalsa* as we did it.

It would be too much to assume that the government was not aware of the irrelevance of the *Sarbat Khalsa* in the context of the existing SGPC Act. One can clearly make out from the events narrated above that the government had different approaches to the *Sarbat Khalsa* in January 1986 and October 1987. In 1986, the government wanted to divert public attention from the failure of the Accord and to support the Taksal in order that it could takeover the reconstruction of the Akal Takht. By the time it banned the *Sarbat Khalsa* of October 1987, the AISSF had already demanded the release of J.S. Rode, and apparently a decision had been taken to install J.S. Rode as the *Jathedar* of the Akal Takht. The pressure by a section of the militants on Darshan Singh to quit as the *Jathedar* of the Akal Takht was to get the post vacated. The other section of militants obviously had got wind of this development but they wanted G.S. Manochahal as the *Jathedar* of the Akal Takht. Hence the *Sarbat Khalsa* on Diwali and the consequent press note. After this, the government discarded the use of the *Sarbat Khalsa* by the militant organisations under its influence. The other terrorist outfits were never interested in this gimmick.

The militants inside the temple had been ordering about the officials of the SGPC. But the SGPC was resisting the pressure of the militants and of the priests with regard to their promotions and transfers. They had secured a sort of forced alignment from the four head priests. The presence of the head priest in the temple, and the vast gathering on Diwali could have been exploited by the militants to claim the support of a well attended *Sarbat Khalsa*. The government, therefore, decided that the priests should be arrested. Incidentally, these priests had been appointed in 1986 when G.S. Tohra was elected as President of the SGPC. Accordingly, they were picked up as a preventive measure to maintain peace and tranquillity. They were later detained under the Terrorist and Disruptive Activities Act.

Their detention deprived the militants of the religious shield they wanted to exploit. I was asked by the government to meet them in the jail and probe if they could disassociate themselves from the violent part of the struggle. I planned a visit to the jail. K.P.S. Gill, accompanied me incognito. The superintendent timed their visit to the jail gurudwara, when we were also there. They agreed to issue a statement that the Sikh religion did not condone violence and that as religious men they had no concern with politics. But they would not agree to 'condemn' the boys. I had to meet them three times, but every time the draft of their statement was not acceptable to the government. I finally asked the Governor why the government was keen on releasing them. I gathered from him that someone, either in Delhi or in Chandigarh, was cautioning the government that if the priests were kept in jail any longer there might be a general uprising of the people.

I told him that there was not the remotest possibility of such a development. Both the militants and the government were overrating the popularity of the priests. In my opinion, 95 per cent of the people were not even aware of their existence. He accepted my word and I did not have to bother the worthy priests any more. The Governor happened to visit Amritsar a couple of days later. Appreciating my assessment, he said that these priests had become irrelevant because things were changing fast in Punjab. I said, 'Sir, when I met them last I felt that, for a change, they are finding the jail more peaceful than the Temple.' They had been kept in isolated quarters.

7

January–March 1988: The Killings Increase

There was growing optimism in the government because of a perceptible decrease in terrorist crimes during the last 10 weeks of 1987. This had been a hard earned achievement of Governor S.S. Ray's administration. The most palpable gain, however, was containing the so-called Social Reform Movement of the militants, and the consequent easing of communal tensions which had been increasing during S.S. Barnala's regime. Governor S.S. Ray had won the confidence of the people and of the administration in a very short time. Hindu migration was restricted within the state. It now centred on safer villages and *deras*, particularly Dera Beas of the Radha Soamis.

Developments on the eve of the New Year were quite ominous, however. On 31 December 1987 around 9.00 P.M., the militants wiped out a family of nine in an isolated farmhouse in Cheema Bath village, off the National Highway No. 1, only 25 kms away from Amritsar. The newspapers called it a 'bloody New Year' and reported five more killings in the rest of Punjab. This elimination of entire families turned out to be a macabre new trend. Five members each of two families were eliminated again on 7 and 17 January 1988. On 2 February, a family of eight was killed in village Sehnsra in Amritsar. Till the end of March 1988, similar gruesome killings were repeated in 11 other villages. The ghastliest shootout was on Holi, the joyful festival of colours, in village Kari Sari of district Hoshiarpur where 35 Hindus were killed and 30 were injured.

The largest loss suffered—18 members—was by a very poor clan who made their living by collecting saltpeter soil in village Theh Ravjja in Amritsar. The usual killings were also on the increase. The gloom engulfing Punjab was so dreadful that the Prime Minister cut short his visit to Tripura and returned to Delhi on 3 April 1988. Even the militants in the Temple seemed scared by the barbarity of the killings. On 4 April, Jagir Singh, spokesman for the Panthic Panel, condemned these killings, particularly those of women and children. He told a news conference held in the *parikrama* of the Golden Temple, that government agents were responsible for the carnage only to malign the militants. He was reading from a hand-written note bearing the signatures of G.S. Manochahal, Wassan Singh and Kanwaljit, which he showed to the press reporters. He named one Ghula from Chohla Sahib, a self-styled Lt. Gen Hira Singh, as being the man behind the killing of these families. For that reason, they themselves were after him.

The monthly killings rose from 57 in December to 143 in January, 141 in February and 265 in March 1988. This spurt in bloodshed was largely stunning for the masses as well as the administration. But the misfortune of witnessing the ghastly scenes was maddening. The explanations that came were quite confusing. It was said that hired killers were being used for revenge killings and to settle disputes of property or to even some other old scores. One view was that the killings were for extortions or to break any resistance to the sheltering and feeding of the *kharkoos* when they approached the farmhouses. Intelligence sources suggested that the spurt in crime was to provoke suppression by the state as a measure to evoke public protest against the government.

The Amritsar police believed that it was the result of inter-gang rivalries. Various militant organisations were attacking each other's relations and associates in a spirit of revenge. Another theory blamed all this on Pakistan which was reported to have sent in more sophisticated weapons and highly trained, ruthless killers to bolster the sagging movement. The foregoing reasons were a constant factor in varying degrees in sustaining the bloodshed. But they do not fully answer the crucial question: why was there a sudden spurt in killings at that particular time and why were they sustained over such a long period? To seek an answer, we have to take note of significant political and other developments that occurred around this period.

Governor S.S. Ray was eager from the outset for political inputs by the Government of India to remove the persisting irritants between the people and the government. For example, he suggested the release of the Jodhpur detainees, the rehabilitation of the army deserters and prosecution of those guilty for the Delhi riots. But the Central Government look no action even during the last quarter of 1987 when the killings were down and peace seemed possible only through such gestures. On the other hand, quite inexplicably, the killings shot up and remained on the increase.

Governor S.S. Ray undertook a tour of all the districts during January and February to address the representatives of the various political parties and eminent citizens. He seemed quite disappointed. The essence of his speech in Amritsar was that the Prime Minister was keen to bring about peace in the state, and a package of economic and other concessions was in the offing, but the sudden spurt in violence had stalled it. He was to conclude his tour on 8 February at Hoshiarpur. Hearing him, one got the feeling that this tour was his farewell to Punjab.

Prakash Singh Badal, after his release in December, was surely available to form a government. He also told the press that people were suffering. There were rumours that he was being approached to head the government but he did not show any interest. The S.S. Barnala group was, however, willing to form a government. Later the P.S. Badal group agreed for a dialogue, provided Balwant Singh—a former Minister in his Cabinet who had ditched him earlier—was kept out. But the two factions could not agree. The alternative of reviving a democratic set-up to combat terrorism seemed to be closed. This suited the Congress lobby which did not want the Punjab Legislative Assembly to elect Simranjit Singh Mann as a member of the Rajya Sabha—in the elections due in April 1988. If the Akalis, who had 73 members in a house of 117, were not willing to form the government it gave an excuse to the Central government to dissolve the Assembly and prevent the entry of two Akalis to the Rajya Sabha where the Congress did not have an adequate majority to get any constitutional amendments through.

The UAD Badal group, began organising rallies at the district headquarters. The first rally was held at Amritsar outside my office on 11 February 1988. It was a chaotic gathering. The All India Sikh

Students Federation (Manjit) boys were the cause of it. The local district head of the party, who came supported by slogan shouting men, was not even allowed to come near the stage by the AISSF. When P. Ś. Badal arrived, the meeting showed some semblance of order. However, interruptions continued. At best it was organised pandemonium. P.S. Badal accused the Central Government of being averse to Punjab and, therefore, adopting an insincere approach. He described Amritsar as a slaughterhouse and he wanted a committee of two men to probe into the alleged fake encounters. This trend was followed at other meetings. In the concluding meet at Ludhiana, the UAD reiterated its faith in the Anandpur Sahib Resolution. These meetings seemingly gave a boost to the militants, which was reflected in a spurt in killings.

On 5 March 1988, Jasbir Singh Rode and four head priests were released from jail. Their freedom completely overshadowed the release, on the same day of the 40 Jodhpur detainees whom Governor S.S Ray himself received individually, on their arrival at Chandigarh Airport. The simultaneous release was not a coincidence but a deliberate act of the Home Ministry designed to belittle Ray's major achievement. His release of the Jodhpur detainees was an important step towards building the confidence of the people during Governor's rule.

The decisions of the *Sarbat Khalsa* of 1986, that apparently made inconsequential news at that time, became meaningful and important at this juncture. Politically, this ploy was a clever move, but it was bound to give impetus to militancy. Darshan Singh, the acting *Jathedar* of Akal Takht, had fled from Amritsar in August 1987 and refused to return. He submitted his resignation to the SGPC which was pending.

The militants held complete sway over the affairs of the Temple. Due to this de facto control, the SGPC was in deep financial crisis with its income dwindling by the day. The gurudwara at Goindwal Sahib had to borrow money from the local Commission Agents to enable the SGPC to disburse monthly salaries. They saw a possible solution of the problem, if, with J.S. Rode's influence, the nuisance of the militants within the Temple could be removed. This would pave the way for the scared faithful to resume visits to the Temple. Even otherwise, to accept J.S. Rode as the *Jathedar* of the Akal Takht was a Hobson's choice for the SGPC. Since J.S. Rode had announced that he would takeover as *Jathedar* at the Akal Takht on 9 March, the SGPC obliged him by clearing the decks by 8 March. Some critics of the SGPC alleged that it had unwittingly, though by implication, accepted the validity of the *Sarbat Khalsa*, which had dismissed the SGPC itself. But the Committee did not make any reference to the *Sarbat Khalsa* of 1986. They accepted the resignation of Darshan Singh and filled the consequent vacancy.

The Secretary of the SGPC, Bhan Singh, told me, 'The Government of India has already accepted Rode as the *Jathedar* of the Akal Takht. We did not make an issue out of it because of the fire that is already burning all around.' The Secretary also said that it was easy then for the government to plant its own men or buy anyone, but such a person, he asserted, 'could not do any good to the people, the government, or the Committee.'

It may be recalled that the *Sarbat Khalsa* of 26 January 1986 was held by the militants after more than a century and a half. S.S. Barnala's Government acquiesced in its being held at the Akal Takht. Perhaps the then Government sought a soft option to manage the situation. We must remember that, originally, Bhindranwale was also patronised by the Government of India even though he later began to defy it. J.S. Rode's brief was presumably to bring down the demand of Khalistan to *Puran-Azadi*, win over the militants to his fold, clear the Temple of the extortionists and killers, and stop the killing of innocent people, with or without issuing a *hukamnama* from the Akal Takht. Governor S.S. Ray and DGP J.F. Ribeiro asked for my opinion when they visited Amritsar. I had not met J.S. Rode till then but his conduct after his release showed that far from having any influence over the militants he did not have it in him to influence even the ordinary people. I told the Governor that in my opinion if J.S. Rode had insisted that he would enter the Temple only after the militants had removed all signs of militancy from the holy precincts, then perhaps he could have made his mark both on the people and the militants. By the time J.S. Rode took charge, opposition to him on the part of a large number of militant organisations was evident. Not all the factions participated in the salute of a 100 rounds of bullets given to him on 5 March. Therefore, in order to further strengthen the support of the militants for J.S. Rode, the Home Ministry also had to release half a dozen terrorists, some of whom had rewards on their heads from jail.

In doing all this, the government had gained absolutely nothing from the point of view of restoring peace in the state. On the other hand, some allegations against the government became apparent. Satya Pal Dang, a highly respected veteran Communist leader, had been alleging that Avtar Singh Brahma, the cruellest of the killers, was in league with the government. There was a similar public perception about some factions of the AISSF. A.S. Brahma was the first to support J.S. Rode's *Puran-Azadi* philosophy. In installing J.S. Rode, the government had unwittingly gone half way to meet the demands of a section of the militants and thereby lent credence to its involvement with that group. J.S. Rode asked the militant organisations to sink their differences and unite. He wanted them to cleanse the *parikrama* of extortionists and stop the killing of women and children.

The Panthic Committee, KCF, Bhindranwale Tiger Force (BTF) and AISSF stuck to the demand of Khalistan, thus clearly notifying their opposition to J.S. Rode's *Puran-Azadi*. Divisions among the militant organisations became dangerous for J.S. Rode. He shifted from the Akal Takht to Nanak Niwas citing a need for 'commodious accommodation'. In desperation, he blamed the Central government for having released him in an attempt to divide the militants. As there was no let up in extortions, he said that government agents were responsible for it and by way of proof he claimed that now more letters demanding money were being received by the Damdami Taksal and by relations of Bhindranwale. This was a candid admission of the failure of his mission. More solid proof was that March turned out to be the bloodiest month in terms of the number of killings till then.

On 5 March 1988, when Jasbir Singh Rode arrived in the Darbar Sahib with all the fanfare, and slogan-shouting of his supporters, a hundred bullets were fired in the *parikrama* as a salute to him. The fusillade of guns of all sorts shattered the peace of the Darbar Sahib, scaring the flocks of pigeons and doves, and disturbing the *Kirtan* being recited within the Harmandar. The deeper implications, however, reverberated all over the *parikrama* and beyond. The slogans of 'Khalistan Zindabad' were being shouted. Yet the political parties in violence ridden and bleeding Punjab welcomed the move in their anxiety for peace.

Even S.S. Barnala, in a press statement, welcomed the release of J.S. Rode but somewhat sarcastically. He observed that since the Central Government had brought together the militants and the priests, it had thereby succeeded in sidelining all the factions of Akali party and putting the SGPC in an awkward position. He suggested that the government should first bring peace to Punjab, for which objective he would not mind the dissolution of the Punjab Legislative Assembly so as to enable even the militants to participate in fresh elections. Curiously, the Punjab Legislative Assembly was dissolved the day after S.S. Barnala's statement.

The dissolution of the Assembly on 6 March 1988 without waiting to see whether or not J.S. Rode succeeded to the post of *Jathedar*, would show either that the Central Government had anticipated J.S. Rode's success, or that it was getting panicky because of the mounting violence. As S.S. Barnala had suggested, it was likely that the prospect of contesting for the Assembly may lure the militants to negotiation. Having known J.S. Rode and having some idea of the thinking of the sleuths of our intelligence, I feel it was a political move, designed by the lobby that had foiled the Punjab Accord, to prolong the Punjab problem—but keeping the violence under check—until the general elections that were due by the end of 1989.

It was in April 1987 that Home Minister Buta Singh, announced that the Punjab militants had their links and bases in Pakistan for the first time. It is unlikely that the government had no such knowledge earlier when violence was rocketing. How could one expect a man like J.S. Rode to wean away the militants from Pakistan? The *Sarbat Khalsa* of 26 January 1986 in which J.S. Rode was named *Jathedar* of the Akal Takht, was the point at which the escalation of violence had begun. Logically, any government would have judged J.S. Rode's effectiveness before dissolving the Assembly.

The 115 legislators were a powerful link between the people and the administration, and an effective channel to disseminate the government's views. They could counter anti-government propaganda and baseless rumours. All the MLAs of Amritsar district visited my office and brought to my notice the excesses and lapses of the police and other departments. After the dissolution of the Assembly, their visits to my office decreased dramatically. Their place was taken by self-styled leaders who were not very responsible people. Nor were they of a representative character. Though, one could gather some useful information from them, they were unable to inform the people of the limitations and problems of the administration.

Sarbat Khalsa, the failure of the Rajiv–Longowal Accord, the division amongst the Akalis, the resultant support to militants by the Badal–Tohra group, the dismissal of the S.S. Barnala Government, the release of J.S. Rode, and the dissolution of the State Assembly, all these factors furthered the cause of militancy. Pakistan had been supporting the militants for quite some time but, around this period, it gave them a foolhardy though concrete plan to attain Khalistan. With so much support given to the militants, it should have been easy to understand the spurt in killings. In releasing J.S. Rode, the government conceded its inability to fight the terrorists. J.S. Rode was there to formalise their victory and work out a truce between the two. Therefore, each terrorist group and every individual terrorist vied with the others to lay claim to a larger share of the grains. The militant organisations opposed to J.S. Rode swore that they would ensure that J.S. Rode did not succeed in bringing about peace. Crime in the month of March nearly doubled compared to that in February. It seemed something of a competition between the Pakistan-based militants and J.S. Rode's supporters.

To answer the questions raised earlier—the spurt in killings and the apparent move of Governor S.S. Ray to quit—we may recall that J.S. Rode was named *Jathedar* of the Akal Takht in January 1986. In April–May 1987, the services of *Jathedar* Darshan Singh became necessary in order to dismiss the S. S. Barnala Government without any reaction by the people. For this purpose Acharya Sushil Muni was chosen to influence the *Jathedar*. In place of G.S. Kaonke, G.S. Manochahal was made the acting *Jathedar* at the *Shaheedi* Conference held on 4 June 1986. He made way for Darshan Singh at the *Sarbat Khalsa* of January 1987. Darshan Singh's optimism that he could strike a bargain with terrorists at the so-called 'World Sikh Conference' flopped when he had to flee from the post on 8 August 1987. One cannot fail to notice a degree of co-ordination between the above named militants and the Central government.

It may also be noted that by the end of December 1987 the situation in Punjab seemed to be under control. At this stage Governor S.S. Ray could validly press for giving up the older idea to induct J.S. Rode and, instead, to ask for political inputs. Avtar Singh Brahma, the terrorist who was alleged to be close to the government, was, behind the sensational killing of the family on New Year's eve in Cheema Bath according to the Amritsar police. This was followed by a chain of similar heinous mass killings. Even if Pakistan's interest in sustaining violence was to be kept in mind, Governor S.S. Ray was seemingly upset by this kind of manipulation. He must have made up his mind either to quit or recommend revival of the Assembly. After his tour of the Punjab districts, his insistence on the release of the Jodhpur detainees was conceded. The release of detainees on 5 March was a substantial achievement of Governor S.S. Ray's from the humane and public relation angle. If they had been released earlier, during December when some improvement had been brought about by S. S. Ray, it would have been a more significant step towards peace. It was not only delayed by more than two months but the Home Ministry ensured that the shine of S.S. Ray's success was consumed in the din and noise of J.S. Rode's visit to the Temple on the same day. And, unfortunately, J.S. Rode's presence as the leader of one group of militants was bound to excite more violence by the groups, which it did.

This kind of politicking apart, numerous shortcomings such as inadequacies in logistics and the organisation of our fighting forces, became highlighted as we struggled unsuccessfully to control the sudden spurt in militancy from January 1988 onwards. The militants moved and committed crimes mostly after darkness. We had an acute shortage of bulletproof vehicles and night vision devices. Therefore, night patrolling by an otherwise overworked force was not adequate. The force also faced a serious deficiency in transport, communications and up-to-date weapons. The officers were overworked. DGP J.F. Ribeiro, during his visit to Amritsar observed, 'I tell you, SSP Alam goes from one place of killing to another and is not left with any time for anything else.' Generally speaking, he was right.

We had arrested a large number of terrorists but we could not prosecute them for want of witnesses. An amendment of TADA made confessions before a Superintendent of Police admissible evidence but paralysis was setting in the judicial system as well. I recall that in the only TADA related conviction until then, the accused was set free because the sentence was equal to the period of trial. Even though the Governor and DGP J.F. Ribeiro visited the border posts frequently, there was no noticeable improvement in sealing the border with Pakistan. Co-ordination between the police, the CRPF and the BSF needed improvement.

Even in the case of the Golden Temple, although we guarded the entries, frisked the visitors and occasionally searched the Guru Ramdas Sarai, we had not been able to develop any effective checking system. We could never be certain which of the terrorists were inside and when they would go out. Terrorists had de facto control of the Golden Temple and some other historical gurudwaras. The

SGPC rued their presence in the Temple and bemoaned the fall in offerings to a quarter of what they used to be. Neither did they complain to us nor could we take any serious initiative, except to take the security closer to the Temple entrances and to patrol the road between the Darbar Sahib and the *Sarai*. The militants continued using the Temple as a sanctuary.

Crime in March increased so stunningly that we were really at our wit's end and could not think of any fresh defensive strategy. On 1 April, after discussing the situation with the SSP Amritsar and the DIG CRPF, I formulated a proposal and took it to K.P.S. Gill, then Additional DGP. This was to impose night curfew in 350 villages of Patti and Tarn Taran sub-divisions. While he agreed to the suggestion, he knew that we lacked the resources to enforce it strictly. Curiously, it worked! Without discussing with anyone, I promptly, extended it to another sub-division, Baba Bakala. The chance breather lasted for three days.

Before moving onto the ultimate strategy adopted to fight the menacing developments, let me dilate upon the 'concretising of the concept of Khalistan' by Pakistan.

In August 1987, the Amritsar Police and the BSF intercepted Aman Deep Singh Dimpy, as he was sneaking into Indian territory from Pakistan. He revealed that he had met top terrorists including Sukhdev Singh Babbar, Ravinder Pal Singh Narang, Kanwar Paul Singh and Daljit Singh Bittu. Many boys were being trained in Pakistan in time-blasting vehicles to kill VIPs. They could also lay mines on *kacha* tracks. They had also acquired a working knowledge of using radio frequencies. According to him, 130 kg of explosives had already reached the Punjab militants.

He revealed that while in the camps in Pakistan the trainees were assured that in Khalistan they would get high posts. To get Khalistan all that they had to do was to intensify killings in a *tehsil* like Patti by killing the Hindus and if need be the Sikhs as well, to compel migration, and to paralyse the administration by eliminating officers. Thereafter, only an announcement would be needed to the effect that the *tehsil* was an independent country—Khalistan. This could be recognised by the United Nations and some other countries. Though an instance of Utopian logic, it was an idea nonetheless.

Two months later, in November 1987, one Canadian national of Indian origin, Balkar Singh, was arrested from a high class hotel in Amritsar. He was supposed to have told the police that he had delivered lakhs of rupees to prominent terrorists, including Labh Singh, Avtar Singh Brahma and the Panthic Committee. He had been given detailed instructions by the World Sikh Organisation, which had been collecting funds from Sikh congregations in gurudwaras in the US, UK and Singapore. A letter from Harjinder Singh, member Council of Khalistan, to Labh Singh, asking him to undertake some major action to boost the morale of the dissidents, was also reportedly recovered from Balkar Singh. After some time, Balkar Singh filed complaints against the police officers of Amritsar through his counsel. Later the government ordered that he should be handed back to the Canadian Embassy. These two incidents made news in the latter part of the year but not much importance was given to them as our control on the situation was increasing progressively.

But in the New Year, violence again spurted suddenly. Around that time, the Amritsar police recovered one of the largest arsenals, comprising of 12 AK 47s and Chinese Stens. The police also discovered two underground cemented bunkers made to hide weapons. Here, they found 12 AK 47s, 14 rockets and other arms. Again, on 14 April 1988 the police recovered another huge arms dump from village Butter of Amritsar district. The underground dumps in the Patti area fitted like a jig-saw puzzle and reminded us of what Dimpy had told the Amritsar police regarding the plan to declare some area as Khalistan. Arms dumps were also recovered in Tarn Taran sub-division of Amritsar, and places in Gurdaspur and Faridkot during April. Jagir Singh, the Panthic Committee's spokesman, again reading from a hand-written statement, had told the media that the recent seizure of arms by the state forces was only the tip of the iceberg; the arms already in their arsenal were enough for a 100 years' war. He also boasted that they were being provided with still more sophisticated weapons.

In the context of these facts, the utterances of the militants and the sequence of events, the formation of the Council of Khalistan, the World Sikh Organisation and announcing their names from the holy shrine, clearly seemed to be part of a systematic plan. The brainpower and experience of professionals behind the Punjab militants could be easily discerned. The manner in which the state administration, particularly the officers in Amritsar, sustained their determination and continued to present a semblance of functioning governance has few parallels.

The gloom, however, had spread so widely by March that the Central government decided to confer with the Deputy Commissioners and the Superintendents of Police while considering the various alternatives before it, such as calling in the army or imposing an Emergency. Two meetings of DCs of six districts each were fixed for 4 and 6 April 1988 in Amritsar and Ludhiana respectively. These meetings became a turning point in the fight against the militants. A detailed look at the proceedings is therefore necessary.

8

April–May 1988:
Measures to End the Killing

By April 1988 we were in a desperate situation. March 1988 had been the bloodiest month till then with 290 killings out of which only 25 killed were militants and 9 were policemen and personnel of the paramilitary forces. This was more than twice the number of casualties in February 1988. Compared to March 1987, however, these were five times higher. I have already mentioned the element of desperation in the decision to impose night curfew on the 1st and 2nd of April and the suggestions placed before the meeting of the State's top police officers on the 3rd April. It was as embarrassing for the protagonists of President's Rule as it was disheartening for the administration that they had left no stone unturned in their endeavour to fight terrorism and yet there were so many casualties. The Governor and the DGP were literally standing shoulder to shoulder with us in this fight.

In the recent past, the Government of India had publicly admitted Pakistan's active role in aiding militants in Punjab, and had felt the immediate need for dispensing an economic package to appease the people of Punjab locked in fighting against militancy. This admission by the Union Government was tantamount to accepting that the turbulence in Punjab was not merely a law and order problem but that it also had political and even international dimensions. It was also an indirect admission that the determined move to install J.S. Rode on the highest seat of Sikh religious hierarchy had not only failed but had turned out to be counter productive. The tenor of the meeting also recognised the principle of 'local primacy', which was well established during the British regime. Only the district heads of the magistracy and the police, who were directly involved had been included.

Governor S.S. Ray told the meeting held in Amritsar that militancy in Punjab had the full support of Pakistan. Training in insurgency and arms and ammunition was being provided to the terrorists. Whenever positive and ameliorative steps, such as the release of priests and of the Jodhpur detainees, were taken, Pakistan ensured a spurt in violence to counter them. The announcement of the economic package for Punjab by the Prime Minister was ready. Therefore, the situation called for a more effective approach. Buta Singh, the Union Home Minister, and P. Chidambaram, Minister of the State in the Home Ministry, who had recently been given charge of Internal Security, asked us to give our appraisal and suggestions without any reservations. 'Nothing should be held back just because there is some element of awkwardness in it,' was the suggestion.

Amritsar was the worst affected district in the state, I, therefore, spoke first. I said at the outset that even after facing terrorism for nearly a decade, we did not have a national policy agreed to by all the political parties. Instead, the political parties were still trying to derive advantage from the situation. Pakistan was trying to provoke communal riots of the scale which preceded the Partition of India. Since there were no memories of strained relations between Hindus and Sikhs, the attempt was bound to fail. The communal tensions which had surged during 1984 and in the latter half of the Akali Government had disappeared during the 11 odd months of the Governor's rule. I had to resort to the imposition of curfew to avoid untoward incidents during the cremation of the dead bodies of Hindu victims when I joined my post in Amritsar. Many old Sikhs told me that they could not visit Hindu homes immediately, not because of any weakening of their ties but because of some mischief mongering Hindus who were not connected with the bereaved families in any manner. We did not have to take this precaution of imposing a curfew prior to the cremation of dead bodies since December 1987.

I also added that in framing policies about Punjab it should be understood clearly that the Sikhs were not separatists, despite the presence of fundamentalists within and outside the Akali party. No greater proof was needed after they had gone to the polls in such large numbers in September 1985. That too, within a year of the massacre of Sikhs in Delhi in November 1984, and more particularly after the storming of the Golden Temple by the Indian Army in June that year.

In this land of wars and warriors, the love of weapons amongst the Punjabis is a legacy of history. The British, immediately after annexing the Punjab, had disarmed them completely. Licenses for arms were the privilege of the aristocracy, and the grant thereof was at the sole discretion of the Deputy Commissioner. The common man could not keep even a spear. Only the carrying of swords by Sikhs was permitted. Unfortunately, recent developments had a catalytic effect in reviving the desire for arms. The partition of the country had created an artificial international border that even cut through the fields of the villages falling in either country. The existing trade between Lahore and Amritsar was suddenly transformed into smuggling amongst the divided people. To begin with, it consisted of innocent items such as betel leaves, bananas, ginger, cloth, etc. But in the course of time, drugs, narcotics and gold became the predominant items of this contraband trade. These villagers became some of the biggest smugglers and couriers.

At one point of time, smuggling had become very widespread. In his election campaign of 1962, on one occasion, the dynamic Chief Minister of Punjab, Pratap Singh Kairon, had announced in one of the villages on the border, that he would soon supply electricity to the villages falling on the border belt. Someone in his rustic way told him, 'Sardar, you are planning street lights, but we do not want even the sun to rise in this area.' The smugglers began with financing the elections and later some of them also joined politics, which made it easier for them to get rid of obstructive police officers. So we had what the Governor termed a 'Smuggler-Politician-Police nexus'. This nexus had an affinity with its counterparts across the border. As a result, the arms markets of Miran Shah on the Pakistan–Afghan Border and Mir Ali Cantonment, are virtually on our doorsteps.

Simultaneous to these developments, one noticed that, unfortunately, a large number of our young men from rural areas, particularly from the border villages, were either unemployed or had idle time on their hands. Expansion of the educational system at the cost of quality produced more dropouts at the lower and middle levels. The mechanisation of farm operations rendered a labour surplus from the traditional chores of ploughing, harvesting, irrigating and transporting the produce to the markets. The ceiling imposed on the expansion of the Indian Army since the 1970s, the restrictions by many countries on the migration of Indian labour, the total denial to Punjab of any heavy industry, all had combined to further reduce employment opportunities. I pointed out how the British had absorbed virtually the entire effective wing of the Khalsa army in their own forces immediately after winning the battle of 1846, and the rest of it was absorbed after annexing the Punjab. Without losing much time, they had also provided an irrigation system, which kept people occupied in procuring an additional crop a year.

The idle youth and smuggling opportunities became an explosive combination, the effects of which we had lately been experiencing. The mishandling by the State Government of the initial phase of violence and the failure of the Government of India to appreciate the causes and developments behind this violence gave it the necessary impetus. Our approach had been that with the elimination of active terrorists, peace would ensure. Such a strategy was effective when thefts and robberies ceased with the arrest or killing of the dacoits in a particular area. But this formula could not be applied in the prevailing situation, because more and more young boys joined the militant cadres.

The weapons and equipment with the Punjab Police had been outdated for a long time. Yet we still had a brave and strong force. But the AK 47 had acquired the reputation of *Ram Baan* (the all-powerful arrows of Lord Ram). This scared the people, and the force also felt demoralised. One police officer told me, 'DC *Sahib*, you have not heard the AK 47 fire. It shakes the earth.'

We therefore had to provide better weapons and equipment to our force to face the militants. The next priority was to stop the inflow of the weapons from across the border. We could not depend on the BSF alone. I suggested the deployment of a force similar to the Assam Rifles, behind the BSF and yet a third line of Punjab Police for selective picketing. Simultaneously, we also had to provide job opportunities for the village youth.

'If we plan to fence the entire border, will you be able to acquire land?' asked P. Chidambaram. Without hesitation, and even without considering the pros and cons, I committed: 'There would be no problem in arranging the land.'

Police colleagues pointed out the difficulties in identifying terrorists when they were without weapons. It was difficult also to identify passive harbourers from the active ones. The police also pointed out many of their handicap; outdated weapons, inadequate transport, outdated communication system, shortage of staff in the police stations, unsuitable buildings for their offices and police stations with virtually no official accommodation for the NGOs as well as poor co-ordination between the paramilitary forces and the police. 'On the other hand the militants not only had better weapons but night vision devices as well,' said Gian Singh, the officiating SP.

Surjit Singh Bains a former SSP of Amritsar, then at Jalandhar, suggested the trifurcation of Amritsar into three police districts and bifurcation of that Gurdaspur. He said that it was difficult to control law and order in Amritsar even in normal times. It was absolutely impossible to handle it now. Rajpal Singh Gill, SSP, mentioned the need for political inputs and measures to appease the hurt Sikh psyche. He named one senior Congressman, notorious for abetting the Delhi riots, who instead of being prosecuted had been made a Union Minister. According to him, it was necessary to remove such irritants to get the willing co-operation of the people. Other colleagues generally concurred.

We summarised the discussion and our agreed suggestions in a note. In the evening, the Governor, the Ministers and the DIB visited two villages to condole with the bereaved families of six victims of terrorist violence and to inspect the improvised SPO post in one village. The parallel meeting in Ludhiana reportedly made broadly similar suggestions. Fortunately, these suggestions were approved by Delhi and their implementation began immediately.

On 19 April I had three 'police districts' in Amritsar, and Gurdaspur had two. Men from the CRPF were made available to depleted police stations. For overall co-ordination, an IG, Chaman Lal, and a DIG were posted in Amritsar. The 'super cop', K.P.S. Gill, took over as DGP on 20 April. J.F. Ribeiro was elevated to the post of Advisor (Security) to the Governor. One hundred and twenty kms of the border for fencing was identified and the erection of a fence commenced. In the third week, a planeload of self-loading rifles, night vision devices and other equipment arrived in Amritsar.

With these steps the police budget increased tenfold. One felt that it was for the first time that a long term and firm policy was formulated to combat the terrorists. These measures became the bedrock for combating violence. Succeeding governors maintained these arrangements, opting only for peripheral modifications in approach.

On 8 April 1988, Buta Singh told the Indian Parliament that the unfriendly act of 'training terrorists by Pakistan, supplying weapons and foreign exchange' to them had been brought to the notice of the government many times. He also said that Pakistani officials propagated secession from India to the *jathas* of Sikhs visiting gurudwaras in Pakistan. The *Nawa-i-Waqt* and *Jang*, two leading Pakistan dailies, eulogised the exploits of Indian terrorists. Those writings were being distributed amongst Sikhs settled abroad. He admitted that the secessionist militants had converted the Golden Temple into a sanctuary. The Prime Minister of India, during his visits to Japan and Vietnam in April 1988 also blamed Pakistan for supporting terrorists.

Though General Zia-ul-Haq, the then President of Pakistan, refuted the charge, it was obvious that Pakistan wanted to avenge the secession of Bangladesh in 1971 when India had supported the Mukti Bahini. I think that the Pakistan officials, provoking and aiding insurgency in Punjab, knew well that Punjab would not secede from India. But the exercise could serve as a model to encourage separatism in Jammu and Kashmir. Otherwise they would have encouraged the Sikh militants who styled themselves as 'Singhs' to adopt the designations of their models—the eighteenth century Singhs—who harassed the Muslim invaders and the last of the Mughals during the last four decades of the eighteenth century. Instead, the Pakistani mentors organised the militants on the lines of army ranks of Brigadiers, Lt. Generals and Generals. These ranks attracted the youth but the different ranks and regiments became a cause of division and rivalries.

The decisions taken at the meeting on 4 April 1988 are a valid commentary on our shortcomings prevalent at the beginning of militancy which, over the years had aided terrorism to spread in Punjab. In the early 1980s not only the SSPs, but even Directors General of Police, were shifted whenever the militants committed a sensational killing. It was quite demoralising for the police force. In fact during the tenure of the Congress Chief Minister, Darbara Singh, (1980–83) a serious study should have been undertaken to assess the needs of the law and order machinery in the face of increasing organised crime. But the dictates of the electoral politics of the Congress could not favour such steps. However, the changes made in pursuance of the decisions of the two district meetings in April proved to be efficacious because, by 9 May 1988 we got an opportunity to free the Golden Temple of the militants. This was absolutely necessary to end militancy.

9

Operation Black Thunder

Writing about the Vietnam War, Robert McNamara in his book, *In Retrospect: The Tragedy and Lessons of the Vietnam War*, admitted his ignorance about Vietnam, its history, culture and values. About the other decision makers in the Pentagon, including the President, he said, 'When it came to Vietnam, we found ourselves setting a policy for a region that was terra incognita.'

It would not be correct to accuse policy makers in Delhi of a lack of understanding of the Punjab, but their J.S. Rode centred experiment showed a total lack of understanding of the man they had selected to make the militants follow his direction. They had also underrated the capacity of the SGPC in facing the odds. It remained a negative move by the government. Only a few militant groups sided with J.S. Rode; others maintained that unless he stuck to the demand for Khalistan they would have nothing to do with him. Those who opposed the Damdami Taksal also opposed him.

All the militant organisations, however, inferred from this move that the government was scared by the killings and was now showing the olive branch through J.S. Rode. This raised their morale which was visible from their behaviour inside the Temple. Besides, the terrorist leaders, who always tried to shift the blame of killings and extortions to the vigilante (the undercover police group), found another scapegoat in J.S. Rode's men.

The militants inside the temple began to brandish their weapons more often. They also began raising brick walls, as a measure of fire cover, at many places. On 10 April 1988, there was an exchange of fire between the militant groups, on 27 April they exchanged hot words (including Punjabi invectives) and on the 29th they exchanged fire with the CRPF that was guarding the temple complex. Among the groups that opposed him, J.S. Rode had a mortal fear of Surjit Singh Penta. It was also known that S.S. Penta had told his colleagues that he had an intense desire to fire a full burst of an AK 47 through the *Jathedar's* heart. I later learnt that a scared J.S. Rode moved out of the Temple to Nanak Niwas for fear of S.S. Penta and his men.

The press reported all this tension with much spice and colour. But it also noted the dangerous propensities of the situation. 'Conditions in Darbar Sahib akin to the pre-Blue Star position,' proclaimed one of the Jalandhar dailies. Though exaggerated, the statement was not entirely without substance. The sensational headlines of daily killings had not shown any decline. Armed militants were already entrenched inside the Temple. Jasbir Singh Rode, the kinsman of Sant Jarnail Singh Bhindranwale, posing as a militant leader, had also moved into the Temple. For the terrorised masses who could not have forgotten the shock of Operation Blue Star, the situation was certainly reminiscent of the nightmare.

The J.S. Rode card, as I had apprehended, was misfiring. I visited the Temple again to see for myself how things were shaping. A view from the roof of the Braham Buta Akhara, housing the headquarters of the 49th Battalion of the CRPF that day was a good vantage point to view the Temple and surroundings. I discovered this only after taking over as DC Amritsar when I first went there to supervise pre-dawn searches of the buildings in the Temple complex. But that early May morning, when I climbed on to the roof of the three-storied Akhara, I saw that some young boys were busy constructing a brick cover with mortar behind the sand bags on top of the two turrets. These turrets were actually the watchtowers of the adjoining eighteenth century building, Bunga Ramgharian.

As soon as they noticed us, they covered their faces with black scarves and trained their guns at us. The Commanding Officer of the Battalion, Nand Lal, a generally relaxed man, smiled. His smile was enough for me to forget them as it assured me that this was a daily routine. Our bodyguards behind us kept a watch on them. I could see the odd looking brick walls under the soothing white domes of the buildings around the *parikrama* of the Temple. 'Is Rode playing to the militant galleries, or is this the work of that group which is afraid of an attack on itself?' was the question in my mind. I also wondered, 'Could it be a part of the plan revealed to Amritsar police by a border-crosser, Dimpy, about declaring some area as Khalistan?'

I had stayed there for quite some time and this aroused the suspicion of the militants on watch inside the Temple. I suddenly noticed two young boys in long flowing *cholas* coming down the northern *parikrama* towards the Braham Buta. An imp of 12 or 13 years, also in a *chola*, tossing an AK 47 in his hands was leading them. I recognised the older boys; they were the same who had accosted me during my visit on 7 July 1987 prior to my taking charge as DC. As I was wondering whether or not they had recognised me, the little maverick, to my utter surprise, pointed his AK 47 at me. I moved my head away from the line of the gun without moving my feet. He repeated his gimmick as I straightened. At that moment with guns all around me, it flashed across my mind that one of these days some trigger would be pulled accidentally. I need to have a plan of action ready for hitting back immediately, failing which wrong signals would go to the public; because of the higher position of the militants entrenched on the towers of the Bunga Ramgharian we would have more casualties.

It was, therefore, necessary to assess the position of our pickets around the temple complex. The CRPF jawans were manning the pickets located near all the entries to the temple. Besides, they also occupied some of the 14 tall buildings acquired by the government after Operation Blue Star. At the top of some of them they had their observation posts. At a few strategic points on the periphery around the complex, the CRPF had also raised brick walls for cover. Nand Lal also told me that the militants inside the Temple had protested against his construction of the wall near the entry to Baba Atal Gurudwara. There was much evidence of tension and the fortifications built by the militants and the CRPF were proof of it. My intuition—not even an hour old—of an imminent conflict due to accidental firing was reinforced by the support of the position on the ground.

Nand Lal not only agreed with me but he went a step further and said 'Not only accidental firing, there could be intended firing as well. We will be beaten in the first skirmish.' I therefore drove back to my residential office to draft a report to the government. I could not bring out in the report all that I wanted to say. While I was struggling with it, I received phone calls from J.F. Ribeiro, the Home Secretary and the Chief Secretary. I shared with them my apprehensions arising out of the position of the militants in the temple and their aggressive postures. I pointed out that a situation could develop which might require immediate action. These fortuitous phone calls spared me the rigour of drafting an unusual report which could have been disposed by some skilful Deputy Secretary in a one line reply, 'Seek instructions as the eventuality arises'. I also telephoned IG Chaman Lal to apprise him of what I had seen in the Temple. I requested him to discuss it with the DGP and other concerned officers, for guidance in case of an eventuality.

I did not keep note of the date I went to the temple. But I remember that on that day a BBC TV team had come to interview J.S. Rode. It was just about a week after that, on 9 May 1988 that S.S. Virk, the DIG of the CRPF, and I got together while visiting the four bereaved families in village Harsa Chhina, where the terrorists had struck the previous night and had killed four persons. We returned together, and within an hour of his dropping me at my office, I learnt that S.S. Virk had been injured in a firing incident. I saw him in the operation theatre of the emergency ward. He could not speak because the bullet that hit him on one side of his face had exited on the other. But he kept a bold face and raised his thumb. On the assurance of the doctors that they had everything needed to handle S.S. Virk's injury, I felt relieved. To save him, Suresh Arora, the SSP of Amritsar, had very boldly hauled the wounded S.S. Virk on a borrowed scooter through narrow bazaars. Some young boys had helped to clear the way through a panicky overcrowded market.

According to Baldev Singh, SP, Amritsar City, the incident occurred where the militants were constructing a small wall as a cover to shield the stairs of a dilapidated building behind the *prashad* point i.e., on the western side outside the Golden Temple. The CRPF picket at that corner objected to it but the militants were in a defiant mood. Apparently, they wanted to use this building as a bunker. From here, they could give cover when required, to the militant leaders and their family members who had taken shelter in the rooms of the first floor of the *parikrama*, located exactly above room nos. 13 and 14 which housed the office of the Panthic Committee and the Office of Khalistan. Besides the stairs from inside the *parikrama*, there was also an approach to these rooms through a staircase landing on the outer side of the Temple, in front of the building which had been damaged during Operation Blue Star. The government had acquired this building. When the DIG was informed by Nand Lal, CO of the CRPF, of the obstinacy of the militants, the DIG, accompanied by the SSP and SP rushed to the spot. Suddenly some militants appeared on the *prashad* building and, unaware of what was happening and the presence of the officers there, they started taking firing positions. SP Baldev Singh noticed their intentions and shouted for cover just in time and everyone escaped the hail of bullets. The casualties, could otherwise, have been quite serious. As it happened, only S.S. Virk was hit.

I located Chaman Lal in one of the buildings in Katra Ahluwalia which was near the main entrance to the Temple. Firing between the militants and the force, which was under S.S. Virk's command, was still going on from their respective safe positions. IG Chaman Lal had not received any instructions from his seniors. Even though there was a substantial decline in the visiting devotees both on account of the harvest season and because of the presence of the militants, a good number of them were still there. The surrounding bazaars, inured to stray firings, had not closed their premises. In April 1983, the DIG of Jalandhar A.S. Atwal was killed by a militant just outside the main entrance of the Harmandar Sahib as he came out of the Temple with *prashad* in his hands. I knew him as a very upright police officer. The then DC, Sardar Singh and SSP Surjit Singh Bains had sought instructions from the then CM. But no action whatsoever was taken then. This had stuck in my mind. I decided that I should not waste any time. The militants could escape even though it was reported that in their jubilation they had performed the Bhangra in the *parikrama* to celebrate the attack on S.S. Virk who, they believed had been killed. S.S. Virk had worked as SSP Amritsar when the movement was passing through the critical phase of rising terrorism. He was at the top of their hit list.

'I think I have to put the town under curfew,' I told Chaman Lal, who was engrossed in directing the firing. As I turned to come out in the *verandah*, the CRPF jawan manning the LMG shouted at me to duck. Before I could understand his instructions a bullet hit the wall over my head. The angry man mumbled something more as I rushed down the stairs. On the wireless from my car, I conveyed orders for imposing curfew in the walled city with immediate effect till further orders. Within minutes, the police were on the job. By the time I signed the orders, the silence of the sacred city was broken only by the sounds of gunfire. Although firing was limited to the area around the Temple, curfew in a wider area was necessary in order to prevent the flow of devotees from rural areas into the Temple. Curfew alone could secure the closure of the crowded markets adjacent to the Temple. We had to take steps to ensure that the supply of basic necessities of life to the people would not be affected. I had an inkling that I would have to sustain the curfew for a long time.

Within two hours, with the brilliant team of officers in the Department of Food and Civil Supplies, Punsup, Milk Supply, Transport and the Civil Surgeon, we finalised the logistics of maintaining essential supplies to the area under curfew. With this, so far as I was concerned, the operation to tire out the militants from the Temple had begun around the afternoon of 9 May 1988.

According to my perception, it was not necessary to stop the normal routine of the Temple during the operation. Accordingly, I got in touch with Bhan Singh, the Secretary of the SGPC. I asked him to give me the names of various persons who performed various duties in the Darbar Sahib either as employees of the Shiromani Committee or as volunteers, so that I could issue some curfew passes to them and also to arrange for transport, if needed. He gave me the name of some other manager who should be contacted for this purpose. No one offered to co-operate. Perhaps they feared that some other action might follow along the lines of Operation Blue Star.

Interruption in the routine of the Temple seemed unavoidable. Some of the *granthis* closed the Granth Sahib that they were reading from that very evening if the next man on duty did not show up. But by the afternoon of 10 May, all services in the Darbar Sahib and the *langar* came to a standstill.

Late that afternoon and then in the evening I ascertained the reaction of various people who came to see me. I wanted to know what their reaction would be if the curfew was continued in order to drive out the militants from the Temple. Everyone, from a *Sarpanch* to an ex-Minister, from a man in the street to a business executive, sants and even teachers from the university approved of the action in the prevailing circumstances. This strengthened my resolution. During the operation, I made it a point to meet the visitors so as to know the minds of the people. A few days later a young *Sarpanch* said to me, 'Now see it through, Sir.'

The firing stopped around 6 P.M. I learnt that all the important press reporters, who had gone to the Temple, their Mecca for news those days, were stranded there. I went to the Braham Buta Akhara to arrange for their rescue. We sent word to the CRPF pickets about this. But the media men kept their nerve and came out waving their identity cards. They reported that some people had been killed inside while some others had been injured.

The next morning we announced on hailers that pilgrims could come out towards the Guru Ram Das Sarai. As per intelligence reports,we had made arrangements for only 200 people but 946 people, including women and children, came out barefoot. They were famished and scared, not believing that they had come out. We were relieved to see them pour out from various rooms into the *parikrama* and head towards the gate on the Sarai side. Contrary to our apprehensions, though slight, the militants had apparently not planned to hold any of them as hostage. SSP Suresh Arora immediately arranged for additional transport. Courtesy the Red Cross, we provided them with bananas to eat and shoes to wear.

A pressman told me that among the young boys there were many active militants. Around 200 of the younger lot, after a brief interrogation, were detained on suspicion and ultimately only 20 odd were kept in custody. The police did a fine job in quickly completing their verification, thanks to the recently improved communications.

J.S. Rode, who was away from Amritsar, returned on the evening of 10 May. He had blamed the Central Government for trying to create a situation similar to Operation Blue Star. 'Recent temple firings were the manipulations of the Centre', he had told the press before leaving Ludhiana. K.P.S. Gill and the DG, CRPF also returned from Delhi the same evening. We discussed various options available to us. It was felt that before taking any decision, I might meet J.S. Rode and the head priests.

The next morning, the SSP Suresh Arora and I met the *Jathedar* of the Akal Takht and the priests accompanying him. The *Jathedar* did not appear to know his mind. He would not commit to the position that he might be able to persuade the militants to come out of the Temple. He wanted to talk to me alone; so we moved to a small ante-chamber. He cautioned me, 'DC Sahib, if you continue your siege of the Darbar Sahib, a flood of people from the countryside will flow towards it and shall take away your curfew, which would be awkward for the government and it would be our moral victory.'

I stared back to reassess the man who was virtually threatening me. In spite of the confident statement he had made, he appeared to be a person who was basically vulnerable and affected by fear. From the way he was holding the sword in his hands, I realised he was relying on the influence of the exalted office of the *Jathedar* of the Akal Takht and his supposed influence with the militants. He also subtly hinted at being backed by governmental agencies besides his kinship with the late Bhindranwale.

For a moment I pitied him and pitied the unknown organisations that had put faith in this person's capability to lead the militants to the negotiating table. The Army Operation of 1984 had physically damaged the Akal Takht which in turn had bruised the Sikh psyche. But in manipulating this man's ascendance to the highest spiritual and temporal seat of the Sikh *panth*, the powers that be had insulted the brave and straightforward Sikh community. The alleged lofty aim of bringing peace to Punjab through this move would not extenuate the appalling insolence of this man. I felt that it was high time that the Sikhs sought a more suitable person to occupy this exalted position. Until a person of such spiritual dignity was found, a council of Panj Pyaras could officiate.

I managed to control my strong reaction and, in as calm a voice as possible, I told him, 'I know the people of Punjab and this area particularly and more intimately, because I was born here and had most of my education here. As DC I have been going to numerous villages, meeting lacs of people during the last one year. I know what people have suffered and what they feel. One, or, at the most one and a half out of a thousand persons may subscribe to your views. In any case, the present action is our responsibility. Please tell me about your own rapport with the militants in the Temple'. He said he could only answer if he or his men were allowed to go to the Temple to meet the 'boys' there. 'We should have no objection to that, but I will confirm this before the evening,' I told him, and hurried to the Circuit House.

We were late for the meeting, which J.F. Ribeiro had called. As soon as I entered, I got the shock of my life when I was told that I should lift the curfew. For the first time in my life, I experienced what being petrified means. I just could not utter a single word. K.P.S. Gill left the room. I followed him. 'Three days of curfew just to disrupt the services in the Harmandar and no achievement,' I rued to myself. K.P.S. Gill told me that this decision had been taken because the Government of India was keeping silent and no decision had been conveyed so far. 'In that case where is the compulsion to lift the curfew?' I asked.

'And what do we gain by persisting with it?' he queried softly.

'Some of them (militants) may surrender'. I said. He kept quiet for a moment and then hurriedly said, 'Let us go back'.

'The DC has a point, we may hear him.' he told J.F. Ribeiro who looked towards me. I knew that from the moment that S.S. Virk was wounded, the police and the CRPF desperately wanted to storm the Temple. K.P.S. Gill also thought along the same lines. Therefore, the meeting presided over by J.F. Ribeiro in which S.L. Kapur, the Financial Commissioner Home, D.C. Pathak, a Joint Director IB, along with Gill, Chaman Lal, A.A. Siddiqqi the DIG Amritsar and other senior police officers were present had to consider that since the Government of India was not in a mood to allow troops to enter the Temple, why persist with the curfew?

I apprised the meeting of the arrangements I had made to maintain essential services and the supply of basic commodities, and the cooperation we were receiving, as well as of the rapport that had developed between the force and the citizens in the past 48 hours since the curfew had been imposed. 'I do not think any complaint from the area has come to your notice. Although petty mischief mongers could have done so.' I added, 'Rode and his followers, including militants, are banking on their supposed popularity and are hoping that people will rise in their support. If we lift the curfew now, we will strengthen this notion of theirs. The continuance of curfew will generate the fear of a bigger action in their minds and most probably some of them may start surrendering in panic.' After glancing at the other officers, 'OK, you continue with your curfew,' J.F. Ribeiro declared.

We were greatly relieved. I had also been spared from adding the fact that in abandoning the action midway we would be confirming the militants' allegation that the extortionists and killers inside the Temple had been planted by the government agencies.

In the afternoon, we went to the airport to receive the Governor. The first thing he asked me was about the reaction of the people. I reported the exercise I had been doing in ascertaining the views of all shades of people. He was satisfied with my conclusions. I added, though: 'Sir, any one of the Akali factions may launch a *morcha* (agitation).'

'We will arrest them.' the Governor's tone was firm enough to sound furious.

Quite dramatically, as we reached the Circuit House, I was informed by the Public Relations Officer that P. S. Badal had given a call to his party members to reach Amritsar to liberate the Temple and that S.S. Barnala had announced that they would *gherao* (surround) the Raj Bhavan at Chandigarh. It was obvious that agitators would be arrested at the place of launching the agitation. I was also certain that the multiple threats were because of the division in the Akali party. Each group was merely trying to score over the other. The newspapers had published the amusing story of an ex-Minister who was manipulating his arrest near Chandigarh because the jail there had some air-conditioned rooms. Not even a feeble attempt on the part of any ordinary Akali to reach Amritsar was reported. They tamely courted arrest.

The governor ascertained the views of the officers and various public men. He told almost everyone that the government had various options and hence would choose the best one. P. Chidambaram, told the press months later that one alternative under consideration was to send robots into the Temple.

Later that evening, on J.S. Rode's assurance that there would be no mischief and that he would be responsible if any one was held up as hostage, we acceded to his request to send some of his men into the Temple complex. They returned after having an hour long meeting with the holed-up militants. Actually, J.S. Rode was trying to ascertain if the group opposed to him, would side with him in the changed situation. They seemed to be disappointed since J.S. Rode remained silent. At the same time the government made it clear that even if J.S. Rode wanted to go into the Temple he would be allowed to do so. Accordingly, I informed him of this.

I had a feeling that eventually the government might change its decision and decide to arrest him. I shared my thinking with S.K. Arora, SSP Amritsar. We decided to make arrangements to arrest J.S. Rode and his group in anticipation.

A few minutes before the time given to J.S. Rode to enter the Temple, I was told that he should not be allowed to do so. The SSP and I rushed to the Kotwali. J.S. Rode and his men were gathered outside the gurudwara, just opposite the Kotwali. We told him to wait for 10 minutes. Later, I asked him to change his mind. TV cameras were focused on us. His men were getting restive, they wanted to show their bravado before the cameras. I was actually waiting for the bus to arrive before arresting them. Otherwise some headstrong militant might make a dash for the Temple, violate the curfew and put us in a quandary. It could have a cascading effect and shooting in such a situation could be an ugly embarrassment. I had to be tough with the TV crews. I did not hear the bus arrive behind me. I could not play for more time. I told the group that they were under arrest. To my surprise, they dashed past me straight into the bus, which I noticed only when I turned around.

Jacob Malik of the BBC asked me jokingly, 'Why this drama?' He had obviously got wind of the change in the government decision at the last minute. I was almost tempted to blurt out the truth. In retrospect, I feel that I was right to treat the situation as sensitive, with the potential to turn ugly. But our prolonged presence at the scene, (I had requested even IG Chaman Lal to be with us) could have enhanced the chances of its becoming ugly and embarrassing. SSP Suresh Arora and I should have remained available but not visible, and allowed the SP to arrest the *Jathedar*, J.S. Rode and his *jatha*. Our presence unnecessarily enhanced the status of the arrested persons. But J.S. Rode's arrest was an important step towards the action. With it, the idea of parleys with the militants was as good as dropped. The government seemed to be turning in favour of tiring out the *Kharkoos*. The governor had asked them to surrender with their arms, clarifying that the action was against the militants and that the government was keen to restore the *Maryada* in the Temple at the earliest.

We restricted the curfew to within about 300 m around the Temple. That night two militants jumped over the wall and a third one went back, but all three had been hit by the vigilant CRPF men on duty. The two who crossed over were found dead the next day; one on the outskirts of the city and the other in the fields of Chabhal. This incident appeared to be a reaction of the militants to the decision of the government to continue the barricade of the Temple. We had to wait for firm and clear orders for further action.

10

The Militants Surrender

On the morning of 13 May 1988, we went to receive Governor S.S. Ray at the airport. He held a meeting with us in the VIP Lounge. He wanted to know the mood of the people, the impact of the call given by the two factions of the Akali Dal and the possibility of any uprising. I told the Governor that earlier on that day I had gone to the routine monthly meeting of my revenue officers, to pose only one question to the 45 odd officers. I asked if any of them had heard even a whisper against the government action against the militants in the Golden Temple. I was informed by them, almost in one voice, that instead of criticism people had appreciated the government's initiative in getting the Temple cleared of the militants.

I also informed the Governor that in Amritsar we had revived the British practice of assessing the political situation based on information conveyed by the *patwari*—the juniormost field officer. The revenue officers systematically ascertained the facts and changing trends of the terrorist situation in the villages and the general public reaction to the same from their *patwaris*. Thus, the information that I had gathered that morning was neither superficial nor given off the cuff. The *patwaris* had actively sought such information. Even in the ordinary course of their duties, they could keep their eyes and ears open and gather public opinion. If adverse opinion was prevalent in the countryside, no one could have missed it.

To further impress this fact upon the Governor, I said, 'Sir, this is not a civil service practice, nor does it behove me to say so, otherwise I can give you an undertaking in writing on a stamped paper, that the people are with us and there would be no reaction at all.' Governor S.S. Ray could not have liked such a silly way of asserting myself, but I think in that sensitive situation I had to convince the government beyond all doubt that the people were with us and that they supported the government's action. In reply to a query from the Governor, I submitted that for at least another 10 days there would be no change in the public attitude. K.P.S. Gill was also present in the VIP lounge during my briefing.

After holding further meetings in the Circuit House, the Governor flew to Delhi to present his latest assessment. Understandably, the Governor had held numerous meetings in Delhi after 9 May 1988. He was in favour of continuing the Operation to tire out the militants, but the Home Ministry, presumably, might have wanted to give J.S. Rode some more time. In the evening, the Prime Minister told the press that the firm action that the government was taking would continue. I was elated to see this report on the teleprinter. My conviction and strong recommendation conveyed to the Governor had been accepted by the Government of India.

Governor S.S. Ray had a good sense of humour; he might have told the Prime Minister that the DC Amritsar had offered to give an undertaking on stamped paper! I had made that offer only to emphasise my point. But I felt I was bound by that undertaking. If this scheme were to fail in any manner, I was sure to be made a scapegoat. Despite some anxious thoughts, it did not worry me unduly.

That afternoon I was late for lunch. I found Baba Uttam Singh waiting, outside the small office at my residence. It seemed a good omen. He was the head of a sizeable *dera* in Khadur Sahib, a town founded by the second Guru.

During those days, he had been supervising the gold plating of the Akal Takht building under construction; he was one of the five Babas to whom the *kar-sewa* of the Akal Takht had been entrusted by the SGPC. He said that his boys were inside the Temple, not because they had any sympathy with the militants but to guard the gold lying there. He wanted me to do something for them. I told him to get in touch with his boys on the telephone, which was still functioning and advise them that, when we announce a ceasefire and I give them the time to vacate the Temple tomorrow at 3.30 P.M. they should come out. The Baba wanted an assurance from me that his men would be handed over to him. I agreed, without considering that some of his men might be killer or extortionists of which even the Baba may be unaware. It seemed that, help from unseen sources had begun to come in even before I learnt about the approval of the scheme by the Government of India.

On 13 May Nehchal Sandhu, Assistant Director, IB, posing as a press reporter, had talked on the telephone to the militants inside the Temple. According to him, the militants sounded dispirited. He, therefore, suggested to them that they should talk to the Deputy Commissioner on the phone for a way out. K.P.S. Gill wanted to be present when I talked to them. Thus, on the afternoon of 14 May, K.P.S. Gill, Chaman Lal, Pathak the Joint Director IB, N. Sandhu the Assistant Director IB, and I went to my residential office. N. Sandhu telephoned them and gave them my number, adding that I was then available at that number. The voice at the other end said that they had already talked with the DC. In a surprised tone, N. Sandhu repeated what he had heard aloud. He was told in reply that Baba Uttam Singh had had a talk with the DC. He added that when the DC would make a call at 3.30 P.M. that day, they would come out from the Temple. It was already 3.20 P.M. Before I could wind up, K.P.S. Gill had already bolted out of my office and was speeding away to the Temple. There was no response to our call declaring ceasefire. We tried for half an hour, repeatedly asking them to come out. I went with Baba Uttam Singh to the back of the *prashad* point where his men, according to the Baba, would be waiting. But the militants had locked that door and we could not contact the Baba's men. Five old men did stagger out, but they appeared to be only stranded pilgrims.

Evidently they were from relatively affluent rural families who had remained confined for almost five days. None of their kin had tried to search for them. Were the old people of no concern to their families or were people accustomed to their older members coming to the Temple for a prolonged stay to earn religious merit? Or had the old men stayed back to support the militants in case of an attack by the state forces which they had seen all around the Temple? How many of those inside the Temple could be young boys who visited the Temple routinely and may also have decided to stay back just to support the militants in case of a fight or just for the heck of it or to kill their boredom born of unemployment? Such questions troubled my mind. Except Baba Uttam Singh and the wife of a doctor who phoned me about her stranded husband, none of the parents, or a village *Panchayat* on their behalf, had come to enquire about any of the boys. Not all of them could have been militants or terrorists. This was somewhat strange. But in the circumstances, for us all those within the Temple were militants until they surrendered and we could verify their antecedents. For the moment, the hopes raised for their surrender had been belied. I had no choice but to ask Baba Uttam Singh to come again the next day before 11 A.M. for another attempt. The Baba promised to come punctually.

On the morning of 15 May 1988, as I drove to the temple I considered possible alternatives other than merely asking the militants to surrender. Some people who had met me at the morning at my office did not seem to expect an early success of the operation that we had undertaken. However, the Central Government albeit reluctantly, had agreed to the continuation of the operation. On 13 May I had estimated, and then told the Governor, that the support of the people for our effort could be expected for about 10 days. I had played safe while giving this figure. My hunch was that the militants would come out by 19 May though I had no idea about the food available in the *parikrama* rooms and the actual number of persons inside. I was also told that some of the rooms had water supply.

In the prevailing situation, I felt that we had only three options: (*i*) To go inside and talk to the militants. (Unlike my risky visit on 7 July 1987, just before taking charge as DC Amritsar, this time I would have needed permission from the government, which I was sure would have been refused for obvious reasons.) (*ii*) Arrange a phone call by Nehchal Sandhu again, posing as their well-wisher to convey to the militants that the government would deal with them within the law and (*iii*) To convey to the militants through N. Sandhu that in case they did not surrender, the government might resort to a night commando action to nab or kill them to clear the Temple.

I found that my car had already arrived at the Braham Buta Akhara. I alighted and ran up the stairs. I enquired from Nand Lal if Baba Uttam Singh had arrived. He shook his head negatively. Chaman Lal soon arrived, followed by K.P.S. Gill. I greeted them both warmly to cover my anxiety that had not only bothered me earlier but was nagging me again, since Baba Uttam Singh had not shown up.

'When do you expect them to come out Sir?' Nand Lal asked me. Earlier, he had mentioned that some women with the militants also

had small children and infants with them. I had not taken any notice
of this information then. But when he posed the question now, the
grave importance of his information struck me. 'Those who go to the
morchas (bunkers) with wives and children cannot remain holed
up for long, what to say of their fight to the last,' I told Nand Lal.
K.P.S. Gill started explaining to Chaman Lal, who was a bachelor,
what a nuisance children were in such a situation.

It was already past eleven. The Baba had not yet come. 'Has he
been threatened out of coming?' I thought aloud in a mood of apprehension. If Nehchal Sandhu and Baba Uttam Singh could talk to
them on the phone, the inmates and their supporters all over the
district must also be taking advantage of the same facility. I thought
I would have to get the telephones bugged and, if need be, frozen, to
be used only when we need to talk to them. We decided not to wait
for the elusive Baba any longer.

Chaman Lal announced the hour of the ceasefire. It was not that
we had been firing towards the temple earlier. The announcement
was only to make it clear to them that, after that hour, if they came
out of their rooms, we would not fire at them.

Taking the mike from him, I tried to make my tone friendly when I
said, 'The *maryada* of the temple is being violated by using the temple as a fort. It is not worthy of "Singhs". Come to the waiting protection of Guru Ramdas in his Sarai.' After a pause, and after alerting
them I repeated the call, telling them about the route they should
follow. I assured them that they would be prosecuted strictly according to law and not harmed in any other way. The reverberations of
the mike died away and merged into the silence that was becoming
eerier by the moment.

I strained my ears for any sound from the temple. My eyes surveyed the closed doors of the rooms of the *parikrama*. But the doors
seemed to be firmly closed. I curbed my urge to repeat the call
immediately. When even the CRPF jawans began staring at me, I
decided to give another call. I gave my name and designation again
and used the same reassuring words. I asked them for the third time
to leave the *parikrama* rooms and come to the 'waiting Sarai of Guru
Ramdas.'

Suddenly, to our surprise, the doors flung open almost simultaneously as if in obedience to a command. A number of men and a
few women poured from the rooms into the *verandah* and the
parikrama. It was a thrilling moment, indeed full of strange delight.

In a few seconds the whole scene had changed. But at that time they did not appear to be the determined, vibrant and fearless mavericks that I had noticed on my last visit to the Braham Buta Akhara. They seemed to be somewhat confused, as ordinary people would be in a strange place. Only some of them seemed to have understood my instructions properly and headed for the eastern gate to come to the Sarai. I had to guide the bulk of them who headed to other gates and repeated my instructions. They then turned about and followed the directed course. I kept encouraging them as they followed my directions.

In a serious illness or when one is under great stress, quite inexplicably a feeling of well-being sometimes envelops one. The surrendering, docile mass of men and women seemed to be taking a long time to cover the *parikrama* but the uplifting feeling like I have described had started welling up in me. But then suddenly, to our surprise, about 50 of them changed direction, crossed the Darshani Deorhi and headed towards the sanctum sanctorum—the Harmandar. I shouted through the mike that they were doing the wrong thing. But they did not heed me and kept moving. They were carrying small bags round their shoulders.

The CRPF officers standing near me asked if they could fire at them. I thought for a second and felt that in the context of my announcement and our declaration of a ceasefire we could not violate our undertaking and, accordingly, replied in the negative. Two teenagers appeared in the large hole made by LMG fire in the turret of the Bunga Ramgharian. This had been done on the very first day to stop militants from operating from its top. This was the same site where they had been seen constructing a pillbox, and from where they had pointed their guns at me two weeks earlier. Today the two teenagers popped their heads out and said, 'Bring Baba Thakar Singh.' They were holding a paper in their hands, which fell in the *parikrama* between the Braham Buta Akhara building and the Bunga Ramgharian. The boys disappeared from the hole and went back.

The group of militants that had entered the Harmandar seemed to have gone in to stay put. The hour of the ceasefire had also expired. They were not likely to take any risk to come out. I could end my vigil here for the time being. I went to the Sarai to have a look at the 'boys' who had surrendered. On my way, one reporter told me that S.S. Penta had also come out. He gave the description of his clothes and the place where he was sitting.

All of them sat in lines. The courtyard of the Sarai was full with them. Doctors from the CRPF were giving treatment and first-aid to the sick and the injured. I told one of my officers to arrange some food like bananas and shoes for their bare feet. After I had done with the detailed instructions, I turned to locating Surjit Singh Penta. I spotted him instantly and stood before him. K.P.S. Gill was talking to Penta's wife. Both looked towards S.S. Penta. That very instant he consumed cyanide. His face reddened as he fell back. His whole body was in convulsions. I shouted for the CRPF doctors who were attending to the injured militants. Two doctors rushed to save him. But in vain.

His wife did not cry for quite some time. Why he committed suicide, I would never know. Maybe he had promised his wife to come out alive. Or maybe he thought that, because a group had gone into the Harmandar, the temple would remain out of bounds. And if he were to commit suicide inside, his dead body would decay there till it was removed. He may also have been in the know of many secrets of his fellow terrorists and their Pakistani contacts. He was also inimical to J.S. Rode, of whose links with the authorities S.S. Penta must have been aware. Because of any or all of these reasons he preferred to end his own life. I had learnt that this man was an ace sprinter of his school in Delhi and had returned to his village Chhajjalwadi after the Delhi riots of 1984. In the countryside around Amritsar it was rumoured that he had managed to escape on two occasions when the Amritsar police surprised him at his haunts in two different villages. On both occasions he had been fired at but was not hit. I was curious to know how he happened to become a militant. But no credible information could be obtained. The police had to complete papers about each one of them. The group that had entered the Harmandar was already on my mind when I returned to the Braham Buta Akhara.

K.P.S. Gill also arrived. He was naturally unhappy over the escape of 50 of them into the Harmandar. I owned up to the decision of not letting the force fire at them. I gave him my reasons: one, that we had not said that they could not go to any other room and two, that they could be going to pay their obeisance before the surrender. At the same time even if we had fired, we could not have killed all of them. I also said that we should get in touch with Chowk Mehta as the two teenagers had shouted from the hole in the turret of the Bunga. 'Then will you go to Baba Thakar Singh?' he asked. 'Of course,'

I said. But on second thoughts K.P.S. Gill suggested I should get in touch with J.S. Rode who was in the Amritsar Central Jail on the outskirts of the city.

J.S. Rode was not very happy to learn about the situation. 'Baba Thakar Singh is the seniormost, you better contact him,' was his expected reply. The group of militants who had stayed back were seemingly of the J.S. Rode group and they mostly owed allegiance to the Damdami Taksal. I returned to the Braham Buta Akhara.

Baba Uttam Singh had arrived and was waiting for me. He got up and said, 'Our Contessa car developed some snag on the way and this took a lot of time.' He was a typical Baba epitomising all the qualities for which the sants of this area are known; simple, soft-spoken, rotund with a ruddy complexion. I took him to the Sarai. His boys touched his feet with great affection and he hugged them. But the delay on the part of the Baba in reaching the Braham Buta Akhara had technically absolved me of my promise to hand over his men to him. The SP, in charge, promised to take up the cases of the Baba's men first and release them as soon as their antecedents were verified. The Baba took it as God's will and was satisfied.

The SSP and I got very late in reaching the airport to receive Governor S.S. Ray and J.F. Ribeiro. They had left for Amritsar by air as soon as they learnt about the surrender of the militants. As if their elation was contagious, the State Government Beech Craft plane also arrived before time due to a favourable wind. The security vehicles for the VIPs had already been dispatched to the airport. Perhaps in their exhilaration, the VIPs decided to squeeze themselves in the front seats of two Maruti jeeps—the security vehicles—rather than wait for us. Our cars met them half way on the road to Amritsar. Both the Governor and the Advisor were not only physically very tall but were also very high on the hit-list of the militants. With their fair complexions turning red in the May afternoon sun, in the front seats of the open gypsies meant for the security staff, they were clearly identifiable. This gave us the jitters, but it also pleased us to notice their involvement at the success achieved.

In the car, J.F. Ribeiro asked me why I was not looking as happy as I should be. I shared my concern about the breakaway group that had moved into the Harmandar. 'They cannot harm the Temple,' both of them said simultaneously. I also believed the same but I had taken too much responsibility on myself from the beginning. Perhaps I had no other option either.

The next morning, i.e., 16 May 1988, before formally asking the recalcitrant group to come out of the Harmandar, K.P.S. Gill thought we should ask the wives who had surrendered the previous day, to plead through the mike to their menfolk to come out when the officers gave a call. Only one lady refused to say anything. The remaining two or three pleaded with their menfolk to relent and assured them that they were being treated well.

Thereafter, Chaman Lal and I went through our exercise. First he announced the ceasefire, then I requested them to come out of the temple. There was no response so I asked them to surrender two-three times again. It seemed hopeless. I had to meet Baba Thakar Singh in Chowk Mehta. Chaman Lal and I left for the headquarters of the Damdami Taksal. Chaman Lal stayed at the police station and the SHO of Chowk Mehta accompanied me into the gurudwara.

Gurudwara Gurdarshan Parkash is a huge complex, surrounded by high walls. Driving into the silent vastness did not give me the feeling of going into a gurudwara. The SHO stayed in one of the rooms and I proceeded further accompanied by a guide, to pay obeisance in the gurudwara. Then we moved towards the residential area. It gave the impression of an institute of Vedic days, with rows of rooms for young students who, along with their teachers were quietly moving about. As a small child, Jarnail Singh Bhindranwale had joined this institution. In order to break the silence, I suggested to the guide that they should either provide general education in addition to the religious education or they should admit only boys who already had such an education. 'We do this,' he said pointing to a teenager. 'He has already studied upto the seventh class and now he has come here for religious education.'

Baba Thakar Singh radiated peace through his bearing. He heard my arguments patiently. His countenance remained placid all along. I felt a bit embarrassed; apparently I had not impressed him. I, therefore, added that we were showing the entire operation on television the world over. If the militants stayed on in the Harmandar it would give a poor impression about our concern for the sanctity of the sanctum sanctorum. When my submission was over, he said, 'We will come', and gave a big smile. A burly one-eyed man standing behind him, instantly blurted, 'But we will not ask the "Singhs" to lay down arms. It would be against Sikh ethics.' His one eye was fixed piercingly on me.

'The question is to stop the defiling of the most sacred Harmandar which we wash with milk, and they have made their dwelling place. They have also asked for the Baba to come,' I argued with much feeling and urgency.

'It is for the Jathedar of the Akal Takht (Rode) to ensure cleanliness of the Temple.' He was speaking in terms of cold logic. But he was also protecting their vested interests of enjoying the protection within the four walls of the complex rather than antagonise the militants. When I reminded him that the Taksal had a responsibility transcending every one else's, he was flustered. 'Let Mohkam Singh come, we will think it over.' He found an excuse for an escape. Suddenly a positive feeling for Baba Thakar Singh overpowered me. I felt that it would be wrong to drag in the Baba if that could be avoided.

On 17 May 1988, after the ladies had again appealed to their militant husbands, we gave them time to come out. Only two boys came out of the Harmandar with raised arms. When they came out of the Darshani Deorhi, instead of turning to their right they crossed over to the rooms on their left, ignoring my warning that they could be fired upon. After a few minutes they came out again and headed for the Harmandar. They seemed to have filled their bags with something from the rooms. They were fired at but they managed to go back into the Harmandar. One man from the Harmandar tried to draw a bucket of water from the Har Ki Pauri. He was simply shouted back into his hideout. It was clear that they were running out of food and water. Noticing this, K.P.S. Gill said we would not extend our offer in the afternoon. He, however, wanted me to visit the Baba at Chowk Mehta again so that I could talk to him in the presence of Mohkam Singh. I agreed to make an attempt if the extremists did not surrender on the next day.

The next morning i.e., 18 May, in the Circuit House, S.K. Sinha, Director, Public Relations, Punjab, wanted me to give an interview to a lady journalist who was going back to Delhi by the noon flight. Answering her last question, I told her that I had a strong feeling that the militants would surrender that day.

As usual S.K. Sinha had placed representatives of the world press, including the electronic media, on the roof of the three-storied Guru Ram Das Sarai. While approving of the operation, the Prime Minister had told Governor S.S. Ray to ensure that the whole operation was shown to the people. He had added, 'I would also like to see what you do there.' Governor S.S. Ray had told us all this to emphasise the importance of sustaining the confidence of the people. Therefore, S.K. Sinha was co-ordinating with the entire media. He had a flair for this kind of a job and had been doing it extremely well.

That day, as a strategy, K.P.S. Gill had decided that we would not renew an offer to accept surrender. He was worried that, if, in the presence of the press from all over the world, the militants did not respond again that day, it would not look good. I assured him that I would frame my offer in such a manner that it would not be embarrassing if they did not come out. 'After that, not only will I go to Chowk Mehta but positively come back with the Baba,' I added.

Chaman Lal announced on the mike that for one hour after the announcement the force would not fire provided they followed the instructions which the DC would announce. I had to go down the Braham Buta Akhara and climb up to the roof of the *langar* building so that I could see the Harmandar and the *parikrama* without any obstruction.

On my way I felt that perhaps K.P.S. Gill was also getting more anxious. May be the Central Government was still anxious to give credit to J.S. Rode and the Damdami Taksal and it might have directly or indirectly suggested to K.P.S. Gill to solicit the Taksal's help once again. But in that case K.P.S. Gill would surely have shared it with me. The reactions of the foreign press to the continued obstinacy of this group did not seem to be a matter of serious concern so long as the people were with us. However, I was aware that some of the options which were available to us before their entrenchment in the sanctum sanctorum were no longer possible. Many people could resent the militants using the Harmandar as their abode, which amounted to defiling it. This could dilute the little support they may have from some sections, particularly from the Sikhs.

It was not possible to talk to them on the telephone, as there was none inside the Harmandar. If we wanted to mount commando action at night, we were now in a very difficult position. The only approach was through the Darshani Deorhi and the connecting causeway. Use of boats, the other alternative, was equally dangerous and more sacrilegious. Any gunfight around the sanctum sanctorum would have appalled the Sikhs. In the June 1984 Operation, the army had made loud claims that they had ensured against any bullet scratching the walls of the Harmandar. That claim was absolutely incorrect but the palliative claim was surely necessary even though at that time no militant had taken any position in the sacred core of the Temple.

In a way my responsibility had increased. Of all the officers some of them much senior to me, I alone had asserted that the people were with us and that there would be no adverse reaction to our sustaining the blockade of the Temple. On 15 May 1988, I had specifically stopped the CRPF from firing on this group as it moved towards the Harmandar. I was technically right to do so but I had miscalculated in not anticipating such a move. There was a sprinkling of hard-core fundamentalists amongst them as seen later, since four of them took cyanide capsules. I should have been mindful of this possibility while formulating my announcement to persuade them to surrender.

Despite all this I remained optimistic, since we now knew that there were only 50 odd people inside the Harmandar. They appeared to have hidden some AK47s under their long *cholas* as they shifted here. They did not have any heavy weapons. They no longer had women with them, and during the last two days, they had betrayed signs of having to face a shortage of food and water. The replenishment of food by two men in two small bags could not sustain many famished people for long. And more important, in the May heat both their resilience and determination could weaken. These were the thoughts at the back of my mind as I climbed that hot afternoon onto the new *langar* building to try my luck again.

I addressed the recalcitrant 'Singhs', in more or less the following words: 'Yesterday, at the time of the end of the cease fire I had told you to make up your mind by the time we announce the "no firing time" again. If you have made up your minds, either wave a cloth or simply your hand. There is no need to come out.' There was no response. Every minute was full of anxiety.

The two-storied new *langar* building, was nearly midway between the Sarai and the Harmandar. The previous day, two of the militants had replenished their stock of gram, by risking their lives. An attempt by another person to steal a small bucket of water from the Har-Ki-Pauri had been foiled by merely shouting him away without firing a single shot. They could have been expecting a ceasefire announcement or Baba Thakar Singh's arrival in the forenoon. Neither had happened. A meal of parched gram with little or no water, the closed doors of the Harmandar, no power supply and the scorching sun of

May must have stretched their endurance beyond the limit. There was no need to give a longer pause.

I made the second attempt rather early. 'I am Sarab Jit Singh, Deputy Commissioner of Amritsar. I assure you of a fair trial according to the law. If the "Singhs" have made up their mind, wave a cloth or your hand.' The lead of the mike I was speaking into was short. I, therefore, could not carry it with me if I wanted to reach the edge of the roof. I put the mike down and took two large steps forward. I saw a window open slowly, a hand holding a yellow rag came out. With the first wave of the hand, the rag fell from what must have been a trembling grip. The next moment saffron pieces of cloth were fluttering from all the windows. They were desperate to come out.

My prayers had been answered. 'I have seen, I have seen, wait for my instructions.' I came back to shout into the mike.

I made it clear that this time they must come out in single file with their hands raised, towards the Sarai by turning right from the Darshani Deorhi. 'According to standing orders, anyone going out of line or to any other room or side will be fired at.' They followed the instructions. But just short of the north-western corner of the parikrama, a youth with broad shoulders and an old man staggered quite awkwardly out of the file. I shouted at them to join the rest but they did not seem to hear my warning. Neither did anyone else in the group seem concerned with them. The young man was slumping to the floor when the police fired. The two fell. None of the surrendering militants looked back or tried to help their staggering comrades. We learnt later that they had consumed cyanide, which is why they had staggered out of the queue and fallen. The youth was Karaj Singh Thande, one of the state's most dreaded terrorists.

With hands still raised above their heads, the remainder walked along the parikrama and came out from the eastern Deorhi. They were made to sit under a shed near the langar building. From the single file of the Kharkoos, K.P.S. Gill pulled out two of them at random; one turned out to be Malkiat Singh Ajnala and the other Nirvair Singh, the spokesman of the Panthic Committee. After the last man had come out, I also came down.

I asked Malkiat Singh Ajnala—who was a terror in his area to the people to whom he had been selling groceries on a cart for years, before he became a militant—'How could you decide to fight the government with absolutely no one to back you, neither the people nor Pakistan?' A CRPF doctor was attending to a bullet wound he had received while trying to scale the temple wall when we had first relaxed the curfew on 13 May 1988. In agony he said, 'Yes sir, no one came to the Temple. The curfew was only for three hundred meters.' They were no doubt depending on the people to rise up in their support. He had a grouse against the Pakistan-based terrorists also. 'We had been assured of many things by the "Singhs" coming from Pakistan. But...'

They did not show any remorse. Some of them, who were younger, appeared to be in a playful mood. We served them bananas. They were hungry and they had to eat, but perhaps from some embarrassment or nervousness were eating while joking with one another. This lot may have stayed back in the Harmandar, in order to be able to surrender to Baba Thakar Singh, but the impression had arisen that they were the stauncher lot compared to those who had surrendered on 15 May. Some Sikhs, who sympathised with the 'Singhs' were unhappy to see their behaviour on the TV. They told me, 'These boys could not be the "Singhs".'

P.P.S Gill from *The Tribune* told me that as soon as the surrender began they were told about my prediction that the militants would surrender that day. Mark Tully was so elated that he embraced me exclaiming: 'Sarab Jit, now you belong to history'. By then all of them had surrounded me and were posing many questions. Jacob Malik asked me the last. Thrusting the mike before me, he queried: 'Are you relaxed?' 'Who isn' t?' I said happily.

But the sense of relaxation was not universal. There were people and interests who were not at all happy. The success of Operation Black Thunder had made a material difference. For example; the role of J.S. Rode, the protégé of the Home Ministry, had become irrelevant as soon as the last batch came out of the Temple. The SGPC must have begun to flex its muscles to regain full control of the Temple. It could now get rid of the four high priests thrust on it. The *kar-sewa* at the Akal Takht, reconstruction of which had been undertaken by the Taksal after it was demolished following the decision of the *Sarbat Khalsa* of 26 January 1986, had been materially disturbed. This had been exploited by the militant leaders to revive terrorism. In the guise of volunteers acquiring construction material for *kar-sewa*, the movement of militants and weapons to and from the temple had occurred. This was the easiest and safest sanctuary for the militants and the venue was also accessible to new entrants. This was also the safest place to summon their victims for extortion, in the fashion of Bhindranwale. The projections and schemes initiated by some agencies, such as using J.S. Rode, were also likely to become redundant and irrelevant. In retrospect, one can have some idea of the considerations which were obstructing the instant approval of the Governor's scheme to tire out the militants by the Government of India. He had to fly to Delhi many times to get approval. Finally, after many meetings on the subject, the operation had been sanctioned on the afternoon of 13 May 1988. And the first batch surrendered within two days. It was like a miracle.

This operation was a very significant success for the S.S. Ray administration. The general impression was that this episode would end militancy in Punjab. Official circles also subscribed to that impression. The spurt in violence, we thought, was like the last flicker of a dying fire. As in the case of most victories we did not immediately think of the ramifications of our earlier offer. Soon we were caught in another vortex. It was then that the question would haunt me. Which assurances and by whom had led the group of 46 militants to move to the Harmandar and not surrender along with the others on 15 May. What concessions were they awaiting in staying behind and by surrendering in the presence of Baba Thakar Singh. On the face of it, it would be clear that there certainly were two camps. The first was anti-Rode, to which Surjit Singh Penta belonged. The second was, in a way, the Taksal group. Some of them may have been in touch with some of the intelligence agencies hoping that the government would save them. There would seem to be no other explanation for this group to have entered the Harmandar. They certainly had no plans to fight to the last man, nor did they have enough food or ammunition.

For handling situations and operations like this, there is no known rule of thumb. One's depth of involvement and common sense alone are the guides. Luck also plays a part to make or mar the reputation of civil servants on whose lot it falls to handle such situations. The then Chief Secretary of Punjab, R.P. Ojha, patted me on the back during this stressful time and had cautioned me about taking too much on myself. I thanked him for his concern, but without some risks I could not have functioned. We have seen how every one was happy at the outcome, including the pressmen. But Delhi thought otherwise.

It was Jean Paul Sartre who observed that, in every book, what is 'unsaid' is the larger more important part. I do wish that I could place Delhi's reaction into the 'unsaid' part. But something impells me to the contrary. I had held it back from Mark Tully who perhaps had got some wind of it. He was eager to know about it right at that time. When I have decided to write about my experience now, I feel that without telling the whole truth, my story will remain incomplete. So here is the tale of my inquisition.

11

Trial at Midnight

The operation to force the militants out of the temple, was such a success that it was universally acclaimed. A comparison with Operation Blue Star was inevitable; the success of Operation Black Thunder underlined the folly of the former. But one must not forget that the two situations were vastly different. The only common point, was the objective, viz., freeing the Golden Temple from fundamentalists and terrorists. While the 1984 event had gravely saddened both onlookers and participants in the operation, the culmination of the 1988 Operation relaxed the general public. What made the difference in the result of the two operations was the fact that in the case of Operation Black Thunder the government had the full support of the local people.

The peoples' support could not be assumed at the time of the earlier operation which was undertaken at night after putting the entire state under a kind of house arrest. Due to the curfew a few press reporters stranded in hotels around the temple, could witness the scene from the slits in windows & doors. In the case of Black Thunder, the media had witnessed the operation from the roof of the Guru Ram Das Sarai. There was quite a sizeable international representation, as some reporters, who had been covering the Russian Army Operation in Afghanistan, had rushed to Amritsar. S.K. Sinha, Direction Public Relations had to conduct them in batches to see the Temple from inside after the militants had come out of the Harmandar.

After Operation Blue Star, terrorist violence remained suppressed for several months, but in the case of Operation Black Thunder it spurted in the wake of the surrender of the first batch of militants and continued to increase. This violence took a gory turn in the mass slaughter of labourers who came to the Punjab from UP, Orissa and Bihar for the harvesting season or to work in industry. On 17 May 1988, 36 migrants were killed; 35 on the 18th and 26, including 7 terrorists, were killed on the 19th. On 20 May, the toll was 45 in bomb blasts in Punjab and neighbouring Himachal Pradesh. The killing spree claimed another 50 lives in the following three days. The militants (and their mentors in Pakistan) seemed to have bounced back on their feet with alacrity. Their new strategy appeared to be aimed at disrupting the state's economy by these killings. To my mind, this time they had selected easy targets to signal their presence, to spread fear in the public mind and to restore the morale of their colleagues and supporters.

The choice of the softest possible targets; the poor labourers who were crowded in small dwellings, however, also indicated their nervousness after losing their sanctuary. So long as they operated from the Temple, they could sustain the facade of a religious war and impress the new recruits who came to them in the Temple to join the movement. They could also control their activities from a central place. The loss of the Temple also meant a loss of control over their cadres. An increase in incidents of extortion, also indicated the militant leaders were already feeling helpless during the previous few months. But they had taken steps, which were reprehensible and unpopular, in the effort to assert the point that the movement was alive.

On the other hand, the victors—the government and to some extent the SGPC—were in a self-defeating mood. Strangely enough, over a period of time, they completely threw away the advantage that they had gained.

The interrogation of the militants who had surrendered revealed that some of them belonged to eight states of India—UP, Bihar, Orissa, Delhi, Haryana, Jammu and Kashmir, West Bengal and Rajasthan. This was not a happy portent. Evidently the militants had the capability of spreading out in the Punjab and possibly to other states as well. It called for a fresh initiative which could be worked out on the basis of firm support by the people. We should have organised a mass contact movement to expose the deeds and morals of the so-called *kharkoos*, Babas and Singhs. It was the time to widen and strengthen our SPO posts by involving the people directly in the defence of their villages. This would have checked the growth of militancy. The irony is that the Government of India appeared keen to chastise not only the SGPC but also the officers responsible for the Operation. The SGPC, despite its being in complete disarray because of the terrorists, would not change its mindset which was primarily opposed to the government. Due to such an approach, the morale boosting potential of the operation was lost in the emerging controversies at times dramatised and exaggerated by the press.

For the sake of religious propriety and respect for Sikh religious sentiments and in order to sustain the support of the public, it was necessary to restore the glory of the Darbar Sahib by restoring the *Maryada* without further delay. But I needed at least two days to get the Temple ready to begin its normal ceremonies and other religious services. The whole of 19 May 1988 was spent in completing the mine detection operation. At the first opportunity, senior and responsible citizens were sent in to have a round of the Temple to see the conditions for themselves. The police (in plain clothes) also had to investigate and take the arms and ammunition found in the Temple into custody.

The police, rightly, did not require the gold-plated sheets meant to adorn the Akal Takht, nor the offerings in gold and cash lying in the *parikrama*, so K.P.S. Gill left them in my custody. I decided to seal the entire lot of gold and cash in the presence of the SGPC. I also decided to keep the valuables in covers bearing the official and the SGPC seals in a vault in the Darshani Deorhi which was also sealed under joint stamps. This sensitive work was done under the supervision of Harbans Singh Pawar and Suresh Kumar (IAS), both very capable Additional Deputy Commissioners. Restoration of electricity took another day because the transformers had been burnt either by the militants to keep the Temple in darkness at night or by some stray bullets that might have damaged the supply. I also arranged for the removal of the doors of the rooms in the *parikrama* to avoid their use again by the militants. The huge expanse of the *parikrama* and the *verandah*, which are normally kept immaculately clean by visiting pilgrims, had also to be washed. Keeping all these considerations in mind, I decided to start the restoration of the *Maryada* ceremony on the night of 21 May.

It was past 11 P.M. on the 19th when I was about to call it a day, that the Home Minister rang up from Delhi to enquire about happenings in the Temple during the day. To me, he did not sound too pleased with what had happened. Maybe it was simply my perception. In the euphoria of success, I thought that he had rung up merely to compliment me. He wanted to know details of the activities in the Temple after 5 P.M. I narrated them in sequence and in detail. He was not happy with my report of the day's events. 'Things are not right in Amritsar, I am coming there, we will land at Amritsar Airport around 1.30 A.M.' he observed. By the time I completed all the arrangements, including the opening of the Amritsar airport which is used to undisturbed nights, it was past midnight. The steps meant for 707 jets fell short by a foot for the door of the BSF's Avro aircraft. Also it was dark. I went up the steps to assist the dignitaries to come down. Buta Singh, the Home Minister, was saying his prayers with his rosary. To my query whether we were to go to the VIP lounge of the airport, or to the Circuit House, he indicated the latter. When P. Chidambaram came down, he congratulated me for the good work done during the Operation.

The drawing room of the Circuit House was dimly lit due to a snag in the electricity supply, like an unhappy augury. Both the Ministers took their seats. I stood facing them. Gopi Arora, the Secretary Information and Broadcasting, M.K. Narayanan, the Director IB, and K.P.S. Gill stood behind the Ministers. When the Home Minister raised the issues on the basis of which it was the government's perception that I had faulted, I felt cheated: I was being tried for my achievements. But K.P.S. Gill, even before the Minister had finished, said to me from behind the Minister, 'Sarab Jit, they have come to spoil what we have done.' I shared his embarrassment but felt some relief as he had given words to the feelings arising in me. He repeated his words once more before discretion overtook his valour.

The charges I was to answer were: 1) Why had the gold and currency been handed over to the SGPC when its place was the Government Treasury? 2) Why did I not give the TV team adequate time when they went into the Temple? and 3) It was alleged that the team of civilians selected by me and sent into the Temple was not proper because they made adverse comments which were contrary to the facts inside and, as a result, 4) distorted reports had been published by the press.

I took up the charges one by one. I explained that the Government was aware that this time the forces deployed around the Golden

Temple did not capture it unlike during Operation Blue Star when the army had entered the Temple. The army had recovered a huge amount of currency notes hidden at some places. The army handed over the valuables recovered to the District Magistrate who had to keep it in the Government Treasury as a case property. In the present case, as District Magistrate of Amritsar, I knew that the *kar-sewa* of the Akal Takht was going on and the gold was meant for the domes of the new building. Baba Uttam Singh, who was useful in facilitating the process of surrender, had also told me the same. Under the circumstances, that alone was the right course.

The gold was weighed, its purity assessed by top jewellers in the presence of the Additional District Magistrate and the SGPC officials, and they signed on the report of the jewellers. The cash and gold ornaments which appeared to be the offerings of devotees were counted and sealed along with the gold in proper packets under our joint seals. These packets were placed in a vault in the Darshani Deorhi, again under our joint seal and signatures. The SGPC would not dare to break open the sealed padlock on the outer door of the room. In any event, I said, if we had shifted these articles outside the Temple we would have hurt Sikh sentiments since these offerings belonged to the Guru and the Darbar Sahib.

The arms and ammunition left behind by the militants had been taken into custody as they were illegal and formed case property. If we had shifted the gold and cash to the District Malkhana we would have given cause for wide public criticism. This would have been enough to tarnish the clean operation which we had shown on the TV. Besides, our action did not amount to handing over the gold and cash or the Temple to the SGPC.

P. Chidambaram asked me, 'You mean to say that only a Panchnama (Recovery Memo) was prepared detailing the valuables?' 'Precisely, Sir, this is what I did and it was necessary to make the SGPC a party to it,' I said, adding, 'Technically and legally the goods are still in my custody.' I was grateful to the Minister of State for summing it up in technical terms for me and for coming to my rescue. I felt like giving a humourous turn to the conversation and tell the dignitaries that I hoped this *panchnama* would not become a *panchnama* in a case against me. But I could not gather enough courage at that moment, although in moments of crisis in the past, I have sometimes made use of such one liners.

Incidentally, going by tradition, the SGPC would not have tolerated the government's putting locks and seals on any of the rooms, howsoever small, in the Golden Temple. But this time such an action suited the SGPC too, for it did not want to hand over the *kar-sewa* of the Akal Takht to the Damdami Taksal who had the support of the government in this matter. Only when this controversy was solved and the Taksal got the *kar-sewa*, did the SGPC ask for the return of those articles in April 1992 that is, after a gap of nearly four years. I was still DC Amritsar. When I talked to Chief Minister Beant Singh on the phone about the demand of the SGPC, he instantly told me that I could go ahead and hand over the gold to the SGPC.

In retrospect, I think that if I had taken the gold to the Government Malkhana, the Damdami Taksal which was actually supervising the reconstruction of the Akal Takht, could easily have claimed it. It could also have been handed over to the Temple with all the paraphernalia to take up the construction. In that case the militants could return to the Temple again. The SGPC had entrusted the *kar-sewa* to five sants including the Taksal. The Taksal could have laid claim to it legally by getting the signatures of the other four sants on their request even though two or three of them had disassociated themselves from the *sewa* long ago. In this way, we would have gone back to square one.

By the time the explanation of the first charge was over, my officers had pulled the TV team out of their beds, and brought them to the Circuit House. We presented the team before the Ministers. In the distraction caused by the shuffling around of the TV team, M.K. Narayanan, whom I had not noticed till then, walked behind me and whispered in to my ear, 'Keep it up, you are doing very well.'

The TV team explained that in the absence of electricity the batteries of the lights of the camera could not work for more than two minutes, and in that duration they could not cover more than they had done. K.P.S. Gill was once again on his feet behind the Ministers. He addressed me and said, 'Look the government's own equipment (TV cameras of Doordarshan) is outdated and they are blaming us.'

Coming to the third charge, I gave the background of each one of the eminent people chosen by me. Dr. Daljit Singh, an internationally known ophthalmologist, the pioneer of intraocular surgery in India is a Padma Shree awardee. He is known for his personal integrity and straight forwardness. Sant Singh was from the Chief Khalsa Dewan, Lal Singh Aujla was a retired IAS officer and a former

Deputy Commissioner of Amritsar, Harbhajan Singh Soch was the Principal of Khalsa College, Amritsar, Mal Singh Ghuman was the General Secretary of the SGPC, Giani Mohinder Singh, an octogenarian and a very popular former General Secretary of the SGPC was also included. This apolitical group representing varied and respected walks of life could not be persuaded to say anything contrary to the actual facts. It was in my presence that the pressmen wanted to know their impression and they had said, 'No comments.' This did not imply that the things were very bad in the Temple; they just did not want to comment.

In the meanwhile the teleprinter clippings from the offices of the two agencies, PTI and UNI, had been procured for their perusal. P. Chidambaram read them aloud and looked at the Home Minister. He appeared to be conveying to the Minister, 'I don't see anything wrong in the reports.' The fourth charge had also been answered.

My trial seemed to be over when a smiling P. Chidambaram got up. He was warm and appreciative. The Home Minister, too, had no option but to show satisfaction though he remained somewhat stiff and reserved. Gopi Arora, Secretary (Information and Broadcasting) whom I had met for the first time, also seemed delighted. Still, the verdict of my midnight trial seemed to have been reserved to be announced later.

We left for the Golden Temple along with the TV team which took shots of the Minister's visit and of the sanctum sanctorum; all with the same 'obsolete' equipment. God's House, that has been a haven of peace and solace for centuries, seemed to be in a meditating trance after the recent disturbing months. The utter stillness of the night engulfed this perennial spring of joy. This visit was rewarding for me in a strange way. Buta Singh explained some details about the Darbar Sahib to his Ministerial colleague which even I did not know till then. I had the opportunity of escorting many dignitaries to this holy place during my long tenure later and I could impress them with my newly acquired knowledge about the Temple.

P. Chidambaram bade me good bye in the Circuit House, saying, 'Don't come to the airport, instead take up the work in the Temple early.' That morning we were to remove the doors of the rooms in the *parikrama*. I had suggested to the SGPC that doors on the rooms behind the *verandahs* were not necessary. When these doors were shut they segregated the Sangat and at the same time hindered the sound of Kirtan inside the rooms. This is against Sikh tenets and the

Maryada of the Temple. They could not rebut my logic. The SGPC also shared my fears and felt that doors could help in the re-assembly of militants in these rooms. They felt that even if the militants did not use these rooms for their offices any more, they could easily have closed-door meetings behind them. Hence the SGPC officials instantly agreed with the proposal and did not object to our removing them. One of them said, 'Yes DC Sahib, this is not a hotel.'

Three hours after the departure of P. Chidambaram, we had to proceed to the airport to receive the Governor. 'What do I do in the meanwhile?' K.P.S. Gill asked me knowing that I had to go to the Temple to begin my day's task. 'Better have some sleep, Sir, before the Governor arrives,' I advised the spirited K.P.S. Gill.

I narrated the Home Minister's phone call and the conversation of the previous night in detail to the Governor as we drove down from the airport. The Governor listened sympathetically and I felt that the state's first lady, Mrs. Maya Ray, was also paying full attention. I got the feeling that the matter was more serious than what I had initially thought it to be. It was also for the first time that Governor S.S. Ray was landing at Amritsar at 8 A.M. That had also alarmed me because, left to himself, S.S. Ray hated to begin his day early. My alarm increased when I realised that the Prime Minister too had to be acquainted with the details of our actions. By ten o'clock we managed to get the Prime Minister on the line and the Governor talked to him for more than half an hour. Smiling, he came out of his room and announced to us, 'The Prime Minister has told me to tell you and Gill that he has forgotten all about this (the alleged charges against us). He expects both of you to continue doing the good work.' A few days later, when the Chief Secretary came to Amritsar, he let slip that we had almost incited action under Article 311 of the Constitution of India. This implied dismissal from service, without trial, in the public interest. Much later, I learnt that some Sikh Members of Parliament had complained to the Prime Minister that K.P.S. Gill and I had handed over the control of the Temple to the SGPC.

Actually, the danger had been posed by the manoeuvring of some self-styled experts on Punjab who have been living in Delhi for decades, whether in office or without it. Their claim of being experts rested only on the fact that they were born in Punjab. Any politician can use such experts to conveniently exaggerate or twist facts and convey them to the higher ups concerned with Punjab affairs.

Governor S.S. Ray's opponents could have made up this story. Those who had visions of ending the Punjab militancy through J.S. Rode must have been upset by the exit of militants from the Temple. They might have conspired to ensure that the complaint reached the Prime Minister.

With the expulsion of the militants from the Temple, the role of Jasbir Singh Rode in managing them had become irrelevant. It seemed that J.S. Rode was the agent selected primarily by the Home Ministry. He had shown signs of failing from the very beginning, but the scenario had now changed completely. Nevertheless, the Home Ministry was unwilling to give up J.S. Rode. And it was because of this difference in approach that we could not take advantage of the changed situation and completely mop up militancy in Punjab. The Home Ministry did not fare too well in its choice of J.S. Rode and continued to give him support despite his failure to control the militants. Anyway, in the important task of restoring the *Maryada* of the Golden Temple, I continued to discern some invisible strings being pulled from behind the scene.

It would be apt to recall another important fact which is perhaps little known here. All the accused amongst those who had surrendered on 15 and 18 May 1988 were acquitted on technical grounds by the trial court in Amritsar. I could not see the file because it got tagged with the appeal against the judgement filed by the government. None the less, it must have lowered the credibility of the government during those troubled times.

12

Restoring the *Maryada*

The SGPC appeared keen to have the *Maryada* of the Golden Temple restored. But out of extreme caution, I felt it necessary to have alternative arrangements in case the Committee changed its stance at the last moment. Some eminent scholars of Sikh theology assured me that there were no rigidities in the observance of Sikh rituals. It would not be objectionable if any 'good Sikh' performed the service in the absence of a regular priest. Home Minister Buta Singh sent a senior priest and a Ragi *Jatha* by air to Amritsar despite my assurance that the two could be managed locally. The SGPC, in a formal meeting with me, assured full co-operation in starting the restoration of the *Maryada* ceremony. They only needed Bhai Mohan Singh, the head priest of the Harmandar Sahib who, according to the Committee, was away in Ludhiana. They reiterated their promise in the presence of K.P.S. Gill when he returned from Delhi the following day. With the help of the DCs of Ludhiana and Patiala, Bhai Mohan Singh was located in Patiala jail. The DC Patiala, B.C. Gupta dispatched Mohan Singh to Amritsar under police escort in time. All was thus set to start the restoration of the *Maryada* ceremony at 2.30 A.M. on the night of 21 May.

Bhai Mohan Singh, on arrival at Amritsar, rang up to say that he wanted to call on the Secretary SGPC right away. I thought that since he was coming straight from jail, he would like to know about the decision of the SGPC. I saw no objection to his request. I told him to speak to Bhan Singh, the Secretary of the SGPC, on the phone and gave the phone number to the police Inspector escorting him. He rang back to say that no one was responding from the Secretary's house. I agreed to their coming via the Secretary's residence to the Braham Buta Akhara where I was.

I smelt a rat when no one answered when I rang up the Secretary's residence. I had also thought it proper to be present at the meeting between Bhai Mohan Singh and the Secretary so I immediately left for his residence. K.P.S. Gill had gone for dinner to the Canal Rest House. I managed to wake up the Secretary SGPC after prolonged knocking on his door. By then Bhai Mohan Singh arrived along with the police escort. I found that Bhan Singh had changed since our last meeting that forenoon. He was hesitant to tell me about the change in the SGPC stand. For the sake of clarity, I pointedly asked him whether the SGPC had changed its mind? In a roundabout manner he showed his helplessness. 'Such a decision could not be taken without the approval of Tohra ji,' the soft-spoken Bhan Singh said even more softly. Even then I could not help blurting out, 'None of your employees waited to seek your or Tohra's permission before deserting their posts in the Darbar Sahib on the 9th of May when the Operation started.'

I reached for the phone to speak to K.P.S. Gill. The plug had been pulled out of the socket. As someone put the plug in, I learnt that K.P.S. Gill had left the Canal Rest House for the Braham Buta Akhara. Instead of wasting time I dashed to the Braham Buta Akhara, telling the secretary and the head priest that in any event the restoration of the *Maryada* ceremony would begin that night, as planned.

It could have been that G.S. Tohra may have sent a message through Bhai Mohan Singh, but this did not seem likely because in that event Bhai Mohan Singh would not have ultimately agreed to join the ceremony. The fact that Bhan Singh had pulled out the plug from the telephone socket gave me an inkling that some militants must have threatened them to keep away from the restoration of the *Maryada*. Even this appeared unlikely because all the militants who were in the Temple had surrendered. Besides, there was no chance of any other militant getting to know of our decision to start the *Maryada*. I suspected that someone bent upon mischief either to minimise our achievements or that some vested interests were attempting to create a situation in which only one person could rescue us and thus get credit from his superiors in Delhi. Possible threats to Bhan Singh must have been manoeuvred by such a person.

On the way I recalled the previous day's meeting with the Governor and Buta Singh in one room of the Circuit House and the SGPC executive in another. On 10 May 1988 I had written to the Shiromani Committee, as desired by the government, to agree to take certain steps to keep the militants out of the Temple in future. To avoid taking any decision, the Committee had informed the press that it was for the general house to decide the points raised in the DC's letter. But in the meeting on 20 May 1988, they had agreed to comply with the main points I had raised. An agreement was drafted by me. Every time I took the draft to the Home Minister he had vetoed it although it was along the lines he had suggested. Frustrated, the Committee agreed to meet the Governor but they refused to face Buta Singh who for them was a *Patit* (offender of the religious code, for his role in the repair of the Akal Takht in 1984) Sikh. They assured the Governor of their full cooperation and to keep the Temple free from militants.

The Acting President of the SGPC told the press after the meeting that Buta Singh had sabotaged the agreement which had been arrived at. The Home Minister, on the other hand, had put the entire blame on the obstinacy of the Committee. The Executive of the Committee had again agreed with K.P.S. Gill and me to start the restoration of the *Maryada* ceremony on the night of 21 May. Hours later their attitude had taken a somersault. The Home Minister had virtually forced their help on me to start the restoration of the *Maryada* ceremony. All these events were confusing and I could not come to any conclusion as to what was actually happening.

K.P.S. Gill's annoyance was understandable. 'There was no need to allow Mohan Singh to see Bhan Singh,' he said. I was very clear that Mohan Singh had to be allowed to see the Secretary. The Committee as well as Mohan Singh could back out even at the last minute. 'I will proceed with my arrangements which I will finalise in the remaining two or three hours.' I said resolutely. I was confident that all we had to do was to continue the Kirtan within the Harmandar till about noon. By then the moral pressure of the visiting devotees would be so much on the officials and junior employees that they would not be able to stay away. There were a number of *granthis*—who read from the scriptures—who had been employed by the SGPC—on daily wages. They had met me a day earlier and had told me about their financial problems because of the break in the Temple's routine. I had promised to pay them for the break provided they turned up when the *Maryada* started on the appointed day. Their eagerness to join reflected their desire to end their financial problems. The SGPC's withdrawal from the revival of the service in the Temple was a matter of concern but not an insurmountable problem.

'Can you bring Mohan Singh here?' K.P.S. Gill asked me. In 20 minutes Mohan Singh, with a placid face, was facing K.P.S. Gill's wrath. Mohan Singh agreed to participate. K.P.S. Gill was reluctant to agree to his going to his house to have the customary bath and put on a new dress for the ritual. I again intervened to say that he should be allowed to go through the ablutions and be in proper dress. 'The option to drink water or not is the horse's privilege,' I said. K.P.S. Gill agreed. Actually, Bhai Mohan Singh's son had been missing for quite some time and K.P.S. Gill promised him that he would do all that was possible to locate him.

K.P.S. Gill and I climbed to the roof of Braham Buta Akhara around 2 A.M. and sat facing the Temple. This was the same place where, three weeks earlier, surrounded by guns, I had a feeling that a clash could begin any time. The fortifications of the militants stood pulled down just as the doors of the *parikrama* rooms had been removed. Only one brick structure still stood at the *prashad* point. A cool breeze started blowing. Baba Uttam Singh and his men, along with the families who had traditionally been serving the Temple had washed the *parikrama* clean during the day. The devotees had finished washing the floor of the sanctum sanctorum with milk mixed with water drawn from the Har-Ki-Pauri. The smaller *parikrama* around it had been washed with water from the holy *sarovar*. They were now busy drying it clean with towels. After 3 A.M. the chanting of *shabads* (hymns), blowing of conches and beating of the huge drum was heard. Under the glare of the lights Bhai Mohan Singh, carrying the Guru Granth Sahib on his head and surrounded by the *sangat* came out of the Kotha Sahib (rest room). He placed the Holy Book in the gold plated *palki*. The *sangat* carrying the *palki* Sahib moved towards the Darshani Deorhi and through it to the Harmandar Sahib.

Sounds of joy reverberated all round the Temple. The procession was led by the Nishan Sahib (religious flag) and a small group of musicians singing *shabads*. They had been doing this for generations. Bhai Mohan Singh again lifted the Granth Sahib on his head from the *palki* Sahib as it arrived outside the door of the Harmandar and carried it inside. With the recital of the *ardas* (supplication) the traditional service stood revived after a break of 12 days. Bhai Mohan Singh read aloud from the Granth Sahib after opening it at random to seek the Order of the Guru—*hukamnama*—for the occasion. The stanza was very apt, it read:

> Without the Name, all, ever wander about in the universe and they suffer loss in the world.
> The wayward persons do the deeds in the pitch darkness of egotism.
> The Guru-wards drink Nectar by reflecting over the Name, O Nanak.
> Slok, 3rd Guru. (page 646) (Translation, Kirpal Singh.)

With the *Maryada* restored the Temple was alive again. It had been revived in the tradition initiated by Guru Arjan Dev ji.

From the morning of 22 May 1988, we permitted the general public to visit the Temple in shifts, ensuring that no one had stayed behind at the end of each shift. The SGPC had agreed to this arrangement. On the first day 12,000 people visited the Darbar Sahib. The number went on increasing every day. The crowd from the villages was not all that small. This spurt in devotees was not because of the closing of the Temple from 9 May 1988. It was primarily because many people had stopped coming to the Temple ever since the presence of the militants in the Temple had increased. The devotees, as far as possible, were allowed in without being searched. We could do it because we had deputed official observers in the guise of devout Sikhs inside the Temple as per our understanding with the SGPC. Frisking at the entry points was done very rarely. As such the goodwill of the government under President's rule was building up amongst the Sikh masses.

My random conversations with visitors from the rural areas affirmed this. One elderly illiterate woman, commenting on the militants, said 'They were fake "Singhs". First they chose to entrench themselves with guns in God's house, then with arms raised above their heads they came out like ordinary dacoits. The shameless rogues kept laughing as they ate bananas served by the government.' About the government, she commented with a sigh, 'Sometimes the government also does some good work, but mostly it remains occupied with wrong ones.'

13

Demoralisation versus a Gun Battle

Operation Black Thunder was not a gun battle as press reports would have the public believe. The decisive factor behind the surrender of militants was neither the superior firepower of the National Security Guards nor the limited rations of the militants. It was their demoralisation because of the total absence of any public support to them. This had completely shattered their self-image of being reincarnations of the 'Singhs' 'Babas' and 'Kharkoos' of the eighteenth century.

The agitation announced by the two factions of the Akalis did not amount even to lip sympathy. Each had announced its manner of protest lest the other faction should score a point. The P.S. Badal and G.S. Tohra factions had been criticising the S.S. Barnala government for having given a free hand to the police in dealing with militants. Now when the governor's administration had put them in a quandary, they had to demonstrate some support for the militants. The G.S. Tohra faction announced a march to the Temple and the P.S. Badal group restricted its agitation to block the Raj Bhavan in Chandigarh. In essence, like most of their agitations, it amounted to courting arrest peacefully to force the government to withdraw the force surrounding the Temple. This could not help the militants.

They must have realised their total isolation. Their associates in the field could not threaten people to take out a procession or to move a few trolley loads of men towards the Temple.

The precedent of the military operation in 1984, and because the current action had begun by a firing incident in the Temple, also created the impression in the public mind that it was another armed operation. The government chose to endorse the impression given by the press. An armed force fighting almost insurgent conditions when one of its respected officers such as DIG, Sarab Deep Singh Virk was hit, could only think in terms of a hot chase.

The imposition of curfew, which prevented the escape of the militants and reduced the chances of civil casualties, extended an assurance to the general public, including the forces that some serious armed action was in the offing. J.F. Ribeiro had told newsmen in Chandigarh the same evening i.e., 9 May 1988, that no decision had been taken regarding entering the Golden Temple which implied that the issue was still open. The cross firing on the 9th was quite fierce; four militants lost their lives and the Red Cross retrieved their dead bodies on the 11th. The CRPF had placed pickets all around the Temple for some time. After the imposition of the curfew, additional policemen moved into the empty narrow bazaars to ensure that the militants did not escape. The next morning, firing remained intermittent as if the militants were waiting for some kind of truce.

The government could not but take time to make up its mind. It had played the J.S. Rode card on 5 March 1988 even though J.S. Rode had failed to bring all the militant organisations under his umbrella. But the government wanted to know if he could persuade them in the changed situation. The delay in deciding the final action kept the option of entry into the Temple alive. Newspaper reports talked of an imminent showdown quoting 'some' officers. Even when it was clear that the militants were to be tired out, the impression persisted and it was believed that perhaps the NSG (National Security Guards) would be closing in, step by step. There was some element of truth in the fact that in the course of such an operation the possibility of entering the temple could also have arisen. In that case, clearance would have been sought from New Delhi. But the final strategy employed was to prevent them from replenishing their stores of food and water and to keep giving them a daily opportunity to come out of the Temple.

Doordarshan Delhi had its broadcasting van stationed outside the Kotwali. K.P.S. Gill held a press conference every evening. Besides me, Chaman Lal, and other police officers would be present at these meetings. K.P.S. Gill told the press on 13 May 1988 that the Bunga Ramgharian was to be neutralised. Both the towers of Bunga Ramgharian had been fortified by the militants so that they could fire from a height. But the boys were held back from using these powerful strategic points. Since the situation had developed suddenly, and because of the curfew, devotees no longer visited the Temple. Thus, the 'boys' lost the cover of mingling with the devotees to be able to carry guns and ammunition to the towers. Nor was there an opportunity for the militants to fire from these towers. Potentially, these towers were real trouble spots for us. Therefore, out of abundant caution, holes were made in the towers to expose the stairs going to the top in order to prevent the boys from occupying the tops where they had built fortifications. The NSG had long range precision firing rifles fitted with telescopes and image magnifiers. They could hit a particular brick, even in starlight, anywhere in the Temple complex. From advantageous positions around the Temple complex it was easy for the NSG to overcome the AK 47 carrying 'boys'. But as it was, the boys had stopped fighting after the first day and had retreated to the various *parikrama* rooms. They were obviously relying on the public to rise in their support. They could also have been hopeful of some kind of truce materialising as a result of J.S. Rode's influence. The entry by a group of 48 of them into the Harmandar on 15 May 1988 and their staying therein till the 18th clearly proves that they were waiting, though in vain, for either possibility to materialise.

The NSG had, however, convincingly demonstrated its fire power. One day, I had protested at its having been unnecessarily heavy and prolonged, without any return fire. There are some other factors and events that contributed to the impression that it was a gun battle. The headlines in the *Indian Express* of 13 May 1988 read as if the news was from a battle front 'Security forces neutralise 2 Temple towers (Bungas).' *The Tribune* headlines on the 14th were 'Manji Sahib and Langar building taken over.' There were no militants inside either building, nor did we move into them though the Langar building had been fired at. One suspicion was that the fortification on the Bungas indicated that Karaj Singh with his six associates was entrenched there.

Even after 146 militants had surrendered on 15 May 1988, the press reported that on the 17th 'Commandos stormed the *langar* building and basement of Bunga Ramgharian.' It also said that 'some weapons and ammunition' and letterhead pads were recovered. There was no point in stocking weapons in the Bunga because the police had searched this building many times; it was not part of the Golden Temple but of the larger complex. It was a private residence of the descendants of Jassa Singh, the head of the Ramgharian *Misl*, before the SGPC purchased it. After the operation had started, terrorists could neither reach it nor was there any logic in doing so. At the time of surrender on 15 and 18 May no one came out of this building. The only action taken there had consisted of making a hole in the third floor wall by the security forces to enable lobbing of a hand grenade into the basement of the Bunga. I think the NSG was excessively suspicious of this building, because of its fort-like appearance.

The Bunga is a five-storied building which was built in the eighteenth century to defend the Golden Temple from invaders. To surprise the enemy, three levels had been built underground, where a larger force could hide. Many Bungas built for a similar purpose by other *Misls* were demolished by the SGPC. This one survived because it did not obstruct the SGPC's plan to improve the Temple's surroundings.

Another fact that served to sustain the theory of a gun battle was, that during the firing on the first two or three days, a transformer and a store of oil caught fire. Clouds of black smoke billowed out. SSP Suresh Arora and I drove quite close to the Temple suggesting over a loud speaker that we could send in a fire fighting team. But there was no response from the holed-up adversaries. Due to damage to the transformer, the lights of the whole complex went off on the second or the third day of the Operation. To ensure that the militants did not replenish their stocks of water and rations under the cover of darkness, the NSG would illuminate the area with Very lights and open fire in case they noticed any movement. Sometimes they fired only to scare them. Those pressmen who heard or saw this believed that actual fighting was going on within the Temple premises.

The details of the weapons and ammunition left behind in the Temple by the surrendering militants and the ammunition they had used indicated that they did not have enough for a prolonged fight.

According to the First Information Report lodged with the Kotwali, the city police station, 56 weapons of all sorts, were taken into possession by the police after the surrender. These included 22 AK 47 rifles, eight sten guns, two machine guns. The rest were only some pistols and .12 bore guns. According to the same record, only 2,825 empty bullet shells were retrieved from the Temple. Of these, only 130 were of 9 mm bore and the remaining 2,695 shells were those of the dreaded AK 47s. The live ammunition recovered was 4,636 rounds. Out of which 1,950 rounds were for AK 47s. The police also took 16 rockets and one rocket launcher that had been left behind by the surrendering militants into custody.

The fiercest firing from inside the temple was after S.S. Virk's injury on 9 May, the day I had imposed the curfew. I think out of 2,825 rounds used, nearly 95 per cent must have been used on the first two days alone and the remaining consumption was on account of stray firing on the 10th and 11th. There was thus literally no fighting after the first day as they had no backup ammunition. They had exaggerated notions of their popularity with the masses and were very hopeful that people would rise up in their support as J.S. Rode had told me on 11 May 1988. Malkiat Singh Ajnala confirmed this impression of theirs after he surrendered on 18 May 1988. Apparently they had preserved their ammunition in the hope that J.S. Rode would be able to avert the fight.

14

The SGPC's Dilemma

The Golden Temple was fast regaining its pristine glory—and devotees began to visit in increasing numbers and with greater devotion. But, ironically, the Shiromani Committee was in a sticky situation. The entire blame for the entry of the terrorists into the Temple, the smuggling in of weapons, the issuance of threatening letters for extortion, the torturing of people in the *parikrama* rooms, the resultant killings and overall planning of terrorist operations, was laid on the heads of the SGPC members. Everyone, except the UAD, blamed the Committee.

Another heinous fact that emerged was the existence of a graveyard of which the SGPC employees could not claim to be entirely ignorant. The surrendered militants confessed to having buried dead bodies under the debris of the Akal Takht. J.S. Rode had also given me a hint about this. The digging of this huge mound, undertaken in my presence on 26 May 1988, yielded six dead bodies in various stages of decay. The number of dead bodies exhumed on subsequent days rose to an unbelievable 46. The teenager militant who had been brought to the site under police custody to point out the spot looked apathetic. I could not help asking him if he did not regret the sordid affair. His reply was reminiscent of the situation of the grave diggers in Hamlet.

'I did not kill them, I only buried them.' He said.

'And why did you bury these sealed polythene bags of common salt with them?' I wanted to know.

'I was told to put four or five kgs. of salt on each body in order to prevent the stink,' he replied. Actually, the deeper portions of the mound being already full, it had become necessary to bury the last victims in the upper layers of the rubble which was too small for 46 graves. If he had cut open the polythene the purpose would have been obvious. The whole thing was so nauseating under the mid-day May sun, with the mercury touching 43°C that my inability to instantly solve the riddle of the sealed salt bags around the buried dead bodies could be understood.

What we were witnessing was profoundly shocking. The SGPC was the caretaker and manager of the Temple. Their officials were on duty, day and night. Regarding the presence of the militants inside the Temple, the official stand of the Committee had been that, since the government's forces were guarding the entrances, the government wanted to defame the Sikhs and the SGPC, and so had planted the armed militants. In private they admitted that theirs was the most miserable plight because of the presence of the militants. The Committee did not publicly condemn the terrorists. Neither Darshan Singh nor J.S. Rode could issue a *hukamnama* to the militants urging them not to kill unarmed innocent people. The Committee was expected to but did not seriously endeavour to try and clean the Temple of the militants. It stuck to its stand that the government had planted the armed militants. Even, after Operation Black Thunder, Baba Uttam Singh, who had undertaken the cleaning of the *parikrama* on 21 May 1988, withdrew the very next day without giving any reasons. Obviously he had been threatened.

The Home Minister was already very angry with their functioning and the Committee started receiving adverse comments from other quarters as well. Satya Pal Dang, the veteran Communist leader, wrote in *The Tribune* dated 25 May 1988, that if the SGPC were to be trusted, the Golden Temple may again become the hideout of the extremists. 'That is why some would like the SGPC to be dissolved and a Board set up to manage the affairs of the Golden Temple. This however is a sensitive matter. It should be solved through a national consensus.'

According to the PTI and UNI reports in *The Tribune* of 24 May 1988, the Home Minister and the Minister of State for Home had already held a meeting with the opposition parties in this regard. The opposition was in agreement with the proposal that if the SGPC was not able or willing to shoulder its responsibility and promise co-operation with the government, it would be expedient to make alternative arrangements. Quoting from the same source *The Tribune* also reported that Lt. Gen. J.S. Arora, hero of the Bangladesh War, also expressed similar views in the Rajya Sabha. Doordarshan Delhi, while making a film on the Golden Temple in the context of Operation Black Thunder, asked me to explain some aspects of what had happened. Towards the end of the interview, recorded during a round of the *parikrama*, I was asked whether the SGPC Act should be rescinded. As far as I remember, I had said, 'This Act has stood the test of time; it should be sustained. However, it should be amended to foist responsibility on the SGPC to keep the Temple free of the criminals, or report about their presence in the Temple to the government.'

I was of course happy to see myself in that documentary which was telecast twice by Doordarshan, but I was apprehensive that the government might throw away the tremendous goodwill earned through the success of Operation Black Thunder by dissolving the Shiromani Committee. I did not like their duplicity and their rigid views; or the trite explanations that some of them put forward. During these critical days they backed out from an important agreement. But there was nothing wrong with the institution itself. We could have identified the officials responsible for letting the militants enter the Temple and even prosecuted them. But substituting it by a nominated Board would not only be a retrograde step but also a highly impractical and risky one. Besides hurting Sikh sentiments, it would have been difficult for the Board to get the co-operation of the officials of the SGPC.

My impression about the SGPC's middle and lower cadres is that they lie somewhere in between the ordinary *granthis* and the lower levels of government bureaucracy, lately spoiled to some degree by their recent contact with the militants. But they are soft-spoken and essentially good. I was in a quandary because I could not volunteer my feelings merely on the basis of the press reports. I must confess that I was concerned and was awaiting for an opportunity to put my views before the government.

The SGPC had announced a meeting to be held on 30 May 1988. The Executive was likely to take up the criticism and blame that was being placed solely on it. It was likely that action would be initiated against the high priests and the Damdami Taksal which had wrested the *kar-sewa* of the Akal Takht from them and, consequently, provided the requisite cover to the militants to re-enter the Temple. The Committee, in order to extenuate itself of its responsibility, was claiming that even the government protégé, J.S. Rode, had failed to rid the Temple of militancy with all its attendant ills.

I did not realise that the opportunity, which I was awaiting for, had come when I met one of the seniormost bureaucrats in the country. The Home Secretary, C.G. Somiah, accompanied by his charming wife landed in Amritsar on the morning of 28 May 1988 to pay their obeisance at the Darbar Sahib and to assess the progress of the restoration of the *Maryada*. On the road from the airport to the city a file of milk vendors on their cycles, carrying two to six pear-shaped brass vessels each, was on either side of us. Mrs. Somiah was fascinated by the golden hue radiating from the *valtohees* (local name of the vessel) in the early morning sun. When I informed her that economic pressures are affecting the Punjabi's love of milk and that some vendors had begun to use tin containers to carry milk, she was very concerned. 'Deputy Commissioners are known for undertaking all sorts of jobs. You must do something to ensure that the *valtohees* are protected. These are unique flower vases for milk,' she said. I was genuinely touched by her cultural and aesthetic concerns.

In the Golden Temple, newsmen surrounded the Home Secretary. He told them that the nerve-centre of militancy was in Pakistan and not in the Golden Temple. I quipped, 'But the Golden Temple has been their news centre for long; a dozen of them were inside the Temple to elicit hot news when I imposed the curfew and they were stranded. They did not write about their escape.'

The Home Secretary asked me, 'Are you aware you are going to Delhi with me?'

'The pilot did tell me about this, Sir.' I had not asked the pilot the purpose for which I had been summoned to the capital. The Home Secretary also did not say anything about it. He told me I should arrange for a night's stay.

In Delhi, M.K. Narayanan, DIB, also joined us. When the car stopped at the gate of the Prime Minister's residence, only then did I realise my destination. I thought the Governor must have wanted me to be available in the ante-chamber. I had missed meeting the Prime Minister in the regular PM–DM conference (PM Rajiv Gandhi had undertaken to meet the DCs/DMs in small groups to prioritise development schemes and implement them faster) at Jaipur on 30 April 1988. The Prime Minister had delivered his keynote address in the morning. After that we were to deliberate on the problem allotted to each group of 15 or so and then discuss our reports with the PM on the fourth day. That evening Governor S.S. Ray and P. Chidambaram flew to Amritsar to meet the victims of a bomb blast in Batala. The victims had been shifted to Amritsar hospital. The relatives of the victims demonstrated before them and *gheraoed* the dignitaries. P. Chidambaram, who had seen me sitting in the conference at Jaipur, remarked, 'What is Sarab Jit doing there? Call him.' I left Jaipur the same night. The plane could not land at Amritsar due to extreme haze, and we were flown to Srinagar where we had to wait for 24 hours. A more meaningful meeting had come my way.

We were ushered into a small conference room at the residence of the PM. The Home Minister, the State Minister for Home, the Punjab Governor, J.F. Ribeiro, the Chief Secretary R.P. Ojha, K.P.S. Gill, Mrs. Sarla Grewal, (a Punjab cadre officer who was Principal Secretary to the PM) and the Secretary, Information and Broadcasting were already present. After a few minutes, the PM walked in. Being a new face he could easily spot me. He was kind to enquire about my well-being and also about the welfare of Amritsar.

In the ensuing discussion, I realised that a consensus to dissolve the SGPC seemed to have already evolved. After discussing the situation for some time the decision seemed to have been confirmed as the names of the five persons who were to be on the Board were finalised. I was also shown the list of the names. At the end of the discussions the PM asked me, 'What have you to say about this, Sarab Jit?'

I had the feeling that in these circumstances, I did not have the option to question the decision. I reflected on the five-year-long historic struggle (1920–25) and of the great sacrifices made for the liberation of the gurudwaras from the Mahants appointed by the British government. I thought of its success in securing their management by a democratically elected Committee which was designated as the Sikh Gurudwara Prabandhak Committee. I could imagine that, in the eyes of the Sikh masses, the proposed Board would be equated with the Mahants. I could also extenuate the SGPC's failure to control militancy by pointing out that the militants had been tormenting it since the *Sarbat Khalsa* of 1986 and, within a year, had killed three of its prominent officials—Giani Pratap Singh, Abnashi Singh and Dr. B.S. Brar—to overcome its resistance. But all these issues were debatable. I therefore, decided to highlight the illegality of the proposal and the inherent infirmity in the possibility of its implementation.

'I have two submissions to make, Sir. One is that the SGPC Act, 1925 will have to be amended, because under the provisions of the existing Act if we dissolve the present house and the executive, the previous one shall stand automatically revived.' There was no reaction. I had no official information about The Religious Institutions (Prevention and Misuse) Ordinance, which was being promulgated, nor could I read the detailed provisions from the newspapers. I therefore, discreetly did not mention all that.

'The second submission, Sir, is that before we announce the names of the members of the proposed Board, we must first sound them.' Again there was no reaction. The PM started looking at the papers before him. After about 15 seconds he looked up.

'You mean Sarab Jit that some one may not accept?'

'As far as my understanding goes, Sir, this may be the rule.' I submitted.

I must mention here that I had no previous experience of participating in meetings at this high level. I had no prior notice of the subject to be discussed. In my routine working, I did not have the occasion to consult the SGPC Act. I had browsed through it while addressing a letter to the Committee on 10 May 1988. The provision I mentioned had remained with me. But I had not made any effort to grasp its intention, nor had I tried to look up the relevant rules. Therefore, I was not 100 per cent sure about the first point that I had made. But I was absolutely sure in my mind that no eminent Sikh would ever come forward to be on the Board in place of the SGPC. The government could not afford to put men of lesser eminence in the manner that they had entrusted the *kar-sewa* of constructing the Akal Takht to Baba Santa Singh. I had a feeling that I had achieved my purpose and, perhaps, spared the government an embarrassment.

The other points on the agenda did not concern me. As I was coming out, I had to pass by the PM. He stopped me and complimented me quite profusely for the initiative I had taken for Operation Black Thunder and the forbearance I had shown during its execution. 'Keep your cool and continue doing the good work.' He said. This was good assurance for me. I came into a small ante-room. Buta Singh also turned up there and, surprisingly, he too congratulated me for everything I had done. I had expected a pat on the back from him much earlier when I had gone up to the plane to receive him. He explained 'I could not say it earlier because of the hurry.' I was not certain what more I had achieved in between. Nor could I make out whether the belated pat was for my not directly opposing the sack of the SGPC. But I was sure that many Sikhs, to please the Minister, would have approved of the idea; to replace the 'incompetent' SGPC with a Board of administrators. Yet I can easily venture to say that the same Sikhs would not be willing to accept nomination to the proposed Board.

After a few days, there were statements from the Home Minister and the Governor to the effect that the SGPC Act was not being amended or replaced. I do not know exactly what made the situation change. But I choose to believe that it was my intervention that helped save the institution of the SGPC and also prevented the government from undoing all the good work it had done in the shape of Operation Black Thunder. Even an extremely eminent Board would have failed to deliver the goods for lack of public approval and non co-operation from the majority of SGPC employees. On the other hand, this would have provided an opportunity to J.S. Rode's militant followers to get employment in the SGPC. I had already sealed the gold lying in the Temple which prevented members of the Damdami Taksal to resume the construction and gold plating of the Akal Takht. I could not visualise any benefit to the government by weakening the SGPC in the prevailing situation of terrorism, particularly after Operation Black Thunder. The eagerness of the SGPC to dismiss J.S. Rode from the post of the *Jathedar* of the Akal Takht, as we shall have occasion to see later, supported my line of reasoning.

15

Jasbir Singh Rode's Dismissal

When the militants were holed up in the Golden Temple, the SGPC had conveniently conceded supremacy to them. J.S. Rode, who had initially been named *Jathedar* of the Akal Takht in a spurious *Sarbat Khalsa* in 1986, and the SGPC under force of circumstances had appointed him in March 1988, put forward an excuse (of inadequate accommodation) to justify the shift to the Nanak Niwas which, in reality, was out of fear of the armed terrorists in the Temple. The Central and State governments did not see a way out of the embarrassing but sensitive issue. When the Golden Temple was finally free from the nuisance of the armed militants, every one had ideas about how to manage the affairs of the temple.

The Central government and J.S. Rode believed that they had an opportunity to play a tune to which all the militant groups would flock. The number of killings during May had become relatively higher, indicating the capability of the militants in the field to strike without the help of their masters in the Temple. The government wanted J.S. Rode to continue as the *Jathedar* of the Akal Takht. The SGPC which had appointed him, had also expected him to somehow rein in the militants. He was no longer needed in the changed situation. The SGPC was obviously not concerned with the militancy raging outside the Temple. Therefore, it wanted to dismiss J.S. Rode within two months of his appointment. The Home Secretary had told newsmen in Delhi, in the context of the dissolution of the Committee that the government would watch the decision of the forthcoming meeting of the Executive Committee (*The Tribune*, 29 May 1988). The Committee bemoaned the fact that the government, instead of fighting the militants, was targeting the SGPC and was supporting the Panthic Committee and the priests who not only supported the militant organisations but had earlier also taunted the SGPC for not joining forces with them. Some priests had even sarcastically suggested that the SGPC functionaries should wear bangles and *salwar kameez* (female attire).

I returned to Amritsar on 29 May 1988 and got in touch with the SGPC. Two members of its Executive met me and promised to see K.P.S. Gill and me before their own scheduled meeting the next day. K.P.S. Gill had also been assured by an Inspector General of Police, who claimed a strong personal influence with the Secretary of the SGPC, that the Committee would meet us the next day before the meeting of its Executive Committee scheduled for 30 May 1988.

The Committee, as I have already said, had let me down on two earlier occasions. Therefore, I deputed a magistrate to reach the venue of their meeting before it began so that he could remind them about their commitment to me. He telephoned to say that the Committee had already commenced their deliberations, half an hour prior to the scheduled time. I felt that this was outright betrayal, as I had earlier assured the Committee that they would be free to take any decisions after we had explained our point of view to them. In a bit of a temper, I dashed to the venue via K.P.S. Gills' camp-office. Suresh Arora, the SSP, joined me. Since he was in his uniform he stayed in an adjoining room. I went into the room where they were meeting. 'We were coming to you after the meeting, DC Sahib,' the secretary made an excuse. 'You had promised to meet us before coming to this meeting. Like gentlemen, now get up and come with me,' I opened the door and pointed the way. Surprisingly, they complied. As we were coming down the ramp from the third storey of Guru Ramdas Hospital, Mal Singh Ghuman, a decent and very upright General Secretary apprehensively asked me, 'Are we under arrest?'

'Not at all. We would have arrested you last night if we wanted to. We do not want to influence any of your decisions,' I told them.

'Why did you try to trick us like that'? I later asked him.

'If J.S. Rode is released from jail it would be difficult for us to dismiss him,' he confessed.

'Why can't you appoint a Committee like the government does, to look into the role of J.S. Rode in defiling the Temple, and use its findings when necessary?' I asked.

'The government can release him any time,' he expressed his fears. To allay his apprehensions, I said, 'If you read the newspapers carefully, you can easily preempt such a move.'

A police official ran up the ramp and advised me to stay there, because a few boys with guns were seen roaming around. The Guru Ramdas Hospital building is a huge one where it is easy for anyone to come and do any mischief. Since it was widely known that the Committee was likely to dismiss J.S. Rode and other *Jathedars* it was quite possible for J.S. Rode's supporters to come with arms to threaten or actually shoot down some members of the SGPC. This thought had occurred to me earlier also but I had dismissed it because at that time the militants could not have gone to the Temple complex where the Committee normally held its meetings.

While I waited on the ramp for the police to clear the way it occurred to me that, had I been five minutes late in barging into the Committee meeting, I would have faced the militants in action in the meeting room. It would have been a chilling situation. It was only a flight of my imagination at that time. But on 25 July 1988, some militants did attack and kill Bhan Singh, the Secretary, Sohan Singh, the Head Priest of the Harmandar Sahib, and seriously injured Mal Singh Ghuman, the General Secretary. All of them on that occasion, had gone for some other meeting in connection with the SGPC's Engineering College in Ludhiana. But God has His own ways! Many a time we are not aware of the dangers we may have escaped. As a tribute to Bhan Singh, I must record that after he was badly wounded he did not panic or cry for help but kept repeating 'Wahe Guru, Wahe Guru…' till he breathed his last on the way to the hospital. Sohan Singh had died instantly. M.S. Ghuman had been seriously wounded. He feigned to be dead. In this way, he survived and told me the story.

Soon the police officer came back to tell us that the 'boys' had slipped away. The danger to us was over. The SGPC members boarded their van and followed us to K.P.S. Gill's camp office.

K.P.S. Gill gave them a bit of his mind. The essence of the discussion was similar to that which had transpired between M.S. Ghuman and me while coming down the ramp. At one stage K.P.S. Gill made a gesture as if he was going to hit *Jathedar* Shiv Singh Khushipur with his reading glasses. Later S.S. Khushipur protested to me, 'In the district, the District Magistrate is higher than the highest police officer, why didn't you stop him?' 'I know Gill. He does not hit anyone with spectacles,' I said with a smile. S.S. Khushipur too had a sense of humour. He understood the point and laughed. 'If he uses his proper weapon, how will you label an old Jat as an extremist?' he laughed again. 'We will have your beard dyed jet black,' I joked. 'Why can't you do that when I am alive.' S.S. Khushipur laughed with a glint in his eyes. 'If you go back on your word with a white beard, how can we trust you with a black one?' I continued the banter. 'If I were one of the two who had promised to come, I would certainly have come, whatever the consequences,' the old man said, thumping his chest.

They conceded that they had not 'passed' any of their items on the agenda. A statement to that effect was made to the TV team and a written press note was issued from the Canal Rest House. Since, according to their own statement, the Committee had not decided any of the items on their agenda that day, there was no question of our coercing them. But such an inference was nonetheless drawn by some people. One of them managed to whisper to a Public Relations Official of theirs that in case they did not return by one o'clock he should issue a press note saying that J.S. Rode and the high priests had been dismissed. The employee did it quite dutifully, and it made the headlines in all the newspapers the next day. In the evening I met the press and told them the facts as narrated by the members of the Executive. The members of the Executive, however, did not reiterate that the priests had been sacked.

It was on 4 June 1988 that they handed over photocopies of their resolution claiming to have passed it on 30 May. Obviously they had forged this resolution. They could easily have passed such a resolution on 4 June itself. The confusion was created by the nimbleness of the Committee members. If they had passed the resolution on the 30th, as claimed, they could have shown the copies to the press on the 31st if not on the 30th itself. The members of the Executive could have done this themselves. There was no need to wait for six days. The Executive of the Shiromani Committee could take any decision it wished, and this new decision may have been the right one. But this speciousness did no credit to its status and reputation. On the other hand, J.S. Rode also managed to deliver a press note from Amritsar jail blaming the SGPC for having connived with the government and yielding to it by accepting all the points raised in the DC's letter of 10 May. He, however, threatened that he would call a *Sarbat Khalsa*. He still believed in his popularity, or perhaps he had no alternative, or maybe the government still believed in the efficacy of its J.S. Rode card.

Apparently, the SGPC was under pressure from the UAD to announce the sacking of J.S. Rode and the priests. As I have mentioned earlier, in the appointment of J.S. Rode as the *Jathedar* of the Akal Takht, the SGPC had taken a decision which had been astutely forced on it. The government's experiment of ending militancy through J.S. Rode had failed miserably. Even if the government's assessment was otherwise, it would have been dangerous to let him return to the Temple. If some militants were prepared to listen to him, it was in his personal capacity and because of his Taksal connections, and not necessarily as the *Jathedar* of the Akal Takht. And if such a status was at all necessary, the SGPC could have been given an assurance that the Committee would not be replaced by a Board, or by the Damdami Taksal.

The SGPC feared the militant part of J.S. Rode's entourage more than the fact of his holding the office of the *Jathedar*. Therefore it was keen on dismissing J.S. Rode before he was released. Second, it could pre-empt its own contemplated dismissal. In view of the predicament, that of the government as well as of the Akali–SGPC combine, I think the latter's act was justified. The fact that on 30 May 1988 armed militants were hovering around the venue of the meeting (and the fact that they had succeeded in killing two of the members later in July) proves that SGPC's fears were not unfounded.

But that was not the end of J.S. Rode. He had announced that a *Sarbat Khalsa* would be held on the Diwali day. He was trying to hold on to his post in whatever way he could. But Governor S.S. Ray did not seem to be concerned with the dismissal of the priests. He told pressmen on 1 June that the dismissal of the priests did not matter so long as 'the spiritual and religious work in the Temple is going on smoothly.' He noted the factionalism in the SGPC but hoped that it would abide by its recent resolutions to keep the Temple free of militants. The SGPC had decided to have its own force and co-operate with the government if the militants tried to return to the Temple.

The Governor that day also announced that the implementation of the corridor plan would commence on 7 June 1988. This plan was yet an extremely sensitive issue. It envisaged the demolition of all construction—residential and commercial—within 30 m around the Temple. Internally, the SGPC welcomed the Corridor Plan; the 100 foot wide clean and beautiful corridor around the Temple would be an effective check against the militants sneaking into it. In course of time, the corridor was to become an aesthetic part of the periphery of the Temple. The SGPC was to get sizeable compensation for its completely unproductive properties falling in this belt which they could not otherwise sell, according to the rules. Considering their financial position, at that time, it was an unexpected bonus. Yet their public posture was different. There were news reports that the SGPC would approach the High Court. It did not pursue the issue seriously. Nor did it have the courage to welcome it. Meanwhile, the Governor had designated a firm date to begin the demolition.

16

The Corridor Plan

With every passing day, the *Maryada* was regaining its full glory. More and more staff returned to duty in the Golden Temple. We could, thus, divert attention to other aspects which had a bearing on the future security of the Temple. The bazaars around the temple were narrow but their business was very brisk. Anything could be thrown over the wall of the Temple or smuggled into it through the various openings in the walls. At the beginning of the year, when crime was getting out of control, Izhar Alam, the SSP of Amritsar, had suggested to J.F. Ribeiro that having a small corridor around the Temple wall would be very useful to check the entry of weapons into the holy precincts. Howsoever pertinent the suggestion, it would not have been possible to implement it in that climate. Now, with the goodwill of the people behind us, after Operation Black Thunder, this plan seemed a possibility.

The SGPC also had a plan to make an arcade all along the outer wall if it could persuade the numerous private owners to part with their properties which were causing an obstruction. Most of the residents were fed up with the recurrence of tense situations, firing and at times the appearance of dead bodies. The Prime Minister magnanimously promised liberal funding for an underground market around the complex. I, therefore, reported in a meeting called by Governor S.S. Ray that it would be possible to acquire the private properties, provided we pay generous compensation. Four thousand rupees per square yard was suggested by I.S. Bindra, Secretary Local Government, and this was accepted by Governor S.S. Ray. The government also decided to recognise the tenancy rights of the occupants, and allot them with accommodation under the new scheme. I arranged alternative sites for the owners and the tenants as well.

The stupendous and sensitive task appeared to run along much smoother lines than I had anticipated. The work of acquisition on behalf of the Amritsar Municipal Corporation was proceeding smoothly while a high powered committee of secretaries to the government monitored the progress. The Government also appointed Indian National Trust for Art and Cultural Heritage (INTACH) to act as consultants for the beautification of the corridor.

Mulk Raj Anand, the famous novelist and an octogenarian thinker who hailed from these very bazaars, also took a keen interest in the beautification of this area. He shared his views with me and, later, met the Prime Minister to suggest that some European architects be selected in the project. He had a deep respect for the Golden Temple and an abiding attachment with the haveli of his ancestors. Such sublime devotion of an intellectual to his place of birth was a tremendous encouragement to me. I did not anticipate any problem in implementing the corridor plan. In my rising optimism, I did not take into account the perversity of some bureaucrats on the staff of the Corporation, and of some petty intriguing politicians.

On occasion, there were copious tears in many an eye, particularly when the residents had to be uprooted. I cannot forget a scene in Gali Baghwali, a lane immediately behind Guru Ramdas Sarai. I had told the Corporation authorities to begin the demolition from that street. The government had declared 7 June 1988, as the deadline to begin the demolition work. All concerned the bodies reported that it would be possible to start pulling down the vacant structures by that day. I went to oversee the onset of 'Operation Vacation.'

An old doctor stood outside his house near the trolley which he had hired to move his belongings. He stood mute and shocked. An unending stream of tears was falling into his beard. The Corporation official stood near him, thrusting a formal release before him to obtain his signature acknowledging that he had handed over possession of the vacant premises to the Corporation. Sobbing like a child and with a great effort, he said that he was crying because he had not been able to arrange any alternative accommodation. I looked at the Corporation official, 'But, Sir, he has taken the full payment and promised to go today.' The Corporation official was technically correct. But here was a classic example of a communication gap in bureaucratic functioning.

There were a large number of State Housing Board flats available for allotment. I knew about them because I had had them vacated from the CRPF who had occupied them. The Board was eager to dispose of these flats. I had, accordingly, apprised the Corporation of this, but they had neither informed the people to be displaced about the availability of these flats, nor did they seem to be aware of the importance of this humanitarian aspect of the exercise. I told the people to stay put in their houses till they heard from me. Within an hour I sent for the persons being displaced and showed them the flats in the presence of the Board and the Corporation officials. Their sense of desolation disappeared at the sight of their new and modern habitat. Their happy relaxed faces and energetic steps gave us the impression that they must have wished for such pleasant environment while living in the congested streets around the Temple. Within minutes, the Board had done good business and the Corporation had discharged its moral obligation.

I did not see any further problem and told the press that the demolition of the acquired properties would commence on 7 June 1988. The Commissioner of the Corporation and the Chairman of the Improvement Trust also sounded confident. They had made all the arrangements, saw no problems and promised to keep me informed of the progress. As I did not hear anything from the site of the operation till noon, I sensed that there might be some problem and left for the spot. On the way I learnt that some people had organised a huge demonstration and the demolition work could not begin. The senior officers of the Corporation and the Improvement Trust had already left the site. As I approached the crowd, a senior Congress office bearer met me and brashly advised me not to go near the crowd as I might be lynched. Pushing him aside I managed to climb on the bumper of the van of the State Public Relations Department, which also had been surrounded by the crowd. S.K. Sinha, Director Public Relations, alone was present at the site and he helped me by thrusting a mike in my hands.

I could immediately make out that till then it was mostly a stage-managed demonstration. But a slight mishandling on my part, however, could have become a cause for genuine grievances. I started with first allaying their fears of the government bulldozing the project against their will. By way of proof regarding the government's intentions, I said, 'I have already dispatched the bulldozers and the mounted police from here. If you did not earlier notice them withdrawing from here you can have a look around you and ascertain for yourself.' Actually, the bulldozers were not required on the first day as the demolition was to begin from the roof on the second floors.

The gathering was in a small square where mounted police could not function. Nor, indeed, was it required. The excessive precautions taken by the officers gave palpable cause for concern to the agitators; and the withdrawal of bulldozers, etc., provided me with incontrovertible proof in support of my statement that the project was for their good and if they did not want to leave, no one would force them to give up their houses. This satisfied the affected persons, and it stole the cause of violent action from the hired agitators. Soon the crowd stopped responding to the slogans of the hired lot. The clamour died. The bulk of black flags and lathis were lowered.

I noticed one man moving about and prompting the younger, hired lot. As someone called him by name I felt it sounded familiar. He was the doctor who had been stranded in the temple in May when I had imposed the curfew before Operation Black Thunder began. His wife had been phoning me frantically to help her husband come out from the temple. I bent 90 degrees from my perch to whisper to him as he happened to pass by the van, 'I still have to square up with you for your deed of 9th May and you are giving me another cause.' This scared him to the marrow of his bones and he simply vanished from the scene. The militants in the Temple had been utilising his services.

His ally, the Congressman, who had earlier rudely cautioned me, stood helpless in the midst of the pacified crowd. I specifically asked five odd agitators who were still holding on to their flags and lathis to articulate their grievances. In case they had none, I told them that I expected them to lower their flags and lathis like the rest. They tamely complied. But someone from the crowd raised a point and I saw its validity at once. It was voiced that on the ground floors of some houses there were business establishments. The demolition work would throw much dust and create much noise to scare away customers, bringing their business to a standstill. I promised to keep this valid point in mind when we took up the demolition work.

I had noticed immediately after my arrival that an *Akhand path* had also commenced at the end of the street towards the square. Using religion is an effective means for defying the authorities. It is another matter that even secular political parties do not hesitate to use the card of religion to gain an advantage, including the buying of votes. The same method had been adopted here to stall the demolition work. One *Akhand path*—reading the whole Guru Granth Sahib without break—takes a little more than 48 hours, and a chain of *Akhand paths* can go on endlessly. In the morcha at Jaito in 1923, the Akalis continued 101 *Akhand paths* because one *Akhand path* had been disrupted by the then British-supported Nabha State administration. Such activity can make it difficult for the administration to implement its programmes. I, therefore, felt it was time to throw the ball in the court of the agitators.

I said, 'Don't you think, you have insulted the Guru Granth Sahib by starting an *Akhand path* in the street near the filthy drains?' I offered to carry the holy book on my head to a cleaner place, and a kind of bargaining started on this. They had a plan to conduct a chain of *Akhand paths* to stop the demolition work. I agreed to the continuance of this *Akhand path*, because they promised not to go in for a second one. By then, all flags and lathis had come down. The press published both the photographs, the peak of the agitation showing lathis with black flags all over; also the moment of peace when the lathis and flags had been brought down.

I had the option of beginning the demolition of some old buildings which were partly damaged in Operation Blue Star and had already been acquired by the government. They were not required by us and had been standing only for lack of a decision. But showing a fake demolition on the TV would have been a mere eyewash. We postponed the demolition by about a week. If I had insisted on maintaining the sanctity of the date given by the government, I felt that I would have had a full-fledged agitation on my hands. And this could have delayed the demolition for a very long period or, it may even have resulted in the abrogation of the scheme altogether. In the evening, J.F. Ribeiro came to Amritsar. He approved of the way I had handled the agitation. He also assured the people in a TV interview that in constructing the corridor the government had no interest other than the security of the people and maintaining the sanctity of the Temple and that the demolitions would be done with the consent of the people. I told J.F. Ribeiro that, as desired by the government,

I would remain involved with the demolition work and with INTACH for the designing and beautification of the corridor, but it would not be possible for me to pay attention to the allotment of alternative sites to the displaced persons.

The very next day we embarked on the work of allotment of alternative sites for business establishments. This gave an incredible boost to the prices of real estate. The demolition work was taken up within a week. The government wanted that the public men of the city to be involved in the rehabilitation work. But because of the divergent political affiliations of the oustees and the public men this idea did not work. The task of rehabilitation was entrusted to a senior IAS officer, J.S. Kesar. I was to be involved with him in disputed cases only.

The rehabilitation work, however, turned to be like a lottery. We left it to the traders to choose the location for each of the trades. Some flourished immediately, others took a long time to come up. Now, by and large, every one is happy. Only the corridor could not come up the way the then Prime Minister Rajiv Gandhi and Governor S.S. Ray had wanted. INTACH submitted a beautiful scheme providing for lawns, springs and walls for depicting the lives and teachings of the Sikh gurus. Dr. Ram of the INTACH wanted the government to acquire another seven acres of land for his plan. Governor S.S. Ray wanted them to implement their project in the 14 odd acres already acquired, as he felt that it might not be possible to dislodge business and dwellings from even another half acre. This little controversy could not be resolved as the parliamentary election of November 1989 had engaged the government's attention.

17

Jasbir Singh Rode Resurrected

The terrorists, in the meanwhile, kept up their killings during the month of May and June 1988 despite the setback caused by Operation Black Thunder. In July 1988, however, reportedly due to internal dissensions, the crime rate declined. In 13 incidents, 104 people were killed, including 14 militants. The killing of Sukha Sipahi, also known as General Labh Singh, in Amritsar on 12 July 1988 was a great morale booster for the security forces. The administration, however, received a setback in the killing of Bhan Singh, Sohan Singh and the injury to Mal Singh Ghuman. The terrorists by now were a discredited lot, for having desecrated the Harmandar and then meekly surrendering to the security forces.

It was a moment when the government should have consolidated its gains by winning over the people and showing an olive branch to both the SGPC and the Akali Dals, prior to making a bid for the final blow. It did make some gestures; the release of 132 Jodhpur detainees, increasing employment opportunities for the youth, and the PM's visit to Punjab, during which he announced allocation of some industries and the sending of 42 more companies of paramilitary forces to the state.

But all this was undone many times over by the government's attempt to induct Jasbir Singh Rode again. What is more, it was done in quite a brazen manner. J.S. Rode was released under TADA in August 1988 but arrested under Section 107/151 (Breach of Peace) on the same day. The SGPC announced the appointment of Darshan Singh Ragi as *Jathedar* of the Akal Takht on 14 August 1988. The government released J.S. Rode along with other priests on 15 August 1988. He visited the Harmandar Sahib the same day. He told pressmen that he would announce his programme after seeking the blessings of Baba Thakar Singh at Chowk Mehta.

J.S. Rode maintained that he had been appointed *Jathedar* of the Akal Takht by the *Sarbat Khalsa* of 1986, but that he did not try to occupy the office. The other priests who had been released along with him, however, forcibly occupied their respective offices at Anandpur Sahib and Talwandi Sabo; the head priest of the Harmandar Sahib sitting in attendance before the Guru Granth Sahib was also forcibly moved. Later, J.S. Rode and his other friends fearing the Panthic Panel as well as opposition by the SGPC, moved into the gurudwara at Talwandi Sabo. He continued staying there forcibly despite the objections raised by the Shiromani Committee. He announced that he would hold a *Sarbat Khalsa* in the Harmandar Sahib on the forthcoming Diwali in October 1988.

To demonstrate his popularity, and perhaps to test it as well and as a curtain raiser to the *Sarbat Khalsa*, J.S. Rode announced that he would march from Talwandi Sabo to the Golden Temple in September to free the Temple from the security forces. He had to postpone the venture to the first week of October due to unprecedented floods in the state. But for his exaggerated notions about his mass following, the 'march' through 250 kms of Malwa and Tarn Taran area of Majha, including the historical gurudwara of Chola Sahib, Khadur Sahib and Tarn Taran Sahib, would have been an ingenious plan to gather a big crowd in his support.

I was of the firm view that he would not attract any sizeable gathering anywhere. But I also apprehended that he may have something up his sleeve; he might stay back in the Temple with his armed supporters or just leave some of his armed men behind in an attempt to recreate the pre-Black Thunder situation. This also signified the possible return of the Damdami Taksal which could takeover the disrupted *kar-sewa* of the Akal Takht by show of force. This could have had many and varied repercussions to the certain embarrassment of the SGPC.

Governor S.S. Ray rang me up to enquire about the latest news of the relief work for the flood victims. For the first time I bypassed the hierarchy, and brought to his notice the trouble that J.S. Rode could pose for us. I also suggested that he could be arrested in any of the districts before entering Amritsar. After a few days, the Secretary to the Governor informed me that my suggestions had been approved in principle. On 7 October 1988, he told me again that orders had been issued for his arrest before entering Amritsar. Accordingly, I told Chaman Lal, and he in turn, informed the SSP of Tarn Taran.

On 8 October 1988 as I was returning from Ajnala after supervising relief work, I learnt on the wireless that J.S. Rode had blocked the traffic on the Amritsar–Ferozepur highway. By 8.30 P.M. the IG and I left for the site. I drove across the confluence of the Beas and Sutlej rivers that separates the two districts. J.S. Rode, with a caravan of about a 100 odd people, was squatting on the road reciting *shabads*. It was quite dark. I sat near him urging him to let the traffic move, 'keeping in view the fact that people were already badly affected by the floods and that we were adding to their miseries.' The location was in the jurisdiction of Ferozepur District. The SDM told me that he did not have any instructions to arrest J.S. Rode and his entourage. There was an impasse.

After deputing some officers to provide at least some water and milk to the bus passengers, we returned to Amritsar. I spoke to K.P.S. Gill on the phone. He asked me how they could stop J.S. Rode from visiting the Golden Temple, 'On what grounds?' he asked. I said, 'Because he and his companions are carrying arms'. If that is your objection, you can disarm him outside Amritsar. K.P.S. Gill told me. I returned to the site. This time DIG S.K. Varma joined me. Because of the delay, J.S. Rode now wanted to proceed to Khadur Sahib instead of Chola Sahib. I readily agreed to the change because it would be easier to handle him there.

The next day Sanjiv Gupta the SSP of Tarn Taran, blocked the road outside the *sarai* where J.S. Rode and his men were staying. Two trucks were parked by him on either side of the *sarai*. All of us, waited in a school building opposite the *sarai*. Around 4.00 P.M., the IG suggested that I would have to take some initiative and talk to them. J.S. Rode could not create any nuisance there such as blocking the traffic. No one came to see him either. I went into the *sarai* and met him in his room where the other *Jathedars* were also present. After pleasantries, he asked if they were under detention. 'Not as yet, but there could be some trouble if you move on with weapons,' I said. He raised the question of his security and also disputed the fact that his carrying of arms could create a law and order problem. After about 20 minutes, on my assurance about his security, he came around. Visibly angry, he said in English, 'Alright...!' The SP Tarn Taran, A.S. Chhetra, had followed me. He was very useful and began making necessary arrangements. During our discussions J.S. Rode suggested that I could takeover their weapons before they entered Amritsar city. I looked at SP A.S. Chhetra. He seemed to have reservations and he was right. 'It won't be possible for the police to take possession of the weapons on the roadside,' I told him firmly. The SP was ready to prepare the list of the arms and ammunition being carried.

J.S. Rode asked if a separate list could be prepared for each priest. I agreed. He again asked, 'Could my weapons be delivered to some of my representatives?' 'Are you intending to stay back in the Golden Temple?' Since I already had such a suspicion, the question came out spontaneously. He had betrayed his intentions through that query. He was nonplussed but he came up with a belated explanation that he wanted to return by a route different from that of his companions. After surrendering their weapons, the entourage left for Tarn Taran shouting slogans of victory.

I did not need any further proof in support of my apprehension that J.S. Rode intended to stay back in the Temple. Therefore, when I rang up the Governor who was in Delhi, to explain why J.S. Rode had been allowed to visit Chola Sahib, I also told him the gist of my conversation with J.S. Rode and the inference supporting my apprehensions. 'He will not be allowed to stay back in the Temple,' the Governor said firmly.

The next morning Chaman Lal and I reached Tarn Taran by eight o'clock. J.S. Rode's PA complained that the local police had whisked away a large number of the trucks that they had hired. 'A sizeable *sangat* wants to accompany us to Amritsar. What should we do now?' he queried. I already knew that they had put up a *shamiana* in the *parikrama* of Gurudwara Tarn Taran Sahib. The huge *sangat* that was pouring into the shrine for a holy dip on *Amavas* (moonless night) had not shown any interest in the pretender *Jathedar* of the Akal Takht. The alleged whisking away of their trucks was only an excuse. I, therefore, told the Sub Divisional Magistrate to provide him with the required transport, and requested J.S. Rode's PA to direct the *sangat* to gather at a designated point.

Traditionally, since the inception of the Gurudwara at Tarn Taran, a large number of people walk from Amritsar on the *Amavas* night and, after a holy dip, return on foot early next morning. J.S. Rode's plan was to give a free ride to the people returning to Amritsar to swell his own caravan. People were not taking much notice of him. Even otherwise, those who had taken a vow to walk to Tarn Taran and back, did not think in terms of saving the fare but to honour their word to God. The tradition of course is from the days when either there was no public transport or it was scarce. Finding no obliging passengers, his own men, had sent away the trucks that they had hired. His entourage, comprising mostly of the men who had come with him from Malwa, walked to Amritsar.

As his caravan entered the city, Chaman Lal and I drove to the Temple to take stock of the situation there before his arrival. We were on the Temple View Hotel building adjoining the Temple complex when we saw J.S. Rode's caravan approaching the CRPF barricade. He had reached here 10 minutes earlier than we had expected. We rushed to the check post which the caravan could attempt to defy. But, before we could reach it, a surge of about 150 people from the rear overwhelmed the men on duty and pushed aside the empty coal tar drums being used as a barricade. The group hurried to a spot beyond the outer boundary railing of the Temple and squatted there. J.S. Rode addressed his men. He had expected that the large *Amavas sangat* would join this group. But, even here no one evinced any interest in what he was saying. After some time he lead his group into the Darbar Sahib. And we moved to the Braham Buta Akhara.

K.P.S. Gill arrived before lunch. We briefed him about the day's happenings. There was nothing we could do except wait in the Akhara building. After a late lunch, we speculated on J.S. Rode's next move. I repeated that he would not come out of the Temple. K.P.S. Gill observed that the district administration seemed to be very keen on hosting the *Jathedar*. I apprised him of my conversation with J.S. Rode at Khadur Sahib, which supported my inference.

After lunch, Chaman Lal walked up to K.P.S. Gill, saluted him, and asked if any action was to be taken. 'I am here till 4.30 P.M.' replied the top cop.

'Thereafter shall I be free to deal with the situation as it develops?' asked the IG.

'I shall leave instructions,' said the DGP. Chaman Lal saluted K.P.S. Gill, again and left.

I had no idea that Chaman Lal's smart salute was a good bye to his tenure as IG Border Range. Nor, perhaps could K.P.S. Gill guess it. He also left at 4.30 P.M. without making me wiser about the situation. I gazed at the Harmandar looking exquisite in the afternoon sun. Its reflection shimmered in the rippling *sarovar*. The *parikrama* was filled with devotees. Many were having a dip in the pool. J.S. Rode or his men did not figure anywhere. The place seemed to be immersed in the sacred music wafting beyond the bounds of the white walls. I could not think of any action that I could take.

Only a few months earlier, K.P.S. Gill and I had watched the revival of the *Maryada* from here. I saw J.S. Rode and his men moving towards the Darshani Deorhi, of course without their weapons. They got lost in the *sangat* on the causeway leading to the Harmandar. What does the Central Government have in mind, I wondered. In May, when it was believed that with the absence of the militants opposing J.S. Rode, he could persuade the remaining groups to negotiate with the government, I had tried to persuade the SGPC not to dismiss him immediately. The move had failed. And that afternoon, perhaps, I had failed to fully understand the wisdom of the move.

I bowed before the Temple and left for my residence. As soon as I stretched out on my bed, and dozed off I was woken by a telephone call from P.P.S. Gill of *The Tribune* Bureau. He wanted to know what had transpired between the two top cops. 'Nothing newsworthy,' I said. He laughed and apprised me of Chaman Lal having proceeded on leave which he had announced at a press conference that he had called. Chaman Lal was not available even to me. But when we met after a couple of days, he asked me if I was with him? 'Entirely,' I said, 'Only I do not understand the logic of the press conference.' Chaman Lal smiled and said, 'As a Gandhian I had to punish myself.'

As Inspector General of Police of the Border Range, Chaman Lal, was entitled to independent functioning in the five police districts falling in Amritsar and Gurdaspur revenue districts. In Amritsar we had the headquarters of two SSPs, and one DIG besides the IG. Many a time I had noticed that some police officer or the other felt stifled in his independent functioning. The Government of India, mostly the Home Ministry, was directly monitoring the goings-on in the SGPC and the Temple. Therefore, the DGP also had to come to

Amritsar frequently. Chaman Lal could not tolerate the manipulations to prop up J.S. Rode. I agreed. It was we, in the field, who had to bear the onus of the blame as one could not go on explaining to the people that it was Delhi's decision.

K.P.S. Gill and some of his SSPs believed that public support would follow provided the police dominated the terrorists, while Chaman Lal and others believed in the efficacy of carrying the people with them. Many people also knew the respective perceptions of the two. They responded to and respected officers who had faith in them. I have already observed that both S.S. Ray and J.F. Ribeiro, because of their faith in the people, became very popular in Amritsar. K.P.S. Gill himself did not make a sustained attempt to try to secure public support. He was an upright police professional, brooking no interference in the functioning of his force. Officers apart, even the lowest functionary in the force felt K.P.S. Gill's encouraging presence. These traits of his had sustained the morale of the police and paramilitary force which was important in the prevailing situation.

Chaman Lal carried a professional openness about him which had endeared him to the people of Amritsar and had also helped to improve the rapport between the two. As DIG in the BSF at Gurdaspur, he had done very well and retained the confidence of the people. He was instrumental in reforming many border crossers and settling them in life. J.S. Rode was ultimately responsible for depriving us of this asset. His appearance on the militant scene had helped only the militants; for the people and the administration he had nothing to offer.

However, the balancing effect of their combined presence augured well in the task to deal with the arduous and sensitive situation. Only a few weeks earlier, I had happened to be present in a meeting held by the Prime Minister in Delhi with the Governor, S.S. Ray the Home Minister, J.F. Ribeiro and K.P.S. Gill. I had pleaded that we needed Chaman Lal too. I apprised the Prime Minister of an incident at Khem Karan, a small town right on the border with Pakistan and in the worst terrorist affected belt. At the inauguration of the upgradation of a power station when we came with the Governor, we found the *pandal* nearly empty. All the people were squatting at some distance from the *pandal*. Two days earlier, in a case of sheer blundering, the police had killed a young boy at night. I had gone to the village and apologised to the gathering and to the father of the boy who also happened to be a national level wrestler. I conceded all their demands, including the construction of a hall and some rooms in the village school as a memorial to the unfortunate boy.

As I was returning, I met a former Minister of Punjab Government on the way. He perhaps intended to take me back to the village. I could not afford to be late for another meeting that I had promised in a Hindu dominated village near Tarn Taran. The inhabitants were on the verge of migrating. I had asked them to wait until I told them about the security plan for that village. If they felt that the security arrangements were not satisfactory, I would not stop them from migrating. My effort succeeded and the population did not leave the village. The next day, the ex-Minister displayed his influence by keeping the people out of the *pandal* at the Khem Karan function. I went to the crowd again but this time with the SSP. He also regretted the blunder and offered apologies. I reiterated my promise of the previous evening and, within a few minutes, people moved into the *pandal*.

My thinking was that if the *pandal* was to remain empty, on such an occasion it would have boosted the terrorists and their supporters. The headlines in the newspapers on the next day would have demoralised the public, the officers and the government as well. People remained with us in spite of the Minister's protest. This had been possible because of our equation with them. Chaman Lal had given priority to the public meetings we organised and had also established a rapport with the people in Amritsar during his brief posting. Chaman Lal's departure was a big loss to Amritsar and Gurdaspur districts.

Around 9.30 P.M. the Secretary to the Governor asked me from Chandigarh about the latest news from the Temple. I had told him that J.S. Rode's men were occupying room nos. 45 and 46 and he himself had broken open the lock of the room of the *Jathedar* of the Akal Takht and had occupied it. Iqbal Singh, a seasoned Intelligence officer, had informed me of this just before the call from Chandigarh. S.S. Ray rang me up from Delhi. He was furious when I confirmed the report I had given to his Secretary. The Governor told me to remain available on that phone, 'The PM may like to talk to you on this matter.' His words took away all my fatigue even though I had had little sleep on the previous two nights.

I did not get a call from the PM but, around midnight, the Intelligence people informed me that room nos. 45 and 46 in the *parikrama* had been vacated. The boys had moved to the *sarai* and

J.S. Rode had vacated the room that he had forcibly occupied. At about 5 A.M., I was woken up again. The information was that the boys had returned to the rooms in the *parikrama*. I thought for a while and told the Intelligence man at the other end, 'It is OK, they must be fearing a police raid in the *sarai* which is always around this hour.' He agreed that this could be the reason.

At about 1.30 P.M. the next day, I could tell the Secretary to the Governor that J.S. Rode was about to finish making payments to the men accompanying him; this was to cover the travelling expenses of their return journey. His mission had failed but he did announce from the Golden Temple that he would hold a *Sarbat Khalsa* on the coming Diwali despite the ban imposed by the SGPC on holding such gatherings at the Akal Takht without its prior permission. The Panthic Panel came down heavily on this announcement. The Panel dismissed all the three *Jathedars* appointed by different authorities: G.S. Manochahal, appointed by the Panthic Committee, J.S. Rode, the appointee of the *Sarbat Khalsa* of 1986, and Darshan Singh, who had been installed by the Shiromani Committee. The Panel also declared that the office would be filled when a decision would be taken, at the *Sarbat Khalsa* to be held by the Panthic Panel.

After J.S. Rode had left, I learnt from the SGPC employees on duty in the Temple that J.S. Rode had wanted them to present him with a *saropa*, which they had refused to do. They even nudged one of the SGPC employees with their swords, handed a *saropa* to him, which they had brought themselves, and tried to make him present it publicly to J.S. Rode, under threat. No one obliged. The SGPC became more cautious and banned the entry of weapons into the Temple. It also announced that thenceforth no one could stay in the *parikrama* nor hold any meeting in the Temple area without obtaining its prior permission. This was the essence of the restrictions proposed in my letter of May 1988. This had come in handy for the SGPC to prevent J.S. Rode's holding a *Sarbat Khalsa* on Diwali day on 24 October 1988.

To help J.S. Rode save face, he was arrested in Bhatinda before he could begin his march to Amritsar for holding the announced *Sarbat Khalsa*. This time I did not have to suggest that J.S. Rode should be prevented from coming to Amritsar. Just a day or two before Diwali, the Panel also called off the *Sarbat Khalsa* announced by it to counter J.S. Rode's game. Actually, the Taksal was now unhappy with J.S. Rode because of Operation Black Thunder which the Taksal believed had taken place because of J.S. Rode's complicity with the government and which had, consequently, deprived it of the *karsewa* of the Akal Takht. J.S. Rode, thereafter, remained in Gurudwara Talwandi Sabo till he was arrested on the charge of supplying weapons to the militants.

J.S. Rode did not possess the slightest stature or character needed to fulfil the role the government expected of him. He would stammer under stress. He did not even have a reasonable knowledge of Sikh scriptures. He had revived an unnecessary controversy over the desirability of retaining the last page of the Guru Granth Sahib which recounts all the Ragas used in the hymns of the holy book. This was only to cover up his scanty knowledge of the scriptures. But, knowing that this man had reportedly been a truck driver in the Middle East, one has to give him credit for the courage he showed in accepting the role he was allotted.

But the foregoing episode clearly shows that someone could pull strings in Punjab without the PM's knowledge. Some persons in positions of power, not happy with S.S. Ray's success, were still out to demolish the advantage gained in Black Thunder. So many opportunities to restore peace were wasted before and since. These deserve to be recounted in detail.

———————

18

Panchayat Elections Postponed: Missed Opportunities

Operation Black Thunder was a tremendous achievement in more ways than one. Besides the smoothness and ease with which it was conducted, it had restored chaste, heavenly peace to the Temple and a situation had been created which was propitious for the eradication of violence from Punjab. Its potential was neither appreciated nor utilised. Delhi, in fact, gave very little importance to the Operation. It almost came to the brink of undoing its achievements, as if the Operation had made no difference to the social climate at all.

On several occasions the militants had taken shelter in the Temple and used it as a base to organise and extend their network of violence. This had first happened in 1983 and the result was Operation Blue Star. They had again entered the Temple in December 1985 to bring down the S.S. Barnala Government by organising violence on a massive scale. In the following year, i.e., 1986, they had killed 520 civilians which was 10 times more than the killings during the year 1985. They achieved their objective—the dismissal of the State government—in May 1987 and believed they had the upper hand when their plans were frustrated in May 1988.

It seemed that the Home Ministry's calculations had also been upset. With the exit of the militants, J.S. Rode had no cause to stay in the Temple complex. The Taksal lost the *kar-sewa* of the Akal Takht. This *kar-sewa* had been exploited by the militants to entrench themselves in the Temple for the second time. This change called for an immediate and fresh approach showing some genuine initiative to tackle the whole problem. There could not have been a more propitious time to introduce some political inputs which S.S. Ray and some saner public men had been recommending and which the Prime Minister had been promising. Many opportunities for peace had been frittered away. I think the blame must be shared by the Central Government, the State Congress, the Akali factions and other religious organisations.

It seems to me that the single most important factor responsible for belittling the potential of Black Thunder is that the Operation did not have its origins in the corridors of the North Block. It was locally conceived and devised in the context of circumstances at that moment. Many firing incidents in and around the Temple had been ignored in the past. On 7 March 1987, a constable was killed by the militants in the *parikrama* and the rescue team of police officials was also injured but the matter was allowed to rest there. Earlier, on 20 April 1983, A.S. Atwal, DIG of Police, was killed in the portals of the main entrance to the Temple but nothing was done by the then elected government. I was unhappy with the inaction of the authorities on both occasions. In the case of A.S. Atwal I was deeply hurt, as he was a friend. He was a devoted and upright police officer. I could not do anything more than express my regret and sorrow on those occasions. But when S.S. Virk was injured by the militants from inside the Temple I had the authority and the responsibility to take action which I did.

I took the initiative on my own responsibility and placed Amritsar under curfew. At the time, I also gave an assurance to the higher authorities that there would be no mass uprising by the people, and that we could tire out and evict the militants from the holy precincts. Governor S.S. Ray instantly approved of it, but he had to make more than one trip to Delhi to get approval for the proposal. The Prime Minister, while sanctioning the plan, asked the Governor to televise it, 'so that I can also see what you do there.' My feeling is that the reluctance was on the part of the Home Ministry whose plan to trap the militants through the fake militant leader J.S. Rode was being thwarted.

After the completion of the operation, the agenda of the Home Ministry was not only different from that of the Governor but was opposed to it. Therefore, no one in Delhi seriously assessed the potential for establishing peace in the dramatically changed situation. The operation was a great setback to the so-called Khalistan movement of the militants. The aura of the eighteenth century martyrs who are associated with the honorific 'Singh', which the militants also claimed, was lost to them with their surrender and behaviour after their exit from the temple. The terrorist movement was deprived of 192 surrendering active members. Out of them, 50 were hard-core terrorists who had spearheaded it. The loss of a central office with telephones, and other facilities to summon people, collect funds, hold press conferences, etc., was quite a major setback to them. Besides, the weapons they had to leave behind in the temple must also have weakened their movement. They now needed a lot of time, an alternative retreat, a matching strategy and new leaders to reorganise themselves. They could not sustain the killings they had stepped up from mid-May to mid-June and thus failed to refurbish their awesome image.

The killing of the migrant labourers had damaged their reputation further. From 19 June onwards, the killings declined steadily. In July 1988, Khalistan Commando Force (KCF) and Khalistan Liberation Force (KLF), two extremely powerful terrorist outfits, accumulated arms in the wilderness of the Mand area with the intention to make it their base. K.P.S. Gill who relentlessly combed it from all four surrounding districts—Amritsar, Jalandhar, Kapurthala and Ferozepur, quickly thwarted this attempt. The BSF pickets, with their motor launches, were also stationed there permanently. The militants could not dig in there in spite of the cover of the tall grass and the existence of various escape routes.

General Zia, the then President of Pakistan, was killed on 17 August 1988 in a plane crash. The support which the Pakistan-based top leaders such as Wassan Singh Zaffarwal, Sukhdev Singh Jhamke, Avtar Singh Brahma, and Kanwar Singh Dhami had been getting from General Zia's regime, had suddenly become uncertain. It was becoming evident that the future Prime Minister would be Ms. Benazir Bhutto, the daughter of Z.A. Bhutto who had been executed during General Zia's military dictatorship. She had hinted that she would reverse General Zia's policy of supporting the militants. She eventually signed an agreement to that effect with Prime Minister Rajiv Gandhi when she became the Prime Minister of Pakistan.

The most significant development was the gradual vanishing of the concept of Khalistan. This was disclosed by the 50 odd militants arrested by the BSF and the police while entering India from Pakistan. Besides the waning of Pakistan's support, developments within the movement eroded the alleged goal of Khalistan. The pretence of a religious war, *Dharam Yudh*, which the militants had managed to sustain despite killings, threats and physical torture inside the Temple, was not available to them after their exit from there.

As the militants moved into the widely spread farmhouses of the border belt, the incidents of extortion and kidnapping for ransom increased. The lure of money added to their numbers, but those who joined them were mostly criminals, bootleggers, illicit distillers and the like whose sole objective was to make money. These criminals virtually took over the movement. The prominent leaders who came up during this period were the dreaded extortionists and blackmailers—Bakshish Singh Sona, Resham Singh, Nishan Singh Makhu and Satta Changiara—not that they did not kill but the killings were carried out to facilitate extortion and not for any ideological reasons. Bakshish Singh Sona killed six persons in a village and left a note that they had been collecting money in his name. He killed them because the extortionists merely used his name and did not pass on the money to him—the usual punishment for violating a franchise in the underworld. This harassment became one of the main causes for the alienation of the militants. By January 1989, it became clear that the people were disgusted with the so-called *kharkoos*.

Governor S.S. Ray was eager to grab this opportunity. He had been strongly advocating the need for political inputs to win over the masses and marginalise the separatists. He invited the Prime Minister to lay the foundation stone of a Rs. 246 crore Paper-Board Mill at Goindwal which was a flourishing commercial centre on the Lahore–Delhi highway during the Mughal days. Guru Amar Das built a gurudwara here where the tradition of *langar* attracted large numbers of the people. But at that moment it was in the middle of the worst affected militant area and, as a result, a large industrial centre planned for this area could not come up.

On 21 September 1988, after laying the foundation stone, Prime Minister Rajiv Gandhi complimented the vast gathering of people for not allowing the communalists and fundamentalists to grow. He recognised their suffering and the need for restoring the political set up. He said that, to begin with, *Panchayat* elections could be held.

He regretted that there was no one of the stature of Sant Longowal who could influence the militants. Of the many projects announced, only the rail link between Beas and Goindwal has come up. This has linked the place with the main railway line.

The economic package which S.S. Ray had been hinting at was not announced until March 1989. The one immediate positive step was the release of 138 Jodhpur detainees which S.S. Ray had insisted upon. S.S. Ray was steadily preparing to hold the *Panchayat* elections in Punjab in 1989 which had been actually due by the close of 1988. These alone would have hastened the return of peace in the state. On New Year's day, 1989, Governor S.S. Ray told the press that the concept of Khalistan had been forgotten by the militants. The cassettes of Bhindranwale's speeches were not being played any more. The *bhogs* of killed militants were no more an occasion for large public gatherings. There is no doubt that the police had been stopping people from going to the *bhogs*. But many people, including some *sarpanches* had told me, they merely wanted an excuse for not complying with the dictates of the 'boys'. The presence of the police *naqas* (check posts) had lent them with the requisite, and credible, excuse.

Governor S.S. Ray also lauded the improved relations with the SGPC who had declared that they would not allow the militants to return to the Temple. The SGPC was not cowed down even after the militants had killed Bhan Singh, the Secretary of the SGPC and Sohan Singh, the head *granthi* of the Darbar Sahib. Earlier, in April 1987, when the Assistant Secretary of the SGPC Abnashi Singh and the medical officer Dr. B.S. Barar were killed, all resistance to the militants by the officials of the Committee had ceased.

What Governor S.S. Ray told the people through the press was correct. Although the fear of killers and kidnappers continued to stalk the Punjabis, the first three months of the year showed a decline in the killings of the civilians and a steep rise in the number of the militants killed. In the first quarter of the year 1989, we lost 286 civilians in comparison to 549 killed in the first quarter of the previous year. But the number of militants killed in that year had gone up to 133 against 51 killed in the corresponding period of the year 1988. It was also being said that Pakistan would not support the militants any more. P. Chidambaram, told Parliament on 6 April 1989 that on 15 March a letter recovered from a border-crosser revealed that in the wake of the Rajiv–Benazir Agreement, the training camps in Pakistan were likely to be wound up. He also stated that it was likely that the ISI may no longer assist Punjab militants in transporting weapons to India. The State Department of USA in its report 'Patterns of Global Terrorism 1988' noted the new Pakistan government's pledge to co-operate with India in fighting terrorism. The Pakistani Prime Minister had also replaced the Chief and the Director of the ISI.

The time was obviously ripe for *Panchayat* elections, which the Prime Minister had suggested in his address at Goindwal on 21 September 1988. In the first meeting of field officers, called by S.S. Ray to ascertain their views about the possibility and desirability of holding the elections, they unanimously supported the need for the exercise and assured that these could be held peacefully. Only one Deputy Commissioner said that in six blocks of his district it may not be possible to hold the polls. His assessment was based on the large number of resignations of *sarpanches* from those blocks. Though the fact of the resignations was correct, they were essentially reacting against the functioning of the SSP of Batala—Gobind Ram. He was ultimately shifted. Such a problem had also arisen in my district. I dealt with it by convening a public meeting of the *sarpanches* and also invited the IGP of the Border Range. In the presence of the SHO, people had complained of his rude behaviour and corrupt deeds. The orders of suspension and transfer of the official were announced on the spot by C. Paul Singh IG, and that was the end of the trouble.

These developments were positive steps towards establishing peace. The *Panchayat* elections would further serve to improve the situation. The involvement of people in these elections was much more direct and intense than in any other election. Although these elections were not on party lines, yet the majority of *sarpanches* were known for their alignment with a political party. Most Congressmen were generally not suspected by the police. Therefore, the militants sought them more eagerly for shelter or help. They either had to migrate from their villages or buy peace with them. The elections could have brought peace in the state but the Congressmen would have been uncomfortable moving about in the villages. Besides, Beant Singh, the then President of the State Congress, did not see eye to eye with the Governor nor was S.S. Ray happy with Beant Singh. During President's rule, invariably, a council is constituted to advise the Governor in his administration of the state. Such a council, naturally, has the largest number of members from the party ruling at the Centre. S.S. Ray, instead, had a council on which equal representation had been given to the various recognised political parties. The angry State Congress, therefore, undertook an operation to sabotage S.S. Ray's moves.

A vociferous campaign was launched alleging that the bureaucracy had become corrupt and the disgusted people stood alienated which had helped the spread of terrorism. People were allegedly very unhappy. Such a vague campaign against an entire administration is simple. Also, it is relatively safe to make such generalised allegations. In any event, people in Punjab were miserable because of terrorism and the increasing incidents of extortion. The corrupt elements in the bureaucracy remain what they are, only changing their loyalties with a change in the regime. When the critics change positions, from the Opposition to the ruling benches, they defend the same bureaucracy, frequently to cover their own corruption. But the allegations were orchestrated at all levels in Delhi so that the complainants could claim that they had convinced the Central leadership. To the dismay of the complaining Congress leaders, the Prime Minister dismissed all the allegations, publicly commended Governor S.S. Ray's handling of militancy and his awareness of corruption at the lower levels, thus ruling out corruption at higher levels. It was evident that S.S. Ray would continue to head the State Government. S.S. Ray's critics began to see their doom in the *Panchayat* elections which he was keen to hold.

Every day deputations would go to Delhi to emphasise that, if the *Panchayat* elections were held, only the militants would be returned as *sarpanches* and that would be disastrous. In the first lap of their campaign, they succeeded in getting the date of the polls postponed. Then they began opposing these elections with renewed zeal. The ground realities and expectations of people, including the militants was different. Most rural people want a *sarpanch* who can accompany them to the police station, hospital, court, and other offices. The police station is the most important place where they need the intercession of the *sarpanch*. A known militant as *sarpanch* would be of no use to them at all. For the militants also, a gentleman *sarpanch*, with some status of his own, would be more useful for protecting them. During interrogation, except for some hard-core militants, the rest would disclose the names of the persons who had supported them or helped them. The militants' supporters who were increasing in number ever since extortion had become widely prevalent. But they always tried to conceal their support since, otherwise, they could be in trouble sooner or later. The *sarpanches* are also responsible for promoting the development work in the villages. No militant could have been useful in this direction. The denunciation of the elections was in fact veiled opposition to S.S. Ray who did not pander to Congress politicians.

In my view, Governor S.S. Ray might have dealt with the State Congress President, Beant Singh, more diplomatically in order to gain his support for the *Panchayat* elections, particularly when the Rajiv Gandhi Government appeared eager to settle the Punjab problem as well as to woo Sikh voters in the forthcoming parliamentary elections. The desperation for support was of the same intensity as had earlier made Prime Minister Rajiv Gandhi forget the Accord and the Punjab problem in an effort to win the Haryana elections of June 1987. As we know, that strategy had failed. The losing trend beginning in Haryana continued in subsequent by-elections. The three politicians—V.P. Singh, Devi Lal and N.T. Rama Rao—who opposed the Congress had got together and in October 1988 had merged into the Janata Dal. The Congress, therefore, decided to woo the Sikhs.

The Akalis had ignored their feelers although the package announced by the Prime Minister on 3 March 1989 had been hailed by the UAD as well as the SGPC. For the Akalis, generally, politics has not been the art of the possible. Perhaps, because their achievements, such as they are, were gained through *morcha* politics. In June, an effort had reportedly been made through P.V. Narasimha Rao, to woo Manjit Singh, Harmandar Singh Sandhu of the AISSF and S.S. Mann. All three were in different jails. The former two leaders responded to an extent. However, it would seem that their motives did not include bringing peace to Punjab.

But no one, from the Government of India to the grassroot politicians of various parties, tried to come out from their narrow mindsets. And Punjab continued to suffer. Sagacity, statesmanship and the ideals of service to the people had all disappeared.

Governor S.S. Ray finally decided to schedule the *Panchayat* elections for September 1989, which incidentally turned out to be the least violent month, with 78 killings. The *Panchayat* elections could have made a world of difference in restoring peace. They could at least have been a verdict against the militants which would have gone a long way towards shaping things for the future. When the February 1992 elections to the Punjab State Assembly were held, the average monthly civilian killings were around 180 but a downward trend had set in and it needed a political set up to activate the masses to combat militancy. Three years earlier (in September 1989), the situation was much better. Elections to the State's three major Municipal Corporations were held in April 1991 when the situation was pretty bad, yet the terrorists could not influence the results. The importance of the *Panchayats* in our villages was realised even by the militants and their organisations. When these elections were finally held in January 1993, the Babbar Akali Dal, organised by the militants, did not try to stop anyone from participation. Dr. Sohan Singh, on the other hand, wanted the Panthic candidates to be returned unanimously. Even the Akalis, who had boycotted the Assembly and the municipal elections during 1992, could not afford to ignore the *Panchayat* elections. They claimed that the large participation was because of them and they also insisted that they had captured more *Panchayats* than the ruling Congress.

But in 1989, the fact remained that in order to oppose Governor S.S. Ray the jealous State Congress frittered away the chances of peace. If the *Panchayat* elections had been held, the people of Punjab, who had suffered the reign of terror of the militants and the security measures of the state, were sure to reject the militant candidates if any.

The *Panchayat* is an age-old institution which has preserved the traditions of rural India through centuries of alien rule. The old expression 'Panch Parmeshwar'—God's Will vested in the five members of a *Panchayat*—is still cited at times of local crisis or conflict. The *sarpanches* generally carry the image of dignified village elders. Very few would have chosen to seek the support of militants, for this would have been tantamount to surrendering their authority and prestige to the gun-wielding boys. The geographical spread of violence, as disclosed by S.S. Ray to the press on 19 May 1989, was that, out of 217 police stations in the state, only 16 were actually affected. In 66 police stations violence had occurred on a very small scale and 135 had been completely free of violence. In the *Panchayat* poll people could have re-established their essential unity for peace. The Prime Minister himself had said on 3 March 1989 that the militants were not a political force but only a band of criminals.

The institution of the *Panchayat* was not in any danger from the extremists. But with its politicisation due to the introduction of a three-tier system at the village, block and district levels, the significance of the ancient institution had no chance to survive. Many public men and politicians made statements toeing the party line without taking a closer look at the situation. The intelligence agencies also did not support the *Panchayat* poll. They were playing safe. Meanwhile the DMs and the SSPs were in favour of the elections. Consequently, the scheduled dates for the elections were postponed three times.

When the Bill to amend the Constitution of India to provide for a three-tier *Panchayat* system, with enhanced powers, was introduced in Parliament, it was obvious that it would fail for lack of a two-thirds majority in the Rajya Sabha. The state of Orissa postponed its *Panchayat* elections to await the fate of the Bill. Governor S.S. Ray, under the pressure of these developments, could not insist on holding these elections. It may be mentioned here that soon after coming to power in February 1992, the Congress Chief Minister Beant Singh announced that the *Panchayat* elections would be held very soon. It was this election that finally changed the thinking of the people and marginalised the militants. Such elections would have been equally useful in the wake of Operation Black Thunder. The delay in *Panchayat* elections only prolonged the agony of the people suffering under the intimidation of both the militants and the state.

19

The Militants and the Police: Between the Two Terrors

Before Operation Black Thunder, targeted 'donors' were summoned by telephone calls or threatening letters to room nos. 13, 14, 45 and 46 of the *parikrama* in the Golden Temple, and politely informed of the 'the contribution assigned to them'. After the operation, some militant organisations tried to establish their headquarters in the Mand area while others looked for shelter with families living in their far-flung farmhouses, in remote parts of the countryside. Unlike the precincts of the Golden Temple these places were not out of bounds for the police. Therefore, the militants could no longer summon their victims. They resorted to kidnapping their targets, thus preventing their victim's friends and family members from informing the police for fear of the hostages being killed. The disastrous results in the initially reported abductions were enough to caution the police and the people. Reports were lodged with the police as a last resort, particularly after private negotiations failed and the demand, possibly, happened to be beyond the means of the family. Thus, the period between Operation Black Thunder and the parliamentary elections in November 1989, witnessed numerous cases of ransom through kidnapping.

It was not difficult to imagine the suffering of the people and the havoc the kidnappings could cause. But what we could not foresee was the depth of misery and annoyance that was to be inflicted on innocent people by the thoughtless and tactless police methods to combat that widespread evil. The affected families faced prolonged trauma which was more demoralising than an actual killing. And we had no sure remedy to give relief or prevent the crimes due to the nature of the situation at the time.

The lure of easy money made the practice of kidnapping spread like a plague. The militant organisations, in order to broaden their base, had to lure young dropouts from school with promises of jobs in the future. The victims, out of prudence, saw their safety lay in co-operating with the abductors, and this encouraged even novices to form their own independent groups. The militants' ranks swelled faster than before. The movement got a spectacular boost when the illicit distillers of liquor bade adieu to Bacchus, for a stint with the extortionists. The Mand area, with its wild elephant grass landscape, that was once a paradise for bootleggers, was denied to the illegal distillers. The police repeatedly raided this area in search of militant hideouts. The distillers in Mand, who had been the only ones to have escaped the pressure of the social reform movement of the militants now voluntarily gave up the manufacture of illicit liqour. For decades these bootleggers had been paying monthly cuts to the local *Thana* (police station), commensurate with the size of their trade. It was widely believed that they changed their old occupation in favour of kidnapping.

The life of farm dwellers became a veritable hell on earth. Fearing the midnight knock at their doors, they could not sleep at night. No one could neither ignore nor refuse them. A group of five to ten young men would materialise from the darkness and announce with icy informality, 'The Singhs need food and shelter.' They would also ask for money if the house appeared to be prosperous. With no help available, the household had no choice and was at the mercy of the strangers who could turn into devils. If the family resisted or showed even a bit of resentment, they were dubbed as police informers. The militants could pick their victims from the villages also with the same ease. No one would come to the rescue of their neighbours.

The state police added to the people's misery when, after the night's ordeal, it marched in during the day, somewhat triumphantly for having found out the harbourers within hours. 'Have you a soft corner for the militants? Why didn't you report to the *thana* about the night visitors?' they would ask, either in anger or in a sarcastic tone. The night visitors—the militants—would at least spare the families sympathetic to them but the police suspected everyone without distinguishing between the active supporters and the involuntary harbourers. Therefore, relations between the police and the rural public bordered on suspicion, which deteriorated into widespread discontentment and undisguised hostility. As crime increased, the police launched an operation against the harbourers without taking adequate precautions to spare the helpless among them. The protest against alleged police atrocities and corruption was getting more strident by the day. Hence the saying became current—the night belongs to the militants and the day to the police. If one died of a police bullet, one was a militant; those who tasted the militants' bullets were dubbed as police informers.

The police also used the same crude methods, language and metaphors for innocent people which the militants had earlier used when anyone resisted or refused to meet their demands. In rural and suburban areas, there weren't many telephones. Those who had telephones could not deny their use to anyone, including the militants. In one case a telephone number noted in the diary of a border crosser arrested by the police belonged to a doctor practicing in a suburban area of Amritsar. The police picked him up. They did not tell the family the reasons for his arrest or the people from whom they could enquire about him. The doctor told the police that he was a heart patient and could die because of the roughing up. 'The sun will not stop rising if you die,' was the sarcastic reaction of the police official. The case was brought to the notice of K.P.S. Gill, and the doctor was released at his intervention.

The police and people were increasingly getting into a Catch–22 situation. As a rule, the affected family did not report kidnappings directly to the police. An effort was made to convey it informally to senior officers through influential persons. If the police remained inactive it was accused of being in league with the militants. Any follow-up action by it was mostly counterproductive, resulting in complaints of harassment and extortion against the police itself. It was through sheer chance or luck that a victim could be rescued from the kidnappers. Some of the *sarpanches*, who were respectable and prosperous farmers, quietly shifted to nearby towns. The militants often traced them out and found their city dwellings safer. And if the migrant was a Hindu, his residence became the safest hideout. They had to buy peace again. The police would come to know about the urban hideouts only from the confessions of arrested militants. The inevitable harassment of the helpless harbourer would occur again and an easy channel would become available to the police to get its palms greased.

In this situation the number of militant gangs increased to the extent that the police began to believe that a large number of trained militants had crossed over from Pakistan. They moved so freely during the daytime that some of the police encounters with them took place during the day. Many people complained to me in Tarn Taran and Patti that the police knew the 'boys' that roamed around during the day, and yet they took no action. In Ajnala, people complained that Satta Changiara's movements were with the full knowledge of the police.

In course of time they began carrying out kidnappings even in Amritsar. Two contractors were abducted from their doorsteps when their cars halted at the gate. Complaints against the integrity of the police began to multiply. Many believed that the police itself was arranging kidnappings and setting the ransom amounts. There was more smoke than fire but one could not say with assurance that the police were innocent. Two Deputy Superintendents of Police were dismissed without inquiry and in the public interest under Article 311 of the Constitution. The police reorganised its patrol system and inducted more vehicles to reduce their reaction time but these facilities could not be fully utilised for a lack of instant complaints of kidnapping. In the course of time the militant organisations developed their own conduits and intermediaries.

Bakhshish Singh Sona, Harbhajan Singh, Pipal Singh, Resham Singh Warian and Nishan Singh Makhu became legends in their respective areas. Satta Changiara, who became a dreaded kidnapper in the Ajnala area of Amritsar, surpassed them all. One of his victims pleaded that the heavy ransom money for him could not be arranged until he was released. So the kidnapper provided a moneylender who would later be repaid by the victim!

The killings could be counted, understood and analysed but this could hardly be done in cases of abduction for ransom. Every affected family preferred to use people who had some influence with the group or a known intermediary rather than report the case to the police. Rumours in circulation painted a picture of total anarchy which was of great help to the criminals. Even novices could snatch any vehicle or car but the policy of painting the number on the doors and its body, besides the number plate—which could easily be changed—reduced such incidents. The militants then commenced borrowing vehicles and generally ensured their return at the promised time. We found it difficult to persuade people to resist paying ransom or report incidents of borrowed vehicles. An idea of the extent to which this malaise had spread can be judged from the following two incidents.

On a complaint of purse-snatching by a lady, the police could trace the culprit because the lady remembered part of the number plate of his vehicle. The culprit was from a well-to-do family and disclosed that it was his 36th snatch. He used to chase his victim on his scooter and, as she stopped her car or scooter to open the gate of the house, he would simply threaten the victim and drive off with her purse. The 35 earlier victims had not cared to report these incidents to the police. In the other case, two teenagers went to a higher secondary school in Patti and, posing as members of the Bakhshish Singh Sona group, threatened 50 odd teachers demanding Rs. 100,000. The deal was finalised at around Rs. 50,000. On the appointed day, when they visited the school to collect the pooled money, they were confronted by the brother of Bakhshish Singh Sona whom one of the teachers happened to know and had requested to intervene. Both the extortionists swooned and fell to the ground.

To restore the sagging morale of the people, Governor S.S. Ray visited all the districts, addressing public meetings even on the roadside. He renamed these meetings as *shakti sammelans* and senior Secretaries to the Punjab government were required to be present at these meetings in order to decide issues on the spot. These meetings drew large crowds but the faces largely remained grave as if devoid of hope. Actually, the general discontent with the attitude of the police was increasing. People suspected that the police gave support to the extortionists. 'If they do not know the whereabouts of the kidnappers they surely know the intermediaries, why do they not take action against the brokers of this unholy trade?' was the question for which we had no convincing answer except that of non-interference for the safety of the victim. Often the kidnapped people, after their release, would approach the police to register a case but the police generally avoided doing so. A couple of cases came to my notice in which the militants had advised their victims while setting them free that they should lie to the police that the ransom amount was much less than what had actually been paid. We also had some cases in which the police had succeeded in freeing the victims after an armed encounter. But such cases were rare.

If the excessive criminalisation of the movement in its early stages damaged the police reputation, with the passage of time, the bulk of the people began turning against the militants. In public meetings, people were encouraged to disclose complaints against the erring officials and the police. The police predicament, in the absence of timely reports about kidnappings and threats of extortion, were explained. Some individuals who had defied the demands of the militants and had taken weapons from the police were also presented at such meetings. But it was difficult to dispel allegations of police connivance in some cases of extortion. In that climate of fear no one was willing to give evidence either against erring officials or the so-called agents who negotiated the ransom deals. However, a sustained campaign to bare the tactics of the militants and their subtle methods of maligning the police to erode the people's confidence began showing results.

Police officers in the field also made special efforts to win the confidence of the people. The SSPs of Majitha and Tarn Taran presented victims who had been raped by the militants at village public meetings to highlight the militant's depravity. The Gurdaspur Police Chief presented the apparently repentant Nishan Singh Makhu and Baldev Singh Dorangla—the two dreaded terrorists—before public meetings. By these methods an effective beginning was made in assuring the suffering people of the governments earnestness. Most people were already feeling greatly harassed by the increasing incidents of extortion and the nightly visits of the militants. The wind began changing. From the beginning of 1989, the police domination in encounters showed some improvement. From June 1989 onwards it kept improving steadily till the announcement of the parliamentary elections in the state in November that year.

K.P.S. Gill explained the alienation of the militants from the people because of their atrocities. Talking to the press in Amritsar, he added that the police was getting more information as a result of which police encounters were taking place during the day as well. In the course of time people became more optimistic and co-operative. But their suffering due to the fear of kidnapping, threats of extortion and action by the police against even passive harbourers continued, even though it abated somewhat. Justice Tarkunde's team of Citizens for Democracy confirmed the police excesses, particularly in dealing with passive harbourers. They also declared that the people were against Khalistan, and that the number of terrorists committed to Khalistan were rare.

Ransom and extortions did give a boost to militancy. In fact these malpractices had spread from Amritsar to adjoining districts and in time to the rest of the state. Militancy followed as a corollary to those malpractices. It was really very unfortunate that no satisfactory remedy could be found immediately. But, with the criminalisation of the movement the seeds of its decline were also sown. It would be interesting to know where the crores of rupees which were extorted during half a decade went! Very few families of the extortionists are known to have thrived after the elimination of this evil. A large number of chit fund companies had sprung up and they mopped up a big chunk of the extorted money. No action could be taken against these companies under the existing law. A Reserve Bank of India team came to Amritsar and after examining the system followed by these companies, told me that the chit fund companies were not violating any of their provisions. Fishing in troubled waters continued, however. But the money extorted was much more than the deposits with these companies. As soon as the public complaints began pouring in, these companies simply disappeared.

Governor S.S. Ray had done his very best to sustain the public morale. To give it a boost he now opted to host the country's National Games in trouble-torn Punjab.

20

The 'National Games'

Governor S.S. Ray, with the courage of his convictions, had offered to host the country's most prestigious sports event, the National Games, in Punjab at a time when the rigours of state action had begun to hurt the people as much as the acts of the militants. The Games were scheduled to be held in November 1989. The Governor had hoped to steer the state towards normalcy by that time. By September the number of killings had came down quite noticeably. The meeting chaired by the Governor on 17 October was the final meeting in connection with the holding of the Games.

The Prime Minister's sudden announcement in Delhi of holding parliamentary elections, also in November 1989, deprived Punjab of the glamorous show, imposing another kind of 'National Games' on the entire country. We could see the change in Governor S.S. Ray's expression as he read the 'Urgent' report placed before him. But Delhi's having agreed to hold the Games in Punjab surely indicated its confidence in Ray and his administrative machinery. Besides this, the intense love of sports of the resilient Punjabis—which could keep any disturbance by the militants at bay—must have been another factor behind Delhi's bold gesture. During all those months, as we were making arrangements for the competitions, not a single voice was heard against holding the Games in such difficult times. Amritsar was to host the wrestling events and the people were very enthused. But now we were to have elections instead.

In a short duration of three to five years, it is unlikely that a government can produce substantial results and convince the electorate about its credentials. Invariably politicians have to find a new vote catching issue. Prime Minister Rajiv Gandhi had sought an amendment of the Constitution to delegate vast powers to the *Gram Panchayats*. The amendment approved by the Lok Sabha failed in the Rajya Sabha, for want of a two-thirds vote. Therefore, the Congress had to go to the ultimate authority—the people of India—to ask for a mandate. The elections were to be held on 22, 24 and 26 November 1989. For the ruling Congress, it was its most difficult election in the context of trends discernible in the results of recent elections in eight State Assemblies. The Hindi belt, its bastion till then, had become its Achilles heel. For the Congress it was literally a question of survival or death and it was sparing no effort to survive.

Punjab, which was specially mentioned in the Congress election manifesto in 1984—the year of Operation Blue Star, of Mrs. Indira Gandhi's assassination and of the massacre of the Sikhs—did not find any mention in the manifesto preceding these elections. Many parties criticised the omission of Punjab. The party's popularity in UP and the areas around it seemed very low. The state of UP had, until then, been its most dependable vote bank. To please both major communities fighting over the Ram Mandir and Babri Masjid, the Congress managed the laying of the foundation stone of the Mandir 100 yards away from the Masjid. But the combination of three stalwarts, V.P. Singh in UP, N.T. Rama Rao in Andhra Pradesh and Devi Lal, in Haryana was too formidable to be countered by such palliatives.

Punjab was also a difficult state for the Congress. But in this state, the Central leaders felt they could still win a majority of the parliamentary seats, provided they could divide the votes of their major opponents, the Akalis. In fact the Central Government had released Manjit Singh, the President of the All India Sikh Students Federation, in July with this end in view.

In June 1989, both Manjit Singh and Harmandar Singh Sandhu had been shifted from Jodhpur (in Rajasthan) to jails in Punjab. P.V. Narasimha Rao, the Minister for Human Resources, reportedly contacted them before Manjit Singh was released. Immediately after his release, Manjit Singh started reorganising the All India Sikh

Students Federation. He organised a conference in Ropar district in August 1989, and an open house session at Manji Sahib at the Golden Temple complex. A large rural gathering was observed at this conference vaguely hoping for some respite, if not peace. A week earlier, Manjit Singh had accused G.S. Manochahal of leading a lavish life in Pakistan while his men were making life miserable for people in the villages (*The Tribune*, 11 September 1989). To the utter dismay of the audience, no mention was made in the session about the people's plight. He asked them to achieve their '*Raj, Darbar and Sarkar*', restore the *kar-sewa* of the Akal Takht to the Damdami Taksal and struggle for Khalistan. The *kar-sewa* would have helped the militants to re-enter the Temple. As the session dispersed, I came down from the Braham Buta Akhara to the road from which the gathering was to emerge. I overheard the comments of an elderly group, 'The whole drama was for *kar-sewa* and to embarrass the SGPC and get the support of the Damdami Taksal. No one is a fool now not to understand their game' was one of the comments.

The youngsters, however, walked out in a jubilant mood. They were happy with the outcome. The AISSF now had the support of the Taksal and Baba Joginder Singh. The four priests dismissed by the SGPC after Operation Black Thunder were again recognised by the session which implied that Jasbir Singh Rode was still the *Jathedar* of the Akal Takht. There was talk of the elections and of agitation against the police interrogation centres which had gained notoriety for torture. Many a young man in the business of extortion could now cloak his demands in terms of respectability (by soliciting funds for electioneering) much before the elections were announced.

As usual, the Akali factions could not agree on joint candidates, nor on the allotment of separate seats to the various groups, and the Federation. Amarinder Singh tried hard but could not bring about any consensus. The AISSF and the Pakistan based Panthic Panel also had serious differences according to a news report in *The Tribune* dated November 1989. The Panthic Committee dismissed Manjit Singh from the Presidentship of the Federation for his dithering stand on Khalistan. The latter threatened the Panthic Committee that if it did not stop criticising him, he would expose the deeds of G.S. Manochahal and his associates. This conflict appeared to be a kind of shadow boxing because both the organisations had a working understanding with each other.

For the forthcoming elections, the Federation announced support to eight candidates of the UAD (Mann) who allegedly believed in the Bhindranwale ideology. Six out of these eight won. As expected, Simranjit Singh Mann, who was still in Bhagalpur jail, swept the polls in the Tarn Taran parliamentary constituency which was affected by the severest onslaught of militancy. Dhian Singh Mand, another youth leader, won from the adjoining constituency of Ferozepur defeating two stalwarts—Choudhari Devi Lal and Bal Ram Jakhar. Bimal Kaur Khalsa, the widow of Beant Singh, an assassin of Mrs. Gandhi, also won from Ropar, which was still comparatively free from militancy. She had earlier lost in both, a parliamentary and an assembly constituency, in the elections of September 1985.

Without analysing the pattern of voting in the multi-party contests (barring Tarn Taran), the AISSF construed it as a sudden swing in its favour. To translate a Punjabi saying into English, the tails of Manjit Singh and his followers were up as never before. The fact was that just a few days before the poll, some Akali candidates were forced to withdraw in favour of the candidates supported by the AISSF. For instance, Charan Jit Singh Walia the sitting MP from Patiala, withdrew in favour of Atinder Pal Singh. His supporters, naturally, voted for Atinder. In Simranjit Singh Mann, the former officer from the Indian Police Service known for his integrity, the people of the worst militancy affected areas saw a messiah of peace. When people harassed by violence voted for the candidates of UAD (Mann) they were voting for Simranjit Singh Mann and not supporting militancy in any manner.

In addition to the hopes for peace from S.S. Mann, it is important to notice the fact that the Federation-supported candidates had an advantage over their rivals, not because the Federation had any widespread support of the people but because of some demographic changes. These changes had taken place in the rural and semi-urban areas. Some of the grassroots leaders, *panches*, *sarpanches*, and accepted opinion builders, had earlier quietly migrated from the villages and small towns. They could not now come back to ask for votes. The canvassing machinery of all the political parties, barring the Left, was thus severely handicapped. In their absence the vehicles carrying canvassing parties comprised of strangers or lesser known individuals who could not strike the same rapport with the voters for they did not know them. Most often they returned after making ineffective appeals through a hailer. On the Federation side, the boys—mostly teenagers who were not real militants but just their admirers—contacted the voters with warmth and enthusiasm in the name of S.S. Mann. Due to their numbers and free time, they met the voters in their homes on the polling days as well, to remind them. The element of fear, if at all it worked, existed to the extent that the people were obliged to show up at the polling booth. There was absolutely no compulsion to cast their votes under threat, as the secrecy of stamping the ballot paper was being fully maintained. Senior civil servants from other states paid surprise visits more than once to the polling booths.

My own assessment for Amritsar constituency initially gave an edge to the Congress candidate in a quadrangular contest. A few days before the polling was due, the *bhog* ceremony of Kanwal Jit Singh, a feared terrorist, belonging to a respectable family, happened to be held in his village, Sultanwind, on the outskirts of Amritsar. Kirpal Singh, a rebel member of Devi Lal's Janata Dal, was also contesting from Amritsar as a member of a new political party formed by him. He had to address the gathering because of his social status and his relations with the family. His fine oration won the hearts of the large teenage presence in the gathering and suddenly the wind changed in his favour while otherwise he, would have been in the third position. When I saw the teenagers canvassing for Kirpal Singh in a number of villages, I revised my assessment in favour of Kirpal Singh and informed the government about the trends having changed. The other three candidates, Dr. Baldev Prakash of BJP, Raghu Nandan Lal Bhatia of the Congress and Manjit Singh Calcutta of the Akali Dal came to see me in the middle of the night in my office. They could not believe the voting trends which were being regularly updated by hourly reports from the counting centres. I told them that there was no booth capturing nor any bogus voting and the real cause was as mentioned above. They were apparently convinced as they did not insist on any enquiry or on countermanding the elections in some of the polling booths.

The Panthic Committee did not want elections to be held in Punjab. Therefore, a spurt in terrorist crime was anticipated. Saturnalia, a cultural festival of engineering students of the north zone was being held in the Thapar Institute of Engineering and Technology, Patiala. On the night of 10 November 1989, 19 students were brutally shot dead by the militants. The students belonged to some colleges in Kurukshetra and Kanpur. On 12 November 1989, the number of killings all over Punjab were 14, including those of 3 terrorists. On the following two days, 3 security personnel and 11 civilians lost their lives. In the third week, 13 civilians, 2 teachers, 3 terrorists, 2 policemen and 6 home guards were killed. In two bomb blasts in Amritsar, on 18 November 1989, 6 persons lost their lives, 40 others were injured.

All killings of the innocent are shameful and the killing of these students left deep scars on us. But judging by the average monthly killings in the first six months, these killings could not be considered as a serious attempt to sabotage elections in the state. In fact the number of killings in the months of October and November 1989 were less than the killings in the same two months in 1988, 1990, and 1991. In October, for 100 civilians killed, 94 terrorists also lost their lives. But in November and December 1989, the number of civilians killed rose to 120 and 121 respectively and the number of terrorists killed fell steeply to 57 and 37. This surely was no doubt, a consequence of the diversion of the attention of security forces to the election process.

It is also a fact that Punjab, where polling was held on 26 November, was perhaps the only state where no poll related violence took place. On 22 and 24 November, the rest of the country witnessed 35 and 30 killings respectively. In numerous polling stations a re-poll had to be ordered. In Amethi, from where the Prime Minister was contesting, a re-poll had to be ordered in 97 polling stations. In Punjab, no such complications arose.

As anticipated, the Congress failed to get a majority though it was still the largest party in Parliament. Rajiv Gandhi did not stake his claim to form the government. Vishwanath Pratap Singh was elected the leader of the Janata Dal coalition and took the oath of office to become Prime Minister of India.

The outgoing government withdrew cases against all the important militants, including the conspiracy case to assassinate Mrs. Gandhi, against Simranjit Singh Mann. Walter K. Andersen, First Secretary, in the American Embassy, who met me in Amritsar, was appalled at the withdrawal of a case of conspiracy to murder the Prime Minister of the country. But the outgoing government seemed to have a devious plan to queer the pitch for its successors. As a result, Harmandar Singh Sandhu, the more aggressive colleague of Manjit Singh and Atinder Pal Singh were both released. The traditional political stalwarts, G.S. Tohra and Prakash Singh Badal, were also released as part of the political strategy of the outgoing government.

A sea change took place in the course of a week's time. The Akalis could hold parleys with an open mind with the new government at the Centre. But the AISSF (Manjit) began to take all the credit for toppling the old order in Punjab. For the first time, they had claims on some of the representatives who would sit in Parliament. They had a solid presence and legitimacy that they had not known earlier. The Panthic Committees, after Operation Black Thunder, existed only in newspapers and had no legitimacy except for the muscle power of the killers under their command. The election had not bestowed anything substantial on them. Therefore, the Committees began to assert themselves more and more in order to contain the AISSF. Manjit Singh, on the other hand, claimed that the AISSF success was the victory of the militants and a verdict against the repressive policies of the outgoing government.

The United Akali Dal seemed to have been pushed into the wilderness. G.S. Tohra changed his support to S.S. Mann. Amarinder Singh wrote to P.S. Badal to follow suit. Baba Joginder Singh, who was heading the UAD, saw the writing on the wall and formally handed the keys to the office of the party to S.S. Mann in a ceremony in the Manji Sahib Hall on 6 December 1989, the day Governor S.S. Ray resigned.

These last acts of the Congress Government give rise to the question whether their parting acts of compassion were to create goodwill for the Congress or was it only the implementation of a premeditated contingency policy to create problems for the succeeding government? In the absence of direct answers, I consider that a brief analysis is required. These measures had a tremendous impact on the prevailing sway of terrorism in the Punjab. It was visible in the steep fall in the number of terrorists killed during November and December.

According to newspaper reports the Congress Government during the year 1989 had contacted Simranjit Singh Mann, Manjit Singh, and Harmandar Singh Sandhu ostensibly to assist in bringing about peace in the Punjab. S.S. Mann who had been brought from Bhagalpur to Delhi had told newsmen that while he was in jail, he could not do anything to ease the Punjab situation. As mentioned earlier, Manjit Singh alone was released and he immediately began organising the AISSF to participate in the elections—'Get your *Raj*, *Darbar* and *Sarkar*,' he had told the large audience in Manji Sahib. The advantage of the division of the votes caused by him surprised everyone, including Manjit Singh himself. Had he anticipated such a response, he would have himself offered to contest the election just as he did in the aborted elections of June 1991. Obviously the Congress had not released Manjit Singh to deny itself the six parliamentary seats which the UAD (M) had won out of a total of 13 seats in Punjab. Therefore, one can conclude that no contingency plan existed for spoiling the game for the opposition if it were to come to power.

The outgoing government could surely have left the withdrawal of the cases against S.S. Mann and Atinder Pal Singh, the two MPs, and Harmandar Singh Sandhu for the succeeding government to decide. If, at the time of the release of Manjit Singh, P.V. Narasimha Rao had met the duo and seemingly had not advised the release of Harmandar Singh Sandhu, one cannot find any justification for his hurried release in the prevailing sensitive situation. To my mind the release of Harmandar Singh Sandhu surely vitiated the release of the other two. Whatever the considerations behind their release, the Congress had only liberated three very inconvenient persons. But unwittingly, their scheme to release Manjit Singh with the objective of dividing the votes, laid the foundation for a fresh growth of terrorism. It also provided the infrastructure. The release of these leaders who were pro-militant and had a large following amongst them, certainly put the security forces in a dilemma.

Governor S.S. Ray, while pressing his case for *Panchayat* elections, had said in August–September 1989 that only 16 police stations in the state were affected very badly. Soon we found terrorist operations of extortion and killings spreading all over the state. This had become possible because of the spread of the geographical base of the six MPs of UAD (Mann) and of the two other MPs who joined them later. The young boys, in fact, had started campaigning for these candidates just for the heck of it, to use a colloquial phrase. In organising the election campaign, an area-wise hierarchy emerges by itself. After the victory of their candidates, the same boys joined the ranks of the militants and became gang leaders. This increased the number of extortionist gangs and killings all over the state. The sudden swell in the ranks of the militants was also the reason for a sudden increase in the number of militant casualties from March 1990 onwards.

21

A New Government at the Centre

Within five days of his taking over as the Prime Minister, V. P. Singh was in the Golden Temple to pray for peace. He was accompanied by three of his senior Cabinet colleagues. The Sikh youth, up in rebellion against the Government of India for more than five years, turned up at the Golden Temple in large numbers to meet and welcome the new Prime Minister with great fervour. Every one in the enthusiastic crowd attempted to converge towards the VIPs. The ring of security around them broke, time and again. K.P.S. Gill and I would lend a helping hand every time the ring was overwhelmed. Half way down the *parikrama*, I told K.P.S. Gill that I would manage in the *parikrama*. But if they were allowed to move like this on to the causeway connecting the Darshani Deorhi with the Temple, chaos would be unavoidable. He walked on to the Darshani Deorhi and arranged to keep the boys back from following the leaders. As a result, the VIPs could pray in peace within the Harmandar while the enthusiastic boys filled the whole area between the Darshani Deorhi and the Akal Takht. By the time V. P. Singh returned, the three storeys of the incomplete Akal Takht building were also packed. The place was jammed with youth as never before.

The SGPC and the Akalis had frequently extolled their decade-long fight as a conflict between the Akal Takht and the Delhi Takht. Now, the Delhi Takht, comprising V. P. Singh, his Deputy Prime Minister Devi Lal, the Minister for External Affairs I.K. Gujral, and the Home Minister Mufti Mohammad Saeed, had presented itself before the Akal Takht to pray in all humility and affirm in all sincerity the government's resolve to find a solution to the Punjab wrangle. It was virtually a tacit agreement implying that henceforth peace would be pursued by both sides. V. P. Singh, with the priority he gave to Punjab and the new era he promised in his address, and the youth (who had since hijacked the Akali agitation) through their rousing ovation at the presence of the leaders from Delhi, seemed committed to end the conflict. 7 December 1989 could have gone down in history as an Armistice Day, but the protagonists of the past were not present. However, the impact of this kind of open interaction and the exuberance of goodwill and hope in the air was real. From the Golden Temple, the dignitaries moved to the adjoining Jallianwala Bagh, to pay homage at the altar of liberty. Sensing the enormous goodwill for the Prime Minister, it was possible for K.P.S. Gill to implement his plan to take him in an open jeep from the historical route through the old Amritsar city to the Durgiana Mandir, where all the VIPs offered prayers again.

The Akalis also responded favourably to this propitious atmosphere. All their factions formally conceded leadership to S.S. Mann through their respective press statements. S.S. Mann himself ensured that Manjit Singh, President of the AISSF, participated in the gathering on 6 December 1989 in the Dewan Hall, Manji Sahib, where the keys of the office premises of the UAD were formally handed over to him. Manjit Singh had taken a tough stand and laid stringent conditions—to be fulfilled by the new government—before his newly elected MPs would take oath. In the beginning the militant organisations also appeared to acquiesce in the new arrangement. Thus, S.S. Mann would appear to have become the acknowledged leader of Punjab.

His popularity had soared even before he had been flown to Amritsar on the late evening of 2 December 1989. I had visited the airport in the afternoon to inspect the security arrangements. A large number of young boys were loitering around. A wishful rumour was rife amongst the enchanted young admirers that S.S. Mann would be given the Home portfolio in the V. P. Singh Government.

They were also optimistic that the elections to the Punjab Assembly would be held in February 1990 along with the Assembly polls in nine other states. The general mood was upbeat and the winners had high spirits. They envisioned themselves as commanding an influence both in Delhi and Chandigarh, all because of S.S. Mann. I very much wish that S.S. Mann, besides other things, had taken note of the aspirations of this section of the youth.

To consolidate all the factions, S.S. Mann attempted to blend the Anandpur Sahib Resolution with the Bhindranwale ideology. He felt that thereby he could bring the militants to the negotiation table. He had already been assured that the Akali unity could materialise only under his leadership. Such consolidation, under a common leader, or at least an agreement of all factions on the stand to be taken in the all-party conference, was necessary before the scheduled all-party conference under the chairmanship of V. P. Singh could be convened. But dissension appeared over the proposed resolution in the very first party meeting held at Amritsar on 11 December 1989. The resolution proposed was a synthesis of the Anandpur Sahib Resolution, and J.S. Rode's *Puran-Azadi* and Sikh Homeland demands, which sought an autonomous region within India. It also sought to include Punjabi-speaking areas of the adjoining states. Three MPs, Bimal Kaur Khalsa, Dhian Singh Mand and Jagdev Singh Khudian, walked out of the meeting as they insisted on Bhindranwale's goal. According to a report in *The Tribune* dated 12 December 1989, they did not recognise Baba Joginder Singh and Jasbir Singh Rode, as representing the ideology of Bhindranwale.

S.S. Mann's charisma at that point of time was at its highest. If he found it hard to carry the militants with him at that time, he could never achieve that after a further lapse of time. The militants had no mass base. Their mentors were the ISI of Pakistan. These organisations had also been infiltrated by Indian Intelligence agencies. They would have continued swearing by Khalistan or Bhindranwale's goal, not brooking any dilution. S.S. Mann, as a former police officer, should have been conscious of this fact. He could have strengthened himself by having a clear understanding with the conventional political parties who were committed to the Anandpur Sahib Resolution which was then under reference to the Sarkaria Commission. Devi Lal, the Deputy Prime Minister, had pretensions of being a national leader. It was, therefore, the most propitious moment to take up concrete demands such as the transfer of Chandigarh to Punjab, the completion of the Thien Dam, the control of the Bhakhra Management Board, the recognition of second language status for Punjabi in Himachal Pradesh and Haryana, the merger of Punjabi speaking areas of Rajasthan and the sharing of river waters, etc. All projects expected from what is known as the Punjab Package could have been taken up. But S.S. Mann had an altogether different approach. He could not properly assess the situation even after the V.P. Singh Government had announced the parameters within which a solution to the Punjab tangle could be found.

The consensus arrived at by the all-party meeting on 17 December 1989, under the chairmanship of V.P. Singh, was quite candid about the approach to the problem. The meeting was for 'toning up law enforcing agencies and administration' and 'to end police excesses'. While the fresh approach to the problem was to be on an enduring basis, all solutions were to be within the parameters of the Constitution. It was also specifically mentioned to extend 'support to those who did their duty to fight terrorism' i.e., the police and the paramilitary forces, and ensure that there was no laxity in action against the extremists. Prakash Singh Badal and Simranjit Singh Mann did not attend the conference but the former subsequently welcomed the move on the Punjab. The Congress (I) also stayed away from the meeting as it allegedly objected to the drafting of the resolution prior to the holding of the meeting. A day before the conference it had been clarified that it may not be possible for Punjab to go to the polls in February 1990. Within a week of the conference, it was clarified that K.P.S. Gill would continue as the DGP Punjab.

'*Savera hoga, zaroor hoga,*' (The morn shall surely come) was the assurance given by the optimistic PM at the all-party rally organised in Ludhiana on 11 January 1990. The PM announced his government's eagerness to remove the various old irritants such as jobs for the army deserters, the speedy trial of the remaining Jodhpur detainees and review of illegal detentions. S.S. Mann had received the PM at Halwara airport in the morning, but he did not participate in the mammoth gathering at Ludhiana. His absence certainly raised suspicions regarding his claims of carrying the militants with him. S.S. Mann was reported (*The Tribune* dated 14 January 1990) to have had a secret meeting and a 'heart to heart', talk with the PM in which he asked for greater evidence of the 'healing touch' to convince the boys about the new era. He also suggested the withdrawal of the CRPF and the BSF from Punjab. According to the same report, at Ram Jethmalani's residence, Devi Lal, like a true Haryana Jat, told S.S. Mann that he could attain a higher stature than that of P.S. Badal if he can wean away the 'boys' from violence. Devi Lal was absolutely right, but unfortunately S.S. Mann did not have a magic wand. He neither tried nor could he have weaned them away from the influence of Pakistan who had intensified its proxy war. An initial step was the repudiation of the Indian Constitution by the militant organisations as a rejoinder to the declaration of the all-party meet at Ludhiana.

At this meeting, Surjit Singh Barnala had made a very meaningful assertion to the effect that the Sikhs were neither separatists nor did they believe in terrorism. This was a necessary reminder to the well-meaning new government who did not have an adequate base amongst the rural masses of Punjab. The majority presence of Sikhs, in the gathering that filled the Guru Nanak Stadium at Ludhiana, belonged to the Akali Dal (Longowal) represented by S.S. Barnala. There were no supporters of the militants. Tactically, therefore, it was necessary for the government to heed the conventional and moderate Akalis and support them to organise the masses against terrorism. It is correct that for quite some time the Akalis had ceased to have any dialogue with the Congress Government in Delhi or with the S.S. Ray administration in the state, but this did not indicate that they approved of militancy. They had been pushed into such a difficult situation because of endemic groupism and frequent humiliating interference by previous Central governments.

The eagerness of V.P. Singh's government to have a dialogue with the militants and S.S. Mann, in a way, gave more importance to the noise of the guns. This certainly strengthened the militants at the cost of the Akalis. The Congress Party which had its own mass base, also had some compulsions to keep the Akalis divided. Hence they could condone such policies. But there were no such limitations as far as the Janata Party was concerned. The Left parties who were a part of the new government were already pitted against militancy. They had no animosity against the Akalis although they were critical of their mixing religion with politics. Nor did the Akalis have any old or new differences with the ruling coalition. However, I also feel that the move to support the new government should have been endorsed jointly by all the factions of the Akalis. Without such a combination, neither the Akalis nor the Janata Government could effectively mobilise the masses against the militants. V.P. Singh seemed to realise this. The choice of N.K. Mukerji, a former ICS officer from Punjab, who had vast experience and considerable ability, as the Governor could have overcome this handicap but his tenure lasted only six months. The government deputed two of its State Ministers to tour Punjab and they did well despite their limitations.

While the government had high hopes from S.S. Mann, the AISSF had different plans. The AISSF (M) did not have any MP of its own. The MPs of UAD (M) had been supported by the Federation. He, therefore, made his concerns clear. In return, he wanted to control the SGPC which was then with UAD (Talwandi). He also wanted Jasbir Singh Rode to be recognised as the *Jathedar* of the Akal Takht and the *kar-sewa* of the Akal Takht to be handed over to the Damdami Taksal. This is what the Home Ministry was working for during the Congress regime, when in October 1988, efforts had been made to reinstall Jasbir Singh Rode in the Golden Temple.

Harmandar Singh Sandhu, the Secretary of AISSF (M), after his release, laid claim to the idea of setting up *Khalsai Panchayats* as a substitute for judicial courts. He also supported Manjit's stand in asserting that the old and the corrupt clergy would be replaced by younger persons to attend at the gurudwaras. It may be recalled that four pro-militant priests, appointed in March 1986, had been replaced by the SGPC when they dismissed J.S. Rode in June 1988 immediately after Operation Black Thunder. Unlike Manjit Singh's statements indicating only a tilt towards Khalistan, H.S. Sandhu made sweeping statements that made headlines such as 'Salute the *Kesri* flag on the Republic Day.' He was not only creating a scare but was overshadowing his president, Manjit Singh. He was shot dead two days before Republic Day at his residence while he was talking on the phone. I visited his house. Someone in the crowd recognised me and in my hearing murmured to the boy next to him that they knew who was behind H.S. Sandhu's murder and they would avenge it soon.

The oblique reference was to the President of the AISSF (M). Outside the gate of the house, boys from another group had gathered. From their conversation, which was not dissimilar to that I had heard a little while earlier, I could make out that the killers had been briefed by militant outfits based abroad to shoot H.S. Sandhu when he answered a phone call from Canada, so that the man at the other end could hear the shot. The killers, on overhearing that the call was from Canada, moved from H.S. Sandhu's drawing room to the adjoining bedroom where he was taking the call and shot him dead. He had married only a week ago and only a day before his murder, a press reporter who had interviewed him, told me that this boy was no ordinary man to be taken lightly. I was curious to meet him but that day he lay dead on the floor of his house with no serious mourner around.

H.S. Sandhu, apparently a principal aide of Bhindranwale was suspected to be a government mole with the code name 'falcon'. He was the only person from the coterie of the flamboyant Sant who had surrendered to the army. By then Bhindranwale had been declared dead. Manjit Singh was the younger brother of Amrik Singh (killed during Operation Blue Star) the main aide of the Sant, for whose release the Sant had combined his *morcha* with Sant Longowal's agitation in 1983. The background of the duo is the only indicator why P.V. Narasimha Rao recommended the release of Manjit Singh alone in July 1989 and why the outgoing government ordered the release of the more flamboyant Harmandar Singh Sandhu in December 1989. We have seen their roles. Both were creatures of the government. It is obvious that both these young men had their own axes to grind and they could never have worked as a team.

A large number of AISSF boys had started indulging in extortions. For that reason, while releasing the UAD (M) leaders who were under preventive arrest, we detained Manjit Singh. Simranjit Singh Mann led all the released persons to my residential office to protest that through this kind of discrimination, the government was trying to divide them. 'Either release Manjit Singh or put us back in jail,' he said. I told him frankly that the SSP Sanjiv Gupta and I had decided to keep him back because of the increase in extortion cases at the hands of the AISSF boys who enjoyed his protection. To convince S.S. Mann and Bimal Kaur Khalsa, I phoned SSP Sanjiv Gupta and asked him to come over to my office to meet the deputation. He corroborated what I had told them. He also showed them some documentary evidence. Satisfied, S.S. Mann left without any further protest and so did the other MP.

After his release, Manjit Singh, accompanied by a very eminent leader, Kirpal Singh, MP, came and protested vehemently against his arrest. I told the MP what I had said to the deputation led by S.S. Mann only a few days earlier. I narrated another incident in which, despite my bringing the details to his notice, his boys kept on threatening a retired Colonel of the Indian Army and his only son till the family left India. The SSP was asked to bring the documentary evidence which he had earlier shown to S.S. Mann. Manjit Singh remained annoyed with me, but did not publicly deny the allegation, despite our assurance that we would not rebut his denial. The other faction of the AISSF (Daljit group) contradicted S.S. Mann's hope that the militants would come to the conference table. This group had the support of the Pakistan based Panthic Committee. An escalation in crime was noticeable. Security personnel were their favourite targets. In December 1990, we lost 41 personnel compared to 20 in October and 28 in November. This was the situation in which Governor N.K. Mukerji endeavoured to give a 'civil face' to the state administration so that it could win back the confidence of the people.

22

The 'Civil Face' of Governor Mukerji's Administration

Nirmal Kumar Mukerji, formerly of the ICS and Cabinet Secretary of the Union Government, took over the reins of administration in Punjab on 8 December 1989 to bring about the changes the Prime Minister desired and promised. Punjab's most disturbed areas of Amritsar, Gurdaspur and Ferozepur were a part of Jalandhar Division where N.K. Mukerji had been Commissioner in the early 1960s. After taking oath as the Governor of Punjab, his claim that it was a 'homecoming for him' was not merely a pleasantry but a reality. He had followed the unhappy developments in Punjab. He was aware of the suffering and the untold miseries of the people at the hands of the militants and the police, and he had thought of a solution: 'Give a civil face to the administration and build confidence in the masses.' It was also rumoured that Governor N.K. Mukerji had told the security forces that he would brook no excesses or killing of arrested militants, in what had come to be known as 'fake encounters' (*The Tribune*, 4 January 1990).

He came to pay his obeisance at the Golden Temple and Durgiana Mandir on 12 December 1989 accompanied by the Chief Secretary R.P. Ojha and K.P.S. Gill. Wreaths were laid at the Jallianwala Bagh. He promised to visit Amritsar more often as the people here were the worst sufferers and he kept his word. Within four weeks he visited Goindwal, where for the previous decade successive governments had tried to establish an industrial complex but had failed. He heard the people both at Goindwal and Tarn Taran where militancy was at its worst. Patti and Khalra were covered in succeeding visits.

From the very inception of the terrorist movement in the Punjab, the police had been at the forefront of the confrontation with the militants, fighting as best as it could. It had earlier made short work of a militant Naxalite movement during the late 1960s under the Akali Government, but it met with mixed success in dealing with the rise of militancy under Jarnail Singh Bhindranwale. The reorganisation of police districts, strengthening of the force and better logistics had enabled us by 1989, to achieve a reasonable control over militancy. With the announcement of the elections in the last quarter of that year, militancy had begun to increase. In armed encounters with the terrorists, though the police retrieved its reputation of bravery, it lost much of its credibility in most other policing aspects of the fight against terrorism. This was because their criterion for success was merely the number of killings. The police logic was that if they succeeded in killing some terrorists, terrorism would end *ipso facto* and the public would come to its side. Conversely, if the terrorists had an upper hand, people would lean towards them.

When Governor N.K. Mukerji said that he would give a 'civil face' to the administration he was emphasising the greater importance of fighting for the hearts and minds of the victims of terrorism. He was responding to the woes of the people who had suffered and were still caught in the crossfire between the militants and the police. The question coming up again and again in his mind must have been, 'What were the District Magistrates doing when people were suffering under such atrocities at the hands of their own police?' And he actually posed the question to me during his second visit to Amritsar while we were touring the most disturbed areas of Patti and Tarn Taran.

'What has happened to the civil services? Is the stuff not up to the mark? Or, has the office of the Deputy Commissioner been denigrated?' He was very soft spoken, and the manner in which he posed the question was, somehow, reassuring as he seemed to imply that I was an exception. Maybe I chose to interpret it that way in conformity with my own self-image.

I recalled the fact of the separation of the judiciary from the executive since 1965, as a result of which the Judicial Magistrates were now fully under the Sessions Judges. Earlier they were under the District Magistrates (DM) where criminal cases were concerned. This channel was, therefore, no longer available to the DM to evaluate the working of the police; nor did the police look up to the DC for help in important cases. Second, the politicians depended more on the police for their day-to-day functioning which included twisting the arms of their opponents. I also submitted that the situation was not as bad as it was being presented. In the terrorist ambience, the police and the paramilitary forces were physically more visible on the ground. Unfortunately, militancy had been increasing all the time. The police force and anti-terrorist operations had to be increased accordingly. It had, therefore, generally acquired an unhappy image of terror rather than one of protectors of the harassed people.

There was, however, another important aspect of this problem which could not be overlooked. Investigations in terrorist cases brooked no interference or moderation. However, this was something that public men expected from the police in accordance with the practice of *sifarish*. Interrogation of terrorists was a very difficult, extremely sensitive and laborious task. Sometimes third degree methods were also used but, more important was intelligent interrogation not only to elicit sensitive information but also to win over the man. Apparently the ISI training also included lessons in the art and importance of how to feed wrong information to the police. In each district, only a few officers could be entrusted with the arduous and trying job of conducting interrogations. It also had to be done with imagination and requisite tact, for long hours at a stretch, so as to tire the suspect to breaking point.

In one instance, two police officers in Amritsar temporarily lost even their voice due to the unremitting stress of long hours of interrogation. Such interrogations, for the sake of secrecy, could not be done in police stations. Separate centres had been established for this purpose. Special officers and isolated buildings marked for this purpose earned notoriety, both because of their location and the person in charge. We cannot say that physical torture was excluded. This had always been around, particularly in cases of smuggling but the notoriety earned by the police during the terrorist phase was much greater. We could not always help the aggrieved relations of suspected militants. Therefore, the impression formed was that the DM's were ineffective.

The incidence of crime and preventive arrests had increased many times which also implied a corresponding increase in paper-work in police stations. The production of the accused persons in court, taking them to the hospital for medical examination, taking the dead bodies for post-mortem and, above all, VIP duties had also increased abnormally. As the workload increased, control within the organisation began to become lax. The revenue districts of Amritsar and Gurdaspur had to be divided into three and two police districts respectively each under the charge of an SSP. But much damage had been done before we could think of effecting this change on 4 April 1988.

I also submitted that, ever since the imposition of President's rule, there had been a tremendous change in the role and authority of the Deputy Commissioner as the head of developmental administration. As a result of this, he enjoyed more influence with the general public than before. This was especially visible when the DC and the SSP went to rural conferences, which we organised frequently in order to promote better understanding between the people and the administration. Due to the dissolution of the State Assembly and, also because of the fear of terrorists, the former members of the Assembly no longer came to see the DCs and SSPs as frequently. But this gap was filled by the grassroots politicians who would throng to the DCs office. Consequently we had developed new and independent sources of information in the form of this new breed of politician. We also received information from various village level workers in the Revenue Department, Block Development Office, Health Department and the village school teachers. Information coming to us was generally more objective compared to the coloured information given to the police.

But all these measures could not give much relief to innocent cases amongst the accused, who had been subjected to torture in the Interrogation centres or who rotted in jails because of unending trials. In many cases, the parents were not aware of the involvement of their wards in militancy. Their harassment and annoyance was natural. The impression of police high-handedness was enhanced if the police officials happened to be unscrupulous and released the innocent, or those marginally involved, after their palms had been greased. The fear that worked on the minds of the parents was not always that the boy may be charged under some law or the other, but that he may be tortured or even eliminated. They invariably looked for an intermediary who could pass money to the concerned official. The only remedy seemed to be to undertake mass contact programmes with the objective not only of getting to ascertain peoples' grievances but also to seek their co-operation to assist the administration to devise less harsh methods. The Governor knew many of the facts of my long narration but he was gracious enough to listen to me patiently. He seemed to be satisfied with my observations and views.

I would like to believe that it was because of his endorsement of my assessments and also because they were the worst affected areas, that Governor N.K. Mukerji frequently toured Amritsar, Gurdaspur and affected parts of Ferozepur. He met people freely and, wherever necessary, he gave them private audiences. Unlike Governor S.S. Ray who had to depend upon interpreters, Governor N.K. Mukerji had been brought up in the Punjab. Therefore people were very much at ease in his presence and loved to meet him. His familiarity with the local language was a tremendous advantage. In Patti and Tarn Taran, we met unending queues. Governor N.K. Mukerji started going to each one of them. Those who wanted secrecy had to wait till the end and were then heard privately. One could notice the beginnings of a fresh confidence in the administration.

He visited the Central Jail, Nabha, which housed the largest number of terrorists after the Central Jail in Amritsar. After hearing the inmates, he ordered the review of all cases in order to identify those which could be withdrawn. This was to be undertaken by the Deputy Commissioner upon getting a recommendation from the SSP. As a result, 600 cases from all over Punjab were recommended to be withdrawn. Fortunately the state government agreed. The *Panchayats* were also to be consulted before releasing the young boys. Since many of the boys accused in these cases were also involved in some other cases, the number of people actually released was much less. The DC and SSP were required to meet every month to review complaints against the police. Although we discussed only the complaints that were received by the Deputy Commissioner, this turned out to be a very useful exercise to redress genuine complaints of harassment.

Governor N.K. Mukerji reconstituted the grievance panels and increased the frequency of their meetings. But the most important institution that had a durable effect in mobilising the masses were the District Planning Boards. Each block elected four representatives. Then there were representatives of political parties. The

Chairman was the Deputy Commissioner. This was one of the measures of the package that had been announced earlier by Rajiv Gandhi and urged by Governor S.S. Ray but it was during Governor N.K. Mukerji's term that this useful institution became operational. In the course of its functioning, this innovation became an appropriate substitute, if there could be any, for an elected government. It evoked great interest in the masses for development in their areas. There was genuine, direct participation by the people in the process of development. The District Planning Boards continued to exist even after the restoration of a democratic government.

The killings which had begun to increase with the announcement of elections in October 1989 continued to rise. When things worsened in March 1990, B.G. Deshmukh, the Principal Secretary to the Prime Minister, came to Amritsar on the 20th to review the situation. He held a meeting with the people of a village and also inspected the working of two police stations. He pointed out the similarity in most of the FIRs in cases of terrorist detention to K.P.S. Gill and me. Each of them repetitiously recorded that the militants, at the sight of the police party, raised slogans of 'Khalistan *Zindabad*'. This had been done in order to apply the provisions of TADA. It was amazing but a lesson to me in particular as I had also examined the same reports and had evidently not been vigilant enough. The fact that carbon copies of the FIRs sent to my office were usually faint and illegible, could be an extenuating circumstance. But it had surely a lapse on my part.

B.G. Deshmukh seemed to be satisfied with the morale of the people living in the worst affected areas close to the border. But the press reported on the same day, that the Home Minister had spoken in favour of revamping the Punjab administration. B.G. Deshmukh reviewed the situation again on 29 April 1990 at Amritsar with me, the IG Police, Border Range, and the GOC of the area. We learnt from him that the NSG would be deployed in the border districts in a couple of days. The National Security Guards had quite sophisticated weapons and training but their deployment, I regret, had not led to any encouraging results. That force was not oriented to the situation prevailing in Punjab. Understandably, it was withdrawn soon after.

The spurt in violence was certainly alarming. The reasons behind this were obvious. Pakistan had begun to give more incentives to the militants to escalate violence in order to stall the expected Assembly elections in the Punjab. The militants had been given weapons, ammunition and RDX. The new tactics they employed were increasing bomb blasts, carrying out killings during daylight wearing police uniforms and organising shootouts in the Malwa region of the Punjab, where neither the police nor the people had seen much violence earlier. At this stage an effort was made by Pakistan to link up the terrorist movement in Jammu and Kashmir with that in Punjab. A statement that, in order to check terrorism, India might attack terrorist training camps located in the neighbouring country panicked Pakistan. Fearing an attack by the Indian Army, Pakistan sent back G.S. Manochahal, Kashtiwal and some other top terrorists to organise sabotage in case of war, and to escalate violence in the interim. Rockets and mines, as well as material to destroy tanks, were also recovered from border crossers.

Although the Punjab administration had taken steps to induct another 10,000 SLRs, its fighting force had been depleted. The paramilitary forces that had been withdrawn in February 1990 for election duty in eight other states, had not been sent back on the reasoning that Punjab had meanwhile raised three battalions of Armed Police. Since the brunt of the militancy was borne by the border districts, Sanjiv Gupta, and I had organised public meetings in vulnerable areas and made the people aware of all the methods of the enemy. As a result, with the help of the Home Guards, they had detected four cases of bomb plants. Such meetings with the people in the affected areas all over the state, consequently, gave a boost to the rapport of the masses with the administration. We began getting more and more information from people. As a result, the number of terrorists killed in the state in May and June 1990 rose to 96 and 100 respectively which was the highest until then. This trend kept on increasing.

Governor N.K. Mukerji was keenly concerned and aware of the long term measures as well—the development and employment schemes—but the Prime Minister could not find time for him. On the contrary, the Home Minister made quite an intriguing statement on 29 May 1990, that he wanted to 'revamp' the administration of the Punjab. The seasoned ICS man, had done his very best without regard for his health or age, and was very satisfied with the progress achieved. Somewhat unexpectedly, he resigned on 1 June 1990.

A very senior and triumphant-looking cop remarked in a tone as if he was talking to himself and not to me: 'Mukerji was a fine and intelligent ICS man with subtle wit, but he could not understand the entity known as Punjab Police.' The Home Minister had certainly been influenced for the wrong reasons. The remark clearly indicated lobbying against him in the Home Ministry. It was really sad that the good work done by Governor N.K. Mukerji, as also the excellent performance of the police under stress, was wasted in this way. Governor N.K. Mukerji had revitalised the people against militancy. He had revived their confidence in the administration. The increase in the killings of civilians and decline in the killing of militants had begun a couple of months before the election, a situation which Governor N.K. Mukerji inherited. The number of terrorists killed began declining. From 94 in October 1989, it came down to 44 in February 1990 after which this graph also began moving upwards. In March 1990 it crossed 80 and in June, for the first time in the entire ambit of killings, a 100 terrorists were killed. Thereafter, this number remained on the increase. Had the security forces been demoralised, they could not have bounced back in just four months. Thus, even in arithmetical terms, the allegations of demoralisation of the force are unsustainable. After he had made considerable efforts in a confidence-building exercise the Governor wanted to know my assessment about the improvement. I said that there was certainly a very discernible improvement.

'How have you come to this conclusion, Sarab Jit?' he asked. It was the month of May and we were touring the areas near Patti again. It was difficult to substantiate my perception offhand. I could recall only one fact, which was that whenever the police arrested any young boy his parents used to send me a telegram adding that the whereabouts of the arrested person were not known. This was to create evidence of his arrest and preempt extra-judicial elimination. 'There is a considerable fall in such telegrams and letters, Sir.' I replied. Governor N.K. Mukerji thought over my reply for a long moment and then observed, 'I think it is a fairly dependable criterion, but what action do you take on such petitions?'

'I immediately write to the SSP concerned by name. If no case has been registered and the arrest is denied or no reply is received, further action is taken; like discussing such references in meetings with police chiefs, ordering magisterial enquiries, and where nothing is feasible, I order a discreet enquiry to be undertaken.'

The Governor picked up the phrase 'discreet enquiries'. 'Discreet enquiries should always be made,' he suggested.

'We may not be able to take any action on the basis of such enquiries,' I submitted.

'No Sarab Jit, you can confront the police at the personal level. This can be a positive help to your colleague in the police and in itself it can go a long way in improving police functioning at the lower levels,' was his sound advice.

Six months was too short a period to give the administration its old face and revive the confidence of the people in a system where terrorists, by and large, called the shots. When the boys with guns appeared on the scene either as dacoits, Naxalites, or the present militants, it was the police's responsibility to meet the challenge. Even though the present movement by then had acquired more dangerous aspects than the use of guns, it was not palatable for the police force under the command of the high profile K.P.S. Gill to surrender the initiative to the civil administration, even if it had been losing it from day one. Yet the mathematician in N.K. Mukerji, with his precise methods and monitoring, succeeded in giving a civil face even to the police. He toured extensively and met a large number of people, privately if they so desired. He invited them to speak up openly and fearlessly against any officer or public man. After hearing them, he would ask for reports and wherever necessary relief was given to the aggrieved persons. During the Congress regime people had a growing feeling that the party had a vested interest in keeping the Punjab issue and the violence alive and that, the administrative machinery from the top to bottom was the same and was against the people. With the change of government those fears had vanished, and Governor N.K. Mukerji's presence did the rest. His presence and extensive interaction with the people had protected the Punjab police of many exaggerated allegations levied by the supporters of militants and human rights organisations, and helped it to regain the confidence of the people. I do not think the Punjab police ever realised this.

In March 1990, a British parliamentary delegation visited Amritsar. Many a Punjabi and human rights activist, from their constituencies in England had been pestering them to do something to mitigate the reported inhuman treatment being meted out to the Sikh boys. The government instructions were that, in addition to meetings with the prominent people of the district, a visit to the Central Jail, Amritsar, should also be arranged for them. Justice Ajit Singh Bains, a former judge of the Punjab and Haryana High Court,

General Narinder Singh (Retd), Inderjit Singh Jaiji, a former Akali Legislator, also accompanied the delegates. I took the foreign guests into the jail and arranged for those accompanying the delegation to sit in the Superintendent's office. The delegates were impressed by the general conditions of the inmates and their morale. I left them to their interviews and asked them to discuss any complaints with me later. I, also, informed them that the matter of a large number of pending trials was already under the consideration of the High Court.

Sitting in the Superintendent's office, Justice Bains was unhappy over the discrimination in not letting them go with the delegates inside the jail. I used to inspect the jail regularly and I also accompanied the High Court Judges when they inspected the prisoners. Only one man had admitted that he had committed the crime for which he had been sentenced. All the other inmates pleaded that they were innocent. If I had allowed the former Judge Bains who was now a human rights activist, to go into the jail, the inmates would have become rowdy. I told him that I did not have anything to hide from them, but that their names did not appear in the list I had received from the government. Justice Bains was quick to point out two cases where the administration 'had not been fair'.

He named two boys who, according to him, had been tortured by the police and implicated in false cases. One was a postgraduate student in Physical Education. The other, he said, had been wounded and was undergoing treatment in the hospital from where he was whisked away by the police in civvies and since then his whereabouts were not known. As chance would have it, in both these cases I had effectively intervened to ensure that the student took his examination and the other boy was traced out. I asked the Deputy Superintendent to bring both the boys to the office. The boys took the delegates to be a Commission that had come for some probe against the police, began relating fabricated stories about their innocence and police torture and of course the planting of false cases against them. The excited Justice Bains stood up and started addressing the members of the delegation who had returned from the prisoners to the office. After he had finished, I asked the boys, 'Why did the police bring about false cases against you?' They looked at each other. When I disclosed my identity and reminded them about my intervention, they completely lost face.

Mr. Madden, one of the members of the delegation, spoke fluent Punjabi. He talked to the inmates of the jail in my absence. According to a report in *The Tribune* (3 April 1990) the members of the delegation, told the House of Commons on their return, that there was no violation of human rights in Punjab. They further informed the House that most of the terrorists were ordinary gangsters who preyed on the Hindus and the Sikhs in the name of Khalistan and people were sick of them. The delegates pointed out that there were instances of excesses in countering militancy which the government admitted. The British Government, according to the same report 'did not equate India with countries where systematic abuse of human rights is (was) part of Government policy.'

Governor N.K. Mukerji's departure from Punjab came suddenly and quite unexpectedly. The result of his efforts in organising people against militancy had begun to show. The militants had been virtually riding the crest of a high wave since November 1989. By March 1990, the people had begun to distance themselves from the militants and information had started flowing to the police once again. By June, for the first time, the death toll of militants reached the 100 mark and kept on increasing till the end of militancy. This was a great boost to the police whose morale was on the decline since November 1989. But we were surely deprived of the long term perspective which Governor N.K. Mukerji had in mind for providing training and employment to the youth. His successor, Governor V. Varma, shifted emphasis in order to restore peace to revive the democratic set up.

We frequently indulged in juggling statistics to point at the silver lining around the dark clouds on the horizon of Punjab at various critical junctures of the struggle. Zail Singh, the then President of India, on his farewell visit to Chandigarh in July 1987 had said that one cannot wash away blood stains with blood. True, the increased killing of militants was not necessarily the decline of militancy. If more militants had kept on joining armed groups, the situation may have worsened. More blood means a stronger odour of it. But before we have a look at such morbid analyses, let us first have a look at Governor Varinder Varma's efforts to restore peace to Punjab.

23

Governor Varma's Tenure

Varinder Varma, a Janata Dal MP, was the choice of Delhi to succeed Governor N.K. Mukerji. 'Peace and fair polls' were the two tasks he set for himself. This was expected of an old Congressman who had been committed to Gandhian principles during his 45 years of public life. He also took pride in being a simple farmer. After the swearing-in ceremony at Raj Bhawan on 14 June 1990, he told the press that the use of bullets for the last eight years had failed to improve the situation. He would, therefore, endeavour to 'win the confidence of the people and the political parties through love and affection and mutual accommodation.' He also intended to restore the civil administration to its pre-eminent position, primarily in order to prevent police excesses. The following day in Amritsar he told pressmen that all factions of Akalis should call on terrorists to stop killing innocent people. He had come to visit the Golden Temple, the Durgiana Mandir and Jallianwala Bagh.

Meanwhile I had made arrangements for the formal handing over of the gold, silver and some precious gems, recovered from the Golden Temple by the Army at the time of Operation Blue Star, to the SGPC. The Governor was pleased to do so, observing that Operation Blue Star was an unfortunate incident. Individuals in some quarters criticised him for this observation. The mindsets had not changed despite so much bloodshed. 'Peace and fair polls', though a very desirable objective, were a tall order in the given circumstances, both within the country and in Pakistan.

Governor V. Varma's approach to the problem was in keeping with the 'new era' policy of V.P. Singh's government which wanted to increase the participation of people at the grassroots to fight terrorism and thus create an environment of normalcy in which to hold elections in the state. By that time the people of Punjab had been deprived of participation in all kinds of democratic institutions. No elections to local bodies had been held in the state's 10,900 odd *Gram Panchayats*, 118 Block *Samities*, 12 *Zila Parishads*, 3 Municipal Corporations and 93 Municipal Committees because of the terrorist activities. The State Assembly had remained dissolved or suspended from 5 October 1983 to 30 September 1985 and again from 11 May 1987 to February 1992. The brief interlude of S.S. Barnala's Akali Government from 30 September 1985 to 10 May 1987 could not come up to that level of people's participation which could give them the feeling of being a part of the government. This happened because of the simultaneous emergence of violence, engineered communal tension and abrogation of the Rajiv–Longowal Accord.

I have earlier referred to Article 356 of the Indian Constitution which empowers the President of India to take over the control of the State Government under certain conditions. But the fathers of the Constitution in their wisdom also restricted the use of such powers for a duration of six months, within which the President was required to ensure the formation of an elected government. The government, and the opposition at the Centre, had however agreed time and again to amend the Constitution to enable a further postponement of the elections. In point of fact this was the longest denial of democracy in any Indian state. By then therefore, the elections had become the most urgent and crucial issue. As long as there was a Congress Government at the Centre, people believed in its unfairness towards the Punjab. The V.P. Singh Government had assuaged such misgivings in the minds of most people. All political parties, the government departments, particularly the police, had to take note of this fundamental change. But the Central Government itself had tripped when in February 1990 it decided not to hold Assembly elections in Punjab along with the elections held in some other states.

The government's aim to bring about reasonable peace in the state before holding elections, ironically, caused greater and more severe violence. Pakistan's directions to the terrorists to perform an all out killing spree were no secret. The prevalence of easy extortion had, on the one hand, became an added attraction to all sorts of criminals to join the militant ranks and, on the other, it had tarnished the image of the police. Many a police officer in the field seemed unhappy with these developments. Elsewhere I have highlighted the commendable police performance during the Governorships of N.K. Mukerji and V. Varma which had not received adequate recognition in the prevailing atmosphere.

The police itself could neither assess nor project its own performance because of the increased killings and its disapproval of changed policies particularly the emphasis on reviving the 'civil face' of the administration. Discontentment had begun to simmer in some sections of the police force.

In this background, Governor V. Varma convened the first meeting of DCs, SSPs and their seniors on 22 June 1990. A day earlier, *The Tribune* had carried a report of the Governor's interview given in Delhi captioned 'Police hand in Extortion.' The DIG G.I.S. Bhullar protested against the observations of the Governor. 'It upset me so much that I could not sleep. I feel humiliated,' he said in an agitated voice. Though the Governor denied having said what was attributed to him, while summing up, he reiterated that the police must stop their own extortions, failing which he would hold them responsible. When this was being discussed, K.P.S. Gill had left the meeting but returned after a while. At that time it appeared to be a browbeating exercise. Suddenly the police officer's remarks made after the resignation of Governor N.K. Mukerji,—that Mukerji did not understand the entity that Punjab police is—came to my mind. The next day the press highlighted the incident. K.P.S. Gill explained and the Governor knew that he had left the meeting to collect some papers from his car. K.P.S. Gill is not so thoughtless an officer that he would disregard decorum and leave a meeting when his officer had raised a serious controversy. The right course was to convey the correct position about extortions to the Governor through proper channels with the request that he contradict the report.

All this clearly indicated the strain under which the police was functioning. Many police officers believed in the efficacy of keeping the confidence of the people but this was not the avowed policy of

244 ◆ Operation Black Thunder

the force. For the high profile professional cop, K.P.S. Gill, such exercises were mostly hollow and without much meaning. The whole incident had appeared in the newspapers and it was bound to make things difficult for the Governor and his administration.

The Governor launched a massive mass contact exercise. In addition to his own tours to the disturbed areas, a core group of Central Ministers, comprising of I.K. Gujral, Subodh Kant Sahai and Goverdhan Bhagey, visited the rural areas frequently and addressed public meetings. They did really well. I.K. Gujral had an advantage, being regarded as a sagacious 'son of the soil'. He was respected by the Punjabis, even before he became Prime Minister.

In his first meeting on 20 July 1990 in Chabhal, a semi-urban village in the centre of the militancy affected areas, S.K. Sahai began his address with the remark: 'Nothing is more powerful than the people.' This captured their attention. This remained the point of emphasis in all the meetings; of course I saw to it that problems raised were sorted out during the follow-up action. I.K. Gujral explained to them in chaste Punjabi that the aim of Pakistan in training our boys in militancy and helping them with arms was only to destabilise India. He exhorted them to keep the boys away from militancy and build an atmosphere for holding elections. These meetings were held regularly and the feedback was very encouraging.

To further involve the youth in nation building activities, a centre was opened for training the youth from the border areas. The Chief Secretary of Punjab, S.L. Kapur, had initiated this scheme and had also been following it up. In fact he had been thinking on the lines of the land armies of China to rope in idle youth from border areas. Left to him, he would have straightaway taken in a few thousand of them as a work force of sorts and sent them to work wherever the demand arose. The programme was ambitious and in course of time was to cover 100,000 youth. The government gave so much importance to this scheme that the first batch of 500 boys was flagged off by the Prime Minister himself.

On 19 August 1990, the PM came to Lopoke, a small border town, for this purpose. He met the boys before addressing the crowd of 5,000–6,000. He made a very emotional speech. 'To share your agony,' he said 'I shall tour Punjab villages on foot for one week without any security. You will be my security.' The people applauded him when he said that if his blood is spilled on this land of martyrs he will be happy. They applauded him again when he said *'Goli se nahin, pyar ki boli se apnana hoga'* (he would like to win back the boys not with bullets but with sweet words). Such sympathy touched the bleeding hearts and people remembered those words for a long time. Months after the event, an ordinary farmer met me in a village meeting and recalled the Prime Minister's magic words and rued the present times when people had to hide their sons both from the police and the 'boys' (militants). 'Our great grand parents had to hide their daughters whenever the Turks and the Abdalis came plundering, but the boys faced them like men instead of hiding.' He mumbled the PM's words to himself in the fashion of a soliloquy and walked away.

For me, this visit of the PM remains a landmark for another reason. K.P.S. Gill rang me up on 16 August 1990 from Delhi to inform me about the PM's visit. I suggested Lopoke, to which he agreed. In two days all the arrangements had been made. A jungle of acacia bushes was cleared, a water channel was filled up with earth and the people of this area were informed about the PM's visit. His first visit was memorable because of the ovation he got from the boys in the Golden Temple. His second visit would remain etched in my mind for another reason. Harkishan Singh Surjit fixed the PM's visit to Amritsar on Baisakhi day—13 April 1990. No one was prepared to listen to my protest that it was a very important festival and people would be busy celebrating it. Therefore, the audience for his public meeting may not be as per our expectations. 'You have to ensure this.' This was an order. When the PM did arrive and we climbed on to the stage, the Chief Secretary looked at the crowd and then at me, 'Let us wait for twenty minutes, Sir,' I said confidently. The ground filled up within half an hour.

'How come?' asked the Chief Secretary. I told him that the police had frozen all traffic on all roads leading to this site an hour earlier and the blockade was cleared after the PM's cavalcade drove in.

'That I could make out, but the crowd is really good for a festival day,' he said appreciatively.

'It is because of the Baisakhi festival, Sir.' I had been cursing Harkishan Singh Surjit all these days, but I had no idea of the lazy fellows who planned to have a dip in the *Sarovar* of the Harmandar every Baisakhi and then put it off to the next. The free lift in trucks, to the meeting and back, prompted all of them to come.

'God is on your side, Sarab Jit,' he laughed.

A day before the PM's visit to Lopoke, the government had invited all the *sarpanches* to Chandigarh for a meeting. Governor V. Varma and S.K. Sahai addressed them. The *sarpanches* assured the government that they were with it in its fight against terrorism but they were unhappy because of the harassment they were facing from the police and other officials. The government expressed regret at having missed the opportunity to hold elections in February. The Prime Minister, before leaving Amritsar, told the pressmen at the airport that the decision about holding the elections in Punjab would be taken soon, after talking to other political parties and the people.

The political parties, however, were pessimistic. P.S. Badal had said that his party would not attend any meeting of the political parties called by the Government. Simranjit Singh Mann, who only a few days earlier had said that, for the sake of Akali unity, other parties could merge into UAD (M), quit as the party president on 21 August 1990. The newspapers reported that he had handed over his letter of resignation to the Vice President of the party. It was rumoured in Amritsar that the main reason behind his resignation was his criticism by the Panthic Committee headed by Dr. Sohan Singh whose press note, however, appeared in many newspapers including *The Tribune* only two days later. On 29 August 1990, *The Tribune* again reported that the UAD(M) had decided to boycott the poll unless it was held under the supervision of the United Nations. S.S. Mann's vice president had not taken advantage of the resignation letter of his president. Such offices had become unenviable.

The Governor and the Central government, however, seemed keener than ever to restore the political setup. The faction headed by Surjit Singh Barnala had challenged the dissolution of the Punjab Assembly, weeks after the dismissal of the government in May 1987. This was now coming up for hearing by the High Court of Punjab. The government had pinned its hopes on the decision of the judges but the High Court upheld the dismissal. Within two days of the court's judgement, Governor V. Varma held a high-level meeting and recommended holding the Punjab Assembly elections on the 4th and 6th of November. The External Affairs Minister, Inder Kumar Gujral, during his visit to Amritsar a few weeks earlier had graciously told me that they valued my opinion and had asked for my views. I had frankly told him that I saw no reason why we could not hold elections, nor did I anticipate any great surge in violence, although some increase would be inevitable. We started preparing for it in earnest. The BJP and the Congress criticised the proposal. Sat Pal Dang of the CPI was also averse to the idea. Mahant Sewa Dass threatened to immolate himself if the elections were held. The Akali Dal (Badal) was in favour of elections but it had earlier observed that the revival of the Assembly by the High Court would be of no help (the S.S. Barnala group dominated that Assembly). The opinions expressed were thus subjective, varied and conflicting.

Towards the end of August 1990 the V. P. Singh Government had decided to implement the Mandal Commission Report. A nation-wide students' agitation against further reservation of vacancies as recommended by the Commission intensified and became a very serious concern. Educational Institutions in Delhi had to be closed for a month. Three hundred youngsters were arrested. To control the situation at various places, the army had to be called out and curfew imposed. Punjab was the least disturbed area and in Amritsar the agitation remained virtually peaceful. One car was burnt, and curfew was imposed only twice for two hours each. I held numerous meetings with the student leaders and their teachers which really helped to ensure that peace was maintained. There was a realisation on the part of the students that terrorists who supported the Mandal Report could attempt a shootout on student gatherings. They did so in Chandigarh.

On 1 October 1990, the Supreme Court of India stayed the implementation of the Mandal Commission Report. Yet the agitation lingered on. The Vishwa Hindu Parishad launched a powerful movement to start a *kar-sewa* to construct the Mandir at Ayodhya. This also led to violence. The Punjab election was really forgotten. The BJP withdrew support to the government. Chandra Shekhar formed a separate party. On 7 November, V. P. Singh was voted out and Chandra Shekhar, who had been an aspirant to the PM's Office for a while, became the Prime Minister of India on 10 November 1990, with the support of the Congress.

Violence was on the rise in Punjab. October and November 1990 remained the bloodiest months of the terrorist movement. The confidence we had gained to end terrorism after the reorganisation of the police on 4 April 1988 and the exodus of the militants from the Golden Temple within six weeks of that, received a setback. The spurt in violence reinforced Pakistan's resolve to sabotage the election and any other effort for a political solution by successive Governors of the state and Prime Ministers at Delhi. It is somewhat strange that the Congress saw a danger to the country's integrity if elections were to be held in Punjab while Pakistan feared the doom of terrorism if democracy were to be restored.

Governor V. Varma stressed the completion of the border fencing and its flood lighting to check border crossing. He remained critical of the functioning of the police. A month earlier he had ordered the shifting of two Senior Superintendents of Police. On 30 November he told pressmen that the terrorists moved freely in Amritsar and Ludhiana and indulged in shootouts in these districts including Jalandhar, because of 'police incompetence and ineffectiveness'. K.P.S. Gill seemed under pressure for the first time. He announced that their policy henceforth would be to chase the militants in an offensive manner and the senior officers would be sent to the field to spend more time there.

An angry Governor V. Varma was in favour of a complete police shakeup. Both the Governor and the DGP were moved out of Punjab; the former as Governor of Himachal Pradesh and the latter as DG of the CRPF in Delhi. Lt. General O.P. Malhotra, a retired Chief of the Army Staff and a Punjabi, took over as Governor on 18 December 1990. D.S. Mangat was tipped to be the DGP of Punjab. Tejinder Khanna succeeded S.L. Kapur as Chief Secretary. The appointment of India's one time top soldier proved very useful. But I am certain that the crime situation was not properly evaluated because of the shock of the increased killings. Let us, therefore, analyse 1990 the bloodiest year in some detail, before assessing General O.P. Malhotra's administration.

24

1990: The Killings Continue

In a terrorist ambience the odour of blood becomes an obstacle in the way of objectively evaluating the situation. The critics, media and the opposition apart, even the statistics of killings may paint a distorted picture which could be misleading.

It is a fact that the number of killings in 1989 declined continuously, but just the announcement of elections in October immediately led to the number of killings rising from 76 in September to 158 in December 1989, and these figures continued to increase.

Throughout 1990 the continuously increasing odour of blood overpowered the flavours of the changing seasons. There were other, related woes such as kidnappings for ransom, extortion, robberies and unimaginable harassment from the terrorists, by forcing themselves on the local people as 'guests' for the night and also some police 'excesses'. Reports of increased killings, however, were more worrying than other terrorist related crimes. In November 1990, the killings had peaked at 364. The odour of blood diluted all logic. Judges sitting in Delhi could not take a comprehensive view of what was happening. Both the Governors who held the reigns of the Punjab administration during this period were made scapegoats as were some top bureaucrats including K.P.S. Gill.

As we have seen, Governor N.K. Mukerji was in favour of giving a civil face to the administration to gain the confidence of the people

and to fight terrorism. His successor Governor V. Varma who endeavoured to bring about some degree of peace, which was enough
to hold polls in the state, had criticised the police on more than one
occasion. The press in a subtle way also attributed the spurt in crime
to the policies of the Governors. The police, as a disciplined force,
did not criticise any of these measures but they did let their reservations be known in one way or another. But an objective analysis of
the period would show that the battles of 1990 put us on the path to
ultimate victory against the militants. The grit, courage and resilience shown by the police during this period left no doubt whatsoever that the security forces were gaining the upper hand. The
increasing alienation of the terrorists from the masses who were getting better organised to resist the militants was also a significant
trend, which continued in 1991. The decline of militancy in the district of Amritsar was discernible from April 1991 onwards.

This silver lining to the darkest clouds was missed by the Government of India, senior officers in the police and by the paramilitary
forces. The media, also failed to take any notice of the changing
wind. This was largely due to the stunning effect of the heavy and
increasing odour of blood all around. The number of civilians killed
during 1990, had risen to 2,437 from a figure of 1,176 during 1989.
But in 1988 the number of civilians killed had been 1,949. The number of terrorists killed during 1990 had also gone up to 1,321 compared to 699 in the previous year. In terms of these statistics, and
despite the prevailing optimism in the militant camps, the police
force definitely had the upper hand.

Public perception, however, was adversely affected by the spe-
cious arguments put forward to refute the 'civil face' approach and
the criticism of police functioning by Governor V. Varma. The departure of the Governors and K.P.S. Gill from Punjab may have absolved
the Home Ministry of the allegation of remaining inactive but it
went a long way in highlighting the darker parts of the picture, ob-
scuring and undermining the significant, healthy and trend-setting
achievements.

A number of factors during this phase had increased the morale of
the militant camps and gave them the impression of a victory. The
most outstanding change was the public recognition that the militants got; for the first time they had their representatives in Parliament. At par with this was a kind of open invitation from an eager
Government of India to have talks with them. The expectation that

the State Assembly elections would be held in February 1990 enthused the youth who had canvassed for the UAD (Mann) candidates. They were responsible for the phenomenal rush to the camps of the militants. Each organisation was eager to claim a larger share of the rewards in case a settlement was reached. They were in search of personal advantage, not peace.

Besides the changed atmosphere, the authority that the militants with their self-acquired title of 'Babas' enjoyed, was a great allurement. To be called a 'Baba', which entitled them to extort money from tractor owners or other well off persons of the village, was the ultimate ambition of the rural youth of all hues. Their base, therefore, widened at great speed. The Akalis had also, apparently, ceded leadership to the militants. This was more than enough for the militant camps to preen themselves in anticipation of the legal authority that they hoped to attain.

The militants were using hostels, preferably of professional colleges, as hideouts and contact points. At times they could leave their weapons with their acquaintances and friends. Some of the boys like Daljit Bittu, a medical student, were emotionally involved with the movement. But during this period, this seemed almost to be a fashion even in these institutions. The boys began using their influence to threaten their teachers to ensure they passed in their examinations. The sensational kidnapping of Liviu Radu, a Romanian diplomat, from Delhi on 12 October 1991 and the son of Ram Niwas Mirdha, a former Union Minister's son from Rajasthan, were the handiwork of this breed of 'Babas' who came from amongst intelligent professionals. Understandably, they did not harm their victims. The killers amongst them had to leave their colleges and most of them were killed in police encounters.

This spurt in volunteers suited Pakistan. It promptly expanded its infrastructure to train a much larger number of Indian youth in the use of weapons and explosives. There was no dearth of volunteers because of increased kidnappings and the lure of ransom, and the Pakistan Rangers started helping the militants to cross over to get training and then return with a heavy load of weapons. New transit camps were set up close to the border. This made it possible for a group to cross over twice a night. There were still many vulnerable points in the long stretch between Khalra and Khem Karan in the Patti area. From Noordiwala, one such point alone, nearly 100 militants carrying weapons, ammunition and explosives were believed to have crossed over to India between 18 and 23 April 1990. The border stretch between Ajnala and Dera Baba Nanak also had many porous points providing cover to the militants crossing the border through the Ravi. The BSF had intercepted many such consignments but not all. By June 1990, according to the police estimates, the number of AK 47 guns had gone up from 700 to 1,500, out of which 1,100 were in District Amritsar and the adjoining sub-divisions of Batala and Zira. P.K. Kathpalia, a former IAS officer from Punjab, who was Advisor to Governor V. Varma at that time, directed me to study the feasibility of mining all the routes of smugglers. But unfortunately such a scheme could not be implemented and the smuggling of arms continued.

Pakistan's main aim was to sabotage any agreement which would bring the militants back into the mainstream through participation in the democratic process. The excessive dumping of arms, ammunition, explosives and trained boys in a very short period was in order to have a fifth column ready in case of attack by the Indian Army which Pakistan feared. In March and April 1990, the possibility of hot pursuit of militants by the Indian forces was in the air which implied that their training schools in Pakistan could also be attacked. In July, the army moved along the Pakistan border for its annual exercise. It was felt that its presence would discourage and hinder infiltration. During this period, I often paid visits to the border from Khem Karan to the north. Across the Ravi, opposite Dera Baba Nanak, groups of youth, most of them Sikh, could be seen camping in the gurudwara, waiting to cross over from Pakistan to the Indian side, whenever they could outwit the BSF.

Directions from across the border to the militants were to target the security forces and destabilise the village defence system. As a result, 43 police and paramilitary personnel were killed during December 1989 compared to 26 in November and 20 in October 1989. Prior to that the average was 10 each month. To sustain this increasing trend they paid money for information about policemen coming home on leave. They also announced rewards for killing police officers. On 28 December 1989, the militants killed four CRPF *jawans* on guard duty at two sentry posts located in the most crowded square outside the Darbar Sahib in Tarn Taran and took away their weapons. This incident all but drove the enraged colleagues of the *jawans* to fight the Punjab Police, and also to kill some civilians that they had taken into custody, just because they were present at the spot. A timely dash to the spot by the IG Border Range, M.S. Bhullar, and me, not only saved the situation but many innocent lives too. During winters, the rural people wrap themselves in thick shawls. The militants could hide their AK 47s under this cloak and could fire at the *jawans* from a handshaking distance.

The CRPF *jawans* got the impression that the shopkeepers, through whose crowded premises the killers had crept to the posts, were party to the killing of their colleagues, and that the covering fire had come from inside the temple. This feeling of acquiescence on the part of the shopkeepers and the temple authorities had enraged the Force to the extent that they were almost ready to kill them. I sent in a team, which included CRPF personnel, to look for themselves for any empty bullet shells in the temple. This removed their apprehensions and they handed over the civilians who had been virtually held as hostages. The militants after committing the crime had gone into the temple and escaped into a street, through an opening from the *parikrama*, where they left the walkie talkie set belonging to the killed CRPF personnel.

The two most shocking acts of subversion were the bomb blasts in the most well guarded citadels—The Punjab Armed Police (PAP) headquarters in Jalandhar and the Police Training School, Phillaur, housed in an old fort of Maharaja Ranjit Singh. In the former, the main victim was Gobind Ram, who had become very controversial as SSP Batala and had been transferred to the PAP only a few months earlier. Some time earlier, the militants had killed his only son when he was returning from college. In the fort the victims were two really brave inspectors who had gone there for advanced training. The tragic irony was that they were sharing the most protected room as they were high on the hit list of the militants. One was from Amritsar district. The people of Jandiala and Gheri Mandi, two suburban towns of Amritsar, used to say that if they did not migrate, it was because of Inspector Harcharan Singh Suri. In both incidents some constables working in the respective offices had been suborned.

Attacks by militants on the CRPF posts and police stations were increasing. The militants had succeeded in winning over some police personnel. The top extortionist gang (Sona group) fired on the Kairon Police Station for two hours to avenge the killing of two of their gang members. They also attacked the CRPF personnel guarding the Central Jail, Amritsar. Although there was no loss of life, the attack on the jail, which housed many militants, had a symbolic message. Till May they attacked the police and paramilitary forces 20 times a month taking a toll of 25 men on average, every month.

These attacks were intensified from the first week of June—the week to commemorate Operation Blue Star. On the night of 7 June 1990 they attacked the police stations at Chhabhal, Patti, Harike, Sarhali and Amarkot (all in Amritsar district) with rockets. In Sarhali one CRPF *jawan* was killed and the SHO and his wife were injured. Another five CRPF *jawans* were injured when their camp outside Patti was attacked. Half a dozen *jawans* were tricked into clearing a road blocked with eucalyptus trees under which the militants had placed some bombs. All of them were injured. On the night of 13 June 1990 a gang of about 40 kept on firing at the headquarters of the 69th Battalion of the CRPF, located at a village in Patti subdivision, until, reinforcements arrived. The trend continued during the rest of 1990, which covered the tenures of Governors N.K. Mukerji and Varinder Varma.

Reportedly Pakistan had also sent back top terrorists like G.S. Manochahal and Sukhdev Babbar to personally oversee this campaign. Besides their presence, the mere act of having attacked the bastions and headquarters of battalions also boosted the morale of the militants. In their campaign against the SPO posts and the Home Guards, many of whom had been employed on daily wages, it was not difficult for them to win over these poorly paid semi-trained local boys. They succeeded in enticing about 600 SPOs and Home Guards by December 1990 to quit or absent themselves from duty. They also succeeded in threatening members of the Village Defence Committees to disassociate themselves from these icons of resistance. But there was no dearth of replacement for the vacancies thus caused. Police patrol vehicles were also being landmined. Because the number of civilian tractors plying on these routes was much greater, this strategy had to be given up. The police also began to force mischievous elements of the village to sit in police vehicles for night movement. They would indicate the landmine spots, which they invariably knew. It was also during this period that close relatives of some senior civil and police officers were kidnapped.

The number of armed encounters between the militants and the police increased every month. For instance, in January and February 1990, the police crossed swords 26 and 20 times respectively with the militants. In March 1990 they faced bullets from each other 50 times. In May and June 1990 such skirmishes exceeded 60 each month. In July 1990 the number was 78, while in August 1990 on 90 occasions fierce battles were fought. In the entire year, 706 such encounters took place.

In many cases these encounters took place during daylight and lasted for hours. In some cases they went on for days. In almost all cases, the police and paramilitary forces succeeded or, at least, had the upper hand. These battles indicated the morale of the force as well as the increasing confidence of the Punjabi people in the police and the CRPF. While the militants and their supporters continued describing every encounter as fake, the people now had the opportunity to see for themselves instances of such cross firings. In Chhabhal an encounter began with the firing by militants on the tail end of a cavalcade of police cars returning from Patti with P.N. Mathur, IPS, who had come to assess the situation in his capacity of Advisor (Security) to the Prime Minister.

Three CRPF *jawans* were hurt on the first day but all the militants were killed in the succeeding days. K.P.S. Gill had to return to the site to see why the shooting was dragging on. The number of militants was not large but they hid in a paddy field and a nearby sugar-cane field and managed to fight for two days. The idea of having bulletproof tractors for combing even tall crops and paddy fields in such situations was adopted immediately after this encounter. It proved useful in future similar situations. However, it would be incorrect to give this method sole credit for a fall in the number of acts of militancy.

The encounters continued. After the deployment of the army in December 1990, their number further increased. An encounter fought in the heart of Ratul village in Tarn Taran area, went on for three days. This village was a frequent haunt of G.S. Manochahal. Therefore, he had made proper defensive plans to fight back whenever the occasion arose. In some buildings, modifications had been made for adequate cover to move from one building to another. It was rumoured that he was in that village when the police and the army cordoned it off on receiving a tip. Reportedly, he succeeded in convincing some members of the cordoning force, that the woman riding pillion on his scooter was his wife who was sick and needed urgent medical attention.

The SSP Tarn Taran, Narinder Pal Singh, who was leading the fight, had very bravely moved into a building close to those occupied by the militants. He was hit on the thigh and shifted to Amritsar hospital. DIG Ajit Singh, also a very brave officer, rushed to the spot to stand in for the district chief. He was also injured fatally and died on the way to Amritsar. Despite these setbacks, the encounter continued until all the militants were killed. People living in the surrounding houses had to be evacuated for their safety. They co-operated and stayed in the gurudwara as long as the fight lasted.

But more illustrative of police morale was the brief encounter of the SSP, Sita Ram, near Batala. The militants had challenged him on the phone to come and face them on the Batala Amritsar road. SSP Sita Ram hastened to the point indicated, only to find himself held up by some trees that the militants had felled on the road. The militants immediately showered bullets from all sides and escaped after injuring nine policemen, including the SSP.

In the hospital SSP Sita Ram told me that if he had held himself back, fearing a trap, he would have lost the right to keep his moustache up, as the saying goes in Punjabi. Self respect was extremely important for him. In another encounter, a police constable was firing at a militant from an open spot. The SSP, Narinder Pal Singh, shouted some invectives and told him to take cover. 'Sir, the man opposite me has an AK 47, his bullets cannot reach me. I will get him with my .303 in a few minutes,' and he did. Only two years earlier I had told the Home Minister that our police feared the AK 47 as if it was a *Ram Ban*. We had surely come a long way.

Anil Sharma, a young IPS officer who was SSP Majitha, was twice fired at during night patrolling on rural roads. Despite the fact that his car at that time was not bulletproof he continued his night patrolling. The high morale of the police during this period was certainly putting pressure on the militants. There were other reasons for the increase in killings. The assessment by the Home Ministry of the Punjab administration was really harsh. There is no doubt that the killings had increased but a rational analysis was necessary, before condemning the state administration publicly. The way this criticism was made public was most inappropriate.

In fact, during this period, some very senior officers also showed great courage. The relations of senior IAS and IPS officers, including M.S. Gill, Secretary to the Government of India, (who later became the Chief Election Commissioner) IG M.S. Bhullar and my cousin were kidnapped by G.S. Manochahal. He wanted the government to release Resham Singh Malmohri in exchange. We recommended rejection of the demand. Neither R.S. Malmohri nor any other militant was released. But when relatives of two politicians were kidnapped, within days, the Government of India bowed to the demands of the kidnappers. The militant, after his release, killed at least a 100 innocent people in Amritsar district before he was himself killed.

Dr. Daljit Singh, an ophthalmologist of international repute, shifted to Bombay when extortionists harassed him. This created quite a stir not only in Amritsar but in the rest of India as patients from different parts of the country had to go back. Some elders of the city came to me and suggested that I should do something urgently lest an exodus of eminent citizens gets underway. I wrote a letter which Kirpal Singh MP, a grand old man of repute, took personally to Dr. Daljit Singh in Bombay. To the great relief of every one, the doctor also showed courage and came back to his hospital.

The new breed of militants, who came up during this period, were responsible for the increased killings and extortions. But many of them showed how amateurish they were in this game and lacked any sense of commitment. It was obvious that this phase could not last long. In many encounters they left behind their weapons while retreating. For example, in Amritsar district, the militants attacked SPO posts at Kotli Nasir Khan and Dhapai. On return of fire by the posts, they ran away abandoning some of their weapons. Similarly in attacks on the SHO of Harike and Jandiala, the militants ran away leaving their weapons behind.

There is no doubt that we were also under stress. Under such circumstances, it was expected that the government would lend us increased armed support. Instead, the Central Government response seemed curiously incomprehensible because it forced us in this trying situation to spare two battalions of the CRPF for the State Assembly elections in other states during February 1990. To add to our woes, after the elections were over, the borrowed force was not returned to Punjab on the excuse that Punjab had in the meanwhile raised two battalions of Armed Police. This force was entrusted with the duty to guard sensitive places. We again had to spare two dozen companies for the rest of the country which was ravaged by the Mandal agitation. The loaned force was returned as late as February 1991, when the May–June 1991 elections in Punjab were in the offing.

Individually as well as collectively in villages, the resilient Punjabis stoically braved adversity, including the loss of their kith and kin, (young and old, even infants) and property. In support of this, and by way of tribute, I must record the instance of village Kotli Nasir Khan. The village decided to resist all the demands of the militants. In spite of repeated firing at their village and manhandling of many villagers, they defied the militants and their threats. SSP Sanjiv Gupta and I kept visiting them. Towards the end of August 1990 when the paddy was almost ripe, and it had not rained for quite some time, the militants burnt all the 13 transformers feeding the village tube wells. To check the growing panic, I urged the Electricity Board Engineers to replace all the transformers. They could spare only one or two. If the crop were to wilt for lack of irrigation, the villagers' resistance was sure to break. The following night was one of the few in my life when sleep evaded me. In the stillness of the second half of the night, I heard God speaking to me through a faint sound of thunder. To make sure that I was not dreaming, I rushed out into the *verandah*. It was already drizzling. In a few minutes, it was pouring. Next morning I rang up the Superintending Engineer and asked him to ensure that all the burnt transformers of the village were replaced in the ensuing week. 'With the eased pressure it would be expedient to replace all of them right now. After a week, the pressure would be more intense if it does not rain in between,' said the relaxed engineer. During the paddy season, transformers often go out of order and farmers squat before the offices of the Electricity Department till it is replaced.

In another incident, some *lambardars* in villages had collected land revenue but were not depositing the same in the Treasury. The revenue staff was threatened if they went to collect the amount from them. Arrears were mounting. I sanctioned some development projects for some recalcitrant villages but withheld the release of grants. When the village deputation came to complain, I told them that the grants would not be released till the entire land revenue dues were paid. The pressure of the whole village was mounted on the mischievous elements and the payments resumed. Similarly, unscrupulous consumers in many villages had not paid their electricity bills and were also instigating others to follow suit. The Electricity Department felt helpless. The stoppage of electric supply to the whole village succeeded in putting pressure on the defaulters and it worked.

People were now increasingly resisting the militants who had come to be regarded as criminals and nothing more. Besides the sympathetic government, the impact of killings in the villages, which had risen to as high as 90 per cent, turned people against the killers. The rise in the cases of extortion had increased the base of the terrorists; consequently, if the killings of civilians increased, the number of militants killed also went up. This graph was a good sign of their unpopularity. But the defiance of the *bandh* call from 5 to 12 November 1990 given by the militants (when Sukhvinder Singh Sangha was killed, allegedly in a fake encounter) was a sure indication of the new trend. The call was not observed fully even in Tarn Taran which S.S. Sangha had dominated for quite some time. His supporters tried to salvage the image of the killed terrorist by extending the call upto 13 and 14 November 1990 but it flopped again.

Militant leaders also realised that the wind was changing against them. On 2 December 1990 they gave an ultimatum to the government to exclusively use Punjabi in its offices. They had also very brutally killed R.K. Talib, the Station Director of All India Radio at Chandigarh, for not complying with their direction to broadcast all its programmes in Punjabi. All these years after the creation of Punjabi Suba in 1966, no serious steps had been taken, even by any of the Akali governments to fully change over to the use of Punjabi in its offices in place of English. The militants ultimatum had been more effective and one may say that they, despite all their black deeds, have something to boast of.

K.P.S. Gill had acknowledged that the militants were being isolated. But his thesis, that if the police had the upper hand the people would come to their side, was not proved. Though this period had witnessed the largest number of civilian killings, yet people were aligning themselves with the administration. The outcry of the people against the police was heeded during Governor S.S. Ray's tenure as well and punishments were awarded to some erring cops. The issue was discussed at our meetings, and corrective action taken, but the subject did not predominate. Governor N.K. Mukerji's insistence on projecting the civil face of the administration was in principle an acknowledgement of people's grievances against the police. An attempt was made to provide special active forums to look into the complaints of the people against the force that was fighting for them. Governor V. Varma's public insistence that it was the responsibility of the police to ease the suffering of the people and his publicly pointing out the failures on the part of the police were reiterations of the fact that there is no sacred cow in the administration, not even the police which was then engaged in fighting militancy. Such announcements did bring about a change of heart in the people vis-à-vis the administration and also put pressure on the police to improve itself.

The migration of Hindus from Bhikhiwind, Chhabal and Patti, the three major suburban towns of the worst terrorist affected area was reported as almost sensational news in the press. In an atmosphere, of panic, such reports gave the impression that the towns were almost deserted and it was the last straw on the camel's back. It cannot be ignored that during November 1990, in Amritsar, out of 56 civilians killed, 33 were Hindus. This was the highest ratio during President's rule. Normally more than 70 per cent of the terrorists' victims had been Sikhs. The increased killing of Hindus logically indicated a more gruesome turn but, even in this episode, the actual facts told a different story.

I was informed on the telephone that the whole Hindu population of the three towns mentioned above had poured into the Durgiana Mandir in Amritsar city. Ever since the deliberate targeting of more Hindus, I had visited these towns many times to be with the people and assess their security needs. I had visited the towns only two days earlier. I was sure of the determination of the people and the commitment of the police officers of the area, particularly S.S. Brar and Paramjit Singh the officers in-charge of the police stations at Patti and Bhikhiwind respectively. It was already dark. The self-styled leaders of Hindu organisations guided me straightaway to the meeting room. On the way these leaders kept repeating to me that Khara Majha (the name of the area of the three towns) was virtually gone.

The would-be migrants packed the small room on the first storey to capacity. I surveyed the gathering. It confirmed my impression that there was some manipulation behind all this. In the crowded room about a dozen lower middle class women, dressed gaudily, sat in front. I told them that they were from Amritsar city, therefore, they could leave the room to make it more comfortable. The migrants' tale of woes was that the militants were roaming around unchecked with their 'Assaults' (AK 47s) and they had told them to leave the town, failing which they would be shot. They had also pasted posters to that effect. But when I asked if anyone among the present group had been threatened or had personally seen the posters, all looked at one another. No one had read or seen any poster nor had any one been directly told by the militants to leave. Since all of them were from Bhikhiwind, I summoned the concerned police Inspector the next evening.

The story as narrated by Inspector Paramjit Singh, in the presence of the migrants, was amusing and somewhat surprising. The facts were that a Hindu boy had a small shop opposite the police station. The militants befriended him. He would pass on information about the presence of policemen in the station to them and on two occasions, the militants had fired at the police station when there were only two or three *jawans* inside. When the police learnt about this, this boy went underground and joined the militants' ranks. After about six months, the police agreed to the request of the parents that the boy should return to his shop but he would now have to give information to the police.

This boy had some differences with one of the militants on the sharing of money extorted earlier by them. He went to see that terrorist. As arranged, at some distance from each other, they took out their magazines from their 'Assaults.' This boy managed to retain one bullet in the chamber and killed the terrorist as he neared him. To avenge this treachery, the companions of the killed terrorist had repeatedly come in search of the Hindu boy. Since they did not find him at his own house, they went looking for him at the homes of his relatives at Chhabhal, Khem Karan and Patti. During these raids, because of the darkness, they took some other young boy to be the one they were looking for and killed him. After narrating the story the Inspector asked the migrants; 'Am I right or not?'

'DC Sahib, he is telling the truth,' several voices spoke as one.

'And is the elder brother of that boy and other black sheep sitting amongst us?' was the second question put by the policemen.

'Yes, Sir,' spoke the worthy migrants. The elder brother was a medical practitioner. He had managed exaggerated reports in the press and he had provoked the Hindu leaders of Amritsar by telling them wild stories. On learning these facts, the local Hindu leaders, who had been incited, were all praise for the Bhikhiwind police. On the previous day, the spokesman of the migrants had ridiculed the police by alleging that fear had made the policemen come at night in their night suits. This was in response to the telephone informing the police that militants were around and were knocking at their doors. The Inspector explained that if they were to put on their

uniforms, the militants within those few minutes, would have succeeded in either killing people or slipping away or both.

With the first stirrings of trouble, I had begun visiting these towns
frequently with the local police officers. I imposed night curfew,
made arrangements for street lighting and arranged for steel gates
at the ends of the streets opening into the fields. I also arranged
more pickets by the police and the paramilitary forces. In accordance with their suggestions for better security, I had ordered more
intensive night patrolling and also subsidised the cost of the civil
works. The DIG of Police had also joined us and we spent one full
day in that area. The people responded enthusiastically and positively all along and agreed to accept weapons from us. Thus there
was no question of their abandoning their homes. When K.P.S. Gill
visited the area, he confirmed that the people were prepared to fight
rather than run away. However, there were cases of sending young
men away for the night as a precaution.

After hearing the facts from Inspector Paramjit Singh, there was
no need of such a precaution. Besides, the killings were now aimed
at delaying or postponing the elections. But even after the episode
described by Inspector Paramjit Singh of Bhikhiwind police station,
the medical practitioner kept on feeding the press with false information regarding the daily return of the migrants. He was doing so
to support his contention that migration had actually taken place.
However, the spurt in the number of killings was definitely of concern. But no assessment of the local situation on the lines indicated
above had been undertaken. The 'shake up' of the Punjab administration, was not justified. Nonetheless the appointment of General
O.P. Malhotra as the new Governor was a happy augury.

We have noted the manipulation in the foregoing story. Another
equally important aspect worthy of note was that the militant was a
Hindu businessman. But this was not a singular example. There
were a dozen Hindu terrorists operating in Amritsar district alone.
Bakshish Singh (Kalyug) and Yadwinder, were sons of petty Hindu
shopkeepers of villages in Majitha and Khalra area respectively. So
were Gulu and Pappu. Three of the militants killed in Majitha Khalra
and Khemkaran areas were from Hindu families. A couple of them
in the Rayya area were rescued from militant gangs and restored to
their parents.

25

Governor Malhotra Takes Charge

Around the end of November or early December 1990, excerpts from a report of experts dubbing the Punjab bureaucracy as 'complacent, smug, insensitive and corrupt' were made public. The competence of K.P.S. Gill was acknowledged. But it was felt that the top cop's superciliousness was an impediment to the desired level of co-ordination with the paramilitary forces, that were fighting terrorism in association with the police. There were whispers about the replacement of the Governor, the Chief Secretary and the DGP. We all had been doing our best but most people missed the silver lining in the cloud. The demand of Simranjit Singh Mann, the President of the UAD (M), to change the repressive state machinery was nearing fulfilment, not for reasons of its repressive attitude but for other 'negative traits'.

In this atmosphere of uncertainly, B.G. Deshmukh, the Principal Secretary to Prime Minister Chandra Shekhar, came to Amritsar. At a get together in the evening he took me aside and asked my opinion on the current situation. I conceded that the killings were very high but added that so was the morale of the fighting force and, equally important, the people were responding to our efforts.

'You have been here for a very long time. Can you suggest some measures which could bring about a noticeable improvement quickly?' I realised the earnestness of his mission.

'We have to stop the flow of weapons and the trained militants from across the Pakistan border by sealing it,' I responded. I was glad that I got this opportunity to talk about this issue. When the decision to fence the border was taken at a meeting chaired by the then Home Minister Buta Singh and his Minister of State, P. Chidambaram on 4 April 1988, I had assured them that I would make land available for fencing along the border, but I had also maintained that the police should be given at least one battalion to man mobile check posts behind the BSF.

'How can it be sealed?' he asked. There was utmost urgency in his tone. It would have been pointless to repeat my earlier suggestion.

'Deployment of the Army between the BSF and the *ditch* cum *band* and other strategic points along the border alone would help, Sir.' I said.

'That I think would be right,' said the Principal Secretary, after a thoughtful pause.

The next day he chaired a meeting with the army authorities headed by Gen. B.K.N. Chibber, K.P.S. Gill and me. Many suggestions came up but none could provide an immediate remedy. I then suggested that deployment of the army alone could be the instant remedy. I also made out a case for its continuation for a reasonable time. There were reservations both on the part of the police and the army. However, after some discussion the concurrence was in favour of deploying the army. The deployment commenced from 10 December 1990. In addition to covering the border, the army spread out in Amritsar and Gurdaspur for routine exercises.

The Akali leaders were critical of the deployment of the army and dubbed it as a blunder. The militants spread a rumour that it was Operation Wood Rose–II. The Panthic Committee gave a *bandh* call which was fully observed on 14 December 1990. That day, I clarified the role that the army would perform during the current phase of deployment to the press. The press reported the assurances that the army deployment was not for dealing with the internal law and order situation and that the army would not search any house or farmhouse in detail. The fear of Operation Wood Rose–II would have scared the militants but it could also have seriously perturbed the villagers because memories of the operation following Operation

Blue Star were highly upsetting. Earlier I had taken some steps to undo the apprehension caused by Operation Wood Rose–II in October 1989, during unprecedented heavy floods, and again when the 9th Division had undertaken an exercise in May–June 1990. The shortage of civilian doctors in the border villages was endemic because the newly recruited doctors for villages kept going away for post-graduation studies or on better assignments. On both occasions I had requested the Div. Commander, General Chibber, to extend medical services to civilians by organising medical camps. I organised the supply of medicines from the Red Cross as per the requirements of the army doctors. The army welcomed the opportunity to help on both these occasions. I assiduously saw to it that memories of Operation Wood Rose–II were not revived in the minds of the people, particularly the youth. In 1984, after Operation Blue Star, the army raided farmhouses to arrest young boys who were allegedly involved with the militants. This fear had driven the youth to seek refuge in Pakistan to escape the vengeance of the then victorious army. The army, presently, continued to organise medical camps and cultivate the people and thus succeeded in reviving their exemplary rapport with the people that had earlier existed during the 1965 war with Pakistan.

At the commencement of the present exercise, I had to impose a dusk to dawn curfew in hundreds of villages along the border, as requested by the army. I toured some of them to assess the reaction of the people. One villager said, 'After a very long time, we have slept in peace and without fear.' Another said, 'The boys have fled within days.' Actually, for the previous few months, the militants had been strengthening their base in the Doaba and Malwa regions of Punjab as also in parts of UP and other states. In the industrial town of Ludhiana, they had found a rich field for extortion. The concentration of the army in Amritsar was much more than at any other place. Most of the militants instantly migrated from Amritsar and those who remained behind became less active for the time being.

Lt. Gen. O.P. Malhotra (Retd.), a former Chief of Staff of the Indian Army, came to Amritsar on 20 December 1990, the day after he took over as Governor. After paying obeisance at the Golden Temple, Jallianwala Bagh and the Durgiana Mandir, we drove straightaway to Bhikhiwind and Chabhal, which had hit the headlines owing to threatened migration. Surprisingly the burden of the people's woes was no more about harassment by the militants but it was the shortage of electricity, which was hindering the working of rice shellers and tube well irrigation. The General was very happy to see the morale of the people who, as per reports in the media, had migrated from the small border towns only three weeks earlier. He began his campaign against militancy on a very optimistic note.

He immediately planned to correct the exaggerated image of militancy being projected by the media. Most newspapers published whatever the militants wanted them to publish. Photographs of killed militants and notices about their *bhog* ceremonies, the *bandh* calls and any other direction always found space in some of the Punjabi newspapers published from Jalandhar. Most of the organisations involved in extortion would sponsor the publication of the photographs to justify their forcible collections. Generally, three to five sets of photographs would be published. In the case of some very important militants, as many as 11 organisations published their photographs. All India Radio and Doordarshan (the state owned TV network) had shown some reluctance to follow the dictates of the militants. The result was direct threats to the employees making announcements in Hindi. The Governor held meetings with all concerned and a code of conduct was evolved to obviate the threats of militants. The employees defied the threatening letters and telephone calls. Soon the militants stopped harassing them. This change was of great help in reviving the confidence of the general public in the administration.

We also began to discourage the gatherings at the *bhog* ceremonies of killed militants. In the changing ambience, we found it easier than before to dissuade people from going to such gatherings. The modus operandi of the militants was to visit the villages surrounding the venue of the *bhog* and personally tell the *sarpanches* and tractor trolley owners to attend the ceremony with a specific number of trolley loads of men and women. Such demands were normally complied with but with reluctance. We set up police checkposts on all approaches to the venue of each *bhog* and stopped people from proceeding. Only close relatives were allowed to go. All the other trolleys were sent back. Keen supporters managed to go through the fields and some trackless paths. The result was that every one could present the excuse of obstruction by the police to explain their failure to show up. Attendance at *bhog* gatherings consequently began shrinking. Photographs of the killed terrorists and notices of *bandhs* and the *bhog*s also started fading away from various dailies.

The Governor decided that the state level Republic Day, function of 1991 would be celebrated at Tarn Taran—one of the most disturbed sub-divisional headquarters. Ever since the creation of the *Punjabi Suba*, the Punjab Government had celebrated Republic Day at one district headquarters or the other. Governor N.K. Mukerji celebrated it in Chandigarh in January 1990 to assert the state's claim to the city; 1991 would be the first time the function was being held at a sub-divisional headquarters located in a highly disturbed area.

I went around Tarn Taran town. The only suitable place I could find was a Sports Stadium, 2 km off the city on the Tarn Taran–Amritsar Road. I learnt that a mild shower not only floods the spot, but underground water also seeps up, waterlogging it. I suggested to the government that it would be safer to shift the venue to Patti even though it was worse affected by terrorism in comparison to Tarn Taran. The venue at Patti was free from the fear of the site being waterlogged. In the flooded Tarn Taran stadium, the celebrations would have been adversely affected. In that climate of terror the terrorists would have hailed it as their victory. In the ensuing controversy, my explaining the real reason for the change would have been ridiculed.

During the celebrations, besides a parade by the police and the paramilitary forces, tent pegging, folk dances like Bhangra and Giddha, and a PT display by the Police Training School, are the usual attractions. These are all best performed on proper ground. But, by then, the decision of the venue had already been made public. The militant organisations called a *bandh* for that day in the whole state. G.S. Manochahal, as per newspaper reports, had declared that in Tarn Taran even a leaf would not stir.

The weather gods were very kind and it turned out to be a beautiful day to be remembered by the thousands of people who came to witness the celebrations. The stadium was overflowing with a very enthusiastic crowd, as I had promised the Chief Secretary that very morning. We lined up to receive the Governor. As he reached me, he patted my chest and observed, 'You have reason to be proud and happy.' The Governor in his impassioned speech exhorted the people to co-operate to end militancy, participate in the task of development and persuade the 'boys' to join the mainstream. The cultural programme, parade and sports were exquisite. Months later when the Governor resigned, I presented him a movie of the function entitled: 'A Turning Point.' In the first week of August 1991 when he left, there was enough reason to justify the title I had given to the parting gift.

Sanjiv Gupta, the SSP Amritsar, and I won another victory related to this very auspicious day, against the terrorists. All militant organisations had banned the trade of liquor, meat and tobacco in the holy city of Amritsar from 26 January 1991. We had held meetings with the representatives of these trades and found them responding to us very positively. We had to sustain the security level for a few weeks. Not a single shop closed for even a day. On same day we also met the bankers to discuss the alleged threats to them to close their clearing house. In the course of discussions, I established the point that the calls were fake and had been manoeuvred by prospective buyers of the property. Unfortunately the bankers did not show any guts. They hired some other premises and shifted. In contrast, the traders mentioned previously, resolved to stay put. 'We do not know any other calling. This level of business is only in Amritsar where we have spent our lives. We shall die here.' Not a single person came to any harm; I was the only one who got the dubious honour of finding a place on the hit list of all the militant organisations. What we had witnessed was sublime courage which, according to many thinkers, is possessed by that class which is too poor to know that they possessed it and too humble for the world to discover it.

Ever since a shopkeeper had been killed in Jalandhar for defying the call, it had been difficult to persuade traders and other business establishments to ignore the *bandh* calls. I learnt that those who could afford to do so, invariably went out of Punjab for a short holiday caused by the *bandh* call. The families of tradesmen in normal times did not have any regular leisure jaunts. They developed this habit during those troubled days. Dalhousie, a hill station, is only three hours drive from Amritsar and the whole route, except for the first 40 odd kms, was free from militants. The Governor wanted us to ensure resistance against the calls for a *bandh*. Explaining my failure, in the very next *bandh* call, I told a somewhat unhappy Governor, that I had earlier only been persuading various traders on such occasions but on the last occasion, I had tried everything, including breaking open the locks for them. Beyond that, I would have been guilty of state terrorism.

I told the traders of Hall Bazaar that after opening their shops, the telephone calls that came to them were from their colleagues and not from the militants. We had already established this. A Punjabi newspaper containing the call for a *bandh* could not reach Amritsar because the vehicle transporting it was detained for some offence by the police at the periphery of the district at Beas. The entire state was closed but Amritsar flourished in its ignorance. We told the traders that if the militants had that large an organisation and had known their telephone numbers, they would have certainly rung up the office bearers of the association of each trade to ask them to close down the shops in Amritsar. They agreed, yet could not be persuaded to defy the call for a *bandh*.

Despite a noticeable and increasing resistance, the *bazaars*, out of abundant caution, would prefer to pull down their shutters if a general call for a *bandh* had been given. Eating places and medical services, both state-owned and private, remained open. Government offices and railways worked as usual. The state owned road transport system also functioned but, for a want of passengers, the frequency of service was reduced. Students or no students, the government and a few private educational institutions in the cities remained open. In villages, only a few schools stayed open. In December there were five *bandh* calls, in January and February there were four calls each. In March 1991, no *bandh* call was allowed to be published because of a mutually agreed decision to censor such news. Therefore, there was no closure.

A general resistance on many fronts bore the stamp of the General. This was achieved due to the firm stand taken by the government and was possible after the deployment of the army. For the first time, militants began leaving Amritsar. Many decided to leave out of fear. Thus the impact of the army's widespread presence (two additional Div. Headquarters at Jandiala and Patti area in addition to the one already in Amritsar) was immediate, in that it reduced the number of killings. While 89 civilians were killed in November 1990 only 36 lost their lives in December 1990 at the hands of the militants. Of them only four were Hindus. The toll of paramilitary forces and police personnel who were killed also came down from 30 to 12. The fall in the number of militants killed was less than other categories; 49 against 94 in November 1990. I had said earlier that the holding of the 26 January 1991 celebrations in Tarn Taran was a turning point of the struggle. This can be substantiated by the figures of civilians killed in the state, quarter-wise. The highest number of civilians killed (840) was in the last quarter of 1990. The number of civilians who lost their lives in the first quarter of 1991 was 656.

In the second, third and fourth quarters of 1991, the number of lives lost were 722, 624, and 589 respectively. The corresponding figures for the year 1992 were 512 in the first and 478, 340, 183 respectively in the ensuring three quarters.

The Governor held peace rallies all over the state, and named them *Sadbhavna* rallies. The first was held on 21 February 1991 in the famous Rambagh of Amritsar (at a spot just 100 m away from the building where General Dyer had camped in the second week of April 1919 at the time of the Jallianwala Bagh massacre). Now, a former General of the Indian Army was trying to remove fear from the minds of a scared populace. All the political parties, with the exception of the Akalis, participated, vying with each other in enthusiasm and numbers. The impassioned speeches by their leaders followed by a march of a nearly 10,000 strong crowd, through the city led by the Governor was a stirring experience for Amritsar city. The boost in people's morale was palpable. In subsequent weeks we went to the smaller towns. In Patti, which was a town worst hit by militancy, the route of the procession was decorated with flags and golden ribbons. Another proof of the positive effect of these rallies was that G.S. Tohra requested people to boycott the rallies. The news about his appeal was published in *The Tribune* on 3 March 1991. There was absolutely no effect of G.S. Tohra's call on the 50 odd subsequent gatherings all over the state. This campaign culminated with the final rally at Hussainiwala, in Ferozepur district.

The Governor introduced the practice of holding open *darbar*s by Deputy Commissioners on every Wednesday, where people could come freely with their problems. He continued the practice of weekly meetings in every Block with the representatives of the people for planning the development of each Block and improving the quality of works undertaken. This exercise was named 'Tuhadi Sarkar Tuhade Dawar', meaning carrying the administration to the people's threshold. These exercises had a remarkable effect on the morale of the people who were getting sick of militancy. With regular monthly meetings to monitor the progress of the redressal of public grievances at the district level and meetings of the Planning Boards at the district and sub-divisional levels, the involvement of people had been considerably widened.

The Governor was moving towards elections and democracy. Years ago, the government had decided to upgrade the Municipal

Committees of the major towns of Amritsar, Jalandhar and Ludhiana to the level of Corporations, since the population of these cities had crossed 500,000 each. The local bodies needed more autonomy for successful municipal functioning. But no election had been held by successive elected governments on one pretext or the other. Governor O.P. Malhotra ordered the holding of elections to the Municipal Corporations in April 1991. The three biggest cities of Punjab thus had their Corporations for the first time. The elections were free from any major incidents. The militants could exert no influence whatsoever. Only in the case of Amritsar, one *sarpanch* of a village falling in the extended area for the Corporation, who had some connection with the militants, was elected as a Councillor. The militants had bought a car in his name and kept it with him. They used to borrow it whenever they needed it. The police did not suspect this vehicle as they remained under the impression that the popular *sarpanch* was its real owner. Incidentally the whole village repeatedly protested against his eventual arrest. Sanjiv Gupta, the SSP, brought him to my office and in the presence of the protesters and revealed the connections of the accused person with the militants. The crowd dispersed immediately.

In April 1991 another interesting development occurred in Amritsar. The harvesting combines available for hire used to move from the east towards the rest of the state according to the pattern of wheat ripening. For the last three years, they had not shown up in Punjab and certainly not in Amritsar because the militants would demand large cuts. That April, some combines turned up. During April, the terrorist crime situation continued improving in the state, but in Amritsar the improvement was considerable. While 84 militants were killed during the month in Amritsar, we lost 47 civilians and 15 police and paramilitary personnel. In the state, the militants took a toll of 237 civilians while 152 militants were killed. In Punjab state the Amritsar trend, of more terrorists losing their lives compared to civilians, was noticed in the month of October 1991, but it got disturbed around the February 1992 election. However, from April 1992 (when 180 civilians lost their lives and 185 militants were killed), the trend continued without disruption till the collapse of the movement.

With such improvements, the Punjab Government had taken an objective decision to recommend the holding of elections to the State Assembly. Similar recommendations made earlier by Governor

V. Varma in October 1990 had been overshadowed by the issue of the countrywide students' agitation which eventually led to the downfall of the V.P. Singh Government. It would be relevant to relate this issue with the idea of 'talks between the militants and the Government of India' ever since the ouster of the Congress Government in November 1989. General O.P. Malhotra had made it a prestige issue for, in his opinion—and many sections of the populace agreed—a representative government was necessary to bring about peace.

26

Attempts to
Restore Democracy

The Akali Dal (Longowal) had challenged the dissolution of the Punjab Legislative Assembly in May 1988 in the Punjab and Haryana High Court. No one took notice of it at that time. Barring Manjit Singh Khera, the party's secretary as well as its advocate, many Akalis were not even aware of it. When the High Court took it up for a hearing, it was a welcome surprise to the Akalis. It seemed that everyone was eagerly awaiting the Court's verdict as if it were the last unavailed remedy for peace in the state. The militants alone wished that the writ petition should fail. Their wish was fulfilled.

Within two days of the Court's judgement, a displeased Governor V. Varma held a high-level meeting on 12 September 1990 and recommended to the Central Government that elections to the Punjab Assembly should be held around 4 November 1990. The then prevalent six-month period of President's rule was due to expire on 10 November 1990. It was true that terrorist killings were on the increase and the anti-Mandal Commission agitation was picking up in the state as well but, every month, more and more terrorists were also being killed. There were reports of the alienation of the militants from the people as well. The three years of President's rule had not brought much relief to the people. More and more of them had increasingly begun to feel that perhaps their woes could be better assuaged in a political set up.

S.S. Mann, who had been talking of elections, had added a rider that these should be held under UN supervision. He also resigned from his Lok Sabha seat on 12 October 1990 because he and some of his colleagues had not been allowed to carry their swords into the Parliament. Rajinder Kaur, another MP of his party, who was abroad, requested S.S. Mann to forward her resignation as well. But he was ready for talks and willing to participate in the Assembly elections.

The AISSF also supported the holding of elections and so did the two Panthic Committees led by G.S. Manochahal and Wassan Singh Zaffarwal. The Panthic Committee led by Dr. Sohan Singh, however, did not support participation in the elections. Its comments on the militants and the conventional political parties seeking power through elections were as objective as they were terse. According to a report in *The Tribune* dated the 23 August 1990, the Panthic Committee recognised the sacrifices of S.S. Mann (his resignation from the IPS and suffering in Bhagalpur Jail for half a decade) but at the same time the Committee felt that he was surrounded by opportunists aiming at capturing political power through militancy. The S.S. Mann Akali Dal, therefore, would be no different from the other Akali Dals and would 'train their guns at us' after grabbing power.

Though reflecting reality, they were, perhaps, a little too optimistic in assuming that the militant factions could capture power through the ballot. The misery, privations and the death dance which the people of Punjab had endured at the hands of the militants, had laid bare the sheer criminality and the cult of violence which had been erroneously projected as a means of social change. The year 1991 was thus not similar to 1989 when the AISSF had been let loose by the ruling Congress at the Centre to queer the pitch for the Akalis. The move had backfired, as militant supported candidates had managed to win some seats because of multi-polar contests in some constituencies and not because of their popularity. If the Sikhs were separatists, Bimal Kaur Khalsa, the widow of Beant Singh—one of the assassins of Mrs. Indira Gandhi—would not have lost the election to both the Assembly and the parliamentary constituencies, which she had contested in September 1985, when the wounds of the Sikhs from Operation Blue Star were still fresh. The same Bimal Kaur Khalsa in 1989, won from Ropar parliamentary constituency, as a consequence, no doubt, of the callous way in which vested interests had manoeuvred to sabotage the Rajiv–Longowal Accord in order to strengthen their interests in the Haryana Assembly election. It was the same vested interests who exaggerated the fears of the militants coming to power through the polls. The Congress at the Centre, whose prospects in the rest of India were enhanced by their image of resolutely fighting militancy in the Punjab, opposed the election while the State Congress leaders were in favour of polls. The BJP and the Left parties, who had a small base in the state at that time, also opposed the election.

Prime Minister V. P. Singh was much too involved in the country-wide agitation against the implementation of the Mandal Commission Report. The recommendations of Governor V. Varma for holding elections in the first week of November 1990 therefore could not be considered. Soon V. P. Singh resigned and Chandra Shekhar, with the support of the Congress, formed the government on 10 November 1990, with Devi Lal as his Deputy Prime Minister. Chandra Shekhar had a good equation with the Akalis and the Sikhs. He had participated in the *kar-sewa* after Operation Blue Star. He had even met the militants holed up in the Golden Temple weeks before Operation Black Thunder in April–May 1988. He had also authored the 'Peoples Accord'—a document listing Punjab's major problems and their possible solutions. Therefore, the emphasis was on 'direct talks' between the Prime Minister and the militants. It appeared to be quite logical.

A vague hope was in the air. It was believed that, somehow, a solution would be conjured up. For the people of Amritsar what mattered was deliverance from violence and all its consequences. These hopes enthused everyone; the Akalis of all sections, the militants, the Sikh Students Federation, the *Taksal*, other political parties and of course the Congress, which was acting as the prop of the Chandra Shekhar Government.

In Amritsar, the media attempted to assess public opinion on the issue of talks and elections. Their conclusion was that people wanted early elections. There were no politicians of significance, belonging to Chandra Shekhar's Janata Dal, who were familiar with the intricacies of the Punjab scene and who could interact with the people. Governor O.P. Malhotra had been meeting the people. He once observed publicly that talks would lead to peace. Mrs. Maneka Gandhi was the first Minister of the new government, to visit Amritsar on Christmas day. She believed that there was no agreed strategy (or objective) amongst the various militant outfits. Elections to the Assembly were, therefore, essential. The only other person who claimed knowledge about the reality was Kailash Samuel, a lawyer practising in our courts. K. Samuel had assumed the role of a mediator. Therefore, he was in touch with the PMO and claimed to have organised the talks. He always carried a letter addressed to him by an OSD from the PM's office which indicated that his offer to be a channel to bring the militants to the negotiating table had been accepted. He had appeared before the Judicial and the Executive magistrates on behalf of the militants in the past. Many young lawyers in Amritsar prided themselves on representing the militants gratis, because they believed, this would give them some importance and could be a step towards building their practice. K. Samuel would not disclose which militants had utilised his good offices and who else, besides him, was working as a channel.

Press reports seemed to belie the hopes that the people and some leaders had pinned on the talks. The main factions of the Akali Dal, the Badal and Longowal factions, acknowledged S.S. Mann as their leader and concurred in his having talks with the Prime Minister, whom S.S. Mann considered anxious to solve the Punjab problem. Tota Singh, a senior Akali leader, brought all other Akali groups to a joint conference under the aegis of Baba Thaker Singh of the Damdami Taksal. The conference was held on 26 December 1990 at Fatehgarh Sahib. This adopted a resolution authorising S.S. Mann to hold parleys with the Central Government, for which, he could take anyone's help (*The Tribune*, 26 December 1990). The resolution also asked for the withdrawal of the army from Punjab and for the recognition of the Sikhs' right to self-determination.

The Panthic Committee led by Dr. Sohan Singh which had earlier been critical of the militants participating in elections took a more lenient stand on talks with the new Central Government. In a press statement, it welcomed the prospect of talks with the 'justice loving' Prime Minister. This concession was allegedly being made for 'valuing human life'—(to stop killings) and to avail of all alternatives before resorting to violence. The octogenarian doctor put forward several impractical conditions such as that the talks should be held at the Akal Takht or UN Headquarters and that, at the negotiating table, the status of the Prime Minister and the delegates should be equal. The release of Harjinder Singh and Sukha Singh, the assassins of General Vaidya, was also sought. The next day S.S. Mann told

PTI that the PM was willing to hold talks with the militants. It all seemed too good to be believed.

Prime Minister Chandra Shekhar, while speaking to the BBC on 30 December 1990, confirmed his willingness for talks which were to be held only under the Constitution of India. He categorically ruled out the extension of Article 370 of the Constitution to Punjab, which accords a special status to the state of Jammu and Kashmir. The next day, the Prime Minister clarified that the talks would not be held at the cost of national unity. According to press reports, S.S. Mann submitted a memorandum to the Prime Minister saying that, 'Sikhs have no choice but to secure their religious, political and other interests which are possible only after self determination'. According to the same report (*The Tribune*, 31 December 1990), S.S. Mann was invoking the assurance given to the Sikhs at the time of the Partition of the country on the basis of which they had decided to join the Indian Union.

The BJP was the first to caution the government against the talks. On 2 January 1991, former Prime Minister Rajiv Gandhi also cautioned Chandra Shekhar and made it known that he was against the talks. The Punjab Human Rights Organisation pointed out that even after the Prime Minister's categorical assertion that national unity would be maintained, S.S. Mann was still harping on the talks (*The Tribune*, 2 January 1991). Two weeks later, the Panthic Committee led by G.S. Manochahal and W.S. Zaffarwal told the press on 14 January 1991 that S.S. Mann should forget about the talks and continue the struggle.

In the month of December 1990, as we have already noted, with the deployment of the army, the militants moved out of the border districts of Amritsar and Gurdaspur. In Amritsar, killings, extortion and kidnappings had come down by about 50 per cent. The militants managed to increase the crime rate marginally during January; however, these evils were much less than what had been seen during November 1990 and earlier. With the migration of the militants, the smuggling of arms and ammunition received a setback. The secret dumps were not known to many, therefore, those weapons were not immediately available. The militants who remained behind, started snatching weapons from wherever they could. In subsequent months they blackmailed and threatened police officials to supply them with weapons and ammunition. The Amritsar police detected six such cases in which police officials had been supplying the militants with weapons and ammunition. On 24 and 25 March 1991, the police captured a big haul of arms and ammunition buried in five ft deep bunkers. Weapons seized in the preceding three months included 150 AK 47s, seven general purpose machine guns and 26 rockets.

The militants, understandably, continued losing their hold in the border districts where they had been firmly entrenched. In the districts of Doaba and Malwa it was not easy for them to prosper despite their initial success in extortion in the industrial town of Ludhiana. Since they were strangers to the area, their presence was easily noticeable. It was also difficult to maintain the flow of weapons to areas away from the border. They started moving to Uttar Pradesh. It therefore became the most opportune time, after Operation Black Thunder, to strike resolutely and secure their surrender. The first batch of 40, surrendered to the army in Tarn Taran. I spoke to all of them and apprised them of the schemes of self-employment. More than a dozen told me that they had nothing to do with militancy, except that their relations and friends happened to be close to some militants. They were absconding because of the fear of harassment by the police. M.S. Bhullar, the IG Border Range, was also present and I entrusted the boys to him. A few days later, on 27 March 1991, the police presented 50 boys before the Governor, Lt. General O.P. Malhotra in the Circuit House, Amritsar. These had, allegedly, surrendered to the police.

Another important change that was noticed was that with the deployment of the army the bulk of militants migrated to the Malwa region. As a result, fresh recruitment to their ranks came down drastically in the border districts.

These were important changes and advantage should have been taken of their positive potential. But this was also, the time for the *tom-tom* of 'talks' and elections. There was a ring of insincerity or misplaced optimism in those who thought that a solution could be found solely' through talks. Many political parties and analysts had, blamed the Congress for initially encouraging the fundamentalists to embarrass the Akalis and to break their alliance of 1977 with the then Janata party. Therefore, at that juncture, the Congress could not afford another suicidal blunder of letting Chandra Shekhar, who was Prime Minister with their support, gain credit for preparing the ground for the defeat of militancy. The Congress would have liked to hold the Punjab Assembly elections itself rather than have the elections held by their proxy.

Similarly, Simranit Singh Mann, in spite of his personal integrity and idealism, was in no way a panacea to cure all the ills of militancy. The charisma that centred around him when he came out from the Bhagalpur Jail gave him the power to cut the Gordian knot. But he failed to capitalise on it by choosing to sail in two boats. This complicated his problems. Optimistic people hoped that the knot would come untied on its own. But this did not happen. The Akali leaders left the leadership of the combined Akali parties to S.S. Mann more than once. Due to the lack of progress, they reasserted their existence. The militants never gave him that status. S.S. Mann knew it well. He did not give a call to the militants to stop the killing of innocent people. He did not accept it as a precondition for talks with militants. His answer, according to press reports, was, 'if the government can talk to the Mizos without their laying down their arms, why such a precondition for Punjab.'

In Mizoram the Mizo leader Laldenga, issued instructions to the Mizo National Front (MNF) to lay down arms by 26 January 1978, and informed the Home Minister of India accordingly. But he faced a rebellion in his party. By April, Brig-Gen. Biakchhunga, Chief of Staff of the Mizo National Army (MNA), became the President of the MNF. His party split and the settlement was delayed by eight years. The accord was finalised and signed on 30 June 1986, and approved by Prime Minister Rajiv Gandhi, within a year of his signing the Punjab Accord with Sant Longowal. S.S. Mann's task was far more difficult. There were three Panthic Committees with a number of militant outfits allied to each. There were a number of Sikh Students Federations. All of them changed shapes and attachments. Many would split to form another organisations including a new Panthic Committee, adding to the number and hierarchy of organisations. It was also difficult to know with certainty which of the organisations was in touch with the various government agencies.

On the government side, Chandra Shekhar who had become the Prime Minister of a minority government on 10 November 1990, resigned on 6 March 1991, though he continued to head a minority caretaker government. On 12 April 1991, the dates (20, 23 and 26 May 1991) for electing the the 10th Parliament were announced. Punjab was not mentioned in the notification for the polls. But demands for talks and polling continued. When Chandra Shekhar had taken over as Prime Minister, the 'talks' implied the holding of a dialogue with the militants for some kind of a settlement and ending the violence. But talks with a caretaker Prime Minister could only be about the participation of the militants in the polls. The Congress, BJP and Leftist parties were averse to the holding of elections in Punjab. Therefore, Chandra Shekhar, in spite of being keen to restore peace in Punjab, had to move cautiously.

To begin with, he also thought of linking the polls in the state with peace. His statement to that effect did not help bring down the number of killings. On the other hand, on the day following his statement, 40 people including two militants and two security personnel were killed breaking a weeklong lull in the killings. This spurt was sustained. Towards the end of March 1991, he left it to the wishes of the people if they wanted any polls. It would appear that the PM was eager that the militants participate in the elections and, if they decided not to contest, he need not trouble himself with a controversial decision. In principle, elections in Punjab should have been held without bothering about the participation of militants for the simple reason that the Central Government had not been able to end militancy, even in four years (Punjab was under President's rule since May 1987). It was high time to give a chance to the people of Punjab, who had resolutely faced violence with the utmost forbearance.

Actually, when the dates for country-wide polls—20, 23 and 26 May 1991 were announced on 12 April 1991, G.S. Manochahal decided the very next day to give political recognition to the AISSF (Manjit); perhaps he intended to get it registered as a political party. When the presidential notification for the Assam and Punjab polls was issued on 18 April 1991, the AISSF was the first to declare that it would participate in the elections. It reportedly had to take the onus on itself because the candidates, who were elected to Parliament with its support in 1989 did nothing to ameliorate the woes of the people. The success of the AISSF in the elections held in 1989, irrespective of the factors behind it, was a great incentive for most of the militant organisations for contesting elections. Nonetheless, Chandra Shekhar proved his concern for Punjab by deciding to hold elections in the state.

The Chief Election Commissioner T.N. Seshan met the political parties in Chandigarh on 5 April 1991. He told the Punjab officers that the parliamentary elections were to be held in all the states and Union Territories as the President had asked him to constitute the 10th Lok Sabha. For holding elections to the Punjab Assembly he needed specific directions as the state was under President's rule. The requisite directions came in a notification dated 18 April 1991.

T.N. Seshan, the redoubtable Chief Election Commissioner of India had made great efforts to cleanse the election process. He had put checks on the party in power so that it could not influence the election in any manner. For this, if on the one hand, he earned the ire of the government, on the other hand, he also earned the gratitude of the people for being firm and fair. He had also been going by rule of thumb, all along in the case of Punjab. But suddenly, he changed the polling date in Punjab from 31 May 1991 to 22 June 1991. It may not have been realised in Delhi but this decision meant giving three more weeks to the militants to eliminate some contesting candidates—which they did—and thereby, sabotaged the election. Against the six weeks given to the candidates in Punjab for canvassing in the May–June 1991 elections, T.N. Seshan reduced it to two weeks when the elections were held in February 1992. He may have learnt the bitter lesson as a result of the killing of 23 candidates in Punjab during May–June 1991 simply because of the postponement by three weeks. By doing so, the CEC had deferred the Punjab election from being held during the term of the caretaker Government of Chandra Shekhar and placed it into the hands of the new government.

However, with the announcement of elections, all the political parties and most of the militant organisations prepared to participate. Beant Singh, the President of the Punjab State Congress, also wanted his party to jump into the fray, but the party high command turned it down. The State Congress, after initial sulking, started shouting 'Wolf'. It appealed to the people, not to go to the polls and to boycott the elections completely because 'it amounted to pushing Punjab into a volcano.' The State Congress formally decided not to contest the Punjab polls. This decision, taken in the context of the party's expectation to form a government at the national level, was devious, for it had the potential to take a decision about the Punjab election to their advantage.

Indian democracy adheres to the form meticulously but lacks the essential democratic spirit. Separating the polls in Punjab from that in the rest of the country by three weeks was both mischievous and indefensible. It was felt that the Commission had done this at the behest of the Congress (I). On 11 June, answering a question on this issue, the CEC ambiguously said, 'No comments'. The Central

Government had categorically stated that it had not asked for the postponement of the date of polling.

The people of Punjab who were disgusted with militancy and were looking for a return to representative government after four years of bureaucratic rule, did not heed the cries of the Congress. Both newspaper reports and the rush for filing nominations portended keen contests. By the closing date, 2,750 candidates had filed their nomination papers for 117 Assembly and 13 Parliamentary seats. 1,330 withdrew from the contest, leaving 1,420 to try their luck. It was going to be a great spectacle and a unique opportunity for a harassed people to give their verdict against the crimes committed against them.

But the mischief had been done. This had also been noticed by those in power in Chandigarh and by the Sikhs in Delhi. The postponement of the date from 31 May 1991 to 22 June 1991 was challenged in the Punjab and Haryana High Court on 28 April 1991. The Sikh leaders of Delhi pleaded for advancing the poll date. Their apprehensions were that if the Congress captured power at the Centre, the Punjab poll would be scrapped (*The Tribune*, 3 May 1991). According to the Representation of People's Act, no one had the authority to annul the election once it had been notified, but the date of polls could be changed if there were some compelling reasons, such as some a natural calamity, non-receipt of ballot papers and other election material; examples mentioned by the CEC T.N. Seshan. Therefore, it was not made an issue by anyone. They were already out in the field with the requisite determination.

The only justification for the separation of the Punjab polls from those in other states, could have been the heavy requirement of additional forces. Punjab had demanded 300 additional companies. One hundred could be sent to begin with and the remainder after they were free from election duty in the northern states. We had already received 59 companies to combat terrorism. Certainly, four weeks were not required to transport the force from other states to the Punjab. It was known that the candidates would be the main target of militants. It was necessary therefore to reduce their exposure. The Chief Election Commissioner had already clarified that the authority competent to postpone elections, could also be authorised to cancel them. The large gap of time provided by the CEC was obviously to meet this requirement. A new government could be formed in Delhi in two weeks after the results were declared at the latest.

The scent of elections, however, renders politicians insensitive to every other consideration. No one had time to heed the intent behind the subtle moves. Simranjit Singh Mann and Manjit Singh (AISSF), were facing the same pressures of those seeking party tickets as were other parties. All were oblivious of the real objective behind delaying the Punjab polls by three weeks. The relations of the slain militants pressed their claims as kin of the martyrs of the present struggle. This was true in the case of both the traditional parties and the militant outfits. Some notorious militants with large rewards on their heads had also filed their papers. S.S. Mann's party alone received 300 applications from the relations of militants seeking tickets. They did not hesitate to file their nomination papers as independent candidates either. They were in the fray in 4 out of 13 parliamentary seats and 40 out of the 117 Assembly seats. The Panthic Committee led by G.S. Manochahal supported the AISSF. Later it forced Manjit Singh to withdraw from the parliamentary contest of Tarn Taran in favour of Resham Singh Malmohri who was in jail. He was the right hand man of G.S. Manochahal. Dr. Sohan Singh was against participation. Some of the militants put up their candidates to ensure that candidates of AISSF (M) did not win. In the meanwhile some organisations started killing candidates. The first to lose his life was the Akali Dal Panthic candidate Amar Singh contesting from Dirba in Sangrur district. By the end of the month, 11 candidates had been killed. Even the AISSF that had not allowed its candidates to seek government protection, withdrew this restriction for the safety of its candidates.

On 20 May, during the progress of polling in Haryana, UP and Bihar, poll violence claimed 43 lives. The army had to be called in Meerut while in 8 constituencies in Haryana a re-poll had to be ordered in 8 booths. In overall terms this amount of violence was more than the poll-related violence in Punjab during that period. On 21 May 1991, the former Prime Minister Rajiv Gandhi was killed by a human bomb in Sriperembudur where he had gone to address an election rally. The whole nation was shocked. The Chief Election Commissioner postponed the polling scheduled on 23 and 26 May 1991 to 11 and 15 June 1991.

Many a civil servant has shown more loyalty to the ruling party than to the laws of the land. That is what caused the fixing of a later date for the Punjab elections. A relevant folk tale comes to mind.

Mullah Nassiruddin was on his deathbed. His son begged him to give him some advice based on his life's experience, as he was leaving no other inheritance. Mullah Nassiruddin said, 'My son, the first thing: You need not trouble yourself to climb a tree, the fruit shall fall by themselves as they ripen. And the second my son: you need not kill a man, for men die by themselves.' If I were to identify a single cause for the spread of terrorism in the state, I would place my finger on 'the fantastic tricks' like this played with Punjab from time to time by the politicians.

Terrorist crime in Punjab did not show any poll-related aggravation till 15 June 1991. Out of the 19 constituencies in which polls had been cancelled, because of the killing of candidates (one candidate died a natural death) the election process in 11 constituencies had to be put into motion again. More than 100 companies of BSF had arrived. Sabodh Kant Sahai, the Minister of State for Home, repeatedly stated that 200 more companies of paramilitary forces would be given to Punjab. He himself was contesting from Ludhiana. On the 16th, the militants struck a ghastly blow to stall the election in Punjab with the massacre of 75 train passengers from two trains at two small stations, Baddowal and Kila Raipur. Around 40 passengers were injured. The compartments had been chosen carefully to ensure that the victims were mainly Hindus. Women and children were made to come out of the compartment before the shooting at Kila Raipur. The killers did not seem to be in any hurry while perpetrating the cold blooded carnage. I consider that it was a complete failure of the Intelligence network not to have anticipated such a possibility. Anyway, the government could not bow to the militants. It did not cancel the polls.

On 19 June 1991, speaking to PTI, T.N. Seshan ruled out the postponement of polls in Punjab. He also confirmed that there was no such request to him by the government either. The state government was satisfied with the additional force. Arrangements were complete in all respects. On 20 June 1991, campaigning in Punjab came to an end. That very day the tenth Lok Sabha had been constituted. The Congress had secured a working majority. P.V. Narasimha Rao had been elected leader of the Congress Legislative Party. Senior civil servants who had been deputed as Observers by the CEC were reaching their constituencies in Punjab. I went to the Circuit House to meet them. K. Sundaram, IAS, had come from Delhi. He told me that in Delhi there were strong rumours that the polls in Punjab were going to be scrapped. It was shocking to hear this but I could not believe it, 'How can they do it at the eleventh hour and on what grounds?' I exclaimed.

I made a last minute check of all arrangements for the next morning. Transport for 1,400 odd polling stations, with the accompanying security, was ready to move. The polling material had been issued and handed over to the polling teams. Everything was ready. The position in all the other districts in Punjab was the same.

Around 3 A.M. my telephone buzzer beeped. Invariably, a buzzer at such an hour is an indication of bad tidings. Fearing some mass killings in the district, I picked up the receiver. A deputy of the State Election Commissioner was on the line. 'Sir, do not despatch the parties. Elections have been postponed,' he said without any emotion. I knew that I had heard the worst news of my stay in Amritsar. I was apprehending a killing of a dozen odd humans, but what I learnt was not only the murder of the whole election but the very institution on which real democracy rests. The very spirit of democracy—'the voice of the people is the voice of God'—in which the world's greatest statesmen have reposed their faith again and again, had been murdered publicly, without pointing out any flaw whatsoever.

'Who has issued the orders, has the notification been published?' I asked him, hoping that someone may have played a hoax on us. The practical official could guess what was going on in my mind, he reiterated, 'Sir, I am not aware of all these details but the news is correct.' He was also in a hurry to inform the other DCs in the state. To cut me short he concluded, 'Sir, you are the first one I have informed.' Around 4.30 A.M. B.R. Bajaj, IAS, the state's Chief Election Officer, rang up to give me the necessary details and final instructions. He was very angry at the government's decision and did not mince his words in expressing his hurt. 'It is treachery with Punjab and the people who have been bleeding for more than five years.' He told me that the polls had been postponed until September which really meant that they were as good as countermanded.

A few militants, close to the hardest core, had won again without contesting, without the casting of a single vote in their favour. Twenty-six candidates had lost their lives at the hands of the militants. They had defied violence and did not flee from the field. New candidates had filed their papers when the election for those constituencies were notified again. People had staked their lives in upholding the democratic principle. No one had suggested such a postponement when 75 innocent train passengers were shot down. But now when there were no such risk involved, the sacrifice of human life was thrown in the waste paper basket. Why? All because the Congress, which was now likely to form the government at the Centre, was not contesting in the state election.

On 10 June 1991, when General O.P. Malhotra, the Governor of Punjab, had met T.N. Seshan, the Chief Election Commissioner told him that he was not going to postpone elections unless the State Government asked for a postponement. On 19 June 1991, in reply to a question by the UNI, he clarified that the Election Commission (EC) had nothing to say on the subject of whether or not a free and fair poll was possible. He asserted that the Commission had not come to any conclusion to the contrary. Explaining the postponement to newsmen, T.N. Seshan said on 27 June, that he had ascertained the views of the government and 'others' (possible only on the 20) and had concluded that 'free and fair' polls could not be held. Therefore, he saw nothing wrong in postponing the polls. T.N. Seshan had certainly not broached the subject with the Governor who promptly met the President and the Prime Minister on 22 June 1991 and submitted his resignation in protest against the last minute decision to postpone the polls and that too without his knowledge.

Home Minister S.B. Chavan wanted him to continue. On 1 August the Governor told UNI that both the Prime Minister and the Home Minister had assured him that the elections in Punjab would definitely be held in November. Presumably, this was to persuade him to withdraw his resignation. But he insisted on the acceptance of his resignation for which he had met the Prime Minister and the Home Minister for the second time on 20 July 1991. In anticipation of this the government was reportedly considering suitable substitutes, namely Vasant Sathe, General K.V. Krishna Rao, General P.N. Hoon, and H.L. Kapoor, Lt. Governor of Delhi. Vasant Sathe alone declined the offer publicly. It was on 4 August 1991 that Surinder Nath—a former IPS officer and Advisor to the Punjab Government during the Operation Blue Star period—consented to takeover the reins of the troubled state. T.N. Seshan continued to maintain, however, that he had not done this to oblige the new Congress government in Delhi.

T. N. Seshan had an open invitation by the Lal Bahadur Shastri National Academy of Indian Administration to address the probationers. He chose to do so on the day that Justice Bains of the Human Rights Commission and I happened to be at the Academy for a panel discussion on militancy. T. N. Seshan in his address did not speak about the stalled Punjab election of June 1991 at all. He did not even clarify whether it was out of his personal assessment or any indication by the Central government that he had decided to postpone the polling only hours before the time of the poll. His power to do so was, of course, upheld by the Supreme Court of India. It is also true that the Congress had declared its intention to stall the elections in case it came to power.

Another familiar apprehension expressed about the elections was that if the militants won the elections, they might embarrass the Union government by moving a separatist resolution. This was improbable. The terrorist leaders had never showed themselves before the people. Nor had they ever bothered about the people's suffering. During the course of a decade, the movement had been more or less hijacked by stupid and unscrupulous people. They were simply indulging in self-delusion hoping to win the election. To visualise themselves as the disciplined 'Singhs' of the eighteenth century was absurd. The 'Singhs' of those days had voluntarily undertaken the duty of guarding the people against the atrocities of the local administration and brutalisation by the predators coming from the north. In return, they charged only one-fifth of the produce. This was known as *rakhi*. Those who combined to defend the people came to be known as *misls*. These *misls* joined to form the *Dal Khalsa* to face the attacking army. However, the present day fake 'Singhs', made the common people the targets of their atrocities. Due to these reasons there was little possibility of a militant winning any seat. If in a multi-cornered contest a couple of them were to find their way to the Assembly it is unlikely that they would have attended any legislative sessions. It may also be mentioned here that six UAD (Mann) candidates who won because of the support of the AISSF were not terrorists.

Amritsar had borne 70 per cent of the brunt of terrorist crime. Militancy was not only born here, it had also flourished here for the longest period. This was the only district where all the police stations were badly affected by militancy. The institutions sympathetic to militancy were all situated in Amritsar. Pakistan, which supported the militants, was just next door. Therefore, if the militants had any chance of winning in the elections it would have been possible only in this border district. Let us have a look at the pros and cons of their prospects.

At the outset, it may be stated that the very grounds responsible for the severest militancy in Amritsar were also the cause of the most determined opposition to the election in this border district. Pakistan and the Pakistan-based Dr. Sohan Singh Committee were against participation in the elections. They could have had the maximum effect through interference in this district. An analysis of the election prospects of the militant candidates contesting from Amritsar and the fairness and freedom of the polling prevailing here could easily be taken as a reliable sample for the entire state.

Let us first look at the killing of one candidate each from two of the 16 constituencies of Amritsar district. Harbhajan Singh, a former Minister in the last Akali Ministry, was contesting from Naushehra Pannuan, a constituency covering the core area of militancy around Tarn Taran. Harbhajan Singh had been my minister too. Unfortunately, the first order that I passed under TADA was for his detention. The allegations were that foreign funds flowed through him to the militants. During the elections the militants had been pressurising him to withdraw. To sort out this issue, he accepted their invitation and met the militants at an isolated place. They managed to separate him from his gunmen and killed him. Had he refused to meet them, it would have been difficult for them to either defeat or kill him. They had reportedly taken off his bulletproof jacket and later took away his weapons too. Similarly, while canvassing, Dalbir Singh Ranike, got separated from his security guards. Before his security vehicles could catch up, the militants blocked his car. D.S. Ranike reportedly came out with his pistol in his hands. They asked for the pistol which he refused to hand over. They shot him and took away his pistol before his security reached the spot. During this phase, the militants in Amritsar were starved for weapons. The conclusion is that both the deceased leaders simply gave away their lives.

There are other significant points pertaining to the campaigning period. The most important of these was that while the political parties including the AISSF, canvassed openly, the militant candidates or supporters could not do the same. They only sent messages to the *sarpanches* and *panches* of the *Gram Panchayats* to vote for them or their candidates. They had exaggerated notions of their influence and popularity. The servility and submission shown by some people was actually out of fear of the gun that the militants wielded. The militants supporters could be counted on one's fingers. Barring a couple of villages which the militant candidates confused with the entire Assembly constituency, no one would have voted to give more power to the usually invisible tyrants. The electorate has always known for certain that the ballot paper remains secret during the whole process of polling and counting. The election results would have cut the militants down to size.

During the first three weeks of June 1991, the killings did come down in the district as well as the state but extortions had been on the increase. The clear inference was that the lower ranks of militants were not under the control of their organisations. Besides, the militants who were for Khalistan found themselves isolated and also lost the cover of the Akali factions who were in favour of elections. The elections had created new dividing lines. S.S. Mann's influence on Akali parties and some militant and pro-militant organisations was only a cover which all were willing to utilise for their personal advancement. Similarly, if the Akalis tolerated the militancy displayed by the terrorists, it was only a tactical move and by no means an expression of a shared ideology. The ideals of the Sikh *panth* were the farthest from their mind. And their observances for them was as impossible as reversing the flow of the Ganga. Despite the surge of terrorism, there were no differences or ill will between the Hindus and the Sikhs any more. The enthusiasm of people for the election and sustained participation by political parties and independent candidates, despite the elimination of 23 of them, was an outright reiteration of the rejection of militancy by the people of Punjab.

Another important, but less noticed, aspect was the increasing distance between most of the militants and Pakistan and also the latter's disappointment with the Punjab militant movement. In a meeting held on 14 or 15 June 1991, the Pakistani mentors showed their unhappiness with such large scale participation in the democratic process. All organisations were pressurised to strictly boycott the election in totality. Those organisations that were not participating in the election vowed to disrupt the elections and work for the withdrawal of support by the militants to any candidate. The relations of militants were also to be asked to withdraw from the contests. The Khalistan Commando Force (KCF) and Babbars instructed their gangs to physically eliminate the members of AISSF and G.S. Manochahal's Bhindranwale Tiger Force of Khalistan (BTFK) if they did not withdraw. Wassan Singh Zaffarwal's group was the only one that actually stopped supporting all the candidates for whom they had been working. An exception was made only for S.S. Mann as he was a Taksal nominee. There was no effect of the directions from Pakistan on any other group. The issue of elections had clearly created a divide amongst the militants. If the elections had been held, the results would definitely have weakened the militant movement further.

The logical outcome in such a situation would have been that no militant would have won as, due to the non-participation of the Congress, its votes would have gone to the Akalis in the rural areas and to the BJP in the urban areas. The teenage vote may have gone to one of the militant organisations and the AISSF. But this would have been ineffective because their votes would have been divided among numerous militant candidates. The AISSF would have secured more votes than any other organisation. But the militants and some of their organisations which were against the polls had put up candidates simply to divide the AISSF votes. Manjit Singh, its President, in Valtoha constituency was opposed by Gurchet Singh who was being supported by KCF out of opposition to Manjit Singh. Manjit Singh must have heaved a sigh of relief at the cancellation of the polls. If a person like him was nervous, no one else in his organisation could have sailed home. If that was the position of the AISSF, no other militant organisation could have won. And if their prospects in Amritsar were so black, they could not have scored anywhere else.

T.N. Seshan, in thus stalling the polls, did not do any service to the nation. He merely served the interests of the Congress and, unwittingly, helped the militants to save their face.

There was general condemnation of the postponement of the polls. *Dharnas*, protest marches and protests were staged by all political parties. The Janata Dal (S) asked for impeachment of the Chief Election Commissioner. The BJP wrote to the President of India to ask T.N. Seshan to quit. Most of the newspapers also condemned the postponement of the elections. *The Tribune* came out with its survey report which concluded that it was a grave blunder to have postponed the polls. It also mentioned that when T.N. Seshan felt that the Congress (I) was going to form the government at the Centre, he postponed the polls. Everyone gave vent to their angry feelings. Beyond that, no one could do anything. Only the pro-Khalistan militants and Pakistan were happy. So were the CEC of India and the Congress (I) who had had their way. And as for Punjab's suffering, there seemed to be end to it.

27

Delhi's Inconsistent Punjab Policy

By all accounts, the deployment of the army had instilled a sense of security amongst the people. The militants had lost their hold on Amritsar where the terrorist movement had originated and flourished. They had vowed to drown the elections in bloodshed but, in the process, more and more terrorists lost their lives every month. In January 1991, the number of militants eliminated was 93 while 319 civilians had been killed by them. From February to May 1991 respectively, 169, 202, 150 and 208 terrorists were killed, while the number of civilian casualties during these months was 265, 309, 237 and 257.

There could not be much doubt about the beginning of the decline and fall of militancy. Instead of garnering strength to give the final push, all those who mattered in this struggle, including the Central Government, seemed to be on the lookout for furthering their personal or party interests. It appeared as if Punjab was being treated as a guinea pig in the laboratory of our brand of politics. While elucidating this point, I may have to repeat a couple of issues which have been mentioned earlier in a different context.

None of the Akali Dal factions had ever appealed to the militants to stop the killing of innocent people. But they repeatedly pressed for the recall of the army. Simranjit Singh Mann would not miss any opportunity to criticise the army. He tried his best to make an issue of the tragic shooting of six persons by the army at village Nathu Ke Burj near Sarhali. The unfortunate victims were going on a tumbrel at about 4 A.M. to fetch diesel. They did not know they were driving to their death. They happened to pass through an area under night curfew. The *jawans* asked them to stop, and simultaneously sent up very lights. Not aware of the unusual light, the ignorant peasants jumped off the cart and ran. They were mistaken for militants and shot. It was indeed a gruesome and tragic blunder. Amongst the victims were a retired BSF Inspector and his only son. The BSF Inspector had retired only a few weeks earlier and apparently he had also got confused. I visited the spot and with unconditional apologies explained the facts to the protesting villagers. They understood and relented. S.S. Mann went to the village and tried to aggravate the situation. Therefore, we detained him to prevent his joining them again on the occasion of the *bhog* when a large gathering of grieving people, as well as mischief mongers and militants, was certainly expected. Everyone condemned this unfortunate and ghastly incident. Some said in passing that if the army were to function in this manner it would be better to withdraw it. The suffering people, as well as the opinion builders of the area did not make it an issue. But for his detention, S.S. Mann would have tried to gain some political advantage from this unfortunate incident.

The government's withdrawal of the army on 6 July 1991, soon after the cancellation of the June election, was an even greater enigma. On the one hand the government said that free and fair polling was not possible and yet the force which sustained the sense of security was being moved out. To fill the vacuum in Amritsar and Gurdaspur districts, 30 additional companies of paramilitary forces were promised. One could not understand the compulsion to withdraw the army. The 30 additional companies promised for Amritsar was a sort of recognition by the government of the need for reinforcement. Then why could the army not continue? The government was fully aware how the presence of the army had not only won the confidence of the people but, because of it, the exaggerated fears of the people from the police had also been assuaged.

It was also a known fact that the militants were moving out of the border districts to other parts of the country. And what was important was that, in Amritsar, recruitment to militant cadres had stopped.

A withdrawal of the army would help no one but the militants. They would not only reinforce their presence in the rest of Punjab but would also return to their old moorings. In June–July 1992, the same Central Government assured the five-month-old Beant Singh Government that the army would stay in Punjab as long as the people wanted it. With the installation of the Congress Government in Punjab the atmosphere had suddenly changed.

In sentimental, farewell, get-togethers with various army units, the implications of the withdrawal at that stage when terrorism was on the decline, would naturally come up for discussion. Someone accused Prime Minister P.V. Narasimha Rao of being unsympathetic to Punjab and recalled that, at the time of the Delhi massacre of Sikhs in November 1984 he was the Home Minister and had allegedly given full support to the alleged machinations of H.K.L. Bhagat. How could the Delhi Police and the administration look the other way when the crowds were mauling and burning Sikhs alive was a question that lent support to the negative role of the then Home Minister.

A few months later, on 23 November 1991, *The Tribune* reported the statement made in Parliament on 22 November 1991 by Hari Kishore Singh, a former State Minister of External Affairs, accusing Prime Minister P.V. Narasimha Rao of involvement in the Delhi riots when he was the Home Minister. H.K. Singh was making the point that the Prime Minister was not interested in the Punjab problem. He alleged that H.K.L. Bhagat had told the then Home Minister '*Ab bahut ho gaya*' (*Now its more than enough*) and, therefore, Bhagat could tell the hooligans to stop the anti-Sikh riot. It is true that after taking over as Prime Minister, P.V. Narasimha Rao had not evinced any concern or emotional feeling for Punjab. Home Minister S.B. Chavan alone seemed to have some concern for the state.

Months before the P.V. Narasimha Rao government was formed, the Chief Election Commissioner had been shuffling the dates of the Punjab polls. These readjustments were not based on security considerations but to enable him to keep both options open—to hold or annul elections in Punjab, as preferred. If a Congress Government were to be formed, it would not have liked elections to be held, not because they would not be in the interest of peace but because that party had not participated in them in Punjab.

It may also be recalled that for the November 1989, the then Central government had decided that Parliamentary elections could be held in Punjab but holding the State Assembly elections would be disastrous. In fact the Congress was desperate to retain its majority in Parliament at that time. It hoped to win more seats in Punjab because of the 'brilliant' move of letting the AISSF loose to participate in the election so that the Akali vote bank could be divided. The surprise victory of half a dozen AISSF-supported UAD (Mann) candidates excited the militants so much that their megalomania sabotaged the sincerest efforts of the V.P. Singh Government to arrive at some settlement. The rush of militants to contest the aborted State Assembly June 1991 election was also because they hoped to repeat their performance of 1989.

If one were to go only by the results of the 1989 Parliamentary elections in Punjab and the large participation by the militants in June 1991, one is bound to get a distorted impression about the popularity of the militants in Punjab in these times. The visibility of the militants in public life was because on both occasions the Congress (I) was fishing in troubled waters (either directly or through its proxies). In the absence of a clear objective ground reality and indepth analysis, the changing policies adopted about the bleeding state of Punjab were tantamount to treating Punjab as a guinea pig.

For instance, the fixing of the date for polls in Punjab would appear to be an experiment. The poll could easily have been scheduled along with that in the northern states on 20 May 1991. Besides the advantages of contiguity, it would have reduced the canvassing time. Instead, the elections were delayed to 22 June 1991. The same Election Commission, gave only 14 days for canvassing before the February 1992 Punjab polls. In the long canvassing period of May–June 1991, 23 Assembly candidates and 3 candidates for the Parliament lost their lives to terrorist bullets. After the poll was further postponed to September, two more Assembly candidates were killed; one of them was a woman from Raja Sansi constituency falling in Amritsar district. For Delhi, however, the experiment of postponement turned out to be a success.

The induction of the army in Punjab in December 1990 had finally tilted the scales against the militants. They began migrating from Amritsar to other parts of Punjab. When they found it difficult to establish themselves in Doaba and Malwa, they tried other states such as Haryana, UP and beyond. The DGP Haryana, K. Rudra, told the press on 26 August 1990 that 29 Punjab militants had been arrested by his policemen. The next day, Prakash Singh, DGP of UP disclosed that 150 hard-core terrorists had sneaked into UP. The crime figures of UP showed that in 1991 terrorist incidents shot up from 40 per year to 180. On 30 July 1991, the day the army was finally winding up in Punjab, Beant Singh, the President of the Punjab Pradesh Congress, while addressing his party workers at Phagwara, said that he was in favour of the army's stay in Punjab. But no heed was paid by the Congress leaders in Delhi to the assessment of their own party President in Punjab.

In July 1991, a relentless campaign had been launched in Punjab against militancy. In 10 weeks in Amritsar alone, 141 militants were killed while in the remaining border belt 59 met their fatal end. About a dozen of them were so-called Lt. Generals. Encouraged by these results, DGP Mangat launched another campaign. The militant ranks in Amritsar had diminished. There had been mass surrenders and the same were continuing. The militants were also short of arms. There were reports of many gangs seeking shelter in farmhouses but without their weapons. It was a big change; the erstwhile tormentors of the people were coming to the people as supplicants. The ISI was reportedly losing interest in the Punjab militants and concentrating on Jammu and Kashmir. The Punjab militants made desperate attempts to hit out, win back Pakistan's favour and regain their sway in their erstwhile domain, the border belt.

They launched a tirade against the police and members of their families living in villages. They started blackmailing police officials for weapons and ammunition. By the end of September 1991, 119 kin of police personnel had been killed. It was a different matter that the Punjab Police, instead of getting demoralised, showed greater determination and resilience. DGP Mangat and I visited all the affected households in Amritsar. According to the government instructions the loss of property was to be compensated and a sum of Rs. 100,000 was to be paid for each life lost. But such visits were really depressing. Houses built or improved over the years with prolonged diligence had been reduced to ruin and the contents reduced to ashes. The grieving old folks narrated their tales of woe. At times the militants had forced the families to destroy their own goods by consigning them to a fire, fed by diesel taken out of their own tractors. But the most heartrending act the victims were forced to do, was to set fire to their tractor.

An aged Assistant Sub Inspector (ASI) who had survived the elimination of his family told us that he had anticipated this trouble.

Therefore, he had put his only son in a hostel. That fateful day, feeling homesick, the boy had come back. A group of militants came within minutes of the boys return. They killed his son and wife. The ASI was saved because he had gone into his room to get his revolver. 'Anything you want me to do?' asked D.S. Mangat, the DGP Punjab. 'I know the killer gang. Allow me three or four days and I will settle the score myself,' said the stone-faced Sikh policeman. Procedurally and going by the rule this could not be permitted, but the man's attitude illustrates the fortitude and the spirit of the victims of terrorism.

The P.V. Narasimha Rao government's decision to withdraw the army was no doubt premeditated. I am sure of this because a news item, dated 22 June 1991 quoting 'official sources', appeared in *The Tribune* announcing the intended withdrawal of the army. Elections had been postponed on the night of 20 June 1991. If the situation was so bad or had suddenly turned grave and it was felt that polling had to be postponed in the entire state, what was the justification for the sudden withdrawal of the army? One wonders if it was because of the army presence that the poll had to be adjourned? If the reason for postponement was in order to issue a fresh notification to enable the Congress to participate in the election process, there was a possibility of grudgingly conceding some rationale to it, even though this would have been devoid of morality. The increasingly brave fight being put up by the people of a bleeding Punjab had been weakened by the politics of the Congress Party. The militants and their supporters, had been effectively contained by the sustained efforts of the police and paramilitary forces together with the army. The recall of the army from Punjab amounted, therefore, to giving a fresh lease of life to the extortionists and killing squads.

Let us have a look at the implications of the Akali factions, AISSF and the militant candidates participating in the elections. Till the last day, the militants had been a part of the contest. The more extreme groups, the pro-Khalistanis, who did not participate had been isolated. Although they had no prospect of winning any seat, the contesting militants had opted to join the mainstream. They were also pitched against the conventional political parties. While filing their nominations they had sworn to abide by and uphold the Constitution of India. If they were to go back on their oath, the law would take care of them.

If the elections had taken place, the non-participation of the Congress in the urban seats would have led to the BJP emerging as the major gainer. The Left parties were also in a much better position to consolidate their strength than ever before. They were the only political activists who had picked up the gauntlet of the militants and had stood resolute against them, for which they had ungrudgingly paid a heavy price. A coalition government of the Akalis, the BJP and the Communists, which had done well in earlier years, could have activated and cemented public opinion against militancy, which was already on the decline. A combination evolving from this alliance could have uprooted militancy from Punjab.

When the V. P. Singh Government wanted to hold elections, the Panthic Committee of Dr. Sohan Singh had said that the political parties in Punjab wanted to grab power through the militants and vice versa. But quite contrary to the Panthic Committee's viewpoint, the June 1991 elections showed that the political parties were pitched against the militants, without any electoral understanding between them and the militants were seeking power through constitutional means without banking on any party.

The absence of the Congress in the Assembly would not have been a serious loss because the Left parties and the BJP were well organised and had their separate ideologies, because of which there would have been an effective inbuilt opposition. The State Congress, as we have seen, had not been able to influence the Central Government of their own party in any of the issues of the state. Even Beant Singh, at the height of his power as Chief Minister, could not boast of having secured a single concession for his state, from his bosses in Delhi. There was no room for the exaggerated fears that if the election were held, some militants could sneak into the Punjab legislature. In the event of things going wrong, the State Government could be dismissed lawfully without taking recourse to questionable methods.

The foregoing account of militancy is replete with details of many experiments made in a tormented Punjab. The first and foremost incident was the the Central government backing out from the Rajiv–Longowal Accord. The final blow was the abrupt withdrawal of the army after declaring that the situation in Punjab was so bad that free and fair polls could not be held. I feel that in this context it would be necessary to have an analytical look at the changes in the crime figures as a result of the induction and the withdrawal of the army. I recall the figures of the Amritsar Revenue District under my charge, which comprised three police districts—Amritsar, Majitha and Tarn Taran:

In November 1990, the number of civilians killed was 89. With the deployment of the army in December 1990, this figure came down to 36. With its withdrawal in July 1991, the number rose to 65. With the Army's re-induction in November 1991, for its Operation *Rakshak*–II, the civilian casualties again fell to 35 and in the following month—December 1991, the number came down to 6.

While one can see a political purpose behind the government's experiment of cancelling the June 1991 Punjab Assembly elections, its withdrawal of the army was clearly a cruel experiment which cost many a precious life. There is little hesitation in my mind in holding the P.V. Narasimha Rao government responsible for treating Punjab like a guinea pig.

28

Elections by February 1992

The visit of Governor Surendra Nath to the Golden Temple on 8 August 1991, just a day after taking charge, was similar to the visits of his predecessors except for the significant pleas of two women who he met during his visit. They must have been fascinated by the unusual sight of a square formed by the security men, in civvies, around the VIP. When they learnt that the new Governor had come to pay his obeisance, they waited near the exit so that they could meet him after he had completed his *parikrama* of the temple. Their nagging woes and anguish had forced them to accost the Governor of the state in the *parikrama* of God's Temple. A mother, in tears, pleaded for the release of her son taken away by the police. The second woman asked him, '*Aman chain kadon mudoo?*' (When will peace and calm return?). Both had come to the Temple seeking peace of mind. The whole of Punjab was yearning for the same more than ever before. Its hopes for the June 1991 elections had been crudely belied. The feeling had grown that the P.V. Narasimha Rao Government was not serious about restoring peace in Punjab. The people's fears were confirmed when the army was also withdrawn.

Governor Surendra Nath, formerly of the Indian Police Service and an Advisor to the Punjab Government at the time of Operation Blue Star, was a deeply religious man and a staunch follower of Sant

Virsa Singh of Delhi. He always had a picture of Guru Gobind Singh on his table in Raj Bhavan and held regular *havans* and chanting of the Jap Sahib as per the advice of the Sant. His words of consolation and hope must have assuaged the feelings of the peasant women.

Every Governor, on taking charge of the troubled state, had reason to believe that he was inheriting a deteriorating crime situation. S.S. Ray took over from Chief Minister S.S. Barnala who had been dismissed on the grounds that the law and order situation was no longer within the government's control. N.K. Mukerji was also aware of the increase in killings due to the November 1989 elections. Governor V. Varma felt that the situation, after his predecessor had left, had deteriorated as the killings were mounting. Towards the end of Governor V. Varma's brief tenure the army had to be deployed and General O.P. Malhotra was acutely conscious of this exigency. Governor S. Nath was aware of the spurt in killings, weeks before the aborted June 1991 elections and again after the withdrawal of the army.

All of them directed us to organise more and more public meetings and conferences for mass contact and to attend to the grievances of the people and quicken the pace of development, as well as we could. After they themselves addressed a couple of such public meetings and noticed the people's response, each one of them had the satisfaction of having set a new trend to attain peace. Each one of them was a seasoned person who had attained eminence as administrators or in public life. All were keen to create conditions in which elections could be held. Governor S.S. Ray was eager to hold even the *Panchayat* elections which were sabotaged by the State Congress. Governor N.K. Mukerji's aim was also to see the end of President's rule. Governor V. Varma recommended the holding of Assembly elections before November 1990. Governor O.P. Malhotra resigned because the June 1991 elections were sabotaged. It devolved on Governor S. Nath to see the election through in February 1992.

In his first conference of civil and police officers in the field and the secretariat, convened on 10 August 1991, the Governor told us that the Central Government was keen to hold elections early next year. To create a climate conducive for the polls, he asked us to win back the confidence of the people by striking a personal rapport with them. 'Speed up the development process and avoid all sorts of harassment in enforcing laws,' he emphasised as all his predecessors had done earlier. On 15 August 1991, at his Independence Day address at the state level celebrations at Ferozepur, the Governor announced that he would strive to hold elections by February 1992.

Besides the threat of militancy, Governor Surendra Nath had to face two more hurdles in holding the election. Most of the factions of the Akali Dal reiterated their decision to boycott the polls, which they had announced at the time of the irrational postponement of elections on 21 June 1991. Since then, Pakistan and the Panthic Committees had convinced the militants that if they and the Akalis did not participate in the elections, it would indirectly be a vote for Khalistan. The militants fell for this line of negative logic not because they were impressed by it but because of their experience of the June 1991 election in which they had come forward to participate for the first time. They were already a divided lot and the election had succeeded in dividing them further. They must have realised in retrospect that they could not have won in any constituency. In boycotting the forthcoming elections they could also side with the conventional parties and thus gain their support for their cause. Hence, they were urging the Akalis to stick to the boycott earlier announced by them. Contrary to their expectations, this common action of a boycott did not bring about any unity in the Akali factions. They remained divided and one of the factions, the Akali Dal (Panthic) headed by Amarinder Singh, decided to participate in the election.

The Governor was keen, and rightly so, that the Akalis should participate. He asked me about my opinion on the issue. I said that, as things stood, it appeared that they were serious about their stand regarding the boycott. I also said that they would surely change their minds if Chandigarh were transferred to Punjab. The other very remote chance was that once the election schedule was announced, it would be difficult for the politicians to resist the lure of this major event of politics.

The Governor did not have to worry much on account of the threat to elections from militancy. The retreat of the militant movement in the border districts—the entire Amritsar district and the adjoining parts of Gurdaspur and Ferozepur—came to prominent notice immediately after the deployment of the army in December 1990. By the middle of 1991, the decline of militancy was noticeable in the entire state. In July 1991, the last month of Governor O.P. Malhotra's tenure, 216 terrorists were killed while 212 civilians had lost their lives. In August 1991, when Governor Surendra Nath took charge, the number of civilian casualties remained at 212, while 221 militants were killed. This was the highest number of militants killed in one month. It was also for the first time that in the entire state, more terrorists were getting killed than their innocent victims. Credit must be given to D.S. Mangat, the DGP, who despite the physical handicap suffered when militants tried to blow up his car in Ludhiana, sustained the pressure on the militants. He remained as mobile as he was before his injury. Yet he kept a low profile.

The army had been withdrawn from Punjab by the P.V. Narasimha Rao government in July 1991. The situation in Amritsar worsened because the militants returned, but, over the rest of the state it remained the same for two reasons: one was that the militants had moved back and the other was that comparatively fewer troops were deployed in the rest of Punjab. However the situation worsened in September and October 1991. The main reason was that the militants, allegedly in retaliation for the killing of the family members of a militant, Balwinder Jatana, embarked on a drive to kill family members of police personnel. The militants halted this drive towards the end of October 1991 after killing 119 kin of policemen, and they made the reasons for their rage against the police known through a press note. The army returned to Amritsar by the end of October 1991 and was deployed in the rest of Punjab by November 1991. The situation improved dramatically, just as it had earlier after the army's deployment in December 1990.

During November and December 1991, the advantage in the ratio of killed militants and the civilians was apparent again, immediately after the deployment of the army. To my mind, this was a sure indication of the reduction of militancy. J.F. Ribeiro, towards the end of 1987 had pointed out the improvement over S.S. Barnala's regime by asserting that, earlier, only civilians were being killed but during President's rule, militants were also being killed. When the number of militants killed continuously exceeds the number of lives that the militants take, the end of the dark tunnel becomes visible. The other indicators of this trend, like the shifting of militants from the border districts, their falling short of men and weapons, fewer *bandh* calls and growing opposition by the people were the more positive indicators. And if these are supported by the arithmetic of killings, there can be no two opinions about improvement in the overall position.

The return of bootleggers to their old profession of illicit distillation and their giving up extortion and kidnapping was another proof of the rejection of militancy by the people. The consequent fall in the ranks of the militants was quite palpable. The licensees of the liquor vends in Baba Bakala, Patti, Tarn Taran and Ajnala were unable to clear their monthly dues like liquor licence fees etc. They had been complaining that because of the sudden increase in illicit distillation, there had been a steep fall in their sales. By September 1991, the mounting arrears of the dues to the government became a matter of concern.

Otherwise, things appeared to be becoming normal under Governor S. Nath. Election to the State Assembly was a simple and straightforward objective. Even though the approach to it was growing rough and more confusing every day, yet there was nothing insurmountable about the task of achieving this objective.

The Government of India could not appreciate the predicament of the moderate Akalis such as the P.S. Badal and Sant Longowal groups. The conventional Akalis had participated in the campaign before the cancelled June 1991 elections despite many of their candidates losing their lives at the hands of the militants. Since many militants were also contesting, it seemed that these killings were at the instance of the militants either opposing them in the election, or by those pro-Khalistan 'boys' who were not in favour of their participation. Every politician, whether an independent or a member of a political party, who staked his life at the altar of democracy—the election— in spite of direct threats and occasionally their implementation, deserves our appreciation. However, when the election was put off to September 1991, just hours before the polling, the dejected Akalis announced their boycott. Maybe, in September, the law was to be amended to cancel the system of election. It had already been announced many times that the polls would be held in February 1992. The militants knew that the Akalis would be looking for an excuse to participate in the elections even after all that had happened. They were mounting all sorts of pressure on them, including threats to their lives, to stick to the boycott. The main purpose of the enclave of 36 Sikh organisations, held on 1 September 1991, was to prevent their participation. According to a report in *The Tribune* dated 2 September 1991, initially all factions of the Akali Dal, i.e., Badal, Longowal, Panthic, Mann and Kabal, were opposed to the boycott. The meeting had gone on for nine hours: and, to reduce the high tension built up, the *Mool Mantra* was recited, followed by *Ardas*. All fell in line with the militants. Only Amarinder Singh of the

Akali Dal (Kabal) could wriggle out on the plea that his party's boycott was subject to the approval of the working committee of his party.

The position that emerged from the conclave was innocuous. The Akalis had been sympathising with the militants but had never joined them nor had they approved of their methods. For the first time, they were being pushed to align with them. The least that the Government of India could have done was to bail out the cornered Akalis. Time and again it had been decided to transfer Chandigarh to Punjab. The latest reiteration was the Rajiv–Longowal Accord. The issue had been hanging fire for identifying some land close to Chandigarh to be transferred to Haryana to enable it to build its own capital there. This exercise could be undertaken once again by entrusting it to another Commission or to the Supreme Court. But at that time, Prime Minister P.V. Narasimha Rao was not concerned with the Punjab situation. It was, therefore, easy for Bhajan Lal the Chief Minister of Haryana to scuttle any move to appease Punjab and the Akalis.

In October 1982, just before the Asian Games, he had sabotaged an understanding between Mrs. Indira Gandhi and the Akalis, minutes before its approval by the Political Affairs Committee of the Cabinet. He was also responsible for manoeuvring the scuttling of the Accord. It would appear that he was also behind the red herring in the form of a suggestion that Amritsar be made the capital of Punjab. But this time the Government of India itself was adding to the confusion. I must recall here the genesis of Bhajan Lal's triumph in scuttling the move of Governor S. Nath and Beant Singh.

On 14 January 1992, Rajesh Pilot, a Minister in the P.V. Narasimha Rao Cabinet, visited Tarn Taran. Beant Singh, the then Punjab Pradesh Congress President, was also there. R.L. Bhatia, a local senior Congress leader and a former MP, had also come from Amritsar. Rajesh Pilot told the gathering that the Centre would talk to the elected representatives of the state about the pending issues of Punjab. I could make out the implications of his statement that no concession was likely to be given before the elections. R.L. Bhatia very casually and seemingly off the cuff, remarked that Amritsar be made the capital of Punjab. R.L. Bhatia has the reputation of being a soft-spoken aristocratic gentleman in love with, and proud of, Amritsar. I could not make out at that time that his remarks were connected with what the Minister had said. But when I read in *The Tribune* dated

28 January 1992, that both Manjit Singh of the AISSF and G.S. Manochahal of BTFK had welcomed the idea of Amritsar as capital, I realised it was perhaps not an innocent slip on the part of R.L. Bhatia. He repeated it in his canvassing for the Amritsar parliamentary seat.

If the idea of Amritsar as the capital of Punjab was to catch the imagination of the people, it would have diluted Punjab's claim on Chandigarh, at least for the time being, and also bailed P.V. Narasimha Rao out of a difficult situation. I have pointed out earlier that the Federation and G.S. Manochahal frequently fell in line with the government, even if it amounted to giving up the demand for Khalistan—though conditionally. We have also noted earlier that P.V. Narasimha Rao as Home Minister of India had reportedly contacted Manjit Singh in Sangrur Jail before he had been released. Whatever the understanding then, the move had boomeranged on the Congress in the election of 1989. Such machinations had never proved constructive. But the government had continued with them. A study of the role of the Akalis and of various political and religious organisations, and also of the various varieties of moles during militancy, calls for a separate book. But here it must be said that such a policy only added to discontentment and misunderstanding, which in turn helped terrorism to flourish in Punjab.

My inference would find support from the rest of the story of postponing the decision on the issue of the transfer of Chandigarh. On 15 January 1992, it was announced in the newspapers that polls were to be held on 19 February 1992. That day, a three day Chandigarh *bandh* began. On 17 January 1992, Governor Surendra Nath, Harkishan Singh Surjit and Beant Singh met the Prime Minister seeking an announcement of the Punjab Package or at least the transfer of Chandigarh. By that time Bhajan Lal had certainly prevailed upon the Prime Minister not to ignore Haryana's claim. The same day, P.S. Badal came to know of it and reiterated the continuance of the boycott of the polls to stress underline the urgency of the transfer of Chandigarh. A triumphant Bhajan Lal strode into Chandigarh on 17 January 1992. In the City Beautiful, which had been eluding Punjab for the last quarter of a century, his party men gave him a rousing reception. According to *The Tribune*, it was the welcome of a hero. The decision of the Prime Minister to take up the Punjab Package after the polls was given to newsmen on 18 January 1992.

Chandigarh is a predominantly Punjabi speaking city which for more than a decade had been the capital of undivided Punjab. The people who built it were mostly from the Punjabi speaking areas of Majha, Doaba and Malwa which are now part of present Punjab. Very few people from Ambala and east of it, which are now part of present day Haryana, invested here. Their preference was for the much faster developing town of Faridabad bordering Delhi. Ironically, even that town had been chosen to be an industrial centre by the great Punjabi visionary, Pratap Singh Kairon. Since Haryana came into being in 1966 with its capital in Chandigarh, a small township of Haryana, called Panchkula, has steadily been growing into an equally beautiful city. There is absolutely no hitch in developing it into another capital city by transferring some land from Punjab. Enlightened opinion in Haryana is that the peasantry of Haryana is more concerned with water which comes from Punjab. The other aspects of the dispute have been blown up by men like Bhajan Lal who were responsible for stalling the Rajiv–Longowal Accord.

I have recounted all these facts to show that in the understanding arrived at between Bhajan Lal and the then Prime Minister of India, P.V. Narasimha Rao, the unstated implication was that the so-called 'Punjab Package' would not be considered even after the Punjab Assembly election. It certainly was a nefarious political conspiracy and a sure way of keeping the Akalis out of the election.

A very casual sort of approach to the issue by Beant Singh, even after he had been made a national hero and a legend as Chief Minister of Punjab, also confirms the above inference. He had been made a member of the Congress Working Committee. It would not have been difficult for him to get back the capital of the state of Punjab. After his first meeting with Bhajan Lal to sort out the dispute, it was reported in the press that they could not agree. That was but obvious. It was a known fact that a large number of Bishnois, the caste to which Bhajan Lal belongs, lived in and around Abohar and Fazilka. For that reason it was an ideal constituency for Bhajan Lal. He would naturally have liked this permanent vote bank to be transferred to Haryana which was possible if it was linked to the transfer of Chandigarh to Punjab. Presently, for every election, he had to hunt for a new constituency. He was right in shifting his constituency every time. He used to boast that he had never lost an election. In 1999 for the first time, under some compulsion, he had to contest again from the Karnal Parliamentary constituency and he was defeated by a margin of more than a lakh votes. I.D. Swami, a retired IAS officer, a favoured officer during Bhajan Lal's Chief Ministership, defeated him.

The P.V. Narasimha Rao government hoped that Beant Singh and Bhajan Lal would come to an understanding about the issue of Chandigarh. One wonders how the disputing parties could settle this issue, when various Commissions could not. But this was the best way to put the issue in cold storage. By mid-May, apprehensions were expressed that the Punjab Package was not likely to come through. A week later it was reported in *The Tribune* dated 22 May 1992, that the CM of Punjab had sent a confidential note to the PM to settle the issues under dispute between the two states. While addressing a local bodies' election meeting on 5 September 1992, Beant Singh said that he was in touch with the CM of Haryana and the Prime Minister regarding the demands of Punjab and that he had already held four meetings. That was all. Thereafter, the issue was rarely raised with any semblance of seriousness.

With all doors closed on negotiations regarding the demands of the Akalis before the election, they had literally no grounds on which to withdraw their boycott and participate in the elections. According to rumours, when they met in Chandigarh a day before the filing of nomination papers, they were inundated with messages from the militants not to join the election fray. Two of the factions, however, came forward. Ultimately, only the Akali Dal (Kabal), headed by Amarinder Singh, remained in the fray. The Akalis had announced a rally at Ludhiana and a march from Anandpur Sahib was planned, to launch their campaign asking people to boycott the elections. As a result, P.S. Badal, G.S. Tohra, S.S. Mann and Manjit Singh of the AISSF were held under the National Security Act (NSA) and other top leaders were picked up under the Terrorist and Disruptive Activities (TADA) the next day. Both the rally and the march were foiled. At the time of the June 1991 elections, the Congress also appealed to the Punjabis not to go to the polls. The Congress leaders had gone about pleading with the electorate that it 'would be a true homage to Gandhi' to keep away from the polls. In that case Governor O.P. Malhotra did not issue any orders for taking action against the Congress leaders and detaining them under NSA and TADA. Surely there was a difference in the two situations. The Akalis had erred in addressing their appeal only to the Sikhs whereas the Congress in 1991 had addressed itself to all Punjabis. In both cases the legal offence—persuading people not to caste their votes—is the same.

Quite intriguingly, the AISSF and G.S. Manochahal candidates filed their nomination papers. Later they withdrew from the contest on 5 February 1992 the date fixed for withdrawal. If the Akalis were to contest the elections, these organisations could have again remained in the contest to queer the Akali pitch, or, maybe, it was to provoke them to join the fray or, maybe both. There was quite a bit of confusion. The Intelligence agencies also confused the Panthic Committees including that of Dr. Sohan Singh. A news item dated 30 January 1992, emanating from UNI Chandigarh, said that Dr. Sohan Singh had decided to participate in the polls 'to teach a lesson to the Panthic candidates'. The source also mentioned that the Doctor was to 'reconsider his relations with Pakistan'.

The fear of the militants disturbing the elections was always present although it was generally acknowledged that they were on the run. K.P.S. Gill, within four weeks of his taking over as DGP Punjab for the second time said, as reported in *The Tribune*, on 19 December 1991 that, 'Given the present conditions, the Army and Security Forces will need four to six months to contain militancy in Punjab'. The State Government was, therefore, of the view that the elections should be held in April and May 1992. But the Government of India had made up its mind to hold it in February 1992. It was expected that the militants would escalate violence even if some of them and the Akalis took part in them; but they were certainly not expected to stall the polling.

The results of the cordon and search operations launched by K.P.S. Gill, were good. But cordoning off a locality before dawn and to continuing it for three to four hours during which every house was searched, was very unpleasant and a great nuisance for the local population. Only a few households harboured the militants and extortionists. These operations soon led to clashes between the people and the police. The police came under severe criticism and faced allegations of theft under the guise of searches. The Bharatiya Kisan Union and some other organisations tried to blow up the situation. This type of haste could be detrimental to the overall campaign against the militants. But the government stuck to 19 February 1992 as the date of polling, which happened to be the birthday of Beant Singh, the then would-be Chief Minister of Punjab.

The killing of 51 train passengers and the injuring of another 30 on 26 December 1991 near Jagraon was the first terrorist killing connected with their effort to foil the elections. About 10 militants fired 300 bullets for 10 minutes and then left in a van. The harrowing act had been committed in the same fashion as the killings before the June 1991 elections. Such a crime should have been anticipated by the administration. On 8 January 1992, the militants killed 18 labourers and injured 23 people in a textile mill at Kharar in Ropar district and at another in Sangrur. Officials assigned to election duties were also targeted. The subordinate services and teachers provide the bulk of the polling and counting duty staff. Their associations announced that they would not undertake the risky election duty unless their pending demands were met by the government. The State Chief Secretary, Tejinder Khanna, persuaded them to withdraw their boycott.

The Governor had arranged for the deployment of employees from Delhi for election duty. This would have been quite a catastrophe and an admission of defeat for the administration and the people of Punjab. An unwilling and scared staff from outside would have been a burden and a liability. Any killing of the borrowed staff would have had 10 times greater propaganda value and the militants would have liked to achieve this. In the final meeting to review the poll arrangements held by the Governor at Ludhiana on 4 February 1992 with the Deputy Commissioners and the Senior Superintendents of Police, I suggested that the staff from Delhi need not come and that we could manage the situation locally. My colleagues supported me and Governor Surendra Nath agreed to take the risk.

The percentage of those who would come out to vote was another area of concern. The consensus was that nearly 50 per cent of the voters may turn out to vote if all went well. That was the last day of filling nomination papers. It was still hoped that the Akalis would come forward to file nominations. We were being optimistic. Army officers, who had been doing a lot of social work in the villages, had been reportedly assured by rural leaders that people would turn up for casting their votes. Canvassing remained very low key particularly in the rural areas. Indeed, there were no signs of enthusiasm or even concern. In the cities, one could occasionally hear blaring loudspeakers. In the old city areas, door to door campaigning went on. The Communists and several other political parties, however, regularly held their small meetings.

There were some cases of violence of various types during the 14 day period of canvassing. On 10 February 1992, six teachers were gunned down in Patiala and Sangrur districts. The same day in Amritsar, terrorists killed H.M. Khosla for refusing to hand over his scooter to them. He was an officer in the Life Insurance Corporation of India and had been deputed to be the presiding officer at one of the polling booths. The killing was not for election duty but for robbery. The next day, four BJP workers were shot dead in Amritsar and one in Ludhiana. In Ludhiana the teachers boycotted the election rehearsal and in Amritsar the Teachers' Union threatened to stay away from election duty. It was not difficult to persuade the Teachers' Union in Amritsar to abstain from announcing or implementing their threat. I had a gut feeling that the election would be completed smoothly. But time and again I would ponder and wonder why it was necessary for me to suggest at the meeting on 4 February 1992 that we would be able to manage without the help of staff from outside the state.

In the villages, there was no sign of a contest, leave alone any heated campaigning. There was absolutely no effort by the militants to scare or warn the people to refrain from polling. I kept inquiring from everyone coming from the rural areas about the visits of militants to threaten them. Everyone confirmed that there had been no threats. About the visit of candidates asking for 'votes and support' most of them would shake their heads vigorously and say, 'No Sir!' in a manner as if they had been missing them. The voters usually welcome candidates coming to them with folded hands, wearing a winsome smile of informality in the presence of others. The women folk also welcome the candidates. Then there are the sections of people whom the politicians generally corrupt. I came across them during my visits to villages. They seemed to be missing the usual payments around every election, at times from more than one party. The money was supposed to be for merry making—some boozing and snacks. Interestingly, the headmen of such groups generally would rue the situation using nearly the same words, 'Nahin DC sahib ji, aitkeen te koi bharua aaya ei nahin.' (None of the 'shameless' have turned up this time!) Even the children in the villages missed the publicity groups distributing small party flags, stickers and badges, around whom they would gather.

It was not the fear of the rural voter that dampened the elections. On the contrary, it was the candidates who were afraid. This was, manifest in the low key canvassing, which in turn caused great disappointment in the countryside. The contesting candidates and their ideology, their manifestos and stirring speeches that appeal to some and anger other sections of the public; as also the flags of the candidates that come up on many a roof in the villages were missing this season. There was neither any debate nor the generation of any difference of opinion. Candidates showed up briefly in the countryside. They feared that voters might not turn up on the polling day, therefore, they would remind them of their constitutional right to vote. Since many a public man had virtually deserted the suffering villagers in the darkest times, they were now somewhat hesitant to face them. They could not even talk of bringing peace and ending terrorism. From that point of view, it was hardly an election. The Congress party talked of militancy indirectly by referring to the unity and integrity of the country. They promised peace and the transfer of Chandigarh to Punjab without ceding any territory from Punjab to Haryana.

The polling day, weatherwise, happened to be murky and dull. There was no sunshine to tempt the voters out of their houses. I drove to some polling stations in the villages. There were no tents of the parties to help the voters locate their names and numbers on the voting list. But for the absence of long queues, the completely lacklustre affair was comparable to elections in totalitarian states.

In rural areas, only 15.1 per cent of the voters turned up. In some villages, only one or two voters exercised their franchise. In urban areas, the average polling was 38.3 per cent. In suburban areas, it had come down to 26.5 per cent. There were rumours of police forcing people out of their houses to the polling booths and making them exercise their franchise. But there were no written complaints.

In the first round of the fray, those who had boycotted the elections could surely claim a moral victory. In effect, however, the Congress had legally won 87 of the 117 seats and was entitled to form an elected government in Punjab after nine years. The Bahujan Samaj Party won nine seats, the Bharatiya Janata Party six, the CPI four, the Akali Dal (Kabul) three, and the CPM, and Janata Dal one each. Independents and others won six. The Akali Dal (Kabul), which was expected to win enough seats to form the government, lamented that the boycott by the other Akali factions was the cause of their failure.

The boycott of the election which the government faced, had two facets. One was staying away by the traditional Akali parties who commanded support from the bulk of the Sikh populace; the other was non-participation by the militant organisations and their supporting parties. The absence of the militants from the election arena was understandable but their rejection by the Akalis was a matter for serious concern. There were factional differences within each organisation and, despite frequent demonstration of sympathies for the militants by the Akalis, they had no alliance or understanding with any. In the denunciation of the elections they had found a common cause. The avowed objective of the militants was: if less than 10 per cent of the votes were polled in the elections it would be virtually a mandate for Khalistan. The Akalis still swore by the Anandpur Sahib Resolution which had been referred to the Sarkaria Commission and which the Akalis had been claiming was not a separatist document. But, in the emerging situation, with their support, the militants could achieve what they wanted.

The militants were not participating because, after the aborted June 1991 election, they realised that none of them would have won. Their mentors in Pakistan had certainly rebuked them for contesting the elections in defiance of their instructions. Now, the Panthic Committee headed by Dr. Sohan Singh was also of the view that it would be better and easier to demonstrate a mandate by keeping the voter away from the polls. After having achieved this negative objective, all of them must have wondered: what next!

29

From President's Rule to an Elected Government: The Return of Democracy

On 25 February 1992, Governor Surendra Nath was able to install a democratic government in Punjab. At 11.20 A.M., on a sunny winter morning on the lawns of Raj Bhavan, he administered the oath of office to Beant Singh as the Chief Minister of Punjab along with a team of 25 Ministers and Ministers of State.

Signs of a continuous decline in militancy were visible in Amritsar as early as April 1991. The same signs—killing of more terrorists than civilians in a month—were noticed in the entire state in July, August, November and December 1991 also. This advantage had been lost around the election time in February 1992 for no fault of the police or the administration and it was quickly restored in April 1992. Thereafter it continued till the end of militancy. Besides, the overall killings, quarterwise, were continuously on the decline. In the third quarter i.e., July, August and September 1991 there were 624 killings. In the subsequent quarters, till the end of 1992, these figures were 589, 518, 478, 340, and 183 respectively. One can see out the rate at which militancy was declining. Peace was surely emerging from the ashes. And by taking into account various other factors such as voluntary surrenders by the militants, stoppage of recruitment to their ranks and the beginnings of their rejection by the people since early 1991, it was simple to predict that, soon, Beant Singh would claim to have fired the final shot and relieved Punjab of a decade long malady. Ironically, no one could have foreseen that Beant Singh, after being an agent in restoring peace to Punjab, would also become the last victim of terrorism. On 31 August 1995, after his day's work, as he got into his car in the porch of the Secretariat, a human bomb blew him up, plunging Punjab and many of his admirers into grief.

Beant Singh, a tall and handsome grand old Sikh had worked hard to come up to the senior-most political position in the state. Like many other Congress stalwarts he too, was initially an Akali. After he became the CM, I met him at 7 A.M. and again at 9 P.M. the same evening. The tireless septuagenarian in white *khadi* looked as fresh in the evening as he was in the morning. He had an unprecedented majority of 87 members in a house of 117, with the largest opposition party, the BSP, having a strength of only 9. The structure seemed too heavy to sustain the democratic spirit. The process of elections had merely conformed to the framework of democracy and not to its spirit. Beant Singh was aware of this shortcoming. He, therefore, convened an all party meet to evolve solutions for the sensitive and major issues by consensus.

The major Akali Dals boycotted this meet as their top leaders were still under detention. In this meeting, the Chief Minister acknowledged that the law and order situation had to be assessed in the context of the political and socio-economic issues. But the very next day in the opening session of the Assembly, right at the commencement of the Governor's address, Vijay Kumar Sathi and two other legislators were physically assaulted by two of Beant Singh's ministers. They had raised the point of the unrepresentative character of the government because of the low percentage of polling. Both the Ministers hailed from the terrorist ridden Amritsar district. The Opposition MLA's rescued the badly mauled V.K. Sathi, and walked out of the Assembly. Democracy had not yet come to Punjab. Not, at least, in its Assembly.

I have mentioned this to emphasise that Beant Singh's foremost problem was to replace the police-like approach of the past five years with a democratic approach. Steps in this direction were urgently needed under a wider policy framework. A mass movement, not necessarily against the terrorists but for the lost peace of Punjab, was needed both at the government and party levels. It could not be achieved immediately but a beginning had to be made at the earliest. The Ministers did begin visiting the districts, but mostly in connection with their departments.

Beant Singh's first visit to Amritsar was on 12 March 1992. The party workers he addressed in the Circuit House were a divided lot, exchanging fisticuffs and abusive language. His task was really a difficult one. That day he also paid obeisance at the Golden Temple, the Durgiana Mandir and the Jallianwala Bagh. Lt. General Chhibber, the Corps Commander, a former Divisional Commander at Amritsar, was also in town to address his officers. At the request of the army officers, the Chief Minister also went to address them as well. In the evening he went to a village around Amritsar to console the surviving widows of the recent killings by the terrorists, who had become active again after the election.

Dilbag Singh Daleke, the Congress MLA from Tarn Taran who had been elected unopposed, had offered to mediate in talks with the militants. He had earlier been accused of sheltering some hard-core terrorists. He was also reportedly opposed to the Chief Minister. The Chief Minister told newsmen that if anyone brings any militants to him he would talk to them and also mediate in their talks with the Prime Minister, if necessary. Such a gimmick had benefited only the militants in the past. Nothing could come out of it. Many militants, on various occasions, had surrendered during President's rule. The last surrender by 11 militants was in Amritsar and Batala on 5 January 1992 to police officers. Two days prior to that, 30 militants had surrendered before M.S. Bhullar, the IG Police at Tarn Taran and 10 at Ferozepur. In my opinion this should have been the only door kept open for them. The offer of talks both misdirected and encouraged them. It also prompted some of them to indulge in more violence to qualify for inclusion in the list of delegates, should talks materialise. In this context, in the first meeting with the state's Deputy Commissioners and police officers held by the Chief Minister in Chandigarh, I had convinced the government that going by the figures of the fall in crime in the Amritsar revenue district, peace could come to the state within a year. We did not have to make any panicky concessions to the militants.

The militants, however, were bound to step up killings in the post election weeks. They were targeting the Dalits i.e., the weaker sections of society for having participated in the election. In the second week of March, while 99 civilians lost their lives, only 29 terrorists were killed. The figures for the next week were 68 civilians dead and 22 militants killed. In Amritsar, the militants came wearing police uniforms and took away the male members from Hindu homes under the pretext of identifying the terrorists, who had committed crimes in those villages, only to shoot them dead. The killings were on the same pattern as in the worst days of militancy but the difference was that, on the one hand, the terrorists were also being killed in large numbers and, on the other, no fresh recruitment was taking place. In Amritsar district, recruitment had come to an end soon after the deployment of the army in December 1990. The killings assuredly, aggravated the gloom and fear of the people but somehow they could not completely cow them and extortion cases were also very rare now.

The presence of the army was a great boost. On 4 April 1992 in Tarn Taran, 40 militants surrendered to the army. Lt. General Chibber could not come on that occasion. The formal surrender was made before M.S. Bhullar, the IG Police, and me. Until then, 160 militants had surrendered and that was the fifth surrender. Most of the militants who surrendered were associates and auxiliaries working for various militant organisations, such as the Khalistan Commando Force (KCF) (Panjwar and Zafarwal) BTFK, Khalistan Liberation Force (KLF) and Dashmesh Regiment. Many of them had absconded because the police was looking for them. The surrendering groups were of great help in giving information about the hideouts and the usual haunts of the militants who were still active. In the first 11 days of April 1992, as many as 87 terrorists, including one Dy. Chief and two 'Lt. Generals' were killed in different encounters in the state.

Going by these trends, and notwithstanding the recent spurt in the killings, I had not been wrong when I had stated that militancy would not last more than a year, in the first meeting held by Beant Singh. From April 1992 onwards, every month, the pre-election trend—of a greater number of militants losing their lives than the number of civilians whom they had killed—was apparent again. Suddenly the militants took up the cause of the Punjabi language once more. They killed the Chairman of the Agricultural Prices Commission in Delhi, hoping to please the Punjab farmers, not realising that the policy and formulae for price fixation was laid down by the government and not by any individual.

On 9 May 1992, five ministers had come to Amritsar city for various meetings. Their security was quite a problem. The SSP Amritsar spoke to me and I shared what I had heard with him. Apparently the CM had admonished the Ministers that they shirked going to Amritsar. Consequently, a horde of them had rushed here to display their bravado. The militants were waiting and they blasted the bulletproof car in which Minister of State Maninderjit Singh Bitta, who was on the top of their hit list, was travelling. The Minister was badly hurt but survived quite miraculously. The site of the blast was a busy market area. Consequently, the blast injured 63 bystanders and killed nine. The security guards of the Minister had also fired when they noticed some boys running away from the rooftops of the buildings on one side of the spot of the bomb blast. Some militants went to apologise to the homes of the victims who were injured or killed in the blast. The militants had shown such concern for the local people for the first time in 12 years. These attempts to woo back the people were desperate gasps for life by the sinking militants.

A move by the militants to manipulate resignations by the *panches* and *sarpanches* was another desperate measure for survival and revival. In June, there were reports of a spate of resignations by the *panches* and *sarpanches*. One report from Ludhiana, maintained that 4,776 of them had submitted their resignations. The Deputy Commissioner admitted the receipt of 270 such resignations which were handed over to him not by the *sarpanches* or *panches* themselves, but by three Panthic leaders.

Actually there was not a single case of voluntary resignation. The 'boys' would approach these gentlemen and they would oblige them by signing the letter only to play safe. The reports therefore did not cause much worry. The Minister of *Panchayats*, however, thought of an effective and clever move. He announced that grants would not be released to the *Panchayats* that had handed over their resignations—a ploy I had actually implemented in the year 1990. This was enough to reverse the pressure of the villages on their representatives. They did not want to lose the grants which are even otherwise quite scant.

This move of securing resignations from the *Panchayats* also had the support of some Akalis. It cannot be denied that the P.V. Narasimha Rao Government treated Punjab as a guinea pig and he gave no respect to the premier regional party of a strategically important border state. But at that time restoration of peace to the bleeding state was the most important task. The Akalis had boycotted the election but their moral commitment to restore peace to Punjab could not be forgotten. They should have worked actively for peace just as they would have done if they were in power. Happily, their support to the resignation campaign was withdrawn in good time. In fact, the boycott of the elections had also been a blunder which was the outcome of a mood of angry frustration. This amounted to political suicide by the Akalis. The party should have debated the issue at length in the prevailing context and taken a rational political decision after assessing people's sentiments across their mass base.

But these resignations were helpful to the state in another way. The Beant Singh Government had been delaying the mass contact programme. It decided to launch it by the end of June, both at the party and government levels. Congressmen organised meetings while inaugurations or foundation stone laying ceremonies by various government departments were also utilised for this purpose. In three huge gatherings organised by the Punjab State Electricity Board, on the occasion of the upgradation of power stations and the inauguration of new power stations, I had the occasion to be present as a Member of the Board. Beant Singh himself was surprised at the response of the people and was quite exhilarated. He told the crowd, 'Sarab Jit Singh has been DC of Amritsar for five years. Ask him how people have suffered all these years. Ask him how many widows and orphans have wailed and cried. Ask him how many parents lost their children and how many families were completely eliminated for no fault of theirs.' Their tears were contagious.

The Chief Minister himself had shed tears when he came to console the surviving members of families killed in March 1992 in a village on the outskirts of Amritsar. He felt that the effect of a chain of such public gatherings on public morale had been tremendous. He sent a special report to the Prime Minister. A Congress spokesman told the press that the ever increasing response of the people in support of the government; has been very encouraging. The small percentage of votes polled in the February elections has no significance.

This confidence building exercise had benefited both the people and the ruling party. The government seemed to be optimistic. The return of democracy encouraged the government to decide to hold elections for the civic bodies. K.P.S. Gill had been regularly disclosing figures of crime to the press. These gave further confidence to the people. In comparison with the previous year, crime from April onwards showed a marked decline while the number of casualties among the militants had increased. With the nuisance of frequent *bandh* calls already becoming rare and kidnappings and extortions having come down considerably, peace seemed to be creeping back into Punjab. This became manifest in various pockets of activity in the state. The psychology of the masses, living under fear for so long, was changing fast.

K.P.S. Gill told the press that, in addition to Majha, the police was getting information from people about the militants in Malwa as well. Many top terrorists were being killed. On 9 August 1992, the Ludhiana police killed Sukhdev Singh Babbar, the man who had become a legend for the militants. The Babbars had the reputation of being the most disciplined, puritanical and committed terrorist outfit. The police bared his lavish lifestyle, living with a comely woman, with photographs of his villa named the 'White House'. His neighbours in a posh residential area of Patiala knew him as a rich contractor. This revelation shocked the Babbars more than their leader's death. This event virtually broke the back of the movement and boosted the morale of the people. The militants, in a desperate attempt to bounce back from the brink of annihilation, made the police its main target once again. In three weeks they killed 75 kin of policemen. But they could not sustain these killings. By then K.P.S. Gill had launched his 'night dominance' plan at Amritsar. This was to curb the movements of the militants and during the night. It was later successfully extended to other districts.

The Chief Minister in the meanwhile had sustained his mass contact campaign. Encouraged by the response of the people, the CM ordered civic elections in the state. This meant, barring the three Corporation towns of Amritsar, Jalandhar and Ludhiana, elections had to be held in all district and sub divisional headquarters, including sub tehsils. The Chief Minister's critics said that he was trying to court more popularity. Even if this was his motive, this mass churning exercise was necessary to strengthen the defiance of militancy.

The Chief Minister found himself on the wrong foot in his inaugural address at the Phagwara civic election rally when he criticised General O.P. Malhotra (Retd.), a former Governor of Punjab, as a supporter of militants. He also maintained that N.K. Mukerji and V. Varma, also Governors of Punjab, were not interested in containing militancy. He was also uneasy in the matter of failing to get the Punjab Package from the PM.

The Central Government, had decided not to concede any of Punjab's pending demands to the state. This could imply, that the Prime Minister was not interested in ending militancy in the Punjab. He must, therefore, have been surprised at the sudden fall in militancy in the state. Politically, this provided the Chief Minister with an opportunity of making sure that the actual credit of ending militancy went exclusively to his government so that his party got a boost in the municipal elections. I have mentioned earlier that, apart from the active rejection of militancy by the people, the fall of militancy in terms of statistics, had begun in Amritsar in April 1991 and in the rest of the state in October–November 1991. This trend got a setback for a couple of months around the elections in February 1992, but was back from April 1992 till the movement finally died out.

When the final results came, the Congress claimed that it had won a majority of seats in 70 out of the 95 Municipal Committees. The newspaper analysis showed that independent candidates had won 75 per cent of the seats; out of 1,067 seats, independent candidates had captured 644 seats, the Congress 360, the BJP 60 and others 3 only. This analysis was supported by the Committee-wise position. But let us ignore the controversy because in small towns people in small wards vote for individuals and not for parties. But if the Congress was now bringing peace to them, they could have, for a change, voted for it. Apparently they were not giving the party any such credit. I feel that this was because of the fact that the people of Punjab, irrespective of their political and religious affiliations, including many Congressmen, felt that the Central Congress Government had not been fair to Punjab and had largely been the cause behind the spread of terrorism.

Happily, the decline in militancy continued at a rapid pace from week to week. K.P.S. Gill had to come up with another action-plan for the rapidly changing situation. In October it was 'Civic Action'— telling the Panchayat and the parents where an arrested boy was being taken and by whom. In November it was followed by 'Chase and Neutralise'. This was being done to instil a greater sense of security to enable people to participate in the Panchayat polls.

The militants continued to surrender. It was only occasionally that they showed their presence. For instance on 1 December 1992 they killed 16 bus passengers near Jagraon. The next day we read in the papers that 19 terrorists had been killed in a 16 hour encounter near Makhu.

The Akalis also participated in the *Panchayat* polls, which began on 14 January 1993. As anticipated, there was heavy polling. There was no need for P.S. Badal to claim that it was because of their call; the polls were expected to be heavy in any case. Beant Singh claimed that he had captured 70 per cent of the *Panchayats*, while P.S. Badal insisted he had won in 60 per cent of the *Gram Panchayats*. I cannot comment on this arithmetical riddle. I would rather maintain that ultimately the people of Punjab had won all the seats. And if there was a price to pay for holding these elections, the people of Punjab had paid it heavily.

On the eve of Republic Day in 1993, Beant Singh thanked the people for curbing terrorism in Punjab. To celebrate the elections and peace, a mammoth crowd of newly elected *sarpanches, panches* and their supporters filled the vast Polo Ground in Patiala. It was a beautiful, sunny winter day. The Chief Minister and his Cabinet colleagues sat on the impressive stage. I was sitting in the third row behind the Chief Minister. Speaker after speaker indulged in fulsome praise of their leader and hero. Everyone seemed to be intoxicated by the joyous ambience.

The Chief Minister happened to look back, I bowed to greet him. He acknowledged me with a wave of his hand, and continued to wave it for quite a few moments. I started wondering, if ever it would occur to him that, four years earlier when Governor S.S. Ray was pleading with the Government of India to let him hold these elections, he was also dreaming of a similar development. At that time, Congressmen from Punjab had gone to Delhi to tell the leaders at the Centre about the havoc that the *Panchayat* elections would cause in the state. They had managed to convince their bosses in Delhi. The sabotage of the elections then had been tragic. How much bloodshed could have been prevented had the elections been allowed to be held in September 1989. But, forgetting the hurt in the true tradition of Punjab, all that we can now say is all is well that ends well.

30

In Retrospect

Odour of blood when Christ was slain
Made all Platonic tolerance vain
And vain all Doric discipline.

Two Songs from a Play, W.B. Yeats

Yeats accurately conveys what happened in Punjab in the mid 1980s. Tolerance slipped out of the world's largest democracy—India—and our leaders lost discipline. The outcome was the projection of Sant Jarnail Singh Bhindranwale, who led a violent movement for three years that culminated in Operation Blue Star. The three connected incidents of bloodletting in 1984—Operation Blue Star, Mrs. Gandhi's assassination and the massacre of Sikhs in Delhi—kept sanity at bay and Punjab bled for another nine long years. For the umpteenth time in its long and troubled history, the land was soaked in blood.

Before we recall the moments when we lost tolerance and discipline, let us note the background which produced the chain of hurtful events. The *Panchayat* is an age-old democratic institution at the grassroots level that has looked after the interests of the individuals and the community even though the country was ruled by kings and monarchs all along. British rule was also a monarchy despite the introduction of elected State and Central Legislative Assemblies in the 1920s. Despite a federal structure, India essentially had a unitary government.

Our Constitution did not end the unitary legacy. The Congress Party, which had led the freedom struggle, also chose to maintain the unitary essence. In the late 1950s, it was rightly felt that the country was lacking in emotional integration. The main reason behind this lack was the absence of a democratic spirit. This was sought to be inculcated by having a strong Centre. In 1959, the first ever elected Communist government in Kerala, was reduced to a minority by manipulating defections, because it was felt that such governments symbolised a weakening of the Central government. The first three non-Congress governments in Punjab were brought down in 1968, 1971 and 1980 for the same reasons. The Janata Dal government (1977–79), the first non-Congress government at the Centre and that, too, a coalition also followed this tradition and dismissed all Congress governments in nine states. In addition to that, the Janata government virtually hounded Mrs. Gandhi, Giani Zail Singh the defeated Chief Minister of Punjab and some other Ministers for their alleged excesses and corruption during the Emergency, which had been imposed by Mrs. Gandhi in 1975.

While politicians swore by democracy, most of them could not either imbibe the democratic spirit or were too autocratic to implement it. Otherwise there would not have been continuing episodes of manipulated dismissals of elected governments in the states nor would there have been engineered resignations at the Centre. Corruption at the highest levels also came to notice during this period, although it was much later that the P.V. Narasimha Rao government (1991–96) had to face charges of bribing some members of Parliament to sustain its majority. In fact the Prime Minister himself and one of his Minister's Buta Singh, have been found guilty of the charges of giving bribes, and sentenced to three years rigorous imprisonment by the trial court. (They have, of course, filed appeals against the verdict and the sentence stands suspended.) If the country's politics had been issue-based and free from various malpractices, terrorism could never have struck root in Punjab or elsewhere. Sponsoring the creation of the *Dal Khalsa*, the AISSF and Bhindranwale was certainly bad politics. So was the role of the Arya Samaj press in opposing Punjabi as the state language even though it had been included as one of the 14 main languages of India in the

Constitution. It was power politics, that created terrorism in Punjab and sustained it with adverse consequences for the people, the administration, the police force and the state as a whole.

In the three years of violence preceding Operation Blue Star (1984), 125 civilians lost their lives—15 (including two security men) each during 1981 and 1982, and 95 (including 20 security men) in 1983. But the scare caused by the killings in the first two years was more oppressive and demoralising than the prowess of the extremists. One reason was that it was the initial stage of killings. Other reasons were the messages and proclamations of Bhindranwale. The high proportion of Hindus amongst the victims was also a matter of concern. In the first two years, out of 26 victims of the militants, 18 were Hindus. In 1983, this changed to 35 Hindus and 40 Sikhs (security men excluded). Such figures, in statistical terms could not be a consolation to any one. Communal tension that had been deliberately instigated, after a few months, fed itself like a jungle fire.

The Congress Party, after it returned to power in 1980, put aside secularism and went on a crusade to win over Hindu votes. The then Janata Party was no less diligent in trying to sustain its hold. The inevitable consequence was the dangerous growth of communal tensions in the Punjab. I may add here that, even if the Hindu–Sikh equation in Punjab was to be strained to the farthest degree, it could not lead to bloodshed between the two communities. Fundamentalists had to be created to cause such an eventuality. Even after that, it must be remembered that, when Sikhs were being brutalised in Delhi in 1984, it was Punjabi Hindus who came to their succour and gave them protection besides initiating the enquiries at the people's level into the excesses perpetrated. Such gestures were not merely a reflection of the strength of Punjabi bonds, or some sense of deeper public morality; they were essentially prompted by the conviction that the Sikhs were not separatists and that the militants were a creation of the government.

Additionally, the sixfold increase in killings during 1983 made the elusive killing squads mythical heroes, and a country preacher, assumed the proportions of a superman with the halo of a saint. One reason, amongst others, for his achieving this image was that he was allowed to stay in the Golden Temple. A senior Sikh Congress leader told me that people were going to remember Bhindranwale in times to come and forget the Congress leaders. The brutal followers of the Sant looked many times taller than their actual stature because they managed to create the impression that the killings were the reaction of a helpless minority against the manipulated politics of a brute majority. For this reason, their ranks also kept on growing, even though their adherents were mostly crooks and criminals.

The police force, which had become obsolete in its composition and impact, due to the lack of intelligent development to keep pace with newer methods to combat crime in the modern world, could not withstand the initial onslaught of the militants. Inevitably, it became demoralised. It was rumoured that relations of some senior police officers bowed before the Sant and begged for the lives of their kin who were on his hit list. Mounting tensions between Hindus and Sikhs could not be effectively countered in such an uncertain ambience. The police force, which was predominantly Sikh came to be dubbed as being communal. The Hindus began looking to Mrs. Gandhi as their saviour. So when the state government of Darbara Singh, a Congress Chief Minister, was dismissed in October 1983, the foundations of Operation Blue Star had been laid.

This situation had developed in less than three years at the cost of 125 killings. After the dismissal of the Darbara Singh Government, to the great embarrassment of the Government of India, the number of killings skyrocketed to 379 (20 security personnel, 237 Hindus and 122 Sikhs) during the first five months of 1984. The compulsions of electoral politics required that the government should put an end to this unhappy situation a month or so before the parliamentary elections due in early 1985. But, to bring it under control, the government obviously could not see a way out other than handing over the situation to the army. Operation Blue Star was the result.

The melancholy situation soon came to a head. But in the euphoria in the aftermath of the Operation, two avoidable blunders were committed. The first was that Buta Singh, who should have known the Sikh ethos well, entrusted the reconstruction of the badly damaged Akal Takht to the *Nihang* leader, Baba Santa Singh. The task should have been left to the SGPC and the Sikh *sangat*. The second blunder, indeed an act of downright stupidity, was to remove very precious manuscripts, books and literature pertaining to Sikh history, from the Sikh library in the Temple to some secret place. These outrageous acts may not have alienated the Sikh community any further but they were seen as evidence of the malicious intentions of an overwhelming majority towards a small minority.

The euphoria had to evaporate and it did pretty soon. In fact, Mrs. Gandhi herself appeared quite gloomy when she visited the battle scarred Temple within a few days of the Operation. In the atmosphere of increasing gloom it was not advisable to hold the general election. However, the tragic assassination of Mrs. Gandhi by her Sikh security guards on 31 October 1984 and the consequent contrived massacre of Sikhs in Delhi and other places, rendered the situation tailor-made for the election.

The unprecedented carnage in November and the electoral victory in December 1984, are already history. But I feel it necessary to highlight the crude manner in which the opportunists and sycophants began to exploit the sad event for electoral gains. The new Prime Minister was still in mourning and mourners were paying their homage to the dead body of Mrs. Gandhi when attacks were being organised on defenceless Sikhs in Delhi and elsewhere. Mourners came as expected, but a stream of young men passed by her dead body not in silence, but shouting slogans, '*Khoon ka badla khoon se lenge* (Blood for blood!).' The crass scene was constantly being telecast by Doordarshan.

It was not clear who wanted revenge and from whom. One assassin had been killed and the other was lying seriously injured and was in police custody. I think that there could not have been greater disrespect to the departed leader. Perhaps nothing like this had happened anywhere else in the world in similar circumstances. In India no one clamoured for revenge even when the Father of the Nation, Mahatma Gandhi, was assassinated. It could not have happened spontaneously on the present occasion. The principal reason behind the contrived carnage would be that it furthered the Congress objective of capturing the Hindu vote.

The unprecedented victory of Rajiv Gandhi in the parliamentary elections called by him to be held within five weeks of Mrs. Gandhi's assassination, was the existence of a strong sympathy wave which was very much at its crest during the polls. We have thus been deprived of assessing the extent of electoral gains to the Congress which it had expected from the impact of its biggest gamble—Operation Blue Star. The party itself, barring the immediate euphoria, mostly remained on the explaining end, and party men privately conceded that it was a blunder and had badly damaged the party.

But, in spite of this, the Congress party did not appear to have learnt any lessons, nor did it analyse all the implications of the unprecedented miscalculation of Operation Blue Star. The Rajiv–Longowal Accord (July 1985) could be formalised because the Prime Minister negotiated it in complete secrecy. The militants increased the acts of violence both within and outside Punjab. The Congress party strategists had covertly begun to sabotage the Rajiv–Longowal Accord as soon as it was made public. It is true that the Congress had also sensed the shift in the minds of the voters against it. It had also noticed the growing challenge from the alliance of opposition parties led by stalwarts such as N.T. Rama Rao, Jyoti Basu, Devi Lal and V.P. Singh. This was no less formidable than the political opposition which had been posed to it in 1977 by Jai Prakash Narayan, Morarji Desai and the BJP.

The next Assembly elections in Haryana were to be held in June 1987. To kill the Rajiv–Longowal Accord, Bhajan Lal quit as Chief Minister of Haryana in June 1986, which gave the impression that he had sacrificed his high office for the good of Haryana. But within months, he secured membership of the Rajya Sabha and a berth in the Central Cabinet. The shrewd politician had evidently foreseen the defeat of his party in the forthcoming elections to the State Assembly.

To meet the challenge of the mid-1970s, Mrs. Gandhi had resorted to the imposition of the emergency in 1975 which had boomeranged on the government in the 1977 elections. It had then resorted to a communal tilt which was continued after returning to power in 1980, which culminated in Operation Blue Star. In spite of these experiences the party persisted with playing the communal card. In 1982, after the Congress lost the Assembly elections in Andhra Pradesh and Karnataka it stuck to the policy of wooing Hindu voters more desperately. This paid rich dividends in the elections to the Metropolitan Councils of Delhi and Jammu. Operation Blue Star was part of the same policy. It was, the same card, that was astutely played, under the subtle and sophisticated cover named *Sarbat Khalsa*, on 26 January 1986—the day the Mathew Commission was to announce its award on Chandigarh.

The so-called *Sarbat Khalsa* held at the Akal Takht was a landmark, no doubt. But it was the beginning of a process to negate the accord. The declaration by the Panthic Committee in April that its goal was Khalistan, contributed towards the sabotage of the Rajiv–Longowal Accord. The resultant occupation of the Golden Temple by the militants and the increased killings, 562 (including 42 security men) in 1986, seemed to lay the foundations for another

Operation Blue Star in a more sinister manner. A formal resolution for Khalistan had reportedly been adopted by the Panthic Committee at this stage. Even Bhindranwale had not done this. The surge of killings almost converted it into an insurgent movement with its nerve centre in the Golden Temple for a second time. Communal tensions started building up once again on lines similar to the pre-Blue Star days.

Many BJP workers in Punjab walked into the communal trap; some Hindu fundamentalist organisations fanned this fire to the satisfaction of the Congress. The Rajiv–Longowal Accord stood formally abrogated when the S.S. Barnala government was dismissed. This was done when the election in Haryana was only two months away. The report of the Eradi Panel which gave much more water to Haryana than its expectations, was made public only days before the polls. Governor S.S. Ray, could fortunately bring down violence in May and June soon after taking over the Punjab administration. But all this did not help the Congress to retain power in Haryana. And the worst news from the Congress point of view was that this victory of an opposition alliance was being considered as the trend-setter for elections due in several other states by election analysts.

By the close of 1987, Governor S.S. Ray achieved what was expected of him—there was a decline in killings, improved communal harmony and greater confidence of the people in the administration. Both Darbara Singh and Surjit Singh Barnala, the Congress and the Akali CM's of Punjab respectively had failed to do so. But the crime graph started shooting up right from New Year's day 1988 as if part of a sinister plan. The Government of India, surprisingly, manipulated the installation of Jasbir Singh Rode as the *Jathedar* of the Akal Takht. J.S. Rode, a relative of Bhindranwale, took charge of the Akal Takht in the second week of March. The government had thus implemented the most important decision taken at the *Sarbat Khalsa* of 26 January 1986, ostensibly to bring down killings and to clear the Golden Temple of extortionist groups.

Paradoxically, J.S. Rode himself had to shift from the Temple to Nanak Niwas out of fear of the terrorist groups opposed to him. The embarrassed Home Ministry had to release another half a dozen hard-core terrorists to reinforce the group already around him. Even then he could not muster enough courage to return to the Golden Temple. All the militants were driven out in Operation Black Thunder. But the government gave J.S. Rode a chance to takeover as the

Jathedar again in October. He failed again. The Intelligence agency that had chosen and groomed him had misjudged him completely and their plan had gone wrong in its entirety. It was assumed that the supporters of Bhindranwale would flock around his nephew. The AISSF had been assigned the task of contesting the parliamentary elections of 1989 to divide the Akali votes. But six of its candidates happened to win. The victory of these candidates remained a major factor behind the spurt in militancy in 1990. Hordes of young boys joined the ranks of the militants. Pakistan increased its support to the militants in order to sustain this trend and also to prevent their joining the expected February 1990 elections.

Something was seriously and fundamentally wrong in the working of this important system of Intelligence agencies and so-called experts, for which Punjab was paying a heavy price. This approach of the Home Ministry remains quite an enigma for me, so much so that at times I shudder when I question myself, 'Was the spurt in violence from New Year's day 1988, onwards also the handiwork of such agencies in order to justify J.S. Rode's installation?' In any case, there should have been some accountability for those officials supporting such an approach to the Punjab problem, in order to ensure that such policies are not continued again in Punjab or tried in other states to solve similar situations. Whosoever was behind these conspiracies was surely leading the government in the wrong direction.

G.S. Tohra had taken similar retrograde steps earlier. Within hours of his election as President of the SGPC in November 1986, he had dismissed the Task Force that had prevented the militants from staying in the Golden Temple. He had also appointed new pro-militant high priests immediately after that. I have recalled all these facts to emphasise that there was a sustained conspiracy by G.S. Tohra to destabilise the S.S. Barnala government. The Home Ministry had also taken many steps to unsettle Governor S.S. Ray. However, G.S. Tohra and the Home Ministry had one aim in common and that was to give support to the pro-militant high priests who, in turn, supported J.S. Rode. What inference can one draw from these complementary moves?

Undoubtedly, terrorism in Punjab had been planted but, despite all the care and nourishment, the soil had not accepted it. For this reason, all these machinations failed and Governor S.S. Ray could rightly claim an adequate return to normalcy in 1989. He urged the holding of *Panchayat* elections which would have further strengthened the rising morale of the people. His efforts were sabotaged by the State Congress which maintained that it would be utterly ruinous for the state. Election dates were postponed twice. The date fixed for the third time in November 1989 had to be cancelled as Rajiv Gandhi announced the holding of parliamentary elections in November in the entire country. What an ironical situation. The State Congress did not see any harm in holding parliamentary elections but maintained that *Panchayat* elections would have doomed the state.

V.P. Singh's promise of a new era was an honest one. Punjabis who, more than any others, wished for it ardently, had no reason to disbelieve him. But it was not to be. V.P. Singh had very clearly and firmly enunciated the parameters for the settlement. Like the Akali factions who acknowledged Simranjit Singh Mann as their leader, the people had also pinned their hopes for peace on him. In the foremost of S.S. Mann's concerns, were the 'boys'—the militants—who respectfully recognised S.S. Mann's sacrifice but none of their organisations was either willing to recognise him as their leader or to unite under him. After the 'boys' were the national leaders, followed by the people, and last were the Akalis. S.S. Mann seriously believed that he was the leader of the *Panth*. Given his priorities it was, therefore, not difficult to infer that the parleys could breed only more militancy, and not peace.

The only relief that could come to Punjab was from the appointment of well meaning Governors, committed to bring peace to the state. Although the entire bureaucracy, the police and the paramilitary forces were the same, yet K.P.S. Gill, the DGP Punjab, alone upset some people and organisations with his image as the icon of the Congress regime. Some others felt safer because of his presence. And oddly enough the police appeared to have manipulated an undercover campaign against Governor Nirmal Kumar Mukerji in the Home Ministry. When it came to Governor V. Varma's turn, his conflict with the Punjab police became quite transparent and did not remain hidden from public view. Despite all this, the police (that includes the Home Guards, SPO's), the CRPF, the BSF and above all the army ultimately won the 'mini war'.

Public indignation against the militants had begun building up in the wake of the brutal killings of 1988. Following the sudden spurt in killings from November 1989 onwards, people finally began opposing the militants openly in 1990. By the close of the year, a discernible sense of disapproval bordering on contempt for the terrorists had built up because of their widespread acts of extortion and senseless killing. Not many people, however, could understand what was happening. Governor N.K. Mukerji's transparency and Governor V. Varma's criticism of the police were very big factors in winning back the support of people for the government. Henceforth, people rejected militancy more actively. As a result, more and more militants were being killed. The senior police officers, however, could not highlight these achievements because some of them in a subtle manner tried to allege that the spurt in crime was due to the policies of the Governors.

General O.P. Malhotra's arrival and the deployment of the army directed the turn of events towards a possibility for peace. The army's presence had lifted the morale of the people and caused panic in the militant organisations. The most telling effect of the army's presence was that fresh recruits stopped joining the militant organisations. The final decline of militancy had begun. From April 1991, militancy was positively on the decline in Amritsar (where it had begun) since every month more militants were being killed than their victims. This trend spread to the rest of the state from November 1991 with an interruption around election time and continued from April 1992 onwards.

In effect, there had been practically no dent in the age-old amity between the two communities. The time was ripe for reviving the democratic set up in the state. After the peaceful elections for Punjab's three Municipal Corporations, the Governor requested the Central Government to hold elections to the Assembly. In the June 1991 election, the Congress did not participate. It turned out to be the only election campaign during which, in addition to a general increase in killings, the militants directly eliminated some contesting candidates in order to sabotage the polls. They did not succeed despite doing their worst. This is what I mean when I say that people had learnt to live with violence just as they do in times of war and deadly epidemics.

But T.N. Seshan, the Chief Election Commissioner of India, and the newly formed Congress Government of India came to the rescue of the militants. Only 24 hours before the polling, without consulting the Governor of the state, the CEC postponed the polls to September 1991 as, in his opinion, the polls would not have been free and fair. Obviously it was because of the militants. Yet, the very next day it was announced that the army would be withdrawn from the Punjab, which was actually done by mid-July 1991. It gave a fresh impetus to the tottering strength of militancy. The election was, however, annulled.

When fresh elections were notified, the militants went on a killing spree again but this time the election was completed successfully in February 1992. The Akalis did not joined the fray. The Congress won 85 seats in the leanest polling in which only 23 per cent of the votes were polled. The results of the 'sham' election of 1992 was reversed in the election of 1997 in which the Congress could retain only 18 seats. That was the people's answer to the tricks that had been played on them.

The Congress has certainly been sobered by its past experience with militancy. Its success in defeating the formidable Akali-BJP alliance in the September 1999 parliamentary polls in Punjab has proved that patience and tolerance do bear fruit. Not only that, these tactics are more successful than intrigue and violence. It also demonstrates that people are more concerned with the issues affecting their own welfare than what concerns the so-called leaders of the community and their religion.

The Akalis and the BJP have realised the importance of taking up the state's problems. If religion has to be mixed with politics, sanity permits only the import of religious morality and not its bigotry. There is no danger to the Sikh religion anywhere in the world. Presently a trend towards liberalism is developing in all religions. So is the reaction to fundamentalists. All parties need to learn to wait while in opposition, like their counterparts in established democracies, not for a year or two, but longer if it becomes necessary, for a change in the people's mandate. The eagerness of the Congress, while in opposition, to bring down governments by undemocratic and questionable means, including violence, has been discredited and has hurt the Indian polity, more than anything else, during recent years. Other parties have also erred but the Congress remains the trend setter.

The police and the paramilitary forces had to fight the terrorists all along. In between, the army was also deployed to assist the state forces. The civil administration and the people faced the entire onslaught of terrorism, including the bullets of the militants and, occasionally, those of the erring forces. The unarmed field officials of the civil administration; government, semi-government outfits and the private sector had the most difficult time.

I have seen the entire staff of a rural bank branch killed by militants' bullets. I have seen senior engineers, as indeed my own revenue officials, killed while seated on their office chairs and no one came to see what happened even after the killers had left. A jeepload of revenue personnel from Tarn Taran was kidnapped and another team was killed in Ropar. An irrigation engineer was thrown into a flowing canal. The expensive machinery being used in laying metalled rural roads was blasted more than once. Threats of extortion, kidnappings and pressures to influence decisions, selections, postings and transfers were also present. There was evidence of lapses and cases of succumbing to threats. Even the police, at the lower levels, was not immune.

The Department of Education was the worst affected. Many Hindu and targeted Sikh teachers migrated from villages to towns. But at no point of time did any of the departments cease functioning. I am afraid that in some places copying could not be prevented, but that was only in some remotely located schools. I had to order the shifting of an examination centre from the village of Valtoha to the city of Amritsar. The Guru Nanak Dev University, Khalsa College and the Government Medical Colleges in Amritsar, and educational institutions in the rest of the state that had a sprinkling of militant supporters nevertheless succeeded in maintaining reasonable discipline. This was despite militant threats.

I happened to be the chief guest at a function at in my alma mater, Khalsa College, Amritsar. A student poet was called to the stage to sing his welcome poem. But a loud demand from the students wanted him to sing his poem about the elimination of a terrorist by the police in a stage-managed fake encounter. 'There is no harm', I told the somewhat embarrassed Principal. The young man sang both the emotional poems. The same poet, at the end of the function, also sang the National Anthem. This was the correct picture of the younger generation. If one were to take note of only the young-man's 'fake encounter' poem and ignore his joining in the National Anthem, it would be a distortion of reality.

The civil and developmental administration remained practically functional all along except that we could not find witnesses willing to depose against the militants booked under the criminal and special laws. Consequently, we failed to secure their conviction. There was no situation that could be called a breakdown of law and order. The Judicial Courts functioned almost normally in respect of the rest of the cases. All other departments functioned even under the severest imaginable strain.

Trade, transport, and the communication systems functioned more or less normally. During this period, we even began extension of telecommunications to the rural areas. There was continuous industrial growth, and an increase in the rate of growth in agricultural produce and its marketing all over the state.

A team of World Bank officials came to inspect the brick lining of minor irrigation canals. I took them to Bhikiwind which was one of the worst affected areas. They were surprised to see the hustle and bustle and huge heaps of paddy in the vast marketing area of this small trading town.

The shortage of doctors was endemic even before the onslaught of terrorism. But to meet this, we introduced mobile dispensaries in the border areas. These served the people well and are still being continued. There were numerous examples of personal courage in defying the militants. A woman ripped up a militant with a scythe. A retired army *jawan*, presently working as a postal clerk, killed three of his kidnappers with one of their Assaults. The Comrades of Bhikhiwind repelled attacks of terrorists, by fighting pitched battles with them. Many others had challenged the militants and they did not dare to attack them. The Punjabis were bled pale, many families lost their bread winners and their kith and kin, during the dreadful trial they went through. But, ultimately they emerged substantially unscathed in spirit and in their zest for life.

From the Bhindranwale days, the police was suffering from the syndrome of being an ill-equipped force especially when it compared its own weapons with those possessed by the militants. This was a serious handicap. The deployment of the CRPF and the BSF did make up for the shortage of men and materials but, to be fully useful, any force alien to a terrain needs time to become effectively functional. The reorganisation of the police and the modernisation of its logistics was undertaken in April 1988. By then militancy had entrenched itself for the second time and had, once again, struck fear in the hearts and minds of the people.

Extortions and kidnappings by the militants shocked the overworked police. Owing to their relative failure to contain them, it lost much of the credit due to it for fighting the militants. The suspicions of the people that the police were involved in the increased kidnappings could not be satisfactorily allayed. The allegation of elimination of militants in police custody or in fake encounters was even more embarrassing. It always made sensational news. For the militants and their supporters it was very easy to allege. They could not, nor did they have to prove these allegations. But at times they embarked on counter campaigns to kill policemen and their family members and they did wreak havoc on them.

Besides supporters of the militants, the general public and village *Panchayats* also complained of police excesses. An IAS officer based in Chandigarh had complained to the Governor that the police had picked up his son, a fresh graduate in Engineering, from his residence at Mohali. Thereafter his whereabouts were not known. The police denied having picked up his son. But most of the time people were not willing to lodge a written complaint. As far as I remember, there were seven such complaints in Amritsar. In two cases one Deputy Superintendent, one ASI and five constables were dismissed by the government under Article 311 of the Constitution. In the case of three written complaints we ordered magisterial enquiries. In two, the police was found guilty and directed to register cases. In the third case, compensation was given to the dependants of the victim because the police was found to have acted in error. The remaining two complaints were verbal and no one was prepared to lodge a complaint in writing. I have not included many applications and telegrams sent to me so as to bring on record that the police had picked up some young boys. This was done as a matter of precaution. Appropriate action was taken on all such petitions to the satisfaction of the applicants. A few writs had also been filed in the High Court during the years of militancy. But the writ petitions including one in the widely publicised J.S. Khalra case have reportedly deluged the High Court and the Human Rights Commissions at the state and national level, particularly after the Akalis formed their government in Punjab in February 1997. A score of police officials have been named in a FIR registered by the Central Bureau of Investigation. The matter is in a way sub judice because the FIR had been lodged on the directions of the Punjab and Haryana High Court. Therefore, instead of commenting on the issue, I would like to recall some facts and figures and the extremes of the police action—the lawful and the alleged wrong actions.

As examples of lawful action we have the instances of two open encounters lasting for many days—one in Chhabhal and the other in Rataul. The alleged disappearance of Jaswant Singh Khalra in

September 1995, can be cited as a classic instance of unlawful action. In Chhabhal only militants were killed while in Rataul, besides a couple of militants, DIG Ajit Singh was killed and SSP Narinder Singh was injured. J.S. Khalra, as a young lawyer, had represented some militants in cases filed against them. He managed to point out quite a few cases of the cremation of dead bodies certified as unidentified by the police in Amritsar. In some cases, he had claimed that the name and number of the police personnel as given in the cremation grand record were fictitious. The constables who accompanied the dead bodies had perhaps done so to protect themselves in the event of any subsequent enquiry. This naturally casts serious doubts on the functioning of the police in this regard. J.S. Khalra's whereabouts, after he was allegedly picked up by the police from his house at midnight, are not known. The police denied having picked him up.

But this was not first time that such allegations had been levelled against the Punjab police. This had happened for instance in the 1940s (in an erstwhile princely state) in tackling the menace of dacoits, in the late 1960s it was the *Naxalites*, in the 1970s it was the *Lal Kurti* organisation in the district of Ferozepur. But the allegations against the police in the eighties were quite severe and oft repeated by the militants and their supporters, and at times, also by the people of the area. Walter Laqueur, who studied terrorist movements the world over, in his book, The *Age of Terrorism* (Little Brown & Co., 1987, Boston), has noted that 'state terrorism' is a concomitant of terrorism.

Despite the erosion of confidence in the police, there was no let up in the commitment of a very high order by the police along with the CRPF and the BSF. J.F. Ribeiro, K.P.S. Gill and D.S. Mangat, toured the remotest parts of Amritsar regularly. D.S. Mangat himself survived the blasting of his car. The militants had killed his doctor son, in the prime of his youth. Yet this man had kept his balance and courage and spared no pains to bring peace to the state. DIG Ajit Singh, two SSPs, many SPs, some with their family members, and all the ranks downwards, particularly the constables and their relatives, had lost their lives. Many of those who fought and survived are now defending themselves in various enquiries and writs filed in large numbers in the High Court. Now they feel let down and insecure.

One SSP, Ajit Singh, committed suicide. Such a development could not have been anticipated even by K.P.S. Gill. The backlash could have been prevented if the police, as a matter of policy, had involved the people in the fight against terrorism. The involvement of the common people remained a matter of personal choice with the field officers. In contrast, the army cultivated the people as a matter of policy to erase the unhappy memories of 'Operation Wood Rose.' The army's presence, during the last years of militancy, made up for its earlier lapse more than adequately. Its presence in the encounters also enhanced the credibility of the police in instances of armed encounters with the militants.

I have recalled this background not to extenuate the evil but to provoke a public debate at the national level, so that a viable solution can be evolved. The police and their family members remained the first target of the militants. Now some of them are facing prosecution. All the allegations of extortion, use of third degree methods and excesses could not be false. In spite of all this they have done a commendable job in restoring peace in the state. The army, paramilitary and auxiliary forces also did well but the police remained the cutting edge of the tool. Justice has to be done to them as well.

I recall the relevant statistics of lives lost in Punjab beginning with the year 1981 till the end of 1993—civilians 11,690, terrorists 7,946, police personnel 1,714. During this period 20,407 terrorists were arrested.

When I came to Amritsar, it was a 'blood, sweat toil and tears', situation. Three days later, on the morning of 10 July 1987, I stood gazing at the five well padded burly Sikhs lying dead on their closely laid cots on the roof of the farmhouse of Satnam Singh Bajwa, a former Deputy Minister of Punjab. The dead body of the host, was amongst them. In their sleep, none of them had stirred when the terrorists shot them simultaneously. Here I met S.S. Virk and Izhar Alam, the DIG of the CRPF and the SSP of Amritsar respectively. Both of them welcomed me to Amritsar with the customary smile. The formalities of courtesy calls and return calls had thus been complied with over the deceased who, even in their death, symbolised warm friendship and a jolly, carefree attitude to life. I realised then what my forthcoming routine was going to be and did not need any time to get inured to the job. Senseless killings continued and I had to live with them.

Pleasant rewards also fell my way in this blood curdling drama. I had a considerable share of both. The ghastly sight of killings, mass cremations, inconsolable families, communities and even whole villages are my dreadful and recurring memories. The comfort, consolation and hope to worried families, the restoration of their boys to them after getting them released from the police or the militants, addressing agitated crowds and students and pacifying them are touching memories which are still fresh in my mind.

The four public meetings I organised for the Prime Ministers, the three meetings with the Prime Minister that I attended, the unconditional confidence of five Governors, five Chief Secretaries, three DGPs and many advisors to the government was quite rewarding. I had no problem in dealing with the four IG's, five DIG's and 14 SSP's with whom I worked during my tenure of five years at Amritsar.

The special compliments, by way of 'accolades' only to me by the President of India after he conferred the National Award of Padma Shri on me, are equally unforgettable. On 13 April 1989, Governor S.S. Ray came out of his plane with a book in his hand. As I received him he presented it to me. It was a historical novel, *Massacre at Jallianwala Bagh* by Stanley Wolpert. The inscription by the Governor read 'To Sarab Jit—a rather efficient D.C. of Amritsar—to warn him of the mistakes that another D.C. of Amritsar had committed in 1919!! Best wishes.' 'Siddhartha Ray'. Above all, the innumerable swords and mementoes presented to me by the village *Panchayats* showing their confidence in me, are a cherished treasure.

Terrorism has been wiped out but many a militant is still around. Most of them are in Pakistan. They keep creeping into India with large quantities of RDX, obviously to revive militancy. Quite a few of them have been falling into the hands of the police. But some must also have escaped. Such incidents sometimes raise the question; can terrorism stage a comeback?

I quite firmly believe that such incidents, even if they increase, cannot develop into a terrorist movement. A revival is possible if any government or its Intelligence agencies, extend support to the militants and provoke inter-community tensions through sectarian and communal politics. The Akalis may take up their agitation for the pending demands of Punjab such as the issues of water and territory, etc., in the course of time. Even this would not take a violent turn in the shape of a militant movement. The possibility of the revival of such a situation, therefore, is not all that likely. But I am sure of one thing; the militants can no longer consider the insanity of starting their activities from the holy precincts of the Golden Temple.

Glossary

Ahuti: (Sanskrit) Literally sacrifice.

Akalis: Literally the followers of *Akal*—the timeless God. The first Sikh newspaper started in 1920, to organise the movement to free their *gurudwaras* from the mahants and the country from the British, was named *Akali*. Those who volunteered to participate in the struggle came to be known as Akalis.

Akhand path: Continuous recitation of the Guru Granth Sahib to be completed within 24 hours by a relay of readers.

Amavas sangat: The congregation that gathers for a dip in the holy *sarovar* on a specific moonless night.

Ardas: Supplication, a prayer offered at the beginning and completion of religious functions. (Also the offerings at such functions.)

Baisakhi: The first day of Baisakh. Guru Gobind Singh founded the Khalsa on this auspicious day in A.D. 1699.

Band: An earthen dam, an obstruction.

Bandh call: A call given by agitators to stop work in support of the cause of their agitation.

Baraat: The guests and relations of the bridegroom who accompany him to the bride's place for the marriage ceremony.

Bhai: Literally brother; a person who looks after the gurudwara.

Bhog: Completion of the reading of Sri Guru Granth Sahib.

Chola: A long sleeved or half sleeved shirt worn over the torso that extends almost to the ankles.

Darbar sahib: The Golden Temple, Amritsar.

Dera: Abode, camp, used for the temporary dwelling of a religious or prominent person, also a unit in the Khalsa army.

Dharam Yudh: Righteous war, fight in the cause of religion.

Doordarshan: The government owned television network of India.

Dukhbhanjani beri: Reliever of all pain and sorrow—name given to a tree alongside the holy *sarovar*. It is believed that a dip at the site heals many diseases of the faithful.

Galiara: One hundred feet free space all around the Golden Temple known as 'Corridor plan'. This was done to prevent militants taking advantage of the clustered bazaars to surreptitiously enter the temple again after Operation Black Thunder.

Gandi bhasha: Crude language.

Gherao: To immobilise by surrounding a person or building with sheer manpower. A method of protest.

Giani: A man of knowledge and learning.

Gram Panchayat: A village council elected by the village.

Granthi:	One who recites the Guru Granth sahib as a profession.
Gurmata:	A decision arrived at by a Sikh congregation in the presence of the Guru Granth Sahib.
Gurudwara:	Literally 'threshold of the Guru'; a Sikh Temple.
Hai hai:	It is an utterance of both sorrow or condemnation.
Har ki pauri:	Steps leading to the *sarovar* on the eastern side of Harmandar, from where pilgrims can holy water...
Harmandar Sahib:	The Golden Temple, Amritsar.
Hartal:	Strike.
Havan:	Religious ceremony involving offerings made to a sacred fire.
Haveli:	Generally a large building, a dwelling in a city.
Hukamnama:	Written directions/ orders issued by the *Guru* to the Sikhs.
Jatha:	Volunteers gathered in groups to press for the attainment of social or political goals.
Kar-sewa:	Voluntary labour in the service of a cause.
Kesri:	Saffron colour, also the Sikh religious flag.
Khadi:	Hand spun and hand woven cotton cloth.
Khalsa:	The name given by Guru Gobind Singh to the baptised brotherhood of Sikhs; it literally means pure or the chosen one.
Kharkoos:	Militants.
Kisan:	Farmer.
Langar:	Eating place attached to a gurudwara where food is served free to all comers irrespective of cast and creed.
Langri bhasha:	Lame language.

Lathi:	Long wooden stick used as a weapon.
Mahant:	The presiding personage of a religious place.
Mand:	Marshy area between the confluence of the rivers Beas and Sutlej.
Maryada:	Decorum and sanctity.
Miri:	Temporal authority.
Misl:	Urdu word for file; in the eighteenth century it was used for the combination of various groups guarding different areas (*rakhi*) to fight a common foe. *Misls* in course of time, were named after the leader of the combination of various groups.
Mool mantra:	The basic tenets on which the Sikh religion was founded.
Morcha:	An extension of Sikh war terminology to their peaceful agitations such as Jaito, Guru ka bag *morcha*. In war terminology it was used for be sieging a fort.
Nihang:	One who shuns unnecessary worldly acquisitions to remain carefree. They are also known to be fearless fighters.
Nishan Sahib:	*Kesri* flag erected in Sikh temples. The flag bearers also lead the religious procession.
Palki:	A palanquin.
Panch:	Members of a *Panchayat*. Also a juror, arbiter, mediator or referee.
Pandal:	A sitting place for a gathering, large tents are also raised at the venue for shade etc.
Parivar:	Literally a family.
Patit:	A Sikh who violates the wows he took at his baptism ceremony for initiation into the *Khalsa panth*.

Patwari:	A government official who keeps a record of land holdings and collects land revenue.
Piri:	Spiritual authority.
Prasad, prashad:	Sweetmeat offered to the Guru, deity.
Rakhi:	Literally 'protection'; it refers to the area under a Sikh Chiefs protection and also the percentage of agricultural produce due to him from that area.
Ram Ban:	Arrows shot by Lord Rama which no enemy could withstand.
Sahib:	Master.
Sangat:	Society; company; congregation, generally religious. The collective body of Sikhs of one place.
Sarai:	A resting place for pilgrims.
Sarbat Khalsa:	Meetings of all the heads of the *misls* and *Jathedars* on the *Baisakhi* and *Diwali* festivals in the eighteenth century.
Saropa:	A token of honour. Generally a saffron cloth.
Sarpanch:	Head of the village *Panchayat*.
Satyagrahi:	Non-violent agitator, passive resistor, one who is wedded to truth.
Shabad:	Word; also a religious verse from the Guru Granth Sahib.
Shamiana:	Tent.
Sifarish:	Recommendation.
Singh:	Lion. The suffix to the name of all Sikhs ordained by the Tenth Guru.
Tankhah:	Religious punishment or penalty.
Toshakhana:	Treasury, room for keeping precious objects.
Zindabad:	Literally 'long live'; usually uttered as a favourable slogan.

Index

Abdus Samad Khan, 35

Abnashi Singh, 173

Abohar: Haryana was to get in lieu of Chandigarh, 41, 66, 68, 77, 307

accountability, 330

administration, morale, 94

Advani, Lal Krishna, 89

Ajit Singh, 256, 337

Ajnala, Malkiat Singh, 145, 167, 189

Ajnala, Punjab: movements, 210, 252

Akal Takht, 37, 71, 72, 74, 106–7, 110, 134, 146, 153, 154, 171, 173, 188, 195, 196, 216, 227; Bhindranwale moved in, 53–54; reconstruction after Operation Blue Star, 24, 25, 30, 32, 71, 72, 326; —donations for, 31, 32; —kar-sewa, 24, 31, 134, 146, 153, 154, 171, 173, 188, 198, 216, 227; see also Golden Temple

Akali Dal, Akalis, 25, 58, 60, 62, 74, 75, 77, 86, 93, 105, 163, 204, 205, 215, 218, 220, 223, 226, 241, 278, 279, 290, 298, 302, 304, 305, 308, 319, 331, 333, 336; agitations 41, 55; demands to Congress government, 48; elections boycott, 308, 309, 313, 315; existence threatened by Bhindranwale, 47; participated in Panchayat polls, 322; split, 78, 109, 302; Sadbhavna rallies boycott, 270

Akali Dal (Badal), 247, 276, 304

Akali Dal (Kabal), 304, 305, 308

Akali Dal (Kalan), 312

Akali Dal (Longowal), 78, 98, 226, 273, 276, 304

Akali Dal (Panthic), 283, 302, 304

Akhand Kirtni Jatha, 46, 64

Alam, Izhar, 89, 90, 91, 111, 181, 338

All India Gurudwara Bill, 60

All India Sikh Students Federation (AISSF), 25, 29, 45, 50, 58, 60, 64, 75, 77, 87, 96, 101, 106, 108, 204, 215–17, 220, 227, 228, 274, 275, 280, 283, 287, 288, 290, 295, 297, 306, 308, 309, 324, 330

All India Sikh Students Federation. (AISSF) (Daljit group), 229

All India Sikh Students Federation (AISSF) (Manjit), 220, 223, 280, 283

All India Sikh Students Federation (AISSF) (Mann), 227

Aman Deep Singh see Dimpy, Aman Deep Singh

Amar Das, Guru, 200
Amar Singh, 283
Amarinder Singh, 68, 78, 216, 220, 302, 304, 308
Amarjit Kaur, 46, 64
Amarkot, Amritsar, Punjab: terrorist attack police post, 254
ambience, 94, 232, 266
Amethi, Uttar Pradesh, 219
Amrik Singh, 53, 228
Amritsar, 25, 199, 232, 233, 234, 275; army deployed, 264, 265, 269, 277, 302; Mandal Commission, agitation against, 247; militants active; — bandh calls, 269; —banned liquor, meat and tobacco, 268; — kidnappings and killing, 50, 82, 116, 210, 212, 213, 248, 257, 260, 287; —decline, lost hold, 250, 292, 295, 296, 303, 314; —bringing weapons from Pakistan, 252; migrations, 257; paramilitary forces, 293; poll violence, 288; proposal to make the capital of Punjab, 305–6; *Sadbhavna* rallies, 270
Amritsar Municipal Corporation, 182, 183, 271
Amte, Baba, 98
Anand, Mulk Raj, 182
Anandpur Sahib, Punjab: flag of so-called Khalistan hoisted, 50
Anandpur Sahib Resolution, 43, 58, 60, 66, 106, 224, 313
Andersen, Walter K., 219
Arjan Dev, Guru, 36, 37, 162
Arjun Singh, 58, 59, 60
Arora, Gopi, 152, 155
Arora, J.S., 170
Arora, Suresh, 124, 128, 176
Arya Samaj, 39
Assam Rifles, 118
Atinder Pal Singh, 217, 219, 221
Atwal, A.S., 26, 126, 198
Aujla, Lal Singh, 154

BSF *see* Border Security Force
Baba Bakala, Amritsar: night curfew, 112

Babbar Akali Dal, 205
Babbar, Sukhdev Singh, 112, 254, 320
Babbars, 65, 290
Babri Masjid, 215
Badal, Prakash Singh, 58, 59, 60, 61, 62, 78, 82, 84, 105, 106, 163, 220, 225, 226, 227, 228, 229, 246, 304, 306, 308, 322
Badal–Tohra group, support to militants, 109
Bahujan Samaj Party (BSP), 312, 315
Bains, Ajit Singh, 64, 238, 239, 287
Bains Committee, 64–65
Bains, Surjit Singh, 119, 126
Bajaj, B.R., 285
Bajwa, Satnam Singh, 338
Bakshish Singh (Kalyug), 262
Baldev Prakash, 218
Baldev Singh, 125, 126
Balkar Singh, 112
Balwant Singh, 59, 60, 105
Banda Singh, Bahadur, 35
bandh calls by militants, 320; public response, 268–9
Bansi Lal, 82
Barnala, Surjit Singh, 24, 26, 37, 44, 59, 61, 62, 63, 64, 66, 68, 72, 73, 74, 75, 77, 78–79, 80, 83, 87, 88, 93, 96, 103, 105, 107, 108, 109, 163, 197, 226, 242, 246, 301, 303, 329; government dismissed, 109, 110
Basu, Jyoti, 328
Batala, Punjab: militants activities, 82, 172; militants bringing weapons from Pakistan, 252
Beant Singh, 154, 202, 204, 206, 281, 294, 296, 298, 305, 306, 307, 308, 309, 314, 315, 317, 318, 319, 320–2
Beant Singh (assassin of Indira Gandhi), 62, 217, 274
Bhagat, H.K.L., 294
Bhagey, Goverdhan, 244
Bhajan Lal, 66, 82, 305, 306, 307–8, 328
Bhakhra Beas Management Board, 69, 225
Bhan Singh, 107, 127, 159, 160, 177, 187, 201

Bharatiya Janata Party (BJP), 76, 81, 89, 247, 275, 277, 280, 297, 298, 312, 321, 329, 333

Bharatiya Kisan Union (BKU), 309

Bhatia, Raghunandan Lal, 59, 218, 305, 306

Bhattal, Rajinder Kaur, 274

Bhikhiwind, 261, 262; migration of Hindus, 260, 265

Bhinder, Mrs., 46

Bhindranwale, Jarnail Singh, 44, 45, 46, 47, 50, 52, 53–54, 55, 58, 61, 64, 72, 77, 107, 108, 123, 141, 147, 217, 224, 228, 231, 323, 324, 329, 330, 335; killed in Operation Blue Star, 56

Bhindranwale: Myth and reality by Chand Joshi, 56

Bhindranwale Tiger Force of Khalistan (BTFK), 108, 290, 306, 317

bhog ceremonies of militants, 266

Bhullar, G.I.S., 243

Bhullar, M.S., 252, 256, 278, 316, 317

Bhutto, Benazir, 199

Biakchhunga, *Brig.-Gen.*, 279

Bindra, I.S., 182

Bishnois, 307

Bitta, Maninderjit Singh, 318

Bittu, Daljit Singh, 112, 251

Black Thunder Operation, 73, 146, 149, 150, 170, 173, 174, 181, 184, 187, 195, 196, 197, 198, 199, 206, 207, 216, 220, 227, 278, 329; Akalis protest, 163–4

Blue Star Operation, 23, 24, 32, 54, 55, 56, 58, 62, 63, 72, 75, 76, 123, 124, 126, 127, 128, 143, 149, 150, 153, 185, 215, 241, 254, 265, 274, 275, 286, 300, 323, 325, 326, 327, 328, 329

Boparai, S.S., 95

Border Security Force (BSF), 80, 111, 118, 199, 200, 225, 252, 264, 331, 335, 337

Bose, Subhash Chandra, 39

Braham Buta Akhara, 27, 28, 30, 96, 123, 128, 135, 138, 140, 159, 161

Brahma, Avtar Singh, 108, 110, 113, 199

Brar, B.S., 173, 201

Brar, S.S., 260

bribes, 233, 234

British: Sikhs conflict, 38; recognised identity, 37

Brown, Percy, 28

Budha Dal, 72

bureaucracy, bureaucrats, 182, 183, 203, 331

Buta Singh, 37, 72, 73, 83, 86, 109, 116, 120, 152, 155, 158, 160, 174, 264, 324, 326

Butter, Amritsar, arsenals recovered, 113

CPI, 247

CPM, 312

Calcutta, Manjit Singh, 218

Catch-22, 209

Census of India, 1961, 42, 44

Central Jail, Amritsar, 234, 238

Central Jail, Nabha, 234

Central Reserve Police Force (CRPF), 32, 80, 87, 89, 90, 92, 99, 111, 112, 119, 123, 124, 126, 137, 138, 139, 144, 145, 164, 183, 191, 225, 248, 252, 331, 335, 337, 338; personnel killed by militants, 253–4, 255, 257

Chaman Lal, 119, 125, 126, 135, 137, 141, 142, 165, 189, 190, 191–2, 193, 194

Chandigarh: *bandh*, 306; Mandal Commission, agitation, 247; was to be transferred to Punjab, 59, 66, 67–68, 77, 302, 305, 306–8, 312; non transfer, 71; made Union Territory, 41–42

Chandra Shekhar, 75, 83, 98, 99, 247, 263, 275, 277, 278, 279, 280, 281

Changiara, Satta, 200, 210

Channake, Punjab: terrorist killings, 90–91

Chauhan, Jagjit Singh, 49

Chavan, S.B., 286

Cheema Bath village, militants strike, 103, 110

Chehru, Manbir Singh, 80

Chhabhal, Amritsar, Punjab, 255; migration of Hindus, 260, 265; militants,

244; —attack police post, 254; police-militants encounter, 336–7
Chhetra, A.S., 190
Chibber, B.K.N., 264, 265, 317
Chidambaram, P., 116, 118, 152, 153, 155, 172, 201, 264
Chohla Sahib, 104
Citizens for Democracy, 213
commission to identify the Hindi speaking areas of Punjab, 66–68
Communal Harmony and Integration Council, 79, 80, 92
communal tensions, 42, 51, 76, 116
Communists, 95, 298
Comrades, 95
Congress, 39, 44, 45, 46, 47–48, 49, 50, 57, 62, 73, 95, 105, 121, 202–3, 204, 205, 215, 218, 219, 220, 221, 225, 226, 238, 242, 247, 274, 275, 278, 279, 280, 281–2, 284, 286, 287, 290–1, 294–5, 296, 297, 298, 306, 308, 312, 321, 324, 325, 327, 328, 329, 331, 333; Hindu vote, 60; sabotaged *Panchayat* elections, 301
Congress Working Committee, 307
Constitution of India, 42, 48, 69, 81, 86, 101, 156, 206, 210, 215, 225, 226, 242, 277, 297, 324, 325, 336
corruption, 203, 209, 324
Council of Khalistan, 113

Dal Khalsa, 36, 45, 287, 324
Daleke, Dilbag Singh, 316
Daljit Singh, 154, 257
Damdami Taksal, 25, 31, 45, 71, 87, 96, 101, 108, 122, 140, 141, 143, 146, 147, 154, 171, 174, 179, 188, 216, 227, 275, 276, 290
Dang, Satya Pal, 108, 169, 247
Darbara Singh, 47, 50, 51, 52, 55, 120, 326, 329
Darshan Singh, Giani, 74, 83, 84, 96, 97, 98, 99, 106, 107, 110, 188, 195
Dashmesh Regiment, 76, 317
Delhi: anti-Sikh riots, 32, 57, 58, 64, 73, 81, 89, 105, 119, 139, 294, 323, 327; victims, in Punjab, 65–66

democracy, 285, 315
depotism, 36
Dera Baba Nanak, Punjab, militants cross over to India through, 252
Desai, D.A., 68
Desai, Morarji, 62, 69
Deshmukh, B.G., 235, 263
Devi Lal, 73, 82, 204, 215, 217, 218, 223, 224, 226, 275, 328
Dhami, Kanwar Singh, 199
Dharam Yudh, 47, 48, 62
Dhillon, Ganga Singh, 50
Dimpy, Aman Deep Singh, 112, 113, 124
Dismemberment of the Punjab by Mohan Lal, 43
Doaba, Punjab: militants, 265; —losing hold, 278, 295
Dorangla, Baldev Singh, 212
Dunnet, 38
Durgiana Mandir, 223
Dutt, Sunil, 98

educational institutions, under militants' threat, 334
Election Commission, 286, 295
electoral politics, 326, 327
emergency, 44
emotional integration, 324
employment opportunities and smuggling, 117–18
Eradi Tribunal, 69, 329
extortions, 108, 203, 209, 211, 212, 213, 216, 221, 228, 243, 249, 257, 259, 265, 266, 289, 303, 320, 332, 334, 335; extorted money and chit fund companies, 213

faith, 31, 37
'falcon', 228
Faridkot, Punjab: arms recovered, 113
Fateh Singh, 41
Fatehgarh Churia, Punjab: militants, 82
Fazilka: Haryana was to get in lieu of Chandigarh, 41, 66, 68, 77, 307
Ferozepur, Punjab: 199, 235; army deployed, 302; Lal Kurti organisation, 337; militant activities, 82

freedom struggle, Sikh participation, 39
fundamentalism, 45, 117, 325

Gandhi, Indira, 23, 41, 68, 69, 89, 215, 274, 305, 323, 324, 326, 327, 328; negative attitudes towards Akalis, 43, 44, 45, 46, 47, 49; assassination, 56, 57, 58, 60, 62, 64, 77
Gandhi, M.K., 38, 39, 327
Gandhi, Maneka, 275
Gandhi, Rajiv, 23, 32, 33, 49, 57–58, 60, 61, 82, 83, 86, 171–3, 186, 199, 200, 203, 204, 215, 219, 235, 277, 279, 283, 327
Gandhi, Sanjay, 47, 58
Ghuman, Mal Singh, 97, 155, 176, 177, 187
Gill, K.P.S., 99, 101, 112, 119, 128, 129, 130, 134, 135, 136, 137, 139, 141, 142, 143, 145, 151, 152, 154, 156, 158, 159, 160, 161, 165, 172, 176, 177, 178, 189, 191–2, 193, 199, 209, 212, 222, 223, 225, 230, 235, 238, 243–4, 245, 248, 249, 250, 255, 259, 262, 263, 264, 309, 319, 320, 321, 331, 337
Gill, Manohar Singh, 256
Gill, P.P.S., 146, 192
Gill, Rajpal Singh, 119
Gobind Ram, 202, 253
Gobind Singh, Guru, 35, 36, 37, 301
Goindwal, Punjab: militancy, 231
Goindwal Sahib Gurudwara, 106
Golden Temple, 27–29, 38, 49, 55, 60, 87, 99, 104, 111, 181, 222; arms recovered, 166, 167; control seized from British, 38; corridor plan, agitation of uprooted people, 183–5; —, rehabilitation, 183, 186; militants presence, 26, 27–30, 31–33, 34; —, hold of, 26, 33, 53, 55, 61, 72, 88, 106, 111–12, 123, 124–6, 157, 175
Goodall, David, 27
government, state and union: bowed to militants demand, 257; ignored the developments, 50, 51, 115–16; objectives coincided with militants, 73–75, 108, 157; Sikhs' faith, 32–33; short-sighted approach, 26, 83, 115; sponsored terrorism, 50–52
gram panchayats, 215, 322
Grewal, Sarla, 172
groupism, 226
Gujral, Inder Kumar, 49, 223, 244, 246
Gulu, 262
Gupta, B.C., 158
Gupta, Hari Ram, 36
Gupta, Sanjiv, 189, 228, 236, 258, 268, 271
Gurbachan Singh, 46
Gurchet Singh, 290
Gurdarshan Prakash Gurudwara, 141
Gurdaspur, 234; arms recovered, 113; army deployed, 264, 277, 302; paramilitary forces, 293
Gurmata, 71
Guru Ka Bagh, agitation by Akalis, 25–26, 100; Sikh resistance, 38
Gurudwara reform movement, 38
Guru Nanak Dev University, 334

Har Gobind, Guru, 36
Harbhajan Singh, 288
Harcharan Singh, 73
Harike, Amritsar, Punjab: terrorist attack police post, 254
Harjinder Singh, 113, 276
Harsa Chinna, Punjab: terrorists strike, 125
Haryana: assembly election, 73, 275; claim for Chandigarh, 306–7; Hindi speaking areas to, 66–67; and Punjab, disputes, 24; —, and Rajasthan, river water sharing, 59; demand for separate state, 41; Yamuna, control given, 42
Hathi, Jaisukhlal, 46
Himachal Pradesh: demand for separate state, 41; and Punjab, merger, 40
Hindu Maha Sabha, 39
Hindus, 23, 32, 47; traumatised by militants, 63, 325, 326; Sikh tension, 50, 51, 55
Hira Singh, 104
Home Guards, 254
Hoon, P.N., 286

Hoshiarpur, Punjab: militant activities, 82
Hukam Singh, 44
hukamnama, 35, 107, 162, 169
Human Rights Commission, 336
Human Rights Organisations, 238

Improvement Trust, 183
Inderjit Singh, 239
Indian Architecture: Islamic Period by Percy Brown, 28
Indian National Army, 39
Indian National Congress *see* Congress
Indian National Trust for Art and Cultural Heritage (INTACH), 182, 185, 186
Indo-Pak border fence, 264
inner-gang rivalries, 104
Inter Services Intelligence (ISI), 26, 77, 202, 224, 232
inter-gang rivalries, 123
Investigations and interrogations, 232
Iqbal Singh, 194
Irving, Miles, 34

Jagat Narain, Lala, 52
Jagdev Kalan, Punjab: killing of Hindus, 89, 90
Jagir Singh, 104, 113
Jagraon, Punjab: militants strike, 322
Jaito agitation, 39
Jalandhar, 199; municipal corporations, 271; Punjab, militant activities, 82
Jallianwala Bagh, massacre, 25, 34
Jammu and Kashmir: terrorist movement, 236
Jan Sangh, 45
Janata Dal, 46, 75, 83, 96, 98, 204, 218, 241, 275, 312, 324
Janata Dal (S), 290
Janata Party, 44, 226, 278, 325
Jandiala, Punjab: militant activities, 82
Jang, 120
Jassa Singh, 166
Jaswant Singh, Giani, 74
Jatana, Balwinder, 303
Jethmalani, Ram, 226
Jhakhar, Balram, 217

Jhamka, 91
Jhamke, Sukhdev Singh, 199
Jodhpur detainees, 60, 65; released, 111, 201
Joginder Singh, Baba, 58, 59, 60, 62, 75, 77, 216, 220, 224
Joshi, Chand, 56

Kabul Singh, 74
Kairon, Pratap Singh, 43, 117, 307
Kandu Khera, 68
Kangra, included in Hindi region, 40
Kanwal Jit Singh, 104, 218
Kanwar Pal Singh, 112
Kaonke, Gurdev Singh, 72, 110
Kapoor, H.L., 286
Kapur, S.L., 130, 244, 248
Kapurthala, Punjab: militants, 199
Karaj Singh, 165
Kari Sari, Hoshiarpur, militants strike, 104
Kashmir Singh, Giani, 74, 97
Kashtiwal, 236
Kathpalia, P.K., 252
Kerala, communist government, 324
Kesar, J.S., 186
Khalistan, 24, 49, 50, 53, 54, 73, 74, 78, 96, 97, 107, 110, 112, 122, 124, 199, 200, 201, 213, 216, 224, 227, 240, 291, 302, 306, 329
Khalistan Armed Force, 76
Khalistan Commando Force (KCF), 108, 199, 290, 317
Khalistan Liberation Army, 76, 98
Khalistan Liberation Force (KLF), 199, 317
Khalra, Jaswant Singh, 336, 337
Khalra, Punjab, militants, 251; Hindu, 262
Khalsa, 35, 37; fraternity, 39
Khalsa, Bimal Kaur, 62, 77, 217, 224, 228, 274
Khalsa College, Amritsar, 83, 334
Khalsai Panchayat, 227
Khanna, Tejinder, 248, 310
Kharak Singh, 38
Kharkoos see militants
Khemkaran, Punjab, militants, 251

Khera, Manjit Singh, 273
Khosla, H.M., 311
Khudian, Jagdev Singh, 224
Khushipur, Shiv Singh, 177, 178
kidnappings by militants for ransom, 207–9, 211, 249, 250, 303, 320, 334, 335
Kirpal Singh, 53, 61, 74, 84, 218, 228, 257
Knit India Movement, 98
Kohar, Tarsem Singh, 80

Labh Singh, 113, 187
Lahore 25; and Amritsar, trade between, 117
Lal Bahadur Shastri Academy of Indian Administration, 287
Lal Kurti organisation, 337
Laldenga, 279
langar, 36
language issue, 39–40, 42, 60; base of Haryana Punjab division, 67, 68
Laqueur, Walter, 337
law and order, 23, 24
Left parties, 275, 280, 297
Liberation Front of Khalistan, 76
Lok Shakti Samagam, 94, 95
Longowal, Harchand Singh, 24, 32, 53–55, 58, 59, 60, 62, 63, 64, 201, 228, 279, 304
Lopoke, Punjab: 245; involvement of youth in nation building activities, 244; PM's visit, 245–6
Ludhiana, Punjab: extortion, 278; militants, 248, 265; *panches* and *sarpanches* resigned, 318
Ludhiana Municipal Corporation, 271

Mahan Punjab Samiti, 40
mahants, 37, 38
Majha, Punjab: militants, 320
Majitha, Punjab: Hindu terrorists, 262
Maken, Lalit, 62
Makhu, Nishan Singh, 200
Malhotra O.P., 248, 262, 275, 278, 286, 301, 302, 308, 320, 332
Malik, Jacob, 146
Malmohri, Resham Singh, 256

Malout, Ferozepur, Punjab: militants, 82
Malviya, Madan Mohan, 39
Malwa, Punjab: militants active, 236, 265, 320; losing hold, 278, 295
Mand area, Punjab: militant organisation, tried to establish their headquarters, 207; police raids, 79–80, 208
Mand, Dhian Singh, 224
Mandal Commission Report, 247, 275; agitation against, 257
Mangat, D.S., 248, 296, 297, 303, 337
Manji Sahib, 220, 223
Manjit Singh, 204, 215, 216, 219, 220, 221, 223, 227, 228, 229, 283, 290, 306, 308
Mann, Simranjit Singh, 74, 105, 204, 217, 218, 219, 220, 223, 224, 225, 263, 274, 276, 277, 279, 283, 289, 293, 308, 331
Manochahal, Gurbachan Singh, 72, 74, 77, 99, 101, 104, 110, 195, 216, 236, 254, 255, 256, 267, 274, 277, 280, 283, 290, 306, 309
Maryada ceremony, 78, 132, 137, 151, 157, 158, 159, 160, 171, 181, 192
Mathew Commission, 328
Mathew, K.K., 67
Mathur, P.N., 255
McNamara, Robert, 122
media, exaggerated the image of militancy, 266
Mehal Kalan, Punjab: ethnic homogeneity, 90
migration, 78, 79, 80, 90, 92, 103, 112, 194, 260–1, 262
militants, 26, 27, 59, 60, 71, 75, 145, 151, 200; boycott elections, 302; killed poll candidates, 288, 295; made *panch* and *sarpanches* resigned, 318; and politics, 70; captured power through ballot, 274; ultimatum to government to use Punjabi, 259; styled as 'Singhs', 120; surrendered, 150, 166, 199
Mirdha, Ram Niwas, 251
Miri, 36, 37
misls, 35, 36, 71, 166, 287

Mizo National Front (MNF), 279
Mizoram, 279
Mohali, Punjab: militants strike, 336
Mohan Lal, 43
Mohan Singh, 158, 159, 160, 161–2
Mohinder Singh, Giani, 155
Mohkam Singh, 142
Moin Ul-Malik (Mannu), 35
morale, 263, 266, 270, 331
Mughals and Sikh, 25
Mukerji, Nirmal Kumar, 227, 229, 241, 243–4, 249, 254, 259, 267, 301, 320, 331, 332
Mukherji, Pranab, 67
Mukti Bahini, Bangladesh, India supported, 120
Murthal, Punjab: militants, 50
My Truth by Indira Gandhi, 44

Nadir Shah, 36
nahar roko agitation, 53, 55
Namdhari order, 38
Nanak, Guru, 36
Nand Lal, 123, 124, 126, 136, 137
Nankana Sahib, Sikh resistance, 38
Narang, Ravinder Pal Singh, 112
Narayan Dass, Mahant, 38
Narayanan, S.K., 154, 171
Narinder Pal Singh, 239, 255, 256, 337
Nassiruddin, Mullah, 284
National Council of Khalistan, declared an unlawful organisation, 51
National Security Act (NSA), 64, 308
National Security Guards (NSG), 164, 165, 166, 235
Nawa-i-Waqt, 120
Naxalite movement, 231, 337
Nehru, Arun, 78
Nehru, Jawahar Lal, 39, 48
Nietzsche, 34
Nihangs, 72
Nirankaris: Bhindranwale conflict, 45–46; traumatised by militants, 63
Nirvair Singh, 145
Nishan Singh, 212
non-violence, 39
Noordiwala, Punjab: militants, 251

O'Dyer, General, 25, 34
Ojha, R.P., 147, 172, 230
optimism, 250

Pakistan: aggression in 1948, 40; 1965; 41, 265; assistance and training to militants, 77, 110, 112, 120, 115–16, 200, 202, 236, 243, 244, 251–2, 254, 287–8, 289, 290, 330, 339; —, weapons, 264; Panthic Comm. 216, 229; intensified proxy war, 226
Panchakula, 307
Panchayat, 323, 339; an age old institution, 205–6; three tier system, 206
Panjwar, 317
Pant, K.C., 42
Panthic Committee, 24, 72, 78, 87, 97, 98, 108, 110, 125, 176, 195, 216, 218, 220, 246, 264, 274, 276, 277, 279, 283, 298, 302, 309, 328, 329
Pappu, 262
Paramjit Singh, 260–1, 262
Partition, 25, 117; Hindu–Muslim riots, 34
Pathak, D.C., 130, 135
Patiala, Punjab: poll violence, 311
Patti, Amritsar, Punjab, 112, 113, 234, 237, 255; migration of Hindus, 260; militants, 210, 231, 251; —, attack police post, 254; night curfew, 112; Sadbhavna rally, 270
Pawar, Harbans Singh, 151
Penta, Surjit Singh, 123, 138, 139, 147
'People's Accord', 75, 77, 83, 96, 275
PEPSU, 40
Pheruman, Darshan Singh, 41
Pilot, Rajesh, 305
Piri, 36, 37
Police force: absenteeism, 94; atrocities, 208–11, 213, 233, 246, 336; discontentment, 243; militants nexus, 261–2, 277–8; morale, 256; and public co-operation, 262
Police Training School, Phillaur, 253
Political Affairs Committee, 305
politicians, 182, 184
politics and militancy, 94–95, 106–9, 111, 116

Prakash Singh, 295
Pratap Singh, 173
prejudices, 42
Punjab: army withdrawn, 297, 300, 301, 303; assembly polls, 60, 271, 274, 275, 277, 278, 281–3, 286, 287, 294–5, 302–13; —postponed, 285, 297, 299, 300, 331; annexed by British, 37; budget increased, 120; communal tension, 78, 80, 81; curfew, 56; deprived of democracy, 242; economic package, 201; Haryana and Rajasthan, river water dispute among, 67, 68–70; language, official, 40; —, division on linguistic bases, 41; anti Mandal agitation, 273; *Panchayat* elections, 200, 201, 202, 203, 204, 205–6, 221, 321, 322; Parliamentary elections, 1989, 214–15; Police, lack of equipment, 118–19; poll violence, 283–4, 311; President's rule, 51, 86, 87, 233, 303; reorganisation on linguistic bases, 40; —, political scenario of Punjab and Delhi changed, 45; terrorism sponsored by Congress, 44, 45, 48; Yamuna control, deprived of, 42; youth being exploited, 34
Punjab Armed Police (PAP), 253
Punjab Human Rights Organisation, 64, 277
Punjab Legislative Assembly, 75; dissolved, 109, 242, 273
Punjab Nagrik Manch, 67
Punjab Package, 225, 306, 307, 308, 321
Punjab Reorganisation Act, 69
Punjab State Agricultural Marketing Board, Chandigarh, 65
Punjab State Electricity Board (PSEB), 319
Punjab State Housing Board, 183
Punjabi language, 39–40, 44–45
Punjabi Suba, 39, 40, 44, 259, 267; demand given up: revived, 40, 41, 42, 44
Punjabiat, 31
Punjabis, 89

Puran-Azadi, 107, 108, 224
Puran Singh, Giani, 74

Radu, Liviu, 251
Raj to Rajiv Gandhi by Mark Tully, 66
Rajasthan: water from Punjab, 43
Rajinder Kaur *see* Bhattal, Rajinder Kaur
Rajiv–Benazir Agreement, 201
Rajiv–Longowal Accord, 24, 32, 60, 62, 73, 80, 109, 275, 279, 298, 305, 307, 328, 329
rakhi, 35, 287
Rakshak II Operation, 299
Ram, 226
Ram, *Dr.*, 186
Ramdas, Guru, 137
Ram Singh, Baba, 38
Ramesh Inder Singh, 33, 34
Ranike, Dalbir Singh, 288
Ranjit Singh, Maharaja, 36, 37, 46, 253
Rao, K.V. Krishna, 286
Rao, N.T. Rama, 82, 204, 215, 328
Rao, P.V. Narasimha, 48, 204, 215, 221, 228, 284, 294, 297, 300, 303, 305, 306, 307, 308, 324
Rataul: police-militants encounter, 336–7
Ravi-Beas system, 69
Ray, Maya, 89, 156
Ray, Siddharth Shankar, 24, 26, 65, 95, 96, 103, 105, 106, 107, 110–111, 116, 140, 142–3, 147, 156, 157, 172, 181–2, 186, 189, 193, 194, 196, 198, 200, 201, 202, 203, 204, 205, 206, 211, 213, 214, 220, 221, 234, 235, 259, 301, 322, 329, 330, 339
Regional Formula, 42; rejected, 40
religion and politics, 102, 333
religious hierarchy, 100, 116
Religious Institutions (Prevention and Misuse) Ordinance, 173
Representation of People's Act, 282
Reserve Bank of India, 213
Resham Singh, 200
Ribeiro, J.F., 76, 79, 80, 84, 87, 88, 94, 107, 111, 119, 125, 129, 130, 140, 164, 172, 181, 185, 193, 303, 337

Rode, Jasbir Singh, 72, 73, 98, 99, 101, 106–11, 116, 122, 123, 124, 128, 134, 139, 140, 142, 143, 146, 157, 164, 165, 167, 168, 169, 171, 174, 198, 216, 224, 227, 329, 330

Ropar, Punjab: AISSF conference, 216; formed part of Punjab, 42; militants strike, 310, 334; Parliamentary polls, 217; —Bimal Khalsa won, 274–5

Roy, Pronnoy, 90

Roy, Siddharth Shankar, 84, 85, 86–87, 92

Rudra, K., 295

SGPC *see* Shiromani Gurudwara Prabandhak Committee

Sachar formulae, 42

Saeed, Mufti Mohammad, 223

Sahai, Subodh Kant, 244, 246, 284

Sahib Singh, Giani, 77

Samuel, Kailash, 276

Sandhu, Balbir Singh, 49, 50

Sandhu, Harmandar Singh, 47, 53, 54, 204, 215, 219, 220, 221, 227–8

Sandhu, Nehchal, 135–7

Sangha, Sukhvinder Singh, 257

Sangrur, Punjab: militants strike, 310; poll violence, 311

Sant Nirankaris, 44, 45, 46

Santa Singh, Baba, 72, 154, 173, 326

Sarbat Khalsa, 24, 71, 72, 73, 74, 75, 77, 80, 97, 98, 99, 100, 101, 106, 107, 109, 110, 146, 172, 174, 175, 188, 195, 328, 329

Sardar Singh, 126

Sarhali, Amritsar, Punjab: terrorist attack police post, 254

Sarkaria Commission, 60, 66, 224, 313

sarpanches, 203–4, 205

Sartre, Jean Paul, 147

Sathe, Vasant, 286

Sathi, Vijay Kumar, 315

Saturnalia, a cultural festival, 218

Satwant Singh, 62

satyagraha, 39

Savinder Singh, Giani, 74

secularism, 48, 325

Sehnsra, Amritsar, militants strike, 103

Sekhwan, *Jathedar*, 97

separatism, 49

Sethi, P.C., 44

Sewa Dars, 247

Shabeg Singh, 54

Shah Commission, 44

Shaheedi Samagam, 76, 77, 79

Shahid, Gopal Singh, 50

shakti sammelans, 211

Sharma, Anil, 256

Shastri, Lal Bahadur, 41, 44, 48

Shaw, George Bernard, 268

Sheshan, T.N., 280, 281, 282, 283, 284, 286, 287, 290–1, 332

Shimla, Himachal Pradesh: included in Hindi region, 40

Shiromani Akali Dal (SAD), 24, 25, 29

Shiromani Gurudwara Prabandhak Committee (SGPC), 25, 29, 31, 32, 39, 45, 46, 52, 71–72, 73, 74, 77, 80, 83, 97, 98, 100, 106–7, 112, 122, 134, 146, 150, 151, 152, 153, 154, 155, 156, 158–9, 160, 161, 162, 175–80, 181, 187, 188, 192, 195, 201, 204, 216, 223, 227, 241, 326, 330; factionalism, 179; militants clash, 177

Shiromani Gurudwara Prabandhak Committee Act, 1925, 39, 100–1, 170, 173, 174

Shishupal Singh, 93

Shiv Sena, 76

Sikh Education Conference, 50

Sikh History, The by Hari Ram Gupta, 36

Singh, Hari Kishore, 294

Singh, V.P., 54, 204, 215, 222–3, 224, 225, 226, 242, 244–5, 246, 247, 272, 275, 295, 298, 328, 331

Sinha, S.K., 142, 143, 149, 183

Sita Ram, 256

smuggling, 117–18

Soch, Harbhajan Singh, 155

social reform movement, 83–84, 87, 103, 208; criminalisation, 212, 213

Sohan Singh, 177, 187, 201, 205, 246, 274, 276, 283, 298, 309, 313

Sohan Singh Committee, 288

Somiah, C.G., 171
Sona, Bakshish Singh, 200
States Reorganisation Commission, 40, 42
Sukha Singh, 76, 187, 276
Sukherchakia *misl*, 36
Sultanwind, 218
Sundaram, K., 285
Supreme Court of India, 287
Surendra Nath, 286, 300–2, 304, 305, 306, 310, 314
Suresh Kumar, 151
Suri, Harcharan Singh, 253
Surjit, Harkishan Singh, 245, 306
Sushil Muni, 83, 84, 96, 110
Swami, I.D., 308
Swaran Singh, 48

TADA *see* Terrorist and Disruptive Activities Act
Talib, R.K., 259
Talwandi, Jagdev Singh, 58
Talwandi Sabo Gurudwara, 188, 196
tankhah (religious punishment), 37, 78
Tara Singh, 40
Tarkunde, *Justice* V.M., 213
Tarlok Singh, 62
Tarn Taran, Nabha, 234; arms recovered, 113; militants movements, 50, 210, 231; militants-army encounter, 255–6; night curfew, 112; Parliamentary polls, 217; Republic, Day celebration, 267, 269; Sikh resistance, 38
Tarn Taran Sahib Gurudwara, 190, 191
Tegh Bahadur, Guru, 36, 37
Terrorist and Disruptive Activities Act (TADA), 77, 101, 111, 188, 235, 288, 308
Thakar Singh, Baba, 138, 139, 140, 141, 142, 144, 146, 147, 188, 276
Thapar Institute of Engineering and Technology, Patiala, 218
Theh Ravjja, Amritsar, Punjab: militants strike, 104
Tohra, Gurcharan Singh, 49, 53, 55, 58, 59, 60, 61, 62, 72, 73, 74, 77, 98, 101, 159, 163, 220, 270, 308, 330

tolerance, 323
Tota Singh, 276
transperancy, 332
truth, 39
'*Tuhadi Sarkar Tuhade Dawar*', 270
Tully, Mark, 66, 146, 148

unemployment and militancy, 65
unitary legacy, 324
United Akali Dal (UAD), 58, 78, 97, 98, 105, 106, 168, 179, 204, 220, 223
United Akali Dal (UAD–Mann), 217, 221, 227, 228, 246, 251, 263, 274, 287, 295, 304
United Akali Dal (UAD–Talwandi), 227
Uttam Singh, Baba, 134–7, 140, 153, 161, 169
Uttar Pradesh: terrorist incidents, 296

'Vacation Operation', 182
Vaidya, A.S., 276
Vaishnav, P.H., 94
Varma, S.K., 189
Varma, Varinder, 240, 250, 252, 254, 259, 272, 273, 275, 301, 320, 331, 332
Venkataramiah, *Justice*, 67–68
Village Defence Committees, 254
violence, 47, 50, 53, 55, 56, 59, 76, 79, 80, 81, 82, 102, 109, 113, 147, 150, 275, 285, 325, 333; mishandling by the Centre state governments, 118
Virk, Sarab Deep Singh, 125–6, 130, 164, 167, 198
Virsa Singh, 301
Vishwa Hindu Parishad (VHP), 247

Walia, Charan Jit Singh, 217
Wolpert, Stanley, 339
Wood Rose Operation, 77, 265–6, 338
Wood Rose–II, Operation, 264
World Bank, 335; overseeing river water allocation to India and Pakistan, 70
World Health Organisation (WHO), 95

World Sikh Conference, 75, 96, 110, 113

Yadwinder, 262

Zaffarwal, Wassan Singh, 104, 199, 274, 277, 290, 317

Zail Singh, 37, 45, 47, 52, 72, 240, 324
Zakaria Khan, 35
Zia Ul Haq, 120, 199
Zira, Punjab: militants bringing weapons from Pakistan, 252

The last of the terrorists who surrendered on 18 May 1988.

On 9 May 1988, hundreds of pilgrims were stranded inside the temple as curfew was clamped on the walled city. The DC and SSP leaving the temple after evicting all the pilgrims on 10 May 1988.

Women relatives of militants who surrendered on 15 May 1988.

Militants watching the movements of the police force after they had fired at the police and injured S.S. Virk.

About the Author

Sarab Jit Singh retired recently from the Indian Administrative Service. Among the posts he held during his career was as Deputy Commissioner of Amritsar from 1987 to 1992. He was awarded the Padma Shri in 1989 for his dedication and courage in the fight against militancy. The citation reads: 'Possessing administrative skill in abundant measure, Shri Sarab Jit Singh has been the guiding star for his officers and men in the struggle against terrorism. By his extraordinary dedication and courage and unstinted loyalty he has proved his mettle and continues to set an example for others to emulate.'